UNRULY LABOR

Stanford Studies in Middle Eastern and
Islamic Societies and Cultures

UNRULY LABOR

A History of Oil in the Arabian Sea

Andrea Wright

STANFORD UNIVERSITY PRESS
Stanford, California

Stanford University Press
Stanford, California

© 2024 by Andrea Grace Wright. All rights reserved.

No part of this book may be reproduced or transmitted in any form or by any means, electronic or mechanical, including photocopying and recording, or in any information storage or retrieval system, without the prior written permission of Stanford University Press.

Printed in the United States of America on acid-free, archival-quality paper

Library of Congress Cataloging-in-Publication Data
Names: Wright, Andrea (Professor), author.
Title: Unruly labor : a history of oil in the Arabian Sea / Andrea Wright.
Other titles: Stanford studies in Middle Eastern and Islamic societies and cultures.
Description: Stanford, California : Stanford University Press, 2024. |
    Series: Stanford studies in Middle Eastern and Islamic societies and
    cultures | Includes bibliographical references and index.
Identifiers: LCCN 2024028152 (print) | LCCN 2024028153 (ebook) |
    ISBN 9781503632578 (cloth) | ISBN 9781503639423 (paperback) |
    ISBN 9781503639430 (ebook)
Subjects: LCSH: Petroleum workers—Arabian Peninsula—History—20th century. |
    Petroleum industry and trade—Arabian Peninsula—History—
    20th century. | Industrial relations—Arabian Peninsula—History—20th century. |
    Strikes and lockouts—Petroleum industry—Arabian Peninsula—History—
    20th century. | Foreign workers—Arabian Peninsula—History—20th century.
Classification: LCC HD8039.P42 W84 2024 (print) | LCC HD8039.P42 (ebook) |
    DDC 331.7/6223380953—dc23/eng/20240716
LC record available at https://lccn.loc.gov/2024028152
LC ebook record available at https://lccn.loc.gov/2024028153

Cover design: Daniel Benneworth-Gray
Cover photograph: Robert Yarnall Richie, *Connecting Pipeline, Arabian American Oil Company, Saudi Arabia*, 1948; Robert Yarnall Richie Photograph Collection, DeGolyer Library, SMU
Typeset by Newgen in 10.5/14.4 Brill

For Evelyn

Contents

Acknowledgments		ix
List of Oil Companies and Major Contractors		xi
	Introduction: Producing Labor Hierarchies	1
1	Building Solidarities	17
2	Contesting Sovereignty	41
3	Advocating for Rights	66
4	Shaping Nationalism Outside of the Nation-State	88
5	Writing Labor Laws	115
6	Curtailing Cooperation	145
7	Securing Oil Projects	169
	Conclusion: Depoliticizing Labor	194
	Notes	199
	Bibliography	257
	Index	279

Acknowledgments

This book has been shaped by my ethnographic research on contemporary Indian migration to the Arabian Peninsula, and I owe so much to the workers, recruiters, and government employees who have shared their time, stories, and experiences with me.

I am very thankful to the many people who have read, commented on, and/or talked through portions of this book with me. This includes Syed Ekhteyar Ali, Hoda Bandeh-Ahmadi, Joel Beinin, William Benton, Chandra Bhimull, Neilesh Bose, David Boyk, David William Cohen, Lawrence Cohen, Juan Cole, Geoff Eley, William Fisher, Nelida Fuccaro, Katherine Hendy, Matthew Hull, Peyman Jafari, Hafsa Kanjwal, Munira Khayyat, Elizabeth Kelley, Mandana Limbert, Matthew MacLean, Austin McCoy, Purvi Mehta, Alexandre Mendelmar, Barbara Metcalf, Lisa Mitchell, Farina Mir, Omar Jabary Salamanca, Sarah Selvidge, Stephen Sheehi, Julie Skurski, Neha Vora, Brad Weiss, and Anand Yang. This book also benefitted enormously from the feedback I received from the participants at the AIIS Dissertation to Book Workshop; the Gulf Studies Symposiums; In and Out of South Asia: Race, Capitalism, and Mobility Conference; Interrogating Infrastructure Symposium; Life Worlds of Middle Eastern Oil Conference; Revising the Geography of Modern World Histories Conference; South Asian Migration in Global Perspectives Workshop; and the Writing History after E. P. Thompson Workshop.

Early in my research, both Aligarh Muslim University and the Dubai School of Government hosted me, and I'm thankful for the support, community, and intellectual engagement I found at both places. I'm also thankful to the staff at the British Library, the British Petroleum Archive, the Hoover Institution Archives, the National Archives of India, the National Archives of the UK, the Petroleum Institute at Khalifa University in Abu Dhabi, and the University of North Texas's Oral History Collection. In order to do research for this book, I received funding from the Fulbright-Hays Doctoral Dissertation Research Abroad Fellowship; the Hoover Institution Archive; William & Mary, including APIA's Jinlan Liu Faculty Research Award, Asian & Middle Eastern Studies Program, the Dean of Arts & Sciences, and the Department of Anthropology; and the University of Michigan's Center for South Asian Studies, Joint Doctoral Program in Anthropology and History, Rackham Graduate School, and the Ross School of Business. I'm thankful to Bloomsbury Academic Publishing for permission to develop discussion in this book from my work "Imperial Labour: Labour, Security and the Depoliticization of Oil," published in *South Asian Migrations in Global History: Labor, Law, and Wayward Lives*, edited by Neilesh Bose (2021); I also draw on material from my work "Shifting Solidarities: Strikes, Indian Labor, and the Arabian Sea Oil Industry, 1946–1953," published in *Life Worlds of Middle Eastern Oil: Histories and Ethnographies of Black Gold*, edited by Mandana Limbert and Nelida Fuccaro, Edinburgh University Press (2023).

I'm very appreciative of the incredible work everyone at Stanford University Press does. I'm particularly thankful to Kate Wahl for her insightful comments and consistent support. And I'm thankful to the anonymous readers who engaged so thoughtfully with drafts of this manuscript.

Writing this book coincided with a particularly eventful time in my own life, and I am beyond thankful for my friends and family who encouraged me to write, cheered me on, and indeed, made this work possible and meaningful.

Oil Companies and Major Contractors

Abu Dhabi Marine Areas, Ltd. (ADMA)
Abu Dhabi National Oil Company (ADNOC)
Abu Dhabi Petroleum Company (ADPC)
American Independent Oil Company (Aminoil)
American Oil Company[1] (Amoco)
Anglo-Iranian Oil Company (AIOC)
Anglo-Persian Oil Company (APOC)
Arabian American Oil Company (Aramco)
Atlantic Refining Company
Bahrain Petroleum Company (Bapco)
Bechtel Corporation (Bechtel) (contractor)
BMC (contractor)
Brown Drilling (contractor)
British Petroleum (BP)
British Petroleum, India
California Texas Oil Company, Ltd. (Caltex)
CBI (contractor)
Continental Oil Company (Conoco)[2]
Compagnie Française des Pétroles (CFP)
Contract and Trading Company (CAT)
Exxon Corporation
Exxon Mobil Corporation (ExxonMobil)

George Wimpey (Wimpey)
Getty Oil
Gulf Oil Corporation of Pennsylvania (Gulf)
IBI (contractor)
International Marine Oil Company[3] (IMOC)
Iraq Petroleum Company (IPC)
Kuwait Oil Company (KOC)
National Oil Development Company, Qatar
Near East Development Company (NEDC)
Pan-American Petroleum and Transport Company[4] (PAT)
Petroleum Concessions, Ltd. (PCL)
Petroleum Concessions, Qatar
Petroleum Concessions, Trucial Coast
Petroleum Development, Ltd. (PDL)
Petroleum Development, Qatar (PDQ)
Qatar National Petroleum Company (Qatar Petroleum or QNPC)
Qatar Oil Company, Japan
Qatar Petroleum Company (QPC)
Royal Dutch Shell Company (Shell)
Shell Oil Company, Qatar (SCQ)
Standard Oil Company
Standard Oil Company of California (SoCal)
Standard Oil Company of Indiana
Standard Oil Company of New Jersey (Jersey Standard or Esso)
Standard Oil Company of New York (Socony)
Superior Oil Company (Superior)
The Texas Company (Texaco)
Turkish Petroleum Company (TPC)
United Geophysical (contractor)

UNRULY LABOR

Introduction

PRODUCING LABOR HIERARCHIES

FROM THE EARLY DAYS OF OIL PRODUCTION IN ARABIAN SEA, OIL was connected to imperial militaries and oil companies were connected to imperial governance. Some examples of how imperialism, the military, and oil were connected include the British acquisition of the majority voting share of the Anglo-Persian Oil Company (APOC, later AIOC and then BP) in 1914; the belief that oil gave the British a strategic advantage during World War I; and financial support from the US government to California Texas Oil Company (Caltex), the parent company of Bahrain Petroleum Company (Bapco), during World War II to restructure its refinery to produce jet fuel.[1] Despite these connections, from 1933 to 1945, the British administration showed little interest in strikes occurring in the Arabian Peninsula. The treaties signed between the British government and local rulers specified that local rulers ran the internal workings of their sheikhdoms, and the British government was responsible for external relations. Prior to 1945, the British administration had a general policy of noninterference with the Arabian Peninsula.

In June 1932, workers at Bapco discovered oil in Bahrain, at what is today known as the Awali oil field.[2] This was the first time oil was found in one of the countries of the Arabian Peninsula. This discovery by Bapco, a Canadian subsidiary of US-based Standard Oil of California (SoCal), came seven years after the sheikh of Bahrain granted the first oil concession.[3] It also came days after SoCal sold half of its shares of Bapco to Texaco, another oil company based in the United States.[4] Almost six years after oil was discovered in Bahrain, the world remained in the midst of a severe economic downturn, and prices were rising throughout the country. Only a small percentage of the population could find employment at Bapco, and those who did work there were housed in bare barracks made of wood.[5] In this context, in 1938, the workers at the Awali oil field held their first organized strikes.[6] A US manager at Bapco reported that for months before the strike, "murmurs of discontent had been mounting," but the company "refused to place guards at various places to keep the workmen on the job." As a result, during the strike "all the drilling wells were idle." The manager also observed that the strike ended after police "swung long wooden clubs—and swung them rather vigorously, according to reports. After a few heads were cracked, the crowd broke."[7]

Strikes were common in the 1930s, and in Manama, the capital of Bahrain, they were a regular occurrence.[8] Indeed, as this book will discuss, workers went on strike frequently throughout oil projects in the Arabian Peninsula from the 1930s through the 1960s. In 1938, there were numerous strikes in the Middle East, the Arabian Sea, and globally. For example, the Palestinian peasant movement was at its height.[9] In India, on November 7, 1938, over 200,000 workers from multiple trades stopped work and took to the streets in protest of a labor bill that aimed to diminish the power of unions.[10] Also in 1938, in the United States, 2,772 strikes began, involving more than 688,000 workers and more than 9 million lost working days.[11] Similarly, in the United Kingdom, over 1.3 million working days were lost to strikes.[12]

In Bahrain, the 1938 strikes involved a coalition of workers that included Bahrainis, other Arab workers, and Indians. After Bahrainis, British Indians (those from parts of India directly ruled by the British Empire) were the largest nationality working at Bapco. The 352 British Indians at Bapco comprised 13 percent of Bapco's workforce and outnumbered all US, Canadian, and British workers combined.[13] These workers were just a few of the increasing numbers of Indians working in the Arabian Peninsula, and by 1950, approximately fifteen thousand Indians worked in oil and related industries in the Arabian Peninsula.[14] Indians worked, and went on strike, alongside local workers as well as those from other Arabic- and Farsi-speaking countries.

In the first half of the twentieth century, worker strikes at oil projects often comprised coalitions of workers of differing religions and ethnicities.

For example, the 1938 strike in Bahrain was, according to British sources, inspired by ideas of Arab nationalism that were "spreading across the increasingly well-educated Bahraini population, and reform movements [that] were emerging in Kuwait and Dubai."[15] A broad swathe of Bahrainis participated in the strike, which also included workers from India. Working together, the strikers sought equal pay for Bahrainis and Indians. After the strike, some of the workers' demands were met, but not that for equal pay. There was another strike in 1943 that did more to further worker demands. Labor organizers focused on common conditions as a way to bring workers together.[16] Working and living together impacted how workers formed solidarities and agitated to improve their conditions.

From the 1940s through the 1960s, however, worker strikes became increasingly fragmented, and workers faced growing restrictions on the right to strike. To understand how worker actions changed, this book examines British imperial policies, oil company management practices, and worker practices at oil projects in Iran and the Arabian Peninsula (the present-day countries of Bahrain, Kuwait, Oman, Qatar, Saudi Arabia, the United Arab Emirates, and Yemen). During this period, labor hierarchies were shaped, contested, and codified as formal British colonialism ended and oil companies implemented new management practices. This book historically interrogates the relationships among governments, oil companies, and workers. Examining these relationships demonstrates the process by which the line between citizen and noncitizen was constructed and how citizenship shaped worker organizing.

In the mid-twentieth century, oil company managers developed practices meant to control workers, including the segregation of workforces by nationality. Simultaneously, states grappled with who was a citizen, and government officials debated how to ensure citizens' rights, both of which influenced how solidarities developed among workers. Exploring the changing ways workers formed solidarities, oil companies managed workers, and governments responded to strikes provides critical insight into how understandings of difference were historically produced and used as tools for domination.[17]

As British bureaucrats and oil company managers responded to worker actions within a context of geopolitical competition, bureaucrats and managers refashioned older colonial labor infrastructure to supply the large numbers of workers needed for oil projects. This system of labor mobility was originally developed in the nineteenth century to move indentured workers from India to plantations throughout the British Empire.[18] Worker actions, considered in conjunction with oil project staffing, management practices, and the securitization of oil, illuminate the messy process that produced the racialized labor hierarchies and precarious working conditions of today's Arabian Peninsula.

COLONIAL TROPES AND ARCHIVAL SOURCES

Accounts of worker actions appear in records written by British administrators and oil company managers in the Arabian Peninsula. As managers and administrators described worker actions, they incorporated existing colonial tropes and stereotypes about the region. Mobilizing these tropes, strikes were described as the result of outside influences and workers' attitudes. Often, these descriptions of strikes erased the role of mobile laborers and obfuscated the role of imperialism and oil companies in shaping contemporary governance and labor practices.

Colonial fictions were central to how the history of the Arabian Peninsula was written. Importantly, those in positions of power, including colonial authorities and oil company managers, worked and reworked certain tropes, and these tropes impacted how British administrators and oil company officials interpreted the events they observed. This included an understanding of labor movements as apolitical. These tropes also obscured the relationship between the British administration and oil companies. We see one example of this during the establishment of states' boundaries in the Arabian Peninsula. In 1938, the British administration asserted that it was "impossible to define boundaries between tribes. In fact, there are none."[19] As a result, the British felt they had to try to draw geographic boundaries prior to offering oil concessions.

Colonial fictions informed governmental administrative practices and served as a means of legitimizing these practices. For example, one officer in the British Indian Army, Lieutenant-Colonel David Lorimer, who visited the Gulf in the late 1890s, wrote of the region: "The general impression of Dohah is unattractive; the lanes are narrow and irregular, the houses dingy and small. There are no date palms or other trees, and the only garden is a small one near the fort, kept up by the Turkish garrison."[20] Such views of the

Arabian Peninsula as desolate and isolated were repeated throughout the twentieth century by British colonial authorities, with isolation conflated again and again with "backwardness" and lack of development.[21]

Even as the economic activity of the region changed, colonial tropes endured. By 1969, in the Trucial States (today the United Arab Emirates) agricultural practices were increasing; there were water cargo jetties, a cement factory, a fertilizer plant, and a flour mill; people had access to health and education facilities; and vocational training for tradesmen had begun.[22] Yet, despite these changes in infrastructure accompanying the commercial export of oil, the British argued the social mores of the region remained stagnant. According to this discourse, the Arabian Peninsula was ostensibly in the grip of unchanging religious practice and traditions frozen in time. One British administrator wrote, "The gaunt stronghold of medieval Islamic thought and tradition still cast its gloomy shadows over every aspect of social life."[23] "Puritanical Wahhabism," as it was often classified by British officials, was understood to be most prevalent in Saudi Arabia and Qatar, whereas the Trucial States were felt to have "stirrings" of liberal ideas.[24]

Colonial fictions such as these were central to how managers and government officials described and responded to worker actions at oil projects. In the archive, we find that strikes were characterized as nonsensical or as influenced by outside groups, including communists and pan-Arab nationalists. Indian government officials, for their part, often saw strikes as representative of Indian nationalism. These varying ways of describing strikes oversimplified and distorted worker claims. Strikes were denied their contemporaneity while increasingly viewed as destabilizing to local rulers, imperial governance, and oil production. Governmental, and particularly imperial, intervention was described simply as attempts to "restore order." Such descriptions of strikes "conceals . . . [the] intentionality and socially constructed significance" of both worker action and responses to strikes.[25]

In order to critically interrogate the archive and to examine the shifting constellation of workers that composed the historic geographies of labor subjectivity, I draw inspiration from scholars in Subaltern Studies, and particularly, Ranajit Guha's work in which he provides a methodological approach for reading and questioning the archives to uncover the heterogeneity of worker practices and motivations.[26] I am also influenced by Shahid Amin's work as a model for close reading of and careful engagement with archives, and Dipesh Chakrabarty's attention to the history of the gaps in the archive.[27] In addition, I use anthro/history to provide perspectives that are "betwixt and between" disciplines. These perspectives allow us to question the production of historical narratives and critically engage with how certain fictions become fixed as "real."[28] Such an approach grapples with dominant narrative structures by examining "the interstitial, intermediate, indeterminate, and unfinished frames of knowledge" that arise in an event.[29] In doing so, the ethics and politics of knowledge production become clearer. In the case of labor in the oil industry in the Arabian Sea, this approach demonstrates the process by which oil company management practices, colonial governance, postcolonial states, and workers themselves shaped the labor hierarchies upon which oil production depends.

THE SCALES OF OIL PRODUCTION

In labor history, strikes are often key events in a narrative that relies on the nation-state as the "main analytic or expository frame," and a diverse set of struggles are collapsed into the story of the nation-state.[30] Privileging the nation-state erases the diverse solidarities that workers formed, projecting contemporary understandings of nationality and ethnicity into the past. Doing so also obscures how imperial governance and corporate practices impacted labor movements.

In the Arabian Peninsula, focusing on nation-states means that worker movements in the oil industry are viewed as separate from both global labor movements and world economic practices, and the possibilities of worker strikes are narrowed.[31] Worker mobilizations were dependent on solidarities that shifted over the course of the twentieth century. Critically engaging with worker solidarities makes clear how strikes and other activities were informed not only by nationalism but also by the process of migration, working and living conditions, and broader anti-imperial movements.[32] Some worker coalitions were new and fostered by the growing oil industry, while other networks built upon earlier relations of trade, imperialism, and cultural exchange that have historically moved through the Indian Ocean.[33] As workers agitated for better working conditions, worker actions shaped and were shaped by governance, citizenship, and laws.

In the mid-twentieth century, materials, ideas, and people were all moving through circuits that cut across empires and nations, solidifying the salience of those political entities in some instances, while challenging them in others. This book explores the ways workers, bureaucrats, oil company managers, and recruiting agents used networks to facilitate and, at times, impede oil production. What emerges is a view of oil that draws on and reconfigures the scales of analysis. I use the Arabian Sea as a geographic framework for this book in order to underscore the multiple scales at play for corporations, governments, and workers. Oil production drew upon and reconfigured networks that moved across regions, throughout South Asia, Iran, the Arabian Peninsula, and the world. Worker actions extended beyond the sites of production to workers' networks of affiliation. By attending to the ways workers formed solidarities and participated in labor actions, we find labor movements challenged the boundaries of organizations, nation-states, and empires.

During the first half of the twentieth century, Indian workers invoked or ignored state borders as they protested the managerial practices common at oil projects. British companies and the British colonial government preferentially sought to hire Indians for oil projects, but Indian workers were not always sympathetic to British imperial projects. In the 1940s, Indians frequently participated in strikes at oil projects in the Arabian Sea, including in Kuwait in 1946, in Bahrain in 1942 and 1947, and in Saudi Arabia in 1943 and 1945. During some of these strikes, workers formed solidarities across national, religious, and linguistic lines. Often these solidarities were informed by workers' proximity to one another—on the job, in the company mess hall, and during their leisure time. At other times, workers formed solidarities based on a shared natal village. These represent, to borrow a phrase from Farina Mir, a highly localized aspect of social lives that workers maintained as they moved from their natal villages to oil projects in Iran and the Arabian Peninsula.[34] In such cases, one sees the formation of a localized politics with transnational implications. These cases also demonstrate that nationalism influenced worker action, but we are reminded that nation-states are only one factor informing labor actions.

Considering worker actions and the role of migrant workers in these actions offers new insights into how the production of oil, the international managerial practices of natural resource extraction, and the politics of new nation-states were developed through engagements among the diverse actors involved in oil production.[35] These interactions shaped labor regimes and oil complexes that in turn impacted global governance practices and international oil companies. Workers' solidarities were formed as they tried to make changes to their working and living conditions, and as they responded to the management practices of oil companies, to shifting political and economic factors, and to their own kinship and exchange obligations.

Workers' strikes, protests, and complaints illustrate that the production of oil was a site where international carbon managerial practices and localized politics met. Focusing on this conjunction presents opportunities to destabilize historical narratives that privilege the history of nation-states and sheds light on how workers' various networks and solidarities invoked, and also helped to shape, the scales of the local, national, and transnational. Through critically following worker activism in the oil industry, we uncover the power of national and transnational institutions to obfuscate power structures, as well as the limits of these power structures.

Attending to migration that crosses state borders does not negate the importance of the nation-state, but it reminds us that nation-states are only one factor informing labor politics. Looking at worker action before and after India's independence in 1947 illustrates when and how workers selectively invoked their nationality or the nation-state. In the years after 1947, when Indian workers did appeal to the state, they often described the racist treatment they experienced while at oil projects in the Arabian Peninsula. They also invoked India's status as an independent country. The dignity that Indians felt they were due after India's independence served to bolster their claims. India's independence also helped Indians form alliances across boundaries of language, geography, and, at times, class.

The Indian government's responses show us that as people moved internationally after India's and Pakistan's independence, the rights of citizens and restrictions on citizens' movement were developed in tandem. Many Indian officials felt it was necessary to push for Indian migrants' rights to religious practice and good working conditions. Developing these transnational citizenship regimes allowed the Indian government to define its borders and its people. Exploring such interactions between states, citizens, and the oil industry reveals how postcolonial states and imperial governments attempted to establish sovereignty and the centrality of citizenship for the effectiveness of worker strikes.

When we look at the role of nationalism in fostering worker solidarities, we see that nationalism, at times, united workers of different job categories and skill levels in protest. Nationalism was also sometimes mobilized in a context of anti-imperialism, and this had the potential to foster solidarities between groups.[36] However, nationalist imaginaries based on a homogenous population limited some solidarities. The resulting racism, as Étienne Balibar explains, is a "supplement of nationalism or more precisely a supplement internal to nationalism, always in excess of it, but always indispensable to its constitution and yet always still insufficient to achieve its project, just as nationalism is both indispensable and always insufficient to achieve the formation of the nation or the project of a 'nationalization' of society."[37] Over the course of the twentieth century, as workers fought to change their working and living conditions, the project of nationalism and accompanying racism were grappled with and taken up by people working within and outside of their country of citizenship.

Nationalism did not exist within a vacuum, and the increasing formation of worker solidarities by nationality was further reinforced by oil companies' managerial practices. Increasingly over the mid-twentieth century, oil company managers in the Arabian Peninsula were effective at segregating workers by nationality in their jobs, living accommodations, and access to leisure activities. In addition, worker camps were based on nationality, located in remote areas, and there were few possibilities for interaction among workers of different nationalities. Managers also gave workers of different nationalities different benefits and pay, thereby spurring conflict between them. Taken together, these management practices decreased the likelihood of workers forming broad, class-based solidarities that had the potential to halt oil production, and strikes were increasingly fragmented along the lines of nationality.

LABOR AND THE STATE

Each chapter of this book begins with a discussion of a strike by workers at an oil project as a way to center labor in the history of oil. Laborers rarely show up in histories of oil, and their presence in the archive is often limited except during moments of collective action.[38] During these moments, workers were characterized as "unruly" by oil company managers, British administrators, and local government officials—it was this unruliness that disrupted oil production. In turn, these disruptions illuminate how governable space amicable to the extraction and commodification of natural resources was developed and given legitimacy.[39]

Oil's importance influenced responses to strikes. From 1940 to 1970, the world's energy consumption grew rapidly, almost tripling. In 1940 and 1950, coal continued to be the world's main source of energy, providing 49 percent in 1940 and 43 percent in 1950. However, oil was quickly replacing coal as the primary source of energy. By 1960, oil accounted for 31 percent of the world's energy whereas 38 percent was provided by coal. By 1970, oil had outpaced coal, providing 43 percent of the world's energy versus coal's 27 percent.[40] In 1940, the United States was the single largest producer of oil, producing 62 percent of the world's oil. In 1971, the United States continued to be the single largest producer, but its share of oil production dropped to 21 percent. In the Arabian Peninsula, oil production grew rapidly following World War II, and by 1971, the countries of the Arabian Peninsula (Bahrain, Kuwait, Oman, Qatar, Saudi Arabia, and the United Arab Emirates) produced 20 percent of the world's oil, and these countries' oil production was continuing to rise.[41]

Examining strikes and responses to strikes illuminates changing relationships among local governments, imperial powers, oil companies, and workers from the 1940s to 1970. By historically contextualizing these relationships, we are able to see that the political economy of the Arabian Sea was actively shaped by multiple participants. Such a perspective helps us avoid the common "slippage between oil as a commodity of indisputable political, economic, and cultural significance and what one might call commodity determinism."[42] In addition, examining these relationships will make clear how the political economy of oil was shaped by colonialism, shifting worker solidarities, nationalism, oil company practices, discourses connecting oil and security, understandings of citizenship, and racialized labor hierarchies.

Responses to worker actions changed rapidly in the years after World War II. Strikes were increasingly characterized as costly for oil companies, threatening to the British economy, and destabilizing to local political leaders. As a result, oil company managers, local governments, and the British administration sought ways to minimize strikes and ensure workforce stability. In examining how attitudes toward strikes change, two key assumptions about oil emerge and gain traction: oil is scarce, and national security hinges on control of Middle Eastern oil. Over the course of the twentieth century, these assumptions became the dominant discourses around oil. While critically deconstructed by experts, including Timothy Mitchell and Robert Vitalis, these discourses have historically served as the ideological underpinning for numerous wars and military interventions, and they continue to shape contemporary US foreign policy.[43]

These assumptions about oil were developed as perspectives on the economy and the responsibilities of the state changed. In the mid-twentieth century, the meaning of "the economy," shifted from "the attitudes and transactions of commercial exchange" to a "distinct social sphere" that was the "realm of social science, statistical enumeration, and government policy."[44] Economies were territorialized onto nation-states. One result of this, Nikolas Rose explains, was that the responsibility of the government "for the security of a nation, a state and a people, came to be understood in terms of their capacity to ensure the security of its national economic well-being."[45] In this context, management practices gained power as oil production became increasingly attached to security; thus governments and oil companies invoked security as they sought to curtail strikes, including through militarized responses.

From the 1940s to 1960s, government officials and oil company administrators increasingly asserted that oil was critical for state security and industry. By looking specifically at labor in the oil industry, we are able to see how these understandings of the state, security, and the economy were formulated and contested. Oil's connection to security shaped governance, company practices, and worker actions. In particular, oil companies, the British administration, and local governments developed forms of governance and management practices that were better suited to working with foreigners whose recourse to government support was tenuous. Also, in order to reduce the risk of wide-scale strikes and other worker action, oil companies increasingly sought to hire nonlocal workers.

Oil company managers and British administrators made concerted attempts to diminish the role of the local government in labor relations and, particularly, to curtail local government's support for workers. Oil companies also increased practices such as contracting that made holding the companies accountable challenging. Fifty-fifty profit sharing helped align the interests of oil companies and local governments. To legitimate militarized responses to strikes, oil companies, the British administration, and local governments wrote labor laws that greatly restricted workers' rights, including their rights to strike, free speech, and collectively organize. In short, workers were denied their rights based on arguments for political stability, in the name of protecting the economy, and through mobilizing dominant discourses about oil's scarcity and its connection to national security.

THE CENTRALITY OF CITIZENSHIP

A US manager reflected on Bapco's role in the 1938 strike, writing that "the great majority of the population had received little benefits" from the company's activities.[46] This perspective, that a population will rise up if they do not receive benefits but be content if they do see the benefits of oil production, is seen frequently in the archive. This assumption is also common in the present, and the allocation of oil wealth is given as a reason for the persistence of monarchical governance in in the Arabian Peninsula.[47] Bahrain, Kuwait, Oman, Qatar, Saudi Arabia, and the United Arab Emirates were, and continue to be, monarchies dependent on the export of oil.[48]

In 1970, Hossein Mahdavy introduced the term "rentier states" to describe the impact of oil rents on countries where oil is a large part of the economy. He defined rentier states as "those countries that receive on a regular basis substantial amounts of external rents. External rents are in turn defined as rentals paid by foreign individuals, concerns or governments to individuals, concerns or governments of a given countries." Because of the income from oil rents, countries are able to invest in large public works without taxing the people. Mahdavy argued that the results include the government playing a central role in the economy and an uneven distribution of wealth within countries.[49]

In his examination of the connections between oil and democracy, Timothy Mitchell argues that the materiality of carbon and the differences between coal and oil production have led to differing forms of political action. He notes that shifts in social relations came with the greater harnessing of energy produced by coal, which helped support cities and large-scale manufacturing. In addition, the manner in which coal was transported and mined—namely, its requirement that laborers work in autonomous underground spaces and that coal transportation had choke points—enabled workers to strike effectively. Coal's materiality and the worker relations it helped foster informed "the kinds of mass politics that emerged, or threatened to emerge, in the first half of the twentieth century." Mitchell argues that the materiality of oil shaped forms of political engagements differently than those made possible by coal. Some key differences between the mining of coal and the production of oil are that oil requires a smaller workforce and workers are continuously aboveground and therefore open to continuous supervision. In addition, oil's lightness and fluidity allow it to be transported through pumping stations and pipelines and/or to be shipped. This flexibility of transportation means that oil is transported in a "grid." This grid-like transportation differs from the "dendritic networks" coal followed via railway. Oil's grid makes it less vulnerable to strikes of the kind that caused choke points for coal's transport. Consequently, Mitchell argues, the transportation and working conditions used in the production of oil curtailed "the democratizing potential of petroleum."[50]

Mitchell's focus on the techno-politics of oil production leads him to the conclusion that oil workers were less likely to exert a democratizing impact on the state.[51] However, this account does not consider the centrality of citizenship in shaping governance practices. Despite the limitations imposed in political action by the materiality of oil, workers in the Gulf oil fields continued to form alliances and negotiate their working conditions through political mobilization. In particular, the period of the 1940s through the 1960s includes a time when large amounts of oil infrastructure were being built. These projects required thousands of workers. This book examines labor across oil's supply chain, with focus on the construction of oil infrastructure, oil production, and oil refinement. Construction, production, and refinement required vastly different numbers of workers. From these variable labor needs, issues emerged around redundant labor and workforce training. In these contexts, oil companies, workers, and governments addressed, fought over, and negotiated the problems intrinsic to the variable labor needs in oil's supply chain.

In addition, although workers from India and Pakistan were not positioned to democratize governance in the Arabian Peninsula, their strikes and other worker actions brought international scrutiny to their situation and resulted in some, admittedly limited, improvements in their circumstances. As examinations of strikes and government responses will show, the key factor was not only the techno-politics of oil production. Rather, citizenship also emerges as a critical factor.

The centrality of citizenship appears in multiple contexts in this book, but citizenship was not experienced in the same way by workers—some workers were imperial citizens, others were citizens of an independent nation-state, and some were stateless. The meanings of citizenship for workers emerged in how laws were written and also how the idea of citizenship was put into practice by government bureaucrats and ordinary people. In Iran, India, and the Arabian Peninsula, questions arose over who should be a citizen. Particularly in the Arabian Peninsula, there were also initiatives—spearheaded not only by local elites but also British administrators and oil company managers—to restrict who was a citizen. These debates and initiatives draw attention to the role of the state as a guarantor of rights—an issue that is even more pronounced when we consider how statelessness negatively impacted workers. Taken as a whole, citizenship was both a vehicle for claiming rights and a process by which worker solidarities were fragmented.

Ultimately, the growing rates of contracting within the oil industry, the writing of labor laws that favored employers and restricted unions, restrictions on worker strikes, the recruiting infrastructure in India, and the increasing securitization of oil all contributed to shaping the labor hierarchies prevalent in the Arabian Peninsula's oil industry. Because oil company managers could replace Indian and Pakistani employees who disrupted worksites, from the late 1940s through the early 1970s, workers from these countries were increasingly hired.

SHIFTING SOLIDARITIES

By considering how workers formed solidarities and how workers made claims on companies and states, we are able to critically interrogate colonial categorizations and document how ethnicity, race, and nationality were conflated and territorially fixed in the mid-twentieth century. In that period, colonial classifications and racism informed labor relations at oil projects. As Robert Vitalis illustrates in his history of the US involvement with oil production in Saudi Arabia, key methods developed by US oil companies to curtail labor strikes included the racial segregation of workers and discrepancies in pay based on race.[52] Of course, the use of racism as a management technique was not unique to the oil industry.[53] The internationalization of such managerial practices provoked worker protests, which, in turn, highlighted the specificities of oil production in the Arabian Sea. Worker actions from the 1940s through 1960s at oil projects in places like Abadan, Abu Dhabi, Aden, Bahrain, and Qatar illuminate how oil companies' managerial practices influenced and were influenced by imperial administrators, workers, and managers, with labor mobilizations increasingly segmenting along national lines.

Capitalism operates based on "antagonistic differences," both within and between societies, and these differences are racialized, ordered hierarchically, and exploited to create profits.[54] Membership in the nation-state, too, is informed by this logic of difference.[55] In a colonial context, there was a drain of wealth, as colonial powers actively sought to profit from colonies, including through the appropriation of labor and natural resources.[56] In addition, colonial governments actively sought to "restrict" the economic potential of their colonies.[57] However, these historical processes were obscured through abstracting social relations, including the dispossession of labor. Such abstractions obfuscated how profits were, and continue to be, generated through inequalities.[58] Instead, global wealth inequalities were explained as a result of racialized difference.[59]

From the 1940s through 1960s at oil projects in the Arabian Peninsula, race and nationality were increasingly conflated. The ideas of difference that underpin capitalism impacted who the state saw as a citizen and who could effectively make claims upon the state for protection. Radhika Mongia argues that "cultural racism succeeds, precisely, in securing an identity between a people and a territory such that both come to be described as 'national.'"[60] This territorialization of culture and racialization of nationality make differences between groups appeared fixed and insurmountable, and they are predicated on a projection of current understandings of the world into a timeless past.[61] This territorialization and racialization also actively obscures the fact that people, ideas, and items were always moving, interacting, and changing.[62]

By the mid-twentieth century, work on the oil fields had become a major source of employment for Indian emigrants, and oil companies were hiring almost one-quarter of all Indian emigrants going overseas for jobs in 1951.[63] Though increasing numbers of Indians were moving to work in the Arabian Peninsula, conditions were far from ideal. Both skilled professionals and day laborers faced discrimination and difficult working conditions. In the 1940s and early 1950s, workers living in Aden, Bahrain, Iran, Kuwait, and Qatar all had similar complaints. These complaints revolved around poor living conditions, lack of medical and recreational facilities, "gross discrimination ... between senior staff which is American or British and the Indian or local junior staff," poor sanitation, and the absence of any means for workers to redress grievances.[64] In order to improve their working conditions, Indian workers in the oil fields deployed multiple tactics—from work stoppages to hunger strikes to appealing to the Indian government for support.

Strikes by *khaliji* (Arabs from the Arabian Peninsula) workers in the oil fields also shaped political structures and labor relations. Oil and its nationalization were key factors in a wave of anticolonial movements. In 1951, following the nationalization of the Abadan refinery, the Anglo-Iranian Oil Company (AIOC) began to build an oil refinery in Aden and began to pursue additional oil projects in the Arabic-speaking Gulf. In the wake of a series of strikes held by khaliji workers in the Arabian Peninsula in the 1960s, government officials and the oil company managers worked together to reduce the impact of these strikes. Because oil company managers could easily replace Indian and Pakistani employees who disrupted worksites, from the late 1940s through the early 1970s, workers from these countries came to be increasingly hired for unskilled or semiskilled positions.

Government officials and corporate managers worked to codify citizenship in the states of the Arabian Peninsula. They also categorized workers through a conflation of nationality and race, and distributed benefits based on nationality. As a result, some solidarities between groups became increasingly challenging.[65] However, it was not only government officials and corporate managers who helped shape and concretize difference. Tracing the shifting politics of difference elucidates how workers also reinforced difference by invoking national belonging as a way to make claims for rights.

Over the course of this book, we will see that the interactions among governments, corporations, and workers produced these politicized identities.[66] Shifting solidarities formed along with the maintenance and revitalization of nineteenth-century colonial infrastructures used to move indentured workers, which were adapted in the twentieth century to bring workers to the oil fields. The proliferation of contracting, the writing of employer-friendly labor laws, and increasingly militarized responses to strikes all contributed to configure axes of unity among workers. The result was an evacuation of politics from the oil fields.

One
BUILDING SOLIDARITIES

BEGINNING IN MARCH 1946, THE EMPLOYEES OF THE ANGLO-IRANIAN Oil Company (AIOC) working at the oil refinery in Abadan, Iran, participated in a series of so-called wildcat strikes, in other words strikes without the approval of union officials. British and Iranian officials believed that the Tudeh Party of Iran was the driving force for these strikes. This communist party had much influence in 1940s and early 1950s Iran, and by 1946, the labor affiliate of the Tudeh Party, the CCFTU (Central Council of Federated Trade Unions of Iranian Workers and Toilers), had unionized 75 percent of the industrial labor force in Iran. In the months following the March 1946 wildcat strikes, the Tudeh Party was able to mobilize tens of thousands of demonstrators in Iran's capital, Tehran, and on the streets of Abadan, where the AIOC oil refinery was located. Worker mobilizations included a May Day parade of 80,000 people in 1946 and, on July 13, 1946, the party organized a strike throughout the province of Khuzestan (in which Abadan is located). Involving 65,000 workers, this was the largest strike to date in Iran and one of the largest strikes to have occurred in the Middle East.[1] During this large general strike in July 1946, 50 employees of AIOC were killed and 170 were injured.[2]

Contemporary scholars have considered these strikes' effects and, in particular, the relations formed by the AIOC, the Iranian government, the British government, and Iranian citizens as a result.[3] One scholar attentive to this complexity is Ervand Abrahamian, who explores the high percentage of minorities within the Tudeh Party and the party's promise of citizenship and secularism.[4] His focus on the multigenerational residents of Iran who supported the Tudeh Party indicates the diversity of workers who participated in the strikes and shows how intergroup solidarities were formed. Abrahamian's emphasis on citizenship, the state, and rights offers important perspectives on the power of strikes by citizens to shape companies' policies and state laws, the role of the state as the securer of citizen workers' rights, and the legitimacy the state gained by defending workers' rights.

In addition to the role of a broad coalition of Iranians participating in the strike, we also see coalitions of workers of many nationalities participating in collective action against AIOC. One place the importance of temporary workers arises is in the case of Indian laborers at AIOC's Abadan refinery, the site where most Indians working in Iran were stationed. At Abadan, four days before the general strike, five Muslim men from the Punjab, in British India, were forced to resign from their positions at the Abadan refinery because they had joined the Tudeh Party. After their resignation, they continued to live in the camps near Abadan. In the coming days, these five men helped organize a coalition of hundreds of Indians who, in solidarity with Arabic- and Farsi-speaking laborers, went on a strike that influenced AIOC and imperial policies in the coming years.[5]

The July 1946 strikes were disruptive for the government of Iran, AIOC, the British government, and the British armed forces. Indeed, in the late 1940s, Abadan was the world's largest refinery. It was also Britain's largest overseas investment,[6] providing a significant source of income for both the British government and AIOC as well as 85 percent of the British navy's oil.[7] Abadan's significance in the mid- to late 1940s draws attention to the historical relationships among the British government, the Iranian government, oil companies, and workers. These relationships were often tense, and in the 1930s, the Iranian government sought to exert influence over the oil industry by invoking the language of nationalism, modernization, and citizenship. In response to both the Iranian government's actions in the 1930s and the 1946 strikes, AIOC managers mobilized and reinforced discourses about national progress and the role of citizens in contributing to this progress, but the accompanying corporate practices rarely benefited workers.

Iranian government officials and oil company managers used the language of nationalism and national progress to respond to the 1946 strikes, showing that national identifications were shaped not only by political leaders, centralized education, and newspapers, but also by corporations.[8] In the early days of the Cold War, national identification was also informed by the rhetoric of national progress and the development of modernizing infrastructure.[9] Both the Iranian government and AIOC managers believed that Iranian citizens were key to this progress. At AIOC, the company implemented policies and practices that emphasized citizenship and differentiated Iranian workers from mobile workers. Despite corporate and government discourses and practices that focused on nationality, workers formed solidarities that cut across national, ethnic, linguistic, and religious borders.

OIL AND EMPIRE IN THE EARLY TWENTIETH CENTURY

In the early twentieth century, British companies began to focus on the possibilities of oil production in the Arabian Sea, and much of their attention was on Persia (now Iran). In 1901, William D'Arcy, an Englishman who amassed a substantial fortune in the mining industry, acquired oil concessions in Persia. In 1908, oil was discovered at Masjid-i-Sulaiman in southwest Persia, and the Anglo-Persian Oil Company (APOC, later renamed the Anglo-Iranian Oil Company) was founded the following year. This company held an oil concession for all of Persia, with the exception of the five most northern provinces, where Russia controlled oil production.

During the first decades of the twentieth century, oil's importance for imperial governance increased as it became central to military actions. For the British government, oil's importance grew after 1911, when Winston Churchill, the newly appointed first lord of the admiralty (and future prime minister), successfully pushed to use oil to power the British navy. The change to oil-powered ships revitalized the British navy.[10] As oil became increasingly important both militarily and industrially, many governments, including the British government, took an active interest in exerting control over oil companies and oil production.[11]

Oil prices were rapidly rising in the early 1910s, but by 1912, APOC had exhausted its cash reserves due to the costs of exploring for oil and developing oil production infrastructure. Unable to develop oil projects, the company sought support from the British government.[12] In its appeal to the government, the company argued that Persian oil was vital for British industry and also that oil held great potential for the development of British colonies, including India. For example, the company suggesting it could supply oil to the Indian State Railway.[13] In 1913, Churchill supported the proposal that the British government should invest in APOC. He supported this because government shares of APOC would allow for the government to acquire oil while maintaining secrecy, which, Churchill argued, was necessary because of oil's military and commercial applications.[14] As the British government debated investment in APOC, the Royal Dutch Shell Company (Shell) emerged as another potential investor. However, from the British government's perspective, Shell was an undesirable investor in APOC, as Shell would only agree to a two-year contract with the British government.[15] In addition, the British government viewed Shell as a foreign company, and the British government was eager to both maintain its position in Persia and also develop oil resources within areas of influence of the British Empire.[16]

It was within this context that, in 1914, the British government gained a controlling interest in APOC.[17] This move was supported overwhelmingly by the British Parliament, with 254 members voting in favor of acquiring majority shares and only 18 voting against.[18] While there was strong support in Parliament, however, the British government was not a monolithic actor. The British colonial government in India declined to participate in a long-term contract with other parts of the British government for APOC oil.[19] The government of India's decision played a part in the administration of APOC. Thus, unlike other administrative places in the Arabian Sea, which were overseen by the Bombay Presidency in India, the Persian oil fields were administered by the Foreign Office in London. Despite differences within the government, the British government's controlling interest in Anglo-Persian Oil Company allowed the government to secure oil production as it moved toward increasing reliance on oil by the military and industry.

By purchasing majority shares of APOC, the British government provided financial support to the company. Government support was not limited to finances, and the British government also provided laborers and security personnel for APOC. At the Abadan refinery, Indian troops enlisted in the British armed forces were, at times, used to supplement the labor force and as security personnel. For example, in the days before World War I began,

Indian soldiers were deployed to protect the Abadan refinery.[20] Not only did the British administration and oil company officials provide security personnel to protect oil projects, but the government also wanted to limit the influence of non-British actors at oil projects. British government interest in maintaining control of Persia is seen in a 1915 secret treaty with Russia that promised Russia control of Istanbul in return for British rule in most of Persia's neutral zone. In the following years, the British government attempted to consolidate its power and limit the influence of other countries, including the United States, in Persia.[21]

The importance of oil grew during and after World War I, and oil technology was seen as a key component of the Allied Powers' victory in the war. Imperial interest in Persian oil intensified, and as Kaveh Ehsani demonstrates, following the war, the oil complex made "lasting transformations that were brought about at the local, national, and regional levels." This included a restructuring of relations between local tribal leaders and the central government as well as between individuals and local authorities.[22] APOC also expanded its spatial control of Persia. For example, APOC framed Abadan as a wasteland, and this allowed the company to take control of area without proper compensation.[23] These interactions created imperial spaces that supported oil development.

COLONIAL INFRASTRUCTURE AND LABOR MOBILITY

As the oil industry grew, the labor needs of oil companies were immense. Oil companies needed skilled and unskilled employees to work in the oil fields, build and maintain refineries, and develop new sites of oil production. In addition, workers were needed for the numerous secondary businesses that supplied the necessary goods and services to the oil industry. This included everything from construction work to manufacturing to service provision. Workers came from throughout Persia, the Indian subcontinent, the Middle East, the Caucasus, and Europe.[24] Hiring workers from India was desirable given the already strong presence of Indians working throughout the Arabian Sea and the availability of thousands of experienced Indians who had previously worked for the British at the Burmah Oil Company.[25] In addition, many of the British managers of oil companies had begun their careers in British India before moving to Iran or the Arabian Peninsula. For example, since APOC's founding, Indians had worked for the company, and British businessmen often moved from working in industries in India to positions as managers at APOC. Notably, the director of APOC from 1909 to 1934 had worked previously at Shaw, Wallace & Co. in India, a whiskey manufacturer with offices in Calcutta (present-day Kolkata) and Bombay (present-day Mumbai).[26]

To hire and then move the large numbers of workers necessary to power the oil industry, APOC relied upon the colonial infrastructure that had been in place since 1833 to move indentured laborers from India to other parts of the British Empire. In this infrastructure, recruiting agents played a central role in moving workers. These agents, often located in large cities, worked through subagents to find Indian workers to travel abroad for jobs. Recruiting agents were overseen by government-appointed "protectors" who were responsible for the welfare of migrants. Protectors ensured migrants were not coerced, were healthy, and that they were treated fairly in their destination country.[27] This colonial infrastructure, which was used to move indentured labor during the nineteenth century, was revitalized in the twentieth century to move workers to the oil fields and continues to be used in the present.

While this colonial infrastructure was effective for moving thousands of workers, it was not always a fast way to do so, as labor migrants were required to receive permission from the protector of emigrants before traveling abroad for work. The speed of the system became an issue near the end of World War I, when APOC wanted to hire additional workers from India. At that time, political officers in Basra and Baghdad asked, on behalf of APOC, for the government of India to suspend the operation of Indian Emigration Act "in view of the extreme importance of the Company's operations for the successful prosecution of war." By suspending the Emigration Act, the company hoped it could expedite the hiring process and bypass some of the constrictions placed on the company by the British colonial government in India. In February 1918, the Emigration Act was suspended "experimentally as a war measure in respect of the recruitment of labour required by the Company,"[28] signifying the importance of labor and oil for imperial military purposes.

By 1920, thousands of Indians were working at oil projects and for the British military throughout the Middle East, and at least 3,700 Indians worked at the Abadan refinery.[29] Labor migration, however, was under scrutiny by nationalist leaders in India. Indian indentured labor was banned in 1917 due to pressure from Indian nationalist leaders, and these leaders continued to express concern for the treatment of Indians who migrated for work throughout the British Empire.[30] In addition, in India, nationalist leaders were critical of the British government's actions in the Middle East. This included the pan-Islamic Khilafat Movement that organized against the British government's plans in Turkey to carve up the Ottoman Empire and abolish the institution of the caliphate.[31]

Given this political climate, the Emigration Act's suspension was called into question by British officials in India who feared that the continued suspension of the Emigration Act would give additional fuel to Indian nationalists. British officials were particularly concerned given the poor treatment of Indians working for APOC. The government received a large number of complaints by Indian workers who reported that they were mistreated while working for APOC.[32] In addition, in 1920, three thousand Indians went on strike at Abadan and were joined by Persian workers.[33] APOC dismissed these workers' complaints, writing that they lacked a foundation and arguing "there will be some individuals who never will be satisfied however good the conditions may be."[34] Despite this argument, the company was unsuccessful in pressuring the government of India to continue the suspension of the Emigration Act. The act was reinstated and then revised in 1922, with the protector of emigrants system still in place.[35]

Even with these emigrant protections in place, Indian workers continued to complain about their working conditions and to go on strike. Tensions sometimes arose between groups working at Abadan. For example, in 1926, there were tensions between Persian employees and employees who spoke Chittagonian (a language spoken in contemporary Bangladesh and eastern India). A quarrel led to a strike being proclaimed, but ultimately, workers on shift did not strike and "the men responsible for both strikes were dismissed and sent back to India together with one or two others who were known to exert a disruptive influence among the men. The Chittagonians are now to heel again."[36] In such instances, tensions among workers emerged. Despite these fractious moments, at other times, workers continued to form collective solidarities in order to agitate for better working conditions, such as in 1929, when nine thousand workers at Abadan went on strike for a shorter working day.[37] As we will see in the following section, in the 1930s worker solidarities were also impacted by the political debates, occurring locally and globally, about nationalism, progress, and citizenship.

NATIONALISM AND LABOR IN THE 1930S AND 1940S

In the early 1930s, the Persian government had hoped the oil payment would help the country avoid the worst of the Great Depression. However, this expectation was not met when the 1931 oil payment from APOC to the Persian government was abysmally small.[38] The problems caused by the low oil payment were compounded by rising costs, as the price of imports effectively doubled between 1929 and 1932. In response, Reza Shah Pahlavi, the shah of Iran from 1925 to 1941, sought to implement changes to the country's relationship with APOC.

In 1933, Reza Shah renegotiated the D'Arcy concession with APOC. Reflecting on this almost a decade later, one US manager working for an oil company in Bahrain described this as a major blow to APOC. He wrote, "The British paid in Iran for the exploitation of the country. After the Iranians woke up to the true situation, the British paid thru the nose."[39] Despite this manager's impression of the high price paid by APOC, in reality, the concession negotiations had mixed results. On one hand, the new lease neither significantly improved Iran's control of oil nor increased the oil royalties received by the government. On the other hand, during the negotiations, Reza Shah put pressure on APOC to train and promote more Iranian workers. As a result, the new concession included a plan, formalized in 1934, to decrease the numbers of foreigners working at APOC.[40] Reza Shah's efforts to promote Persians within APOC's workforce contributed to the growth of the middle class as more Iranians began working in better-paying jobs in the oil industry that required technological expertise.[41] To explain his demands for decreasing the numbers of foreigners working at APOC and the promotion of Persians, Reza Shah connected Persian nationalism with modernization, which was understood to include increasing education initiatives and lessening discrimination against religious minorities.[42]

The push to replace APOC's foreign workers with local workers reflected Reza Shah's belief that oil was an avenue for "national progress."[43] Signifying a new beginning for the country, Reza Shah asked the international community to use the name *Iran* instead of *Persia*, and Anglo-Persian Oil Company was renamed the Anglo-Iranian Oil Company (AIOC). As Reza Shah imagined the future of Iran, he put forward an understanding of the Iranian people as a homogenous group, which contrasted with conceptualizations of the Persian nation in the early decades of the twentieth century that had focused more on the country's diversity.[44] As Farzin Vejdani writes, "Race, civilization, and religion became constitutive historical categories that necessarily defined Iranian collective identity against its perceived Others."[45] History textbooks used in schools reinforced this homogeneous view of the Iranian people, and they described Iranians as a race (*nezhad*). While a racialized view of Iranians was not uncontested, in the 1930s, Iranian citizens began to increasingly imagine Iran to be an ethnically and linguistically homogeneous place.[46]

Reza Shah's views on the Iranian nation and the Iranian people resonated with Indian nationalists' engagements with the nation. In India, leading nationalists, including Muhammad Ali Jinnah and Mohandas Karamchand Gandhi, operated from the assumption that India was a "natural territory, inhabited by communities defined above all by religion." But, before the partition of British colonial India into the countries of India and Pakistan, leading nationalists proposed differing relationships among nationality, religion, and territory. Many Muslim leaders argued for both a pan-Islamic identity and simultaneously a loyalty to one's homeland—a homeland that was defined territorially. These included Maulana Husain Ahmad Mamdani's differentiation between communities based on shared textual tradition (*millat*) and communities based on shared residence or territory (*muttahidah qaumiyyat*), and Muhammad Ali Jinnah's argument that Muslims were not a religious community but a nation. What tied together various nationalist views, including the views of Indian nationalists of other religions, such as M. K. Gandhi's view of nationalism, was the understanding of a nation-state to be a territory free from imperial rule.[47] Thus, colonialism and imperialism impacted nationalist discourse not only because they were forces to fight against but also because membership in the nation often replicated an Orientalist ideology that posited essential, unchanging distinctions among peoples.[48]

As who was considered Iranian was debated, AIOC agreed to increase the number of Iranians working at AIOC. However, following this decision, AIOC managers reported that it was challenging to fulfill the company's commitment to hire and promote more Iranians. In part, this was because, in the 1930s and 1940s, increasing numbers of workers were needed due to the rapidly growing pace of oil production in Iran. From 1930 to 1945, the Abadan refinery's throughputs almost quadrupled, with the most rapid expansion occurring between 1943 and 1945 when annual throughputs went from 10.49 million tons to 16.82 million tons of crude oil.[49] One key reason for increased production was that the British armed forces needed oil to fuel military operations during World War II. Oil production during the war was further spurred by Japan's entrance into the war. Japan's involvement meant a loss of Asian oil resources for the Allied forces, and oil, particularly Iranian oil, became of greater military importance. Increased demand for oil meant more workers were needed in the oil industry, and AIOC continued to recruit large numbers of Indian workers for oil projects in Iran. The numbers of Indians employed by AIOC and its contractors grew from 1,709 workers in 1939 to 2,498 workers in 1945.[50] By 1946, approximately 2,560 Indians worked for the company, making AIOC one of the largest employers of Indians in the area.[51]

Indian skilled tradesmen, in particular, were in high demand both at AIOC and at other oil projects.[52] While colonial labor mobilities and government support helped AIOC hire Indian workers, the company still had trouble retaining the number of Indian skilled tradesmen required for projects. One reason managers faced problems with staffing was due to issues workers experienced when they applied for emigration permission in India. In addition, the social upheaval and violence that occurred around the partition of British India in August 1947 meant that many workers, especially workers from the Punjab, did not return to their jobs after their home leaves ended. Trouble hiring Indian workers was further compounded by fierce competition for skilled workers among oil companies. For example, jobs at Kuwait Oil Company (KOC) paid higher salaries than jobs at AIOC, and as a result, AIOC was losing workers to KOC. In response, AIOC managers began fingerprinting workers and asked the protector of emigrants offices in Bombay and Karachi to check these fingerprints against workers seeking permission to work in Kuwait, thereby using the Indian government's emigration system as a way of ensuring workers complete their contracts. While there was competition for Indian skilled tradesmen, Reza Shah's push for the Iranization of AIOC's workforce did influence staffing: Indians were decreasingly hired for laboring positions, and Indians who were employed as laborers were either redesignated or discharged from their jobs.[53]

NATIONALISM AND THE 1946 STRIKES

Given these debates on corporate policies, hiring citizens, and national development within an imperial context, it may not be surprising that British officials, Iranian officials, and AIOC managers focused on the treatment of Iranian workers in their analyses of the 1946 strikes. For example, when Manucher Farmanfarmaian, a high-ranking Iranian official, visited the labor camps near Abadan, he was appalled at the conditions in which workers lived.[54] His critique pointed to the stark disjuncture between the treatment of British workers and Iranian workers: "Wages were 50 cents a day. There was no vacation pay, no sick leave, no disability compensation. The workers lived in a shanty town called Kaghazabad, or Paper City, without running water or electricity." He contrasted Kaghazabad to British management's accommodations, which included air conditioning, swimming pools, and tennis courts.[55] In addition to criticizing the difference in treatment between British and Iranian workers, Farmanfarmaian also sought to differentiate between the Iranian government and AIOC managers, and he focused on the role the Iranian government played in ending the strikes. Specifically, Farmanfarmaian emphasized that, upon arriving at Abadan, Iranian government officials promised workers better pay and a shorter work week.[56] In contrast, AIOC managers focused on the roles of the Iranian military and the Tudeh Party in ending the strike.[57]

AIOC managers, as they looked to the causes of the strike, focused exclusively on Iranian workers. One manager who wrote extensively on the strike was Donald MacNeill, an oil field labor superintendent at AIOC who was appointed in 1939 to be manager of technical personnel. In this role, MacNeill was tasked with hiring foreigners only when "necessary for the maintenance of the efficacy and economy of the Company's operations in Iran."[58] In MacNeill's report on the 1946 strikes, he described why he believed Iranization hindered AIOC managers' ability to maintain positive relations with workers. In addition, in his report, MacNeill argued that the lack of both economic development and formal trade unions meant that agents of the Tudeh Party were able to use the discontentment of workers to their advantage, thereby allowing a foothold for communism in Iran.

MacNeill illustrated his viewpoint on the strikes by writing a fictional story about an imagined Iranian employee of AIOC named Ali. Ali, MacNeill wrote, was frustrated with his job, and his treatment by his manager. In a dark coffee shop, Ali met "a stranger," who was an agent of the Tudeh Party. The agent was "a small man with flashing dark eyes, who was squatting on the rough wooden seat and talking in low earnest tones . . . words include capitalism, class war, 'out oil,'" and he tells "strange stories about lands where there were no 'Sahebs' [sirs] or 'Aghas' [masters or chiefs], but comrades all." After hearing the Tudeh agent, Ali exclaims, *"Allah, ensaf nist"* [God, there is no justice!] and joins the Tudeh Party. In this story, MacNeill drew upon Orientalist tropes and fear of communism to demonstrate how Tudeh Party agents were spreading a Tudeh "propaganda machine" that drove worker strikes.[59]

MacNeill believed the ability of the Tudeh Party to gain traction and the dissatisfaction of workers were both because of poor relations between Iranian managers and British staff. He blamed these poor relations largely on Iranization policies that had begun in the 1930s. He argued, "We have inserted an insulating layer of semi-educated Iranian Junior Staff between British Staff and Iranian labour." The consequence of the Iranization of the workforce, MacNeill wrote, was that managers were not close to their employees. This distance meant that managers did not treat workers well, and company policies were not properly attuned to workers' cultural practices, such as the need to support many dependents.

MacNeill contrasted the labor situation in the 1940s with what he believed labor relations were like at APOC in the 1920s. In the 1920s, MacNeill imagined, managers "worked along with his small gang of Iranian laborers and, because of the primitive forms of transport then, often in comparative isolation." As a result, managers knew the men they supervised well, "took a genuine interest in their welfare," and relations between British staff and Iranian laborers were "satisfactory." This closeness, MacNeill believed, was central to good labor management in the colonies, but Iranization did not allow for these relationships to continue. MacNeill also argued that labor relations were further harmed because British managers were upset because of the shah's treatment of AIOC and the "contemptuous way" Iranian staff treated British staff. However, while managers, including MacNeill, were critical of the impact of Iranization, they were also mobilizing similar logics as the Iranian government about nationality, race, citizenship, and development. As we will see in the following two sections, these logics were put into practice using a rationalization of colonialism as a civilizing mission as well as US perspectives on human resources that focused on employees as citizens who were central to national development.

THE COLONIAL LOGICS OF CORPORATE MANAGEMENT

MacNeill was critical of Iranization, and he also believed AIOC practices informed the 1946 strikes. Specifically, he argued that AIOC managers were not attentive to Iranian workers' economic, psychological, and cultural needs; instead, they relied on the military to control workers at job sites. Given the political uncertainty in Iran, MacNeill contended that guiding workers was a better course of action than military intervention. Looking forward, MacNeill advised, AIOC must not "cling too much to the security which martial law appears to give us and we are only able to maintain an uncertain peace by the periodical weeding out of undesirable elements who would be considered more or less harmless cranks in a more stable and contented society."[60] Rather, MacNeill proposed that AIOC should cultivate the development of Iran and its citizenry to address these issues. MacNeill's analysis and suggestions reflected many of the logics of British colonialism from the nineteenth century, including a model of the world in which countries were hierarchically situated with Britain at the apex.[61] Also similar to colonial rule during the nineteenth century, imperialism was justified by paternalism and progressivism.[62] Central to the logics of colonialism were the beliefs that populations living in areas that were colonized were "not yet" ready for liberty and that it was the duty of colonial governments to teach or "civilize" these populations.[63] While such colonial logics have been studied by many scholars, analyzing MacNeill's report shows that oil company managers understood national development to come about not only through colonial governance but also through corporate practices.

MacNeill's perspectives on progress built upon discourses mobilized by British government officials, politicians, and British East India Company officials regarding colonial India in the nineteenth century. In colonial India, a corporation, the British East India Company, governed most of the colony until 1857, when the British government assumed formal control of the colony. Officials in the British East India Company rationalized that the company was helpful to India because of its role as an educator.[64] This education was meant to make India more like England and Indians more like the English. This was famously articulated in Thomas Babington Macaulay's

1835 "Minute on Education," in which Macaulay argued for teaching Indians in English and using English as the administrative language of colonial India because this would help "form . . . a class of persons Indian in blood and colour, but English in tastes, in opinions, in morals and in intellect."[65] Similarly, in the nineteenth century, citizenship was seen as "a faculty to be learned and a privilege to be earned."[66]

MacNeill's description of the 1946 strikes indicates that he saw AIOC playing a similar role in Iran. MacNeill argued that Iranians looked to the company for this learning, and he reported that workers habitually called AIOC their "father." He further wrote that workers described feeling "very sad about being 'put out of their father's home,'" after workers lost their jobs following the 1946 strikes. Given AIOC's importance, MacNeill believed the company should play a key role in educating Iranians to be more like the British. Critiquing AIOC managers who thought that "Oriental and Occidental psychology" differ, MacNeill asked, "Is not human behaviour and reaction basically the same the whole world?" In this model, through proper instruction, MacNeill asserted that Iranians could be taught to be more like British workers:

> If we have succeeded in teaching Iranian "hill-billies" to drive cars, manipulate files, spanners and screwdrivers, wear sun helmets and congregate in clubs to drink beer, all of which are quite foreign to their way of life, surely we can teach them to organize themselves into trade unions very little different from our own.[67]

Ultimately, MacNeill believed AIOC must encourage social relations like in England, such as clubs and cinema halls. These social relations, he wrote, will "naturally lead to social improvement" when implemented in conjunction with training and economic improvement.

MacNeill also proposed that AIOC should reduce pay differences (but not as much as in the UK), pay workers enough to cover food and children's clothing, foster anticommunist trade unions, and encourage sports like football. Critically, he refuted common justifications of poor pay and abhorrent living conditions, specifically critiquing AIOC managers who rationalized these things by arguing that workers' standard of living was higher than it would be if they didn't work for the company. In his critique, economic development and social development were closely connected:

We may claim such accommodation is good enough for our Iranian workers. Were not most of them living in holes in the ground, black tents, or, at best, mud huts before they joined us? Quite true, but they were in their own environment then and they were not working for the great Anglo-Iranian Oil Company.[68]

Here, MacNeill points to global wealth inequalities as the justification used by managers to explain the poor living conditions at AIOC projects in Iran. The problem, according to MacNeill, is that AIOC had promised better and did not live up to its promises.

HUMAN RESOURCES MANAGEMENT, DEVELOPMENT, AND CITIZENSHIP

MacNeill's analysis of the 1946 strikes reflected colonial logics, and it also was informed by new ideas and practices in human resources management in Europe and the United States that were developed to assist governmental war efforts during World War II and combat communism. Following World War II, oil company managers and British and US government officials believed countries had two possible futures: communist or free.[69] Given these two possible futures, workers were seen as citizens with crucial roles in the state's economic and social development. Both human resources management and colonial paternalism shared central assumptions about nationality and progress, and MacNeill was able to combine new trends in management with his understanding of the colonial relationship between British managers and Iranian workers. MacNeill articulated this perspective through arguing for institutional changes as well as a focus on the development of individual workers. The emphasis, in the mid-twentieth century, was increasingly on citizenship as duty to one's country.[70]

Institutional changes, according to MacNeill, included the development of trade unions. In particular, MacNeill believed workers would see trade unions as operating as their "mother" because these unions would intercede with the company for workers.[71] Thus, MacNeill argued, trade unions would decrease the influence of the Tudeh Party. Trade unions would also strengthen the government, with union officials moderating between workers, companies, and the government, therefore stabilizing the status quo. This was a popular postwar view of trade unions, and they were seen to mitigate communism not only by MacNeill but also by government officials.

However, trade unions were not always successful in strengthening state power. For example, during World War II, in Egypt the British had attempted to co-opt trade unions to spread pro-British propaganda and support British policies. This had questionable success given that, by 1947 and 1948, there was "rapidly accelerating radicalization within the ranks of the trade union movement" as well as "increasingly sharp challenges to the authority of the state."[72]

MacNeill's understanding of the need to cultivate workers into good citizens reflected insights he gained after taking an industrial relations course in the United Kingdom. The program he completed, Training Within Industry (TWI), was paid for by AIOC, and by the late 1940s, most AIOC managers were being taught the TWI theory of job relations, which was developed in 1940 in the United States to help respond to war needs.[73] TWI then spread globally through organizations like the International Labor Organization, Standard Oil, and the United Kingdom's Labour Department. By end of World War II, almost 2 million supervisors had received TWI certifications.[74]

C. R. Dooley, the director of TWI, described its "common goal" as individual education. According to the developers of TWI, education would not only help an employee's company, but job training was also a benefit to a worker's country:

> We all want to meet the demands of war—maximum production through best use of our facilities and talents. But we can also build for the future in meeting the present challenge. The training we give the worker to do a good job *now* for war production can be more than an expedient means of getting the job done. It can be suitable to the individual and in line with his native talent and aspiration. Then it becomes education because the worker placed in the line of work he desires, and trained in accordance with his talent and aspiration, is a growing individual—mentally, morally, and spiritually, as well as technically. Training done from this point of view promotes production now and builds better citizens for a greater national stability afterwards.[75]

Thus, TWI sought to optimize worker productivity as well as strengthen governance. In order to do so, TWI's guidance for supervisors included remembering, "Employees are human beings. They are all individuals. It is important to find out how they feel."⁷⁶ This was premised on universal assumptions concerning worker desires, which were described as "recognition as an individual; to know how he is doing; some 'say' about things which affect him; credit when due; to make the best use of his abilities; [and] recognition as an individual."⁷⁷ Thus, workers across the globe were imagined as fundamentally the same, and state development was seen to move along a standard trajectory. Within this model, workers were understood to be key components of their countries' development and security.

The focus on citizenship, industry, and security, as well as the centrality of the individual and an individual's growth, are present in MacNeill's analysis of the 1946 strikes as well as his recommendations for AIOC's future management. This emphasis on the development of a free labor force as tied into national progress and development was part of imperial logic, in which areas under imperial control are "readied for self-rule while simultaneously asserting that the empire's continued presence is essential for maintaining this direction."⁷⁸ Citizenship was a central component of this understanding of progress, because managers trained workers who, as citizens, contributed to their country's development. Critically, as TWI's training for managers demonstrates, it was not only the government that mobilized narratives of national progress. Rather, discourses about national progress were also mobilized and strengthened by corporate practices, and in turn, they were used to legitimate corporate practices.

THE DANGERS OF COMMUNISM

Given that countries were seen to have one of two futures (communist or free) and the role of laborers as citizens, British government officials and oil company managers saw communist movements to be dangerous, and this belief grew from concerns over how these movements disrupted business as well as larger geopolitical tensions. Specifically, British government officials were concerned about the Tudeh Party's connection to the USSR. British officials based in India, Iran, and the Arabian Peninsula saw the Tudeh Party as symptomatic of the USSR's growing influence in the Arabian Sea and harmful to British companies' businesses, especially the oil industry. This view by the British was reinforced when, also in 1946, the Iranian government, in response to pressure from Tudeh Party leaders, gave the USSR concessions to the northern Iranian oil fields.

British government officials were not alone in thinking the Soviets were behind subversive actions in the Arabian Sea. During this period, Americans were also convinced that the Soviets were behind the strikes by AIOC workers in 1946, and they believed the Soviets were sponsoring strikes, sabotage, and other hostile actions at US oil projects in the Middle East. This belief persisted, despite the fact that there was no confirmation of Soviet influence at US projects.[79] British and US officials saw communism to be dangerous due to the Cold War and because communist movements were able to mobilize broad coalitions of workers.

In Iran following the 1946 strikes, AIOC managers recognized that strike organizers were not only Iranians but also mobile workers from outside of Iran. Indeed, managers were so concerned about the influence of Indian workers that a few days after the July 1946 strikes, the company paid for five Tudeh Party labor organizers from the Punjab, in colonial India, to fly back to Karachi as their "continued presence on the oilfields was considered so undesirable."[80] This solution, however, presented other problems as some government officials worried about the spread of communist ideas.

In 1946, as the British colonial government was preparing to depart from India, one British military intelligence officer based in Karachi was not devoting his time to the upcoming independence of India. Rather, Lieutenant-Colonel Thomas was focusing on Iran and the Arabian Peninsula, and the Indian workers based there. In the letters he wrote to his superiors in New Delhi that year, Thomas detailed his travels and long hours spent investigating the strikes discussed above, as well as other strikes in the Arabian Sea. Thomas spent most of the year locating the men who were dismissed from their jobs in these strikes, interviewing workers on leave who worked at oil projects in Iran or the Arabian Peninsula, and searching for the organizers of the strikes at their homes in northern India.

British agents such as Thomas were troubled by the return of the strike leaders to India and feared the consequences of "Tudeh propaganda" in the subcontinent. While many British officials in the Arabian Sea were concerned with maintaining Britain's access to oil, Thomas was also worried about the rise of communist sentiments among workers in India. He believed the communist ideas that spurred the strikes came to workers based in Iran and Kuwait via the Soviet Union, and he feared such ideas would spread throughout India. Thomas reported that many of the participants in the strikes were "fervent admirers" of the Tudeh Party. He wrote repeatedly to warn his superiors that the workers would continue to disseminate information on communism in India.[81] The danger, according to Thomas, was that Indian workers in Iran were more pro-Soviet than pro-British, and these attitudes were spreading to oil companies throughout the Arabian Sea, including Kuwait Oil Company (KOC).[82] Communism, from both British government officials' and oil company managers' perspectives, had the potential to undermine British imperial power and halt oil production.

Thomas's concerns were mirrored by oil company managers in the Arabian Peninsula, where workers were also collectively organizing and going on strike. Some of these strikes, like those in Iran, were directly informed by the Tudeh Party. In 1946, KOC workers in Kuwait carried out a series of strikes that were reported to be influenced by the Tudeh Party. These strikes utilized multiethnic, multilinguistic solidarities and in many ways appear similar to strikes that occurred at AIOC in Iran that same year. Also, like the strikes in Iran, the Indian organizers of the strikes at KOC were all from the same area of India and shared a linguistic background. KOC, too, deported these workers before they could cause further disturbances.[83]

A few years later, KOC and British government officials continued to worry about the Tudeh Party and other communist influences at KOC. At that time, six workers were dismissed for communist activities, which company managers compared to the activities that had occurred at Abadan. Also like at AIOC, the workers were immediately sent out of the country—in this case they were all put on a ship for Karachi, Pakistan. One KOC manager described the situation:

> Four members of the Tudeh who were expelled from Iran are working at KOC under assumed names but not yet identified. Two small and abortive strikes which have taken place may perhaps be attributed to them. Some of the Indian members of the Company receive the Communist paper called "BLITZ" from Bombay and are reported to indulge in a certain amount of wild talk but up to date there is no sign of any serious subversive movement.[84]

This description points to some of the challenges in identifying what motivated strikes. For example, the manager reported that members of the Tudeh Party were working at KOC, but the fact that the company is unable to identify these workers allows us to see how rumor shaped assumptions about worker activities. We also see that communism was used to categorize a wide variety of activities. For example, the presence of the Indian paper *Blitz* was used by the manager to reinforce concerns about the spread of communism. However, while some of the columnists at *Blitz* had communist sympathies, overall, the paper espoused "populist rather than class politics."[85]

Despite the lack of clarity over the Tudeh Party's actual role in worker action, by invoking it, managers were able to justify aggressive responses to worker actions. This included immediately dismissing Indian and Pakistani workers at KOC who tried to form a union.[86] Oil company managers' allegations of communist activities and aggressive responses were not limited to Kuwait. In Bahrain in 1948, managers at the Bahrain Petroleum Company (Bapco) accused Adenese employees of making communist speeches. Shortly after making these speeches, the Adenese workers traveled to Saudi Arabia where they were deported by plane.[87] In Saudi Arabia, communist parties were also thought to hold sway over workers, and two magazines published by the Lebanese Communist Party, *al-Sarkha* and *al-Nida*, were circulating among workers at the Arabian American Oil Company (Aramco).[88]

BEYOND THE NATION-STATE

As workers sought to improve their working and living conditions, both communism and nationalism facilitated collective action. Similarly, in the first half of the twentieth century, nationalism had the potential to both articulate differences between workers and aid in the coordination of anti-imperial actions among groups.[89] However, while nationalism and communism were both used in anti-imperial movements, at times these movements used competing logics for solidarity building and had differing goals.

As Indians traveled abroad for work in the first half of the twentieth century, some debated nationalism and communism as ways to agitate against British colonialism. Newspapers that focused on Indian anticolonial movements served to bring Indians together and also influenced nationalist activities in India.[90] Not all Indian anti-imperial activity occurring outside of India in the twentieth century was nationalist. Indeed, the Ghadar Movement, operating in both North America and India, had as a goal national liberation, but it was primarily an anarchist movement and was transnationally focused.[91] Other Indian anticolonial activists were influenced by the writing of Karl Marx, including Manabendra Nath Roy. While working in the United States, Roy moved from "revolutionary nationalism" to imagining anticolonial liberation beyond the nation. Roy cautioned against harking back to ideas of a precolonial India or creating an Indian nation-state that used the same structures and forms of repression as were used in colonialism.[92] Similarly, internationalist movements in the 1930s also warned about the dangers arising in nationalism. Indeed, a representative of the Communist Party of Great Britain wrote to Indian communists and advised them against becoming too nationalist for fear that it would foster fascism.[93]

Globally, communist movements at this time largely operated by "speaking a language of national democracy."[94] And despite the internationalist goals of communism, discourses of nationalism by political leaders carried ideological weight and erected barriers to internationalism.[95] The tensions between nationalism and internationalism were reflected in the composition and interests of members of the Tudeh Party. The main sphere of activities for the Tudeh Party was among trade unions and industrial workers. The party was also able to mobilize workers across class divisions in Iran, and British government officials thought middle- and upper-class Iranians were attracted to the Tudeh Party because of their feelings of nationalism.[96] However, the Tudeh Party was also international in its leadership and membership, and workers of many nationalities participated in collective action against AIOC. Indeed, while all twelve leaders of the Tudeh Party came from working-class or lower-middle-class families, they were internationally diverse, and leadership included one Armenian and six Azeris.[97] In the 1946 strikes, five Indian Tudeh Party leaders helped to organize the participation of Indians in the strike.

Regarding the Indian workers who participated in the 1946 strikes at Abadan, there were two key characteristics that exemplify how local and international politics and solidarities were engaged with by workers. First, the coalition was class based. Indian managers did not participate in the strike and remained "loyal" to the company.[98] While they lived in similar conditions as the striking workers, their managerial position influenced their actions and oriented them toward a set of politics that was not tethered to their class, place of origin, or native language. The coalition for the July 14 strike gained momentum from shared ideological (Tudeh) and class sympathies, and workers formed multilingual and multiethnic alliances. Despite this broad coalition of actors, the five men who were considered the Indian organizers of the strike all came from a few districts in the Punjab near Lahore. These men shared a natal village, religion, and language. This points to a second key characteristic of the strike: While workers were forming broad coalitions, local affective ties rooted in British India influenced Indian worker actions. These actions were both based on and formative of a political sensibility that had local roots and followed, but was not limited to, the contours of the British Empire.

It was not only Tudeh Party ideology that fostered solidarity and motivated workers, but shared living conditions in Abadan also helped inform collective action. Indeed, given how poorly non-British employees lived, mass agitations in response to working and living conditions were not surprising. As one AIOC manager wrote, "The vast majority of our labour force are still living in scandalous accommodation in urine-tainted squalor— in little *manzels* [houses]." These houses, the supervisor explained, were "without sanitation, water supply or lighting, and with either too much ventilation or no ventilation at all." Housing for laborers was poorly made, and there were not enough accommodations for all workers. "Overcrowding is rampant and up to 10 persons sleep on the damp floor of a 10 foot room, huddled together to keep warm in the winter or to keep out of the sun in the summer afternoons."[99] British government officials largely agreed and characterized the living conditions of laborers as "'a penal settlement in the desert' with accommodation 'little better than pig-styes [*sic*].'"[100] Living conditions were so poor that AIOC managers cautioned against recreating similar living conditions at oil projects under development in nearby countries.[101]

Not only did workers live in dreadful conditions, but AIOC managers did not control the areas where workers lived. AIOC managers officially reported that Indians lived in "enclaves," and British officials understood Indians to be an intermediary group that operated as a "buffer zone" between Iranians and the British managers.[102] However, in practice, AIOC managers did not actually know where their workers lived in Abadan.[103] As William Glover's work on colonial Lahore demonstrates, spatial separations existed far stronger in colonizer imaginaries than in practice. Such spatial separations were largely discursively constructed within an Orientalist framework and, in practice, were frequently transgressed as workers move through colonial spaces.[104] Through these transgressions and shared experiences, workers were able to collectively mobilize.

CONCLUSION

For workers at Abadan in 1946, communism's strength derived from its ability to effectively mobilize workers through an inclusive logic of membership based on class identity. Such a movement could be contrasted with nationalist movements, which often limited participation based on citizenship. AIOC managers, for their part, acknowledged the possibilities for international solidarities while continuing to engage with workers based on nationality. In contrast, shared working and living conditions and circulating anti-imperialist discourses allowed for workers to forge international solidarities. Attentiveness to the temporary workers at oil projects in Iran and their role in collective action expands the implications of the July 1946 strikes by decentering the nation-state in narratives about labor and, instead, shows the potential of moving toward the construction of a global working class.

Despite this potential, from workers' perspective, the government's responses to the 1946 strikes were mixed. Reforms included new rights for peasants and anticorruption legislation.[105] For laborers, the first minimum wage law came into effect and day rate workers (or unskilled workers) were converted into a more stable form of employment.[106] While AIOC followed new labor laws for factories and the new minimum wage structures, they also increasingly contracted out jobs "to small firms that did not comply."[107] The result was that many did not experience changes to their working and living conditions. The government also implemented martial law and began the regulation of unions.[108] From 1946 to 1949 in Iran, many union leaders were arrested and Tudeh Party leaders removed from the government cabinet. Despite this, in 1949 the Tudeh Party a still had influence at Abadan, and AIOC managers estimated that 95 percent of the Iranian employees at Abadan were members of the Tudeh Party.[109]

For Indian laborers, local networks intersecting with international carbon politics continued to inform worker attempts to renegotiate their working and living conditions. However, additional attempts to strike had trouble gaining support from other laborers at AIOC, perhaps due to the deportation of the Indian Tudeh Party leaders. On August 4, 1947, Indians again tried to strike in the hope of negotiating better working and living conditions. The Indian organizers of this strike were able to get between four hundred and five hundred Indians to participate. Despite the success of mobilizing Indian workers, however, organizers were unable to bring Iranians or other nationalities into the strike. The result was that the Indians returned to work on August 6 without any changes in their labor conditions. This second, smaller strike at Abadan indicates the importance of international solidarities for worker actions to be effective. It also points to the power of a regional or national identity to mobilize workers from all over the Indian subcontinent. Like the earlier July strikes, the suspected organizers of the strike were dismissed.[110]

During strikes and other moments of collective action in the first half of the twentieth century, workers in the Arabian Sea's oil industry often formed alliances across ethnic, national, and linguistic divisions. However, by midcentury, worker solidarities increasingly segmented along national lines. As we will see in the following three chapters, especially influential for informing labor actions were the codification of citizenship in the Arabian Peninsula, India's and Pakistan's independence in 1947, Iran's nationalization of oil in 1951, and the development of new oil projects throughout the Arabian Peninsula.

Two
CONTESTING SOVEREIGNTY

LIKE IN IRAN, IN THE MID-TWENTIETH CENTURY, WORKING AND living conditions at oil projects in the Arabian Peninsula were challenging, and workers frequently went on strike to try to change these conditions. While some of these strikes were directly influenced by communist parties, including the Tudeh Party, others were not. Despite not being explicitly communist, many of these strikes were similar to communist strikes because the striking workers often formed coalitions across linguistic, national, and religious lines. One place where such strikes occurred was at Kuwait Oil Company (KOC) in 1948. That year, a coalition of junior staff, including Indian, Pakistani, Arab, and Iranian employees, went on strike at least three times because of their substandard working and living conditions.[1] The intergroup solidarities during these three strikes are notable, particularly given claims by KOC managers that Indian workers did not get along with Arab workers.

During the first strike at KOC in February 1948, workers complained that the food quality was poor, and workers asked that they be allowed to run their own mess hall, arguing that the junior staff could do so more economically and serve better food than did the current contractor.[2] During a second strike in June 1948 and a third in September 1948, junior staff at KOC, including Indians, Pakistanis, Arabs, and Iranians, again complained about their food. They also had several additional complaints, which pointed to the interconnections between working and living conditions. Workers accused a

European employee of KOC's food contractor (Spinneys) of abuse, and workers asked that managers not speak to them harshly.[3] Workers were also outraged by the refusal by the company to give August 15, 1948, off from work so that employees could celebrate the second anniversaries of India's and Pakistan's independence from British colonial rule.[4] In addition, workers demanded improved working and living conditions, including drinking water to be delivered to their tents, shade and ventilation—especially for those working with "bad gases," and clean bathrooms with doors. Finally, drawing on their experience working for the Anglo-Iranian Oil Company (AIOC), workers asked for ration slips when working in Kuwait, like the ones they received while working in Iran.[5]

As workers at oil projects in the Arabian Peninsula frequently went on strike, oil company managers and British government officials sought to quickly stop worker actions, and their responses draw attention to the different political situations in the Arabian Peninsula and Iran. In Iran, the British government exercised a strong diplomatic influence throughout the first half of the twentieth century, but the British government's formal role in governance was small.[6] In contrast, the treaties signed by the British government with the rulers of the countries of the Arabian Peninsula in the late nineteenth and early twentieth centuries gave the British government additional powers. These differences in imperial governance shaped oil company operations and were shaped by them in turn. As one US employee of the Arabian American Oil Company (Aramco) observed after visiting Kuwait:

> The relations with the government differ from those in other Middle Eastern states in that this is a small country consisting, in effect, of only one city completely controlled by a single Sheikh who is enjoying a relatively enormous personal income. This state has not developed with a bureaucracy, legislation, and other machinery of organized government. Consequently, generally speaking, the [Kuwait Oil] Company is able to proceed according to its own wishes with complete freedom and believes that it can place reliance on British interference should this freedom be challenged by the local government.[7]

As described in this quote, oil company managers believed that local governance structures, small populations, and the British imperial protectorate system allowed oil companies to rely more heavily on British military and diplomatic support than was possible in countries like Iran.

Strikes by workers, both those from the Arabian Peninsula and mobile workers, brought to the fore questions regarding governance, security, and sovereignty. As oil company managers, the local government, and the British government attempted to respond to these strikes and minimize future work stoppages, they debated and attempted to codify rights, jurisdiction, and citizenship for the countries of the Arabian Peninsula. Examining these interactions demonstrates how the state "arises from techniques that enable mundane material practices to take on the appearance of abstract, nonmaterial form."[8] As the state expands to "fill a particular space, encompass all aspects of culture, and stand above all other elements of society," it creates governable spaces through making people and places legible.[9] Like in many colonial contexts, power in the Arabian Peninsula was made visible through "officializing procedures," which included censuses, map making, and record keeping.[10] Exerting the rule of law drew new areas into the colonial orbit and helped create a context in which racial hierarchies were expressed through legal forms.[11] Despite this codification, state and corporate power were neither uniformly asserted nor experienced.[12]

In the Arabian Peninsula, interactions among local governments, the British administration, workers, and oil companies shaped state practices and institutions. This is seen throughout the area historically, as state governance, imperial power, and oil development were closely intertwined. Despite this closeness, tensions arose among local governments, the British administration, and oil companies. Looking specifically at the operations of KOC, we will see that legibility was not created by the state and then used by corporations. Rather, legibility and other features of the state were actively constructed through interactions among local and imperial governments, oil companies, and, crucially, workers.

TREATIES AND CONCESSIONS IN THE ARABIAN PENINSULA

The governance practices and understandings of citizenship that were being worked out on the Arabian Peninsula in the mid-twentieth century were extensions of processes that began in the nineteenth century. From the late 1800s, rulers in the Arabian Peninsula began conceding their external affairs to the British government.[13] Operating out of Bombay, the British signed treaties with local rulers in hopes of creating a "buffer zone" between British India and the Ottoman Empire.[14] These treaties became the foundation for later oil concessions.

The British government signed treaties in 1880 and 1883 with the sheikh of Bahrain, 1886 with the Mahra Sultanate of Qishn and Socotra (creating the Aden Protectorate), in 1892 with the sheikhs of the Trucial Coast (contemporary United Arab Emirates), in 1899 with the sheikh of Kuwait, in 1915 with the ruler of Saudi Arabia, and in 1916 with the sheikh of Qatar.[15] These treaties prohibited the rulers from establishing any contact with foreign powers without British permission and also required the rulers to end all hostilities at sea. In return, the British government recognized the rulers' independence and promised to protect them if attacked.

These treaties bolstered the rulers' internal authority, while relying on government structures already existent in the area. With this type of administration, the British Empire in the Arabian Peninsula was, as historian James Onley argues, largely indigenous.[16] Administratively, British governmental interests in the Arabian Peninsula were overseen from the Bombay Presidency in India. After India's independence in 1947, the administration of this system was overseen by the British political resident and local political agents under the supervision of the British Foreign Office.[17] By the early 1950s, the Trucial system was made up of Bahrain, Qatar, and the Trucial sheikhdoms of Abu Dhabi, Dubai, Ras al Khaimah, Sharjah, Umm al Quwain, Ajman, and Fujairah. These Trucial States were described as British protected states or "independent sheikhdoms with special treaty relations with the United Kingdom."[18]

The benefits of the Trucial system were not limited to protecting colonial India—the system also secured British trade routes. Importantly, these earlier treaties gave the British government an advantage after the Arabian Peninsula rose to prominence for its potential oil reserves in the early 1900s.[19] Seeking to maintain and extend Britain's control in the Arabian Sea, the British government signed additional agreements with the governments on the Arabian Peninsula that specified that if oil was found within their territories, the rulers would not give concessions to foreigners except those approved by the British government.[20] The first of these treaties was signed with the sheikh of Kuwait in 1913. Rulers of the Arabian Peninsula signed similar treaties with the British throughout the following decade: The sheikh of Bahrain signed in 1914, the sheikh of Qatar in 1916, the sheikhs of the Trucial States in

1922, and the sultan of Muscat in 1923. Lord Curzon—whose career included serving as viceroy of India from 1898 to 1905, as a member of the House of Lords, and as the foreign secretary—spearheaded many of these treaties in an effort to gain control over Middle Eastern oil for Great Britain and mitigate other imperial powers' influence in British India.

During the first half of the twentieth century, Britain was not the only country interested in oil reserves in the Arabian Peninsula. The British government felt its oil interests were threatened by both US and USSR oil projects in the area, by pan-Islamic and pan-Arab movements that argued for an end to British colonialism, and by hostile foreign powers that attempted to halt oil production as a means of harming British military capacities. As described in the previous chapter, the USSR had influence in Iran, particularly in the northern provinces, and British government officials feared the USSR was also interested in the Arabian Peninsula. In addition, the British government was concerned about the influence of the United States, as US companies were openly vying to develop oil projects in the area.

These factors influenced the contours of oil concessions in the Arabian Peninsula. Concessions were also influenced by agreements made by imperial powers about oil production in other parts of the Middle East. Particularly, following upon the discovery of huge quantities of oil in Iraq in 1928, French, British, and US oil companies—the Anglo-Persian Oil Company (APOC), Royal Dutch Shell (Shell), the Compagnie Française des Pétroles (CFP, later Total), and the Near East Development Corporation (NEDC)—signed the Red Line Agreement in order to coordinate the development of oil resources in the former Ottoman Empire.[21] Under the terms of the agreement, each of the four parties received a 23.75 percent share of all the crude oil produced by Turkish Petroleum Company (TPC, later renamed the Iraq Petroleum Company or IPC).[22] TPC was allowed to operate anywhere in the Middle East between the Suez Canal and Iran, with the exception of Kuwait.

Oil companies that had not signed the Redline Agreement were not constrained by its terms. Thus, US oil companies that had not signed the agreement could pursue oil concessions where other companies were unable to do so. For example, in 1930, Standard Oil Company of California (SoCal) obtained the concession for Bahrain through its Canadian subsidiary, Bahrain Petroleum Company (Bapco).[23] In 1937, SoCal and the Texas Company (today Texaco) created the California Texas Oil Company (Caltex), of which Bapco became a wholly owned subsidiary. In Saudi Arabia, SoCal was able to negotiate concessions in 1933, and the company formed a subsidiary company, the California Arabian Standard Oil Company, to hold these concessions. Three years later, in 1936, Texaco purchased 50 percent shares of the California Arabian Standard Oil Company, and in 1944, the company was renamed the Arabian American Oil Company (Aramco).[24]

The British administration in the Arabian Peninsula had differing opinions on the fact that US companies held oil concessions in Bahrain and Saudi Arabia. On one hand, the British wanted to stop Americans from moving farther south into the peninsula. On the other hand, they also saw the benefits of increased revenue in the region, and this was one reason Bapco was allowed to search for oil in 1932.

In parts of the Arabian Peninsula, British and US companies worked together to develop oil projects. In Kuwait, in 1934, joint concessions were negotiated by the Anglo-Persian Oil Company (APOC) and Gulf Oil.[25] A year later, international cooperation was again used to explore oil opportunities—this time on the Trucial Coast, when Petroleum Concessions, Ltd. (PCL) was formed by the shareholders of Iraq Petroleum Company (IPC).[26] This cooperation was necessary because, under the Red Line Agreement, APOC could not operate concessions in Qatar and the Trucial Coast except when it was working in conjunction with its partners in the IPC. Thus, after the formation of the new subsidiary, APOC transferred its rights to PCL. After other concessions were acquired by PCL, the concessions were then transferred for development to a sister company, Petroleum Development, Ltd. (PDL). Even though a number of companies had ownership stakes in PCL and PDL, British administrators in the Arabian Peninsula considered both British companies, because they operated as such in "personnel, finances, and outlook." In the absence of fully owned British companies, PCL and PDL served to exclude some types of foreign competition. The political agreements signed between PCL and local rulers also reinforced British control over oil production in the area, safeguarding British interests especially in case of "emergency or war."[27]

LABOR, OIL, AND GOVERNANCE

As oil operations expanded on the Arabian Peninsula after World War II, key issues emerged around state borders, the legitimacy of the British governance in the region, and the control of mobile labor forces. As these issues were debated and policies were put into practice, security and citizenship were worked out within a context of imperial sovereignty. This included British attempts to mitigate Soviet and US influence at oil projects in the Arabian Peninsula and to control which nationalities were employed at oil projects.

British government officials legitimated the British role in governance of the countries of the Arabian Peninsula through emphasizing the part the administration played in fostering security and rule of law, including for oil companies. The British government in the Arabian Peninsula actively defined and enforced borders, decided court cases involving nonlocal individuals, and regulated travel. The drawing of boundaries in the Arabian Peninsula helped cement sheikhs' authority over certain areas and facilitated oil concessions. In turn, oil operations brought large amounts of capital to the rulers of the region. The British administration also hoped that these boundaries would ensure the sheikhs' compliance with the policies of the British government and the oil companies. Signing oil concessions required clear territorial boundaries, and the British government facilitated the drawing of these borders.[28] Disputes over boundaries caused costly delays for oil companies and, in years where some oil companies had record profits, other oil companies suffered due to holdups on the agreements for oil concession boundaries.[29] One example of the delay in oil production arose with a dispute caused when the sheikh of Kuwait granted a concession to American Independent Oil Company (Aminoil) for three islands that KOC believed were part of the KOC concession.[30] Trying to distance the British government from oil companies, the British political resident named an arbiter to decide the issue.[31] However, disputes over Kuwaiti concessions, particularly seabed concessions, continued to arise, and British government officials tried to ensure concessions went to British companies.[32]

The British government also provided some security to the oil companies. For example, in Kuwait, KOC managers worried that if there were a breakdown in Saudi Arabia, then there could be tribal incursions. As a result, they discussed with the British administration plans to protect KOC's camps and installations "similar to that which has recently been prepared for Bahrain." Following these discussions, KOC officials decided that managers should keep a small reserve of pistols and rifles and have a group trained on how to use them. The British armed forces also provided advice, and a senior naval officer suggested that KOC should "obtain some tear gas bombs."[33] In Qatar, the British administration supported oil company operations, and when employees of an oil company had trouble building infrastructure in Qatar due to internal disputes, British government officials threatened a local sheikh into cooperating with the company.[34]

Not only did the British administration provide protection and security advice to companies, but they also regulated travel and provided legal infrastructure necessary for oil company operations. In 1948, the political agent in the Trucial Coast issued travel documents to nationals so they could go work at oil projects in Kuwait, Saudi Arabia, Bahrain, and elsewhere. The political agent's office estimated that it received and approved two hundred applications a day, and that these individuals were readily hired once they traveled, given the oil companies' great need for workers.[35] The British administration also oversaw many court cases, and in 1949, the British courts decided 1,629 civil cases and 279 criminal cases in Bahrain. The number of cases the British courts heard was expected to rise, as increasing numbers of British, US, Indian, and European workers, over whom the British had jurisdiction, moved to the Arabian Peninsula.[36]

In addition to activities like demarcating borders, advising on security matters, and overseeing court cases, the British government also exerted imperial sovereignty as it regulated who could work at oil company projects. As the number of oil projects in the Arabian Peninsula grew, more and more workers were needed to staff them. The concession agreements limited who could work at these projects. Oil concession agreements signed in the 1930s specifically stated that the workers brought in to work for the companies would be locals and people from neighboring countries on the Arabian Peninsula. This was important to local rulers given the depressed state of the economy after the global economic downturn and the collapse of the pearl market due to the spread of pearl farming in the 1930s.[37] Ensuring jobs for locals also reflected rulers' sovereignty, and at this time, "dominion over persons ranked before territory as the operative criterion of Arabian sovereignty."[38] Despite rulers' requests that local subjects be hired for the oil company operations, oil company managers argued that locals did not have the appropriate technical training to meet oil company requirements. As a result, oil companies reserved the right to hire foreign workers; a nationality clause in the concessions, which had been insisted upon by the British government, dictated from which countries oil companies could hire workers.[39]

British government officials expressed concern that large numbers of workers moving to the area could potentially cause political destabilization. Americans owned 100 percent and 50 percent shares in Bapco and KOC, respectively, and the British worried that too many Americans living in these countries would undermine British political authority. They also worried that US workers would be the "tough guy" type, and the British government would have to police these men or there would be general lawlessness.[40] In addition, the British were concerned that the oil companies would bring in Iranian workers, and this influx of Iranians would reopen Iranian claims of sovereignty over Bahrain. Skilled Iraqis, too, were thought to potentially cause problems by organizing worker action. For example, in the early 1940s Iraqi foremen bricklayers went on strike.[41] In the case of Qatar, British officials asserted that the "backward" nature of the people meant that only British-government-approved foreigners should be employed there. More specifically, the British worried that unrest among local workers could lead to the deaths of foreign workers and that these deaths would lead to demands that the British government be responsible for adjudicating these incidents.

To prevent unrest and maintain British influence, concessions stated that British subjects, including Indians, should be preferentially hired for projects. Like the hiring of Indian workers for projects in Iran, large numbers of workers were able to be moved due to a reworking of the colonial infrastructure originally created to move indentured laborers throughout the British Empire in the 1800s. Thus, throughout the 1940s, the number of Indians working in the Arabian Peninsula rose rapidly. Some of these workers had first worked at oil projects in Iran for AIOC. Still other Indian workers were recruited in Bombay by a British recruiting agent based there, using the same recruitment system that was used to recruit workers for oil projects in Iran. Even after India's independence from British rule, companies were encouraged to hire Indians, and Indians made up a substantial portion of oil companies' labor force. For example, at PCL (Bahrain) in 1947, Indians composed almost one-quarter of the labor force and worked in skilled positions as well as manual laborers.[42]

As Indians were hired for oil projects, there emerged a growing division of labor based on nationality. For example, in Qatar, PCL had multiple construction projects and required a much larger workforce than in Bahrain. At PCL (Qatar), Qataris made up the vast majority (84 percent) of daily laborers and Indians were the second largest group of daily laborers, constituting 9 percent of this employment category. The composition of the workforce changed for more skilled positions. Out of the 85 monthly paid employees, there was only 1 Qatari in contrast to 72 Indians. This shows the division of labor along national lines—a division that is further made clear when looking at the nationalities of people working in the top management and professional positions. These positions were held exclusively by Europeans and Americans, including 106 British, 17 US, and 1 Swiss employee.[43] As we will see in the following chapters, labor hierarchies based on nationality became increasingly rigid over the next two decades.

OIL COMPANIES AND SOVEREIGNTY IN KUWAIT

The relationships between the various oil companies operating in the British Protected States and the British administration were complex: Oil companies were reliant on the work done by the British administration to govern the Arabian Peninsula, but they also actively contested attempts by the British administration to curtail their own activities. Thus, while they were able to collaborate on some activities, oil company managers and government officials often operated with differing goals. As one administrator wrote, "oil men, particularly in the opening of a new field, are always in a hurry to achieve their immediate aims—which are not necessarily ours [i.e., the British government's]."[44] The tensions between the aims of oil companies and the British government were exacerbated as oil projects rapidly developed after World War II. There was also tension among companies, as they competed to sign concessions and develop oil projects on the Arabian Peninsula. A monthly letter from the Persian Gulf Residency described the situation: "We have had a number of oil company representatives wandering round the Gulf, most of them watching each other's movements with deep suspicion."[45] As companies sought new areas for oil development, questions were raised about sovereignty, jurisdiction, and boundaries, and contestations over these issues demonstrate both the tensions and collaborations among the local government, British administrators, and oil companies.

Relations between the British administration and company officials were particularly fraught in Kuwait, and British administrators argued that KOC was undermining British authority. British administrators saw this issue as extremely pressing given that KOC ownership was split evenly between

US and British companies. KOC had acquired oil concessions in Kuwait in 1934.[46] The following year, oil was discovered at the Burgan field. However, like in other areas of the Arabian Peninsula, World War II delayed oil production. The field was not developed until 1945, and Kuwait first exported oil at the end of June 1946. In 1947, construction began for a new refinery at Mina al-Ahmadi, and the refinery began operations in November 1949.[47]

As oil production intensified, the British administration was "perturbed" by the actions of managers at KOC. The central issue, according to British administrators, was that KOC was not complying with Article 4 of the political agreement between KOC and the British government. Article 4 required the oil company to "conduct its local relations through the Political Agent except as regards routine business." However, KOC frequently cut the political agent out of the loop.[48] The issue was further compounded because KOC was not the only company that failed to comply with Article 4 of the political agreement; another oil company operating in Kuwait, the American Independent Oil Company (Aminoil), was also out of compliance.[49]

British administrators believed the actions of KOC and Aminoil were subverting British authority in Kuwait, and they found this frustrating because other oil companies, including Bapco, complied with this agreement. To clarify which interactions between oil companies and local rulers fell under Article 4, British officials used the correspondence between Bapco and the ruler of Bahrain as an example. They categorized these correspondences into three categories. The first, "important matters with political aspect," included concession areas, royalty payments, and the company's annual report. All of these should go through the political agent. The second type of correspondences were "less important matters which bear on relations of company and local government." Copies of these correspondences should be sent to the political agent. Third, routine correspondences, like the registration of cars, did not need to go through the political agent.[50]

British government officials gave three reasons that companies ought to follow the political agreement's provisions concerning company relations with local governments. First, British government officials argued that by following the agreement, the companies would avoid political troubles, thereby allowing a company to "operate at its maximum effectiveness through the absence of friction." Second, harkening back to the role the British argued they played in the development of the state in colonies, following the political agreement would ensure that the Kuwaiti "affairs develop on proper lines." Finally, government officials argued that following the political agreement would ensure that British "rights as regard jurisdiction were maintained."[51] Ultimately, the British government suggested that KOC "canalize" their dealings with the Kuwaiti government.[52]

KOC managers resisted the British government's attempts to insert itself into the relations between the company and the ruler. They responded to the British administration that they would like to comply with the British government's wishes, but that two issues stood in the way. First, KOC managers argued for the sovereignty of the Kuwaiti ruler, who, they wrote, "has the right to address the company directly on all matters affecting his relations with the company irrespective of their importance or of the degree to which HM [His Majesty's] Government may be interested." Second, KOC managers argued, the wording of the agreement was vague, and therefore it was challenging to differentiate what types of matters needed to go through the political agent.[53]

While KOC managers actively contested the British administration's attempts to limit relations between the ruler of Kuwait and the company, they worked with the British administration on other matters, particularly regarding company actions that managers anticipated would cause friction between the company and the ruler. For example, KOC deferred to the British administration over compensation for Kuwaiti workers. In 1949, KOC was particularly upset by "absence of decision" by the political agent regarding compensation for Kuwaiti subjects' families when Kuwaitis died on the job.[54] KOC also appealed to the British administration during disputes with other companies over concessions and when they found themselves to be in conflict with the ruler of Kuwait. For example, KOC appealed to the political agent regarding the presence of Kuwaiti police at KOC. When the company had begun its operations, KOC managers had allowed Kuwaiti police at KOC worksites and camps. By the late 1940s, however, managers did not want Kuwaiti police in these areas because KOC was being forced to pay these police officers. In addition, both KOC managers and British administrators agreed that local police officers were overstepping their authority, at times arresting those who were out of their jurisdiction. Anticipating conflict with the ruler if they prohibited the police from entering KOC property, managers asked the British administration to intervene.

British officials foresaw negatives consequences arising, particularly for the British administration, if KOC continued to selectively follow parameters of the political agreement. British officials believed KOC's lack of compliance "amongst other things adversely affects our influence over the Sheikh. As he can get almost anything he wants by applying direct to the oil company we have nothing to bargain with when we want something out of him such as the appointment of British advisers." British officials' fears that they were losing influence and bargaining power with the ruler was compounded by the fact that administrators thought that the current local representative, who was appointed by the ruler of Kuwait, was "in the Shaikh's pocket."[55] British government officials believed that oil companies were not complying with Article 4 of the political agreement "due to fear of offending" the ruler, who wanted "all oil matters brought to him directly—not to Political Agent." For the British administration, this meant it was "impossible" to insist on Article 4 of the political agreement "so long as the Shaikh continues to bully the Oil Company in this manner and the Oil Company continues to stand for it."[56] Such questions over jurisdiction and sovereignty became increasingly important as more and more workers arrived in Kuwait.

MOBILE WORKERS AND GOVERNANCE

British officials based in the Arabian Peninsula saw labor at oil companies to be a particularly fraught topic, as it brought to the fore questions about sovereignty, legitimacy, and governance. In Kuwait, how to manage workers was a pressing concern given the large numbers of people arriving to work on oil projects, including construction of the new refinery at Mina al-Ahmadi. In September 1948, there were 4,938 Kuwaiti laborers and 2,574 Indian laborers.[57] Indians composed 88 percent of the junior staff and 58 percent of the skilled laborers employed by KOC.[58] This workforce was also rapidly growing, and the British political agent estimated that, by the end of 1948, KOC would employ more than 1,600 British workers, 800 US workers, and 6,000 Indian and Pakistani workers.[59] As large numbers of workers were hired for oil projects, issues arose around composition of the workforce, jurisdiction, and the treatment of workers.

The administration argued that the British government should help inform the composition of the workforce. Sometimes KOC successfully influenced the British administration, like when, in 1946–1947, KOC managers used rapid wage inflation as a justification for bringing in Indians to perform manual labor.[60] At other times, KOC acted without coordination of the British government. British officials were particularly concerned, in the late 1940s, that KOC, at the ruler's request, fired all of the company's Iraqi skilled tradesmen working in Kuwait. British administrators believed they should have been consulted, as they argued this staffing choice had the potential to impact relations between Iraq and Kuwait.[61]

In addition, the British administration argued that KOC and the Kuwaiti ruler were bypassing British jurisdiction. In Kuwait, the ruler of Kuwait had jurisdiction over Kuwaitis and people from neighboring countries of the Arabian Peninsula, and the British administration held jurisdiction over all others. British managers complained that British jurisdiction was ignored, and they gave the example of a Pakistani employee of KOC who was arrested and fined by Kuwaiti authorities, even though the British government understood Pakistanis and Indians to fall under British jurisdiction.[62] Another way the British administration argued that their jurisdiction and sovereignty were undermined was when KOC settled compensation claims out of the British courts. The administration argued that by settling out of court, KOC was not only ignoring the role of the British in arbitrating disputes, but they were also harming other British companies by raising the rates that other British companies would have to pay.[63]

Arguing that that they needed to secure the rights of workers who fell under British jurisdiction, British administrators insisted on playing a role in managing the workforce. Specifically, British administrators expressed concern over the denial of workers' rights by the ruler of Kuwait. Regarding the role of the Kuwaiti government in a dispute between Indian workers and KOC managers, a British administrator wrote:

> Indians employed by the Kuwait Oil Company had been denied by the Shaikh the right of free association for joint consultation with the management. It should be the function of the Political Agent to try to see that our views prevail in such matters. Indeed, any question affecting the real value of wages or the conditions of work of the Company's labour force is one in which the Political Agent is interested if only because by improving conditions of work we can do so much to combat communism. The Shaikh has not shown himself particularly enlightened in this respect and we cannot afford to have important

and far-reaching questions of this nature negotiated direct between the Company and the Shaikh.[64]

In cases such as these, British officials in the Arabian Peninsula selectively mobilized claims of protecting the rights of those under their jurisdiction, and they argued that mediating worker disputes with the company and ensuring workers' rights would help combat communism in the area. Through such arguments, British officials maintained that imperial sovereignty, political stability, and continued oil production required the British administration to play an expansive role managing labor at KOC operations.

WORKER ACTIONS AND MANAGEMENT RESPONSES

While the British administration saw the way KOC handled their large numbers of foreign workers to undermine British jurisdiction and authority, KOC also struggled to manage its large workforce—particularly given the abysmal working and living conditions that workers experienced. Many workers had been hired from oil projects operating in Baghdad, Basra, or Abadan.[65] When workers arrived at Ahmadi, they found that they were housed in tents in substandard conditions.[66] Also, like at Abadan, in Kuwait camps were overcrowded, and it was estimated that one thousand men were living in a camp that only was supposed to house six hundred.[67] Indeed, the arrival of new junior staff from India and Pakistan had to be paused for a brief period in 1948 because managers thought the accommodations situation was so dire.[68] In that year, when a broad coalition of junior staff at KOC went on strike three times, managers refused to deal with any worker organizations. Managers did, however, respond to workers based on their nationality, and they were aware of the role the Indian government could play in protecting the rights of Indians abroad. To mitigate the role of the Indian government in protecting workers' rights, managers suggested hiring stateless workers who had less recourse when unhappy with their working and living conditions. Overall, managers' responses denied the political potential of collective labor action and helped establish labor hierarchies based on nationality at job sites.

When considering the three strikes that occurred in 1948, some managers were sympathetic with the striking workers. One noted that fresh water had not been delivered to Indian workers for two days.[69] They also pointed to the fact that in Qatar, a country they considered to have comparable working conditions to Kuwait, PCL and Petroleum Development (Qatar), or PDQ, provided free food. Finally, given the high cost of living in Kuwait, these managers argued for an increase in starting pay and worker allowances in order to recruit good-quality Indian tradesmen.[70]

Other managers agreed that most Indian tradesmen and junior staff were "of a desirable type," but they dismissed worker requests. They did this by arguing that Indians lived better in Kuwait than in India and claiming that the strike was not specific to KOC's conditions. Rather, managers said that the strikes were because there were "always some individuals whose sole purpose in life is to make trouble."[71] For this reason, these managers stated that they did not want to deal with any organizations formed by workers. KOC managers' position was that they could not deal with worker associations based on nationality, because "each 'headman' would consider himself a minor labour office, there would be inter-departmental jealousies and friction."[72] In addition, some managers suggested that the US and European managers at KOC were "handicapped" by not being accustomed to "controlling Oriental workmen and by not knowing their language."[73] According to these managers, British managers were a better choice because of the experience many British managers had working in the area.

Managers, wary of organized worker action, felt the easiest response would be to identify the leaders and "without fuss or fanfare, quietly ship them back to India."[74] These managers also cautioned against hiring new Indian workers. They argued the strikes meant that hiring additional Indians was a "grave concern," and they worried these strikes signaled "the beginning of the end." These dire warnings came as managers feared that strikes by Indians could force a shutdown of production. To restart production, the company would be forced to accommodate worker demands, thereby encouraging additional strikes and raising the operating expenses for KOC.[75]

Strikes by Indian workers threatened production, and they jeopardized the company's ability to hire replacement Indian workers. Oil companies not only had to deal with local governments on the Arabian Peninsula and the British government, but also with the Indian government. This was because the Indian government could potentially stop Indian emigration to job sites. AIOC recruiters in Bombay warned KOC about a ban that the Indian government had temporarily imposed on Indian workers traveling to Iran to work for AIOC. Drawing on their experience with the disruptions this ban had caused, AIOC recruiters cautioned KOC to avoid such a ban being put in place because, they reported, "should there be any great number of complaints, legitimate or otherwise, the Indian government is capable of suddenly imposing a temporary ban on recruitment of Indians for work in Kuwait." To protect against this happening, AIOC managers in Bombay offered to help KOC by interceding on its behalf with the Indian protector of emigrants and by correcting misinformation spread by Indian workers who had been discharged from KOC for "misconduct or insubordination."[76]

Given the threats posed by Indian strikes, some KOC managers suggested workers from other countries be hired. Building on the experiences of Aramco managers, KOC managers suggested the company hire European or US women for clerking and secretarial jobs. For other positions, managers were particularly keen to hire individuals who did not have a state that could advocate for their rights. Managers suggested that KOC try to hire Palestinian Arab refugees, Italians from Eritrea, and "displaced persons from Europe."[77] Managers' preference for hiring stateless persons underscores the potential impact that a state's intervention on behalf of its citizens could have on oil companies.

Even though some managers were cautious about hiring Indian workers and feared the consequences of strikes by Indians, KOC continued to hire workers from the subcontinent. This was because oil company managers and the local government wanted political stability, and they feared that workers from Iran and Iraq were more likely to organize large-scale work stoppages. In addition, the ruler of Kuwait agreed that if foreigners must be hired for KOC projects, then Indians were best to hire after subjects from nearby states, in part because Indians were thought to be more likely to follow local laws.[78] Indians also continued to be hired because the ruler did not want KOC to hire workers from China, and he wanted KOC to replace Iraqi workers with Indian workers.[79] He also asked that Iranian workers, too, be replaced following a strike that began after a fight among Kuwaiti, Iraqi, and Iranian workers.[80] The company was happy to comply with this request, even though the British government expressed concerns that refusing to hire Iraqis and Iranians would negatively impact Kuwait's relations with Iraq and Iran.[81]

In addition to political factors, economic considerations also contributed to KOC managers continuing to hire Indians to work in Kuwait. Indian workers accepted lower wages than workers from other countries. In contrast, managers reported that workers from Iraq and Iran were "prohibitively expensive."[82] Also, in India, KOC managers knew the labor market was "full of people looking for jobs," and with the Indian government putting domestic oil development projects on hold, more individuals were expected to seek jobs abroad.[83] Thus, Indians continued to be hired despite the power of Indian workers to form broad coalitions and to call on their government to protect their rights.

NATIONALITY AND WORKFORCE MANAGEMENT

Managers at KOC also worried about the potential for disruption of strikes by local workers. By 1949, 13,566 people worked for KOC and its contractors,[84] and it was estimated one-quarter of all Kuwaiti men worked for KOC.[85] After construction of the refinery at Ahmadi was completed, however, fewer workers were needed, and managers hoped to radically reduce the number of employees to around five thousand.[86] As the company turned to reducing the number of employees after construction, oil company officials directed that non-Kuwaitis should be removed from the payroll first.[87]

Managers hoped that firing non-Kuwaitis would help to mitigate local unrest,[88] in part because foreign workers could be deported immediately when their jobs ended. In addition, retaining Kuwaiti workers would also allow the company to meet the obligations put forward in the concession by "ensuring that they are given the opportunity of carrying out as good jobs as they can hold down." One manager wrote of the "difficulties of this problem and the care you will have to exercise so that we do not disrupt of economic life of our Kuwaiti friends by too drastic reductions, but the fact remains that we are nearing the end of a very intensive construction programme and reductions in our labor strength will have to be made." KOC managers suggested that one way of addressing this problem was gradually replacing the one thousand non-Kuwaiti Arabs working as laborers with Kuwaiti workers. This policy of gradually replacing foreigners with Kuwaitis was also to be put in place for skilled and semiskilled positions whenever Kuwaitis "can perform the work in a reasonably satisfactory manner or can be trained to do so whether on the job or in a training school."[89]

While the policy of hiring Kuwaitis initially seemed straightforward, the company immediately ran into issues determining who was a citizen of

Kuwait. The Kuwaiti Nationality Law of 1948 was expansive in who was or could become a Kuwaiti citizen. The law made provisions for citizenship for one born in Kuwait whose father was a foreigner but was from a country where the majority of nationals were either Muslim or Arabic speaking, and it also provided ways one could become a naturalized citizen of Kuwait.[90]

Oil company managers argued that the law was vague and unevenly applied, and they continued to question who should be considered a national. For example, in the late 1940s, KOC managers noted that nationality certificates were given without local officials actually differentiating who was Kuwaiti or non-Kuwaiti. Specifically, they argued that the Kuwait government was issuing nationality certificates to workers who were actually from Saudi Arabia, Bahrain, Oman, and the Trucial Coast.[91] In addition, managers noted that some people, especially Iranians, were not given Kuwaiti nationality certificates even though they had "probably resided in Kuwait for all of their lives."[92]

While KOC managers critiqued the lack of clarity over who was a citizen, at other times the messy boundaries between citizens and noncitizens were beneficial for oil companies. One clear example of this occurred in Qatar, where, in 1948, 2,712 of PDQ's employees were listed as "Qataris." However, upon examination, only 1,580, or 58 percent, were actually subjects of Qatar. The remaining 42 percent were khalijis from outside of Qatar, Iranians, and Baluchis.[93] In this case, the lack of clarity over who was a citizen was used by the oil company to argue that it was upholding the terms of its concession that required preferential hiring of nationals, while not actually doing so in practice.

As KOC managers attempted to reduce the company's overall workforce, additional issues emerged. First, Kuwaitis had not been trained by KOC for advanced positions. KOC had relied heavily on Indian workers and little thought was put "toward Arab development. The organization is groping for administrative and personnel policy and meanwhile leans heavily on A.I.O.C. philosophy partly because their second man in charge of all such matters is a former A.I.O.C. employee."[94] This was compounded by a second, closely related issue: Managerial stereotypes about Kuwaiti workers were prevalent and impeded training and employment. For example, managers reported it was challenging to oversee Kuwaiti workers, because, they said, these workers had high rates of absenteeism.[95]

Another issue, according to managers, was that the lack of services provided by the state hindered workforce reductions. Regarding workforce size, issues arose because there were more employees at KOC than at similar projects in the United Kingdom or United States. The reason for the larger number of employees, managers argued, was due to the need for "non-effectual" labor, which they differentiated from "effectual" labor.[96] Here, "effectual" workers were those who were carrying on the normal company operations, and "non-effectual" workers were defined as those who were employed by the company to "render private service to employees or to carry on public utility service which in other areas and countries would be furnished by public authorities."[97]

Finally, KOC managers believed that oil contractors exacerbated tensions, because these contractors fired redundant employees without consideration for an employee's nationality. For example, when contractors such as IBI or Wimpey needed to reduce their redundant employees, they reportedly did so based on job type and job performance, and these contractors were resistant to keeping workers based solely on their nationality.[98] To maintain good relations with the ruler of Kuwait, fulfill concession terms, and maintain general stability, KOC supervisors advised KOC's Labour Department to replace men who were discharged or who resigned by drawing on Kuwaiti workers who had been previously employed by contractors. But, because 37 percent of bulk contract labor was Kuwaiti, implementing this policy was challenging, and the rapid reduction of employees by contractors meant the further swelling of KOC's total workforce.[99]

THE KUWAITI GOVERNMENT, KOC, AND LOCAL WORKERS

As KOC managers attempted to reduce their overall labor force, the government of Kuwait advocated for Kuwaiti businesses and workers in multiple ways. This included the government's insistence that KOC should work with fewer non-Kuwaiti contractors. In addition, the Kuwaiti government said that KOC should end contract work, or work that was on a temporary basis, and that KOC should employ full-time Kuwaitis who had been previously hired as contract workers. KOC managers sought good relations with the Kuwaiti government, but managers did not fully comply with these government requests, citing the need for efficiency and economy in the workforce. KOC managers also sought to foster positive relations with the government of Kuwait through instituting management practices that would not cause disturbances among local workers. These good relations between the government and KOC proved useful when local workers went on strike.

In its discussions with KOC, the Kuwaiti government specifically wanted to protect Kuwaitis from what it described as the exploitive practices of contractors. The ruler was "very mindful of the interests of his people and does not want his subjects to be exploited by a handful of persons (contractors)." Contractors paid less than KOC paid for the same job, and they did not train their employees. Indeed, the government of Kuwait was upset that contractors played such a large role in employing Kuwaitis. Given these issues, the ruler argued, "it is imperative that except in the case of contractors engaged on any constructional work requiring labor assistance, no contractor be authorized to recruit labor in bulk for supply to the Company." But, while foreign contractors were seen as problematic, the Kuwaiti government did advocate for KOC working with more Kuwaiti contractors, a preference that we will see became increasingly formalized in the 1950s.[100]

In response to the Kuwaiti government's request that KOC work with fewer non-Kuwaiti contractors, KOC managers responded that they agreed with the ruler in principle, but they argued they could not fully comply. In part, this was because they did not have enough accommodations or staff to directly hire all the workers who were employed by contractors.[101] However, KOC did hire some local workers that contractors had fired, and managers believed this practice improved the relations between KOC and the Kuwaiti government. This was because hiring Kuwaitis previously employed by contractors reduced the overall number of Kuwaitis who lost their jobs and because employees of contractors reported greater levels of dissatisfaction than employees of KOC.

Kuwaiti government officials also saw contract, or temporary, labor to be detrimental to Kuwaiti workers, and the government urged KOC to reduce contract labor. When oil production resumed in 1945 following World War II, Kuwaiti officials and KOC managers agreed that contract labor would only be used on a temporary basis in order to supplement permanent labor. By 1948, the ruler felt the need for temporary labor had passed. Therefore, he argued that Kuwaitis and workers from nearby states should be hired as permanent workers and paid a minimum of four rupees per day.

KOC managers, in contrast, believed there were benefits for KOC to continue to use contract labor. They argued that contract labor was desirable for construction and other short-term jobs and that some job types were particularly well-suited to contract labor. For these types of jobs, managers said that the continued use of contract labor was necessary because it would make company operations "efficient and economical." For example, managers argued contract labor was necessary at the jetty, where laborers were needed to load and unload boats, but only at certain times. Managers explained the benefits of using contract labor at the pier:

> In slack periods, weather delays, ship delays, small tonnage periods, etc., we are thus able to lay off a third of our labor. In fact efficient and economical operation of the jetty will not be achieved until all labour, with the exception of about 40 experienced men, is available on a daily basis, since once the local becomes on the permanent strength of the KOC, he rarely gives the same results as a contract employee and during slack periods is merely a burden to the Company economy.[102]

Furthermore, managers said that employing contract workers at jetties had been the norm in the United States and United Kingdom, where all dock workers were contracted laborers until unions changed this employment pattern.[103] Managers characterized this change as negative for companies. Overall, managers argued that contract workers were cheaper, because they were only employed when they were needed, and after a short debate, KOC received permission from the ruler to hire contract workers based on the cost savings to the company.[104]

KOC managers also sought to foster good relations with the Kuwaiti government by implementing management practices that they understood as fair to Kuwaiti workers. For example, supervisors were told to not physically strike their workers or threaten to hit them. The reason was that such actions were "liable to provoke disturbances far out of proportion to the nature of the incident," and company managers said they would "severely discipline" supervisory staff who threatened or carried out physical violence against workers.[105] Instead of physically punishing workers, supervisors were told to implement a system in which workers were given warning slips and, after receiving three warning slips, a worker would be fired. This, KOC upper-level managers argued, would be "entirely fair in handling our Kuwaiti labour, and that when [they] are discharged there has been sufficient cause."[106] Managers saw multiple benefits in using this system. As one manager wrote, "By using such a method we tend to correct bad habits and thereby save good men, or if they are undesirable and cannot be correct then they are released, which finally of course, leaves a better type of workmen with KOC. Releases at the present time are not objectionable as it is an easy way of still bringing the payroll down without mass discharges," while also reducing absenteeism.[107] Thus, managers saw the system as a way to encourage Kuwaitis to learn on the job. Workers who could not improve were fired. Through using such a system, managers shifted the responsibility for workplace performance from the company to Kuwaiti workers themselves.[108]

It was not only Kuwaiti workers who were part of this system, and workers who did not have Kuwaiti nationality certificates were also given warning slips, but at much lower rates. In August 1949, 556 warning slips were given to local employees and fifty-nine were given to Indian workers.[109] In other words, despite comprising approximately 35 percent of the laborers working at KOC, Indian laborers only received 10 percent of the warning slips. The fact that Indian workers received a disproportionately small percentage of warning slips does not necessarily reflect on their overall performance at their job. Rather, it points to the fact that there were many Indians looking for jobs and the Indian workers who were hired for jobs at KOC had often received job training at other oil projects. In addition, Indian workers were much easier to fire than Kuwaiti workers. For example, when Indian tradesmen were not performing at the level desired by managers, they were "sent back" using the "regular channels."[110] Similarly, domestic workers who were asking for better conditions were deported to India, and the company decided to look to other countries to fill such positions.[111]

British government officials thought that KOC management's policies would benefit oil production in Kuwait by contributing to political and workforce stability. Specifically, British officials believed that by retaining local employees, they "doubted the 'population' will make demands for a larger share in the royalties."[112] Despite these predictions, local workers did go on strike, and during their strikes, these workers appealed to the Kuwaiti government to intervene on their behalf.

At moments when local workers did go on strike, KOC's efforts to meet the local government's requests concerning contract labor and contractors, along with the company's other efforts to cultivate positive relations with the local government, proved to be beneficial to the company, and the local government often acted in support of KOC. For example, in November 1949, local workers went on strike because their payday was postponed. Workers also reported they were on strike because they were not being paid as much as other workers for the same job, specifically Pakistani workers—a fact that illuminates how KOC used pay hierarchies based on workers' nationality to structure its worksites. During the strike, members of the ruling family came to the job site. When they arrived, they instructed the striking workers that they should tell their grievances to the local government and that they were never to go on strike as a first measure. The members of the ruling family then listened to workers' grievances. Finally, they directed workers to return to their jobs. When some workers showed reluctance to return to their jobs, the Kuwaiti government asked for the names of those who refused to return to work.[113] In cases like this one, good relations with the local government helped the KOC managers handle labor disputes with local workers without creating disruptions to oil production.

CONCLUSION

Given that one quarter of all Kuwaiti men worked for KOC and its contractors, managers and British government officials wanted to decrease the workforce and enforce company policies without causing large-scale work stoppages or political upheaval. Nationality was a key consideration for company managers—it determined hiring and retention at oil companies as well as how companies responded to worker issues. Deciding who was a national was not always clear-cut, and oil company managers believed that nationality certificates were haphazardly issued.[114] Questions around citizenship were compounded by debates over sovereignty and jurisdiction. Across the Arabian Peninsula, jurisdiction differed according to concessions and treaties, and it was contested by local governments, the British government, and oil companies. Borders, too, were contested and debated, often within the context of oil project development and oil concessions. While there were tensions among local governments, the British administration, and oil companies, they had shared aims of political stability and continued oil production. These common goals helped align their interests, often to the detriment of workers.

The interactions among oil companies, local and imperial governments, and workers helped shape governable spaces that facilitated oil production.[115] In these governable spaces, nationality was territorialized; cultures and languages were mapped onto places and racialized.[116] National hierarchies increasingly became a central structure for governance practices *and* corporate management. In the mid-twentieth century, nationalism was seen as a threat to both oil production and political stability. As we will see in the following chapters, India's and Pakistan's independence from British colonial rule, the growing popularity of pan-Arab nationalism, and outrage following the partition of Palestine were extremely influential in how workers agitated for changes to their living and working conditions. As workers mobilized citizenship and petitioned their governments to protect their rights, labor solidarities increasingly fragmented along national lines.

Three
ADVOCATING FOR RIGHTS

IN 1948, THE BAHRAIN PETROLEUM COMPANY (BAPCO), WHICH employed over 1,500 Indians, fired eight Indians who were working as chemists for the company. According to managers at Bapco, the chemists were dismissed from their positions because they failed to follow orders. The chemists disputed the company's reason for their dismissal. Instead, the chemists claimed that they had been fired from their jobs because they had complained about the racist inequalities they faced at their worksite in Bahrain, and they argued that their firing was a violation of their human rights.

In their letters, the chemists described the racism they experienced working at Bapco, and they equated the racist treatment they experienced from US managers with the former treatment of India under British colonialism. In one letter they wrote, "The Americans are careful not to over-step the boundary as far as the sentiments of the Arabs are concerned. But an Indian remains a slave of the Company, segregated, discriminated, and snubbed on account of his colour."[1] They then explicitly compared their experiences with those of Indians in South Africa—only the chemists made the caveat that racism in Bahrain was much worse than in South Africa.[2] This comparison undoubtedly resonated with the Indian public and government officials given that Indians in South Africa faced racism, discrimination, and exclusion from social spaces. Referencing South Africa also invoked the history of India's nationalist movement, as the treatment of Indians in South Africa was one of the key factors that inspired M. K. Gandhi, a leader of India's independence movement, to begin his work to end British colonialism in India.[3]

In addition to describing the racism they experienced working at Bapco, the chemists also argued that their dismissal by Bapco was a breach of contract and a violation of their human rights. Specifically, the chemists believed the real reason they were fired was that they had coordinated among themselves when they filed their complaints with management, and this, the chemists pointed out, violated their fundamental rights of association and free speech. The chemists called upon the Indian government to intervene on their behalf with Bapco, and they based their petition on the interconnected principles of citizenship, universal human rights, and the equality of Indians on a global stage.

The chemists' actions in Bahrain differed from the actions of Indians in Abadan and in Kuwait. Notably, the chemists appealed to a country outside of the country in which they were working, and they insisted on labor rights as part of human rights. The effectiveness of this argument depended on the Indian government's response to the chemists and the ability of the Indian government to intervene on workers' behalf. These criteria were new, given the Indian state's recent independence from British colonial rule. The chemists' appeal to the Indian government and the Indian government's response demonstrate the role Indians working abroad played in contestations over sovereignty in the Arabian Peninsula. They also show how Indian government debates over citizenship were impacted not only by the partition of British India in 1947 into the states of India and Pakistan but also by Indians working abroad.[4]

As citizenship and rights were debated throughout the Arabian Sea, there was an increasing racialization of nationality at oil projects in the Arabian Peninsula. This racialization occurred as US racecraft, in which individuals are classified by and their identities reduced to their race, became increasingly prevalent in corporate management.[5] According to Karen Fields and Barbara Fields, *racecraft* is a social fact that informs both people's imaginations and their actions.[6] Socially, racecraft "transforms racism into race, disguising collective social practice as inborn individual traits, so it entrenches racism in a category to itself, setting it apart from inequality in other guises."[7] In the Arabian Peninsula, difference was racialized, collapsed with nationality, and made real through management practices that impacted working and living conditions. In this context, the meanings of citizenship and rights emerged in the tensions between the state, as a governing apparatus, and the nation, as an imagined community.

RACISM AT US OIL PROJECTS IN BAHRAIN AND SAUDI ARABIA

In their letters to both the Indian government and Indian newspapers, the chemists argued that a key problem was that they were not treated fairly by the management at Bapco due to rampant racism, and that the Americans fostered a racist attitude toward Indians. In one news article, Bapco managers were accused of treating Indians at the company with "racial hatred."[8] Overall, the chemists blamed their unfair treatment on the attitudes of Americans and the managerial techniques in use at Bapco. Newspapers took up this issue, and one article described the situation for Indians in Bahrain as a "horrid colour war that has been raging on the Island [of Bahrain]."[9] However, experiences of racial discrimination were not unique to the chemists, and workers of many nationalities complained about the racism they experienced at US oil projects operating in the Arabian Peninsula.

In the late 1940s and early 1950s, two US companies, Bapco in Bahrain and the Arabian American Oil Company (Aramco) operating in Saudi Arabia, were frequently accused of racism by workers.[10] The fact that workers saw both Aramco and Bapco as companies with similarly racist attitudes and practices should not be surprising given the close connections in ownership and management between the companies. Bapco was owned by Texaco and SoCal, both of which also had a 30 percent stake in Aramco.[11] Upper-level managers and technical personnel at both Bapco and Aramco were primarily Americans. US managers circulated regularly between Aramco projects and Bapco projects, and both companies worked frequently with the same contractors.[12] As Robert Vitalis describes, US managers at Aramco imported racist Jim Crow policies to manage and train workers in Saudi Arabia.[13] The use of racism and segregation as management techniques were not unique to the oil industry in the Middle East, and racial labor hierarchies were also mobilized in, for example, the oil industry in Mexico and factories in India.[14]

In the late 1940s, both Aramco and Bapco were operating with high numbers of employees, and as in Kuwait, nationality informed the job one held. In 1949 at Bapco, the labor force was 7,004 workers, comprising 93 Americans, roughly 800 British and other European employees, approximately

1,500 workers from India and Pakistan, and nearly 4,500 Bahraini and other khaliji workers. The majority of clerical, skilled, and non-European supervisory jobs were held by Indians. In addition, approximately 300 Indians and Pakistanis were engaged in semiskilled jobs comprised principally of domestic duties.[15] At Aramco, there were 12,111 Saudi Arabian workers, 498 Pakistanis, 495 Indians, and 428 Sudanese. In addition, there were 1,190 Italians and approximately 2,595 Americans.[16] Similarly to the job hierarchies prevalent at Bapco, local workers at Aramco were primarily employed as laborers, and Indians and Pakistanis worked as tradesmen. Thus, a system was being established in which employees' jobs were hierarchically ordered by nationality.

Job hierarchies meant that even when workers from the Middle East or South Asia were hired for highly skilled positions, they were not given positions of authority. Only Europeans were in positions of authority. This, the chemists argued, was because of racism; specifically, they asserted that at Bapco managers were in charge not because of their skillset, but because they were white. The strict labor hierarchies at Bapco, the chemists reported, differed from other oil projects they had worked at in the Arabian Sea. In particular, the chemists described their experiences with US managers at Bapco and contrasted these experiences directly with their experiences working at the British-run Anglo-Iranian Oil Company (AIOC), where they felt racism was less prevalent.[17]

Not only did one's nationality inform the type of work one was hired for, but US managers at Bapco and Aramco used highly racialized and racist terms to describe workers based on their nationality. As managers interacted with workers, they used US racial categories. This included references to skin color, and Indian workers were described as having a "dark body" and as "almost black" or having "nearly black skin." Sometimes this was explicitly referenced within a pseudo-scientific description of race and skin color. Thus, skin color and nationality were conflated, and nationality racialized.[18] Managers used this classificatory discourse to insert workers into racialized hierarchies similar to the ones prevalent at that time in the US South, and this was used in day-to-day interactions with workers. For example, Indian workers were addressed by the derogatory title of "boy."[19]

Saudi Arabian and Bahraini workers, too, were racialized based on skin color and put within racialized labor hierarchies.[20] When discussing Arabs from Saudi Arabia, managers mobilized their understandings of tribal membership to lend credence to these categories. In particular, US managers understood Saudi society to be segmented into three hierarchical categories, and these categories were described as genealogical, related to skin color, and related to the type of labor that an individual performed.[21] By mobilizing such descriptions of Saudi society, managers invoked US racial categories and made it appear that these categories existed globally.

Managers categorized workers by race and conflated race with nationality, but they denied that racism was the cause of different treatments of workers. Rather, they argued that "racial discrimination is unknown in the Company's operation." In response to complaints by Indian workers that they were paid less than workers of other nationalities for the same job, one manager at the company wrote:

> Benefits given to one nationality usually extended to all others. Saudi Arabs are handled on an equal basis and we seldom find any one nationality being given any preferential treatment. . . . This follows the principle laid down by Saudi Arabian Government requiring that the company treat the Saudi Arab on an equal basis with personnel recruited from countries located east of the Atlantic.[22]

These types of claims sought to naturalize differences in treatment between US management and workers hired from the Middle East or India.

Racialized descriptions perpetuated stereotypes, and managers used these stereotypes to justify labor hierarchies, such as describing both Indian and Arab workers as less capable than US workers.[23] Such discourses around racialized difference were one way in which the myth of race as a biological fact was (and continues to be) perpetuated. By invoking racialized differences and mapping races onto nationalities, managers shaped and made sense of the labor hierarchies that underpinned Aramco's and Bapco's operations.

SEGREGATION AT US OIL PROJECTS

At Bapco and Aramco, job hierarchies were increasingly based on nationality.[24] Living conditions were also impacted, and conditions were substandard for employees who were not from the United States and Europe. Workers' accommodations and leisure spaces were segregated by nationality, and there were few opportunities for interactions among workers of differing nationalities. As one observer noted, "There is no mixing [among employees] in social events nor sports events, with the exception of an occasional cricket or soccer match."[25] Such restrictions, in conjunction with hiring workers of specific nationalities for specific jobs, helped to prevent workers from forming intergroup alliances and solidarities.

Worker segregation was strictly adhered to both on the job and off the job, and recreational facilities were poor for most workers. One Aramco manager visited Bapco and described the situation: "No recreation facilities provided for other than US and European employees, with the exception of a few playing fields."[26] In contrast, British and US employees had access to a club for a nominal fee of five rupees a month, until 1953 when the company made it free. The club offered multiple amenities, including squash courts, tennis courts, cricket fields, soccer/football fields, hockey pitches, swimming pools, a golf course, a baseball diamond, a barbecue pit, a billiards room, a shooting range, an auditorium, a cinema, and a library.[27] Access to these better facilities depended upon an employee's nationality and the lack of facilities for non-European and non-US employees must have informed how the chemists understood their treatment as unequal with Americans and Europeans.

At Aramco, too, workers were kept segregated while at work and during their leisure time. US managers at Aramco argued that segregation was specifically due to the requirement by the ruler of Saudi Arabia that Saudis be treated the same as workers "recruited from countries located east of the Atlantic."[28] While the Saudi Arabian government hoped these regulations would protect Saudi workers, instead, the regulations served to create an illusion of equity through the reification and conflation of difference via nationality and racism. Aramco managers used the requirement as justification for not providing basic necessities to workers. For example, when Indian workers were unable to purchase food at fair prices in the local market, Aramco managers stated that they could not help provide food for them, because if the company provided food to Indian workers, then the company would also have to provide food for Arab workers.[29]

Managers used the ruler's requirement that Saudis be treated equally with other workers also as a rationale to keep workers segregated. Managers saw multiple benefits to segregation, and they argued it ensured workforce stability and helped retain American workers, as managers believed integration would lead to Americans quitting en masse.[30] Segregation was a policy that other companies, including large contractors, were also keen to follow. When Stephen Bechtel, owner of the US contracting company Bechtel, arrived to discuss building the refinery at Ras Tanura, he agreed that contractors should be separate from Aramco employees, with Bechtel employees "held behind a high fence and not permitted beyond it except in small supervised groups."[31]

Separate food, poor working conditions, and separate living quarters meant that there was antagonism between groups of workers, despite the fact that they all faced racism and similarly poor working and living conditions. One place these tensions emerged was around the differing benefits given to groups—with workers from India, Pakistan, and the Middle East being unable to watch films at the camp, but Italian and other European workers were allowed this leisure activity. One manager described how workers responded to this situation:

> [The ruler of Saudi Arabia] wants no Moslems [*sic*] watching the movies. He has ordered that the Indians be treated the same as the Arabs, so when the Indians come and punch holes in the matting in order to watch the movie, the Arab soldiers on guard, to stop such practice, descend with vigor. Apparently, they particularly like to take a crack at the Indians. At first, the Indians tended to be sullen and hold their ground, but now they get out of the way of the police. Besides, the police want those holes to look thru themselves.[32]

Managers reported that police officers from the Middle East were prejudiced against Indian workers. In addition to prejudice from police officers, managers also described situations in which Saudi workers made false accusations against Indian workers and committed physical violence against Indians.[33] As these examples document, not only were workers dissatisfied with the restrictions that they lived under, and but these restrictions also fostered intergroup conflicts.

Government officials, managers, and workers collapsed race and nationality, but with differing ends. For managers, the racialization of nationalities served to structure the workforce. Workers also collapsed nationality and race as a means of critiquing their treatment. However, worker actions were also limited by this practice. Unlike the initial policies at AIOC and KOC that enabled diverse workers to form solidarities through the proximity in which employees worked and lived, the racialization of nationality and segregation created tensions between employee groups. These tensions, at least in Bahrain in 1948, proved effective at preventing workers from forming the broad political alliances that resulted in large general strikes. However, with India's independence from British colonial rule in 1947, the chemists appealed, as Indian citizens, to the Indian government to ensure their rights.

THE BRITISH GOVERNMENT AND INDIAN WORKERS ABROAD BEFORE 1947

Indian workers had been unhappy with their working and living conditions at Bapco and Aramco seemingly since the beginning of those companies' operations. Prior to India's and Pakistan's independence in 1947, the British played a role in protecting Indian workers, as Indian workers were subjects of the British empire,[34] and they were considered imperial citizens.[35] Imperial citizenship largely hinged on Indians being treated equally with others who were also subjects of the British empire.[36]

Until 1947, the British colonial government in India oversaw emigration through Emigration Act of 1922. This act gave the British colonial government the power to negotiate workers' contracts, provided means to arbitrate worker disputes, and established guidelines that Indians could use to sue oil companies in the Agency Courts.[37] Arbitrating contracts helped the British government extend some control over oil projects throughout the Arabian Peninsula, including at US oil projects and in areas outside the scope of the treaties signed between the British and the local governments. However, as discussed in the previous chapter, companies sought to minimize and, at times, directly contested the influence of the British government in company operations.

In the first half of the twentieth century, there were frequent disputes over contracts and the recruitment of workers. In 1936, after receiving intense pressure to hire more Indians from both the British authorities in Bahrain and the colonial British government of India, Bapco sent a representative to draft a Foreign Service Agreement and open a recruiting office in Bombay (now Mumbai). Before drafting the agreement, the representative began recruiting workers with a paper contract. The protector of emigrants in Bombay refused to allow workers to travel to Bahrain on this contract and threatened the Bapco representative with imprisonment for breach of the Emigration Act. The representative then drafted a Foreign Service Agreement, but it was rejected as unfair to Indian employees. The contract was viewed as unfair because it gave the company the ability to fire Indian workers without notice and did not have provisions for migrants' return to India. It took five months for the protector of emigrants to give permission for workers to travel. During these five months, Indian workers bypassed the ban on hiring by paying for their own fare to go to Bahrain. Once in Bahrain, these workers were then hired directly by the oil company.[38]

As the British government attempted to exert control over both India and the countries of the Arabian Peninsula, oil companies actively undermined the ability of the government to protect workers. One example of both the poor working conditions at Aramco and of an oil company undermining the British administration's role in arbitrating contracts occurred in Saudi Arabia in 1944, when hundreds of Indian workers employed by Aramco ran into trouble with the company. Earlier that year, over two hundred Indian tradesmen traveled from India to Bahrain and then to eastern Saudi Arabia for work on the refinery at Ras Tanura. Initially, their job performance was praised by managers. However, trouble erupted when Indian employees were unable to purchase food at a fair price from the market and their rations were insufficient to cover their nutritional needs. One Aramco manager described the situation:

> A day or so later, they [the Indian tradesmen] all struck. Refused to work unless they were given proper food which included meat and vegetables, unless we placed guards in their area to prevent thievery, and unless we gave them electric lights. They come home after dark and have to cook in the dark. All of these demands are reasonable—but we are unable to comply. We haven't the power to furnish lights, we have no one suitable as guards (Arabs couldn't be trusted to refrain from stealing from Indians), and meat and vegetables simply aren't available.[39]

Aramco managers explained there were two underlying causes of the strikes by Indian workers. First, World War II was wreaking havoc with shipping, and a ship carrying supplies had recently been torpedoed and sunk off the coast of Aden.[40] Second, managers argued that they were limited in what they could provide workers because the Saudi government required that Saudis be treated the same as Indian employees. Regarding workers' demands for food, managers felt they were unable to comply. One manager wrote, "If we feed the Indians, we have to feed the Arabs—and we simply haven't the food and facilities yet." However, they told Indians the company would try to improve conditions as fast as possible. While Indian workers waited for these improvements, the company arranged a truck to bring vegetables to sell to higher-paid Arab and Indian workers.

Despite the purported attempts by Aramco managers to ameliorate the complaints of Indian workers, "about 35 [Indian workers] held out, apparently a group that knew each other and were ring leaders in the strike. The others expressed themselves as willing to return to work." These workers who "held out" were told by managers that they would be sent back to India. Shortly after this incident, another thirty-eight Indian workers complained, arguing that they couldn't keep up their strength on the food available. This group entered an Aramco office building, "scuffling, shouting, and creating a general disturbance," and demanded more food. The workers then gathered outside of a building to "shout and argue." Reportedly, when a manager tried to leave the building, he was "besieged," and the workers stood in front of the car and would not move. Finally, the company called the police, and managers told the workers that their services were no longer needed. Aramco managers argued that after being fired, the Indian workers backtracked and requested to keep their jobs, which the company refused.[41]

When these Indian workers were dismissed, they demanded that they should be allowed, as British subjects, to go to talk to the British political agent in Bahrain. However, Aramco managers denied this request, stating that the political agent had asked that no more Indians be sent to Bahrain until the first group of workers who had quit were repatriated to India.[42] After being told they could not travel to speak with the political agent, the Indian workers wrote to the British political agent in Bahrain and the protector of emigrants in Bombay.[43] In their letter, the workers explained that they had not refused to work. Rather, they wrote that they "were abused, and annoyed in every manner, and their future ruined." For this reason, they argued, they should be given three years' salary for their termination. While managers anticipated that Aramco would "get plenty of bad publicity in India from this,"[44] they also dismissed worker claims, describing these claims as "a typical Indian device of lies and distortions."[45]

Upon receiving the workers' letter, the British political agent sent a staff member to Saudi Arabia to investigate. When the representative of the political agent met with this group of Indians to hear their grievances, the representative was particularly surprised to find out that the workers were forcibly prevented from going to Bahrain to share their grievances with the political agent. Upon learning this, the political agent wrote a memo to Aramco, clarifying that when the company said they were going to repatriate over one hundred Indians via Bahrain, the political agent said there were concerns over "'rationing and housing' in Bahrain, and the company needed to arrange the entire trip back to India. But never meant representatives of workers should be prohibited from coming to air their grievances."[46] Thus, the political agent attempted to reassert his oversight of labor relations.

Ultimately, the British political agent's office found that the Indian workers were treated disgracefully and dismissed without cause. In addition, the office said Aramco's reports did not accurately reflect the circumstances. In India, the Bombay-based protector of emigrants also got involved, with mixed results. He asked the political agent to persuade the workers to return to work and also to advocate on behalf of workers with the company.[47] However, the power of the British government to influence Aramco policy was limited, and in response to the political agent's interventions, Aramco managers did not change their course of action. Instead, Aramco decided to temporarily stop recruitment from India.[48]

THE INDIAN GOVERNMENT AND INDIAN WORKERS ABROAD AFTER 1947

At the end of British colonial rule in 1947, British India was divided into the countries of India and Pakistan. The line between the countries was hastily drawn, partitioning majority-Hindu and Sikh districts in the Punjab and Bengal from majority-Muslim districts.[49] The logic of partition was informed by British rule in India in which communal or religious identities were used as a "colonial form of knowing."[50] Historically, British governance practices had codified religious identities and used communal violence to legitimate British colonial rule.[51] In the wake of the upheaval and violence of the partition of British India, Indian government officials debated who was a citizen of India as well as the Indian government's obligations to Indian citizens working abroad.

After 1947, the British political agent continued to have some responsibility for Indian and Pakistani workers, including jurisdiction over Indians and Pakistanis working in the British Protectorates of the Arabian Peninsula. However, the overall responsibility of the British administration for Indian and Pakistani workers decreased as workers were no longer considered British imperial citizens but rather Indian or Pakistani citizens.[52] Contracts were one site where the British political agents played a diminished role for workers from India and Pakistan. While European and US contracts needed approval from the political agent, Indian and Pakistani workers' contracts were not submitted to the political agent for approval.[53] For issues that needed arbitration regarding Indian or Pakistani nationals, contracts only had to specify that settlements would be submitted to the political agent. British subjects, on the other hand, were required to have a clause in their contracts that made the political agent the arbitrator.[54]

After India's independence, the British political agent was also less proactive in advocating for Indian workers' rights.[55] This change can be seen when we contrast the experiences of Indians at Aramco in 1944 with the case of the Bapco chemists. Initially, the chemists directed their complaints about their treatment by Bapco managers to the British political agent based in Bahrain. However, the political agent's office was not eager to take up the case. Using the excuses that the letter was unsigned and that the office did not recognize the worker organization, the political agent simply ignored the chemists' complaints.[56] The difference between the response in 1944 and the lack of a response in 1948 signals both the limits of the British government's ability to control practices at oil companies, and a shift in the involvement of the British government in ensuring the rights of Indians. Thus, while the British administration still had jurisdiction over Indians working in the Arabian Peninsula, British officials' attitudes and obligations were changing in light of the fact that Indians were no longer British subjects.

Receiving no support from the British political agent based in Bahrain, the Indian chemists turned to the new Indian state to protect their rights, but officials in the Indian government were divided in how best to respond.[57] Some bureaucrats, working from an understanding of citizens as rational actors, contended that the Indian government was not in a strong position to negotiate contracts or take action against oil companies. Those bureaucrats asserted that the government should not take a role in contracts because Indian workers decided to take these positions of their "own free will."[58] Others argued against this idea of free will, and they said that Indians decided to migrate in response to internal pressures in India, including a lack of jobs. They pointed out that unemployment was strongly felt in the oil industry and that there were no positions for oil workers in India. In contrast to the situation in India, oil companies abroad paid higher wages than the same job fetched in India, and workers could save more during one contract period than they could hope to save "in a lifetime of work" in India.[59] The multiple responses by government officials indicates that in the years after India's independence, there was not a consensus among Indian bureaucrats as to what the best circumstances were for Indian workers abroad.

Indian officials also debated the government's duties to citizens abroad. Some argued that Indian laborers working in the Arabian Peninsula needed to have their rights ensured not only for the protection of workers themselves but also for the protection of India's reputation. According to these officials, many Indians abroad were not "sufficiently well educated, occupy comparatively only minor and inferior categories of service and do not have such a social and official status as to provide them with sufficient guarantees (unwritten) to be able to take care of their interests."[60] In addition, these officials also asserted that emigrants should not be allowed to travel to places that were not conducive to their "health and happiness and [were] derogatory to their country's name." The implication of this type of argument was that the Indian government should refuse oil companies the permission to recruit labor if those companies did not agree to certain key issues. These officials felt that oil companies would be quick to cooperate, given that Indian workers performed high-quality work, and they could be paid less than workers of other nationalities.[61]

Eventually, in response to the chemists' letters and press coverage of the chemists' experiences, the Indian government launched an investigation into the conditions of workers in the Arabian Peninsula and, in particular, Bahrain.[62] One Indian official, based in Baghdad, visited Bahrain, Kuwait, and the Trucial Coast in order to ascertain the position of Indians in the oil fields. In his letters to Indian government officials in New Delhi, he indicated that workers took oil jobs because there were no jobs in India, and they were thus compelled to sign contracts that were unfavorable for them. In his opinion, the lack of jobs in India, however, did not excuse the horrible conditions that workers experienced at oil projects in the Arabian Peninsula.[63]

As they investigated the complaints of Indians working abroad, Indian government officials understood the end of colonialism in India to be a strong factor in mobilizing Indian citizens and motivating them to challenge their employers when experiencing poor treatment. One official wrote, "As soon as they reach these places, they find themselves in an inferior position, and being discriminated against. This could be endured in the past, but the change over in India makes these young men feel humiliated."[64] Here, the official indicated that India's new independence altered how workers understood their position internationally, and they recognized that India's independence was a central for workers as they appealed to the government to protect their rights.

GOVERNANCE AND HUMAN RIGHTS

The Indian chemists formerly employed by Bapco asserted solidarity based on their profession and their citizenship in the new Indian nation, and they called upon their government to protect their rights. In their complaints, the chemists specifically asked the Indian government to protect their "fundamental Right of Association and of speech recognised even under the U.N.O. [United Nations Organization] charter,"[65] and they argued that collective worker action was protected as a basic human right. Indian newspapers also covered the story of the chemists and connected rights to collective action and citizenship. Journalists wrote that the Indian government should support Indians forming trade unions in Bahrain and that the government should appoint a representative in Bahrain to "look after the interests" of Indians there.[66] These calls for action point to the importance of a strong state to support citizens' rights, and they make explicit what the chemists and others saw as to be the obligations of the Indian government to its citizens.

In appealing to the Indian government to protect their human rights, India's independence from colonial rule was essential. This was because, according to the United Nations, human rights were given to most peoples but not to colonized subjects, who were understood to be protected by their colonial governments.[67] Rights were ensured through states recognizing citizens, acting within their territories, and negotiating with other states and interstate actors.[68] Thus, the chemists' demand for rights could only be successful when they, as citizens, appealed to their own, independent state to act on behalf of its citizenry.

The rights to which the chemists referred were first articulated on an international stage with US president Franklin Roosevelt's 1941 State of the Union address. In this speech, Roosevelt outlined four freedoms: freedom of speech, freedom of worship, freedom from want, and freedom from fear. These freedoms, Roosevelt argued, were the right of every person in the world. The Allies adopted these four freedoms as their war aims during World War II, and these freedoms formed the basis for Eleanor Roosevelt's work in the United Nations on the Universal Declaration of Human Rights. Later, US president Harry S. Truman reiterated these freedoms to the United Nations in 1946, and the Universal Declaration of Human Rights was adopted by the UN General Assembly in December 1948. When the chemists argued for the protection of the human rights, they did so to engage with the racist policies originating out of US oil company policies. Thus, two seemingly disparate discourses—racist US managerial practices and a universal discourse of rights—were simultaneously circulating in the oil arena and informing oil production.

The chemists' appeal to the Indian government to protect their human rights mobilized current political discourse that was being developed and propagated in the United Nations. In the late 1940s, the same period that the United Nations was focused on ratifying the Declaration of Human Rights, such a strategy was not uncommon, and Pakistani workers in Saudi Arabia made similar claims.[69] In addition, both Saudi and Pakistani workers discussed US racism and the treatment of African Americans in the United States in order to critique Aramco management practices.[70]

For the chemists, appealing to the Indian government on the basis of human rights had two implications. First, it made the implicit argument that ensuring the recognition of such rights was one of the duties of a liberal democratic state to its citizenry. Second, it banked on the notion that the Indian state would be particularly invested in protecting these rights given the country's own anticolonial struggles. The Indian state, for example, had encouraged the International Labor Organization, even before India's independence, to develop a Declaration of Human Rights in 1944 as a tool to critique colonial rule.[71]

After India's independence from British colonial rule in 1947, Indian leaders, including India's first prime minister, Jawaharlal Nehru, saw the internationalism of the United Nations as holding promise for critiquing imperialism and forming international communities. At the same time, Indian leaders were also wary of the potential the United Nations had for reasserting imperial power.[72] They were not unique in this regard; other leaders around the world saw the UN as a means of maintaining imperial power.[73] For areas still under colonial rule, particularly in Africa, many African anti-colonial activists saw some structures in the UN as the best tool to advocate for an end to the human rights violations occurring under colonial rule.[74] For the chemists, who were citizens of the new state of India, human rights were discursively mobilized to argue for the improvement of their working conditions and address inequalities. Such arguments point to the centrality of the state in protecting the rights of citizens, and citizenship was strongly associated with individual rights within a rule of law framework.

CLASS, RELIGION, AND CITIZENSHIP

Citizenship in a newly independent Indian state informed the chemists' complaints and the government's response. Other skilled, professional Indians working at Bapco also appealed directly to the Indian government for support. However, not all Indian citizens appealed to the government to protect their rights. Rather, class and religion were key factors in who appealed to the Indian government and in how the government responded.

In the late 1940s, other skilled workers at Bapco also wrote directly to the Indian government in hopes of improving their working and living conditions. Some skilled workers, who were employed as clerks, reported that they were terminated because of their participation in collective action. Specifically, these workers, along with three hundred other Indian employees, had collectively written a petition requesting medical facilities near their camps, a provision that was guaranteed in their contract. In writing to the Indian government, these workers hoped that the government would act to enforce their contract with Bapco and contest their unjust dismissal. Other skilled workers complained to the Indian government that they were treated with racism. These complaints, like the complaints of the chemists and those seeking medical facilities, came from well-educated, professional employees.

Skilled workers made up one-third of the Indian workforce at Bapco, and the other two-thirds were daily wage laborers. Unskilled workers at Bapco were also unhappy with their working conditions, but this only came to light after the Indian government arranged interviews with them. The government found that unskilled workers' complaints included being injured on the job, not being paid a full salary upon termination, and being terminated without due cause.[75] While many of these workers filed complaints with the company, they did not attempt to contact the Indian government to negotiate on their behalf or enforce their contracts.

In these cases, class differences influenced who mobilized language about their citizenship and made claims on the state to protect their rights. While workers at all levels, from those employed in professional positions to skilled positions to unskilled positions, were all unhappy with their working conditions, only educated, higher-skilled workers appealed to the government by invoking both their citizenship status and human rights. In the wake of independence, migrants with higher educations and income levels than the majority of Indians in the Arabian Peninsula rhetorically situated themselves within a cosmopolitan and international workforce. In addition, they were able to garner the attention of newspapers, compelling the government to respond to their petitions.[76] Skilled workers were uniquely situated to appeal to the government and to have their cases taken up by the government.

For the chemists, their position as well-educated, middle-class citizens of the newly independent state of India facilitated their interactions with the Indian government and press. In their letters, the chemists also connected Bapco's violation of their rights with the racism that they experienced from company managers. These claims of racial discrimination conflated race with nationality and served to lend discursive strength to their argument. As race and nationality were conflated by oil company managers, workers, and government administrators, religion also emerged as an important factor. The chemists were all well-educated Hindus. However, they came from a diversity of geographic areas of India and spoke different languages: one was Sindhi, two Bengali, and five Malayali. Here, we see nationalism was able to overcome some internal divisions, as language was used by the British colonial government as a way of categorizing the peoples of India.[77] But at this time, not all workers with Indian citizenship identified primarily as Indians. Indeed, other Malayali workers at Bapco from the princely state of Travancore (now part of the Indian state of Kerala) donated over one thousand rupees toward a movement advocating for the state to remain separate from the federation of India.[78] In the case of the chemists, their religion and class helped them effectively approach the nation-state for the protection of their rights. By advocating for their rights as citizens of India and complaining of discrimination, the chemists were engaging with a conversation about rights as being guaranteed by one's state, while simultaneously reinforcing the collapsing of nationality, race, and religion.[79]

COMMUNAL VIOLENCE FOLLOWING THE PARTITION OF COLONIAL INDIA

Indian government officials believed that the treatment of the chemists fired by Bapco was due to rampant pro-Pakistani and anti-Indian sentiments among oil companies and governments in the Arabian Peninsula.[80] Government officials were also concerned about communal violence in the Arabian Sea following partition. The partition had displaced approximately 17 million people and was accompanied by mass violence, including the rape of at least 75,000 women and the deaths of at least 1 million people.[81] Aware of this violence and wanting to ensure violence was also not occurring abroad, the Indian government sent a letter to the Bahrain Residency asking if there was persecution of "Indian nationals by Muslims" in the Arabian Peninsula—a formulation that both conflated Indians, or citizens of India, with members of the Hindu religion and positioned Muslims outside of the Indian nation. This slippage calls attention to the tensions around citizenship and religion in post-1947 India.[82] During this time, some Indian government officials tried to argue for a secular state while other government leaders argued for a Hindu one, an issue that has continued to be debated in subsequent decades.[83] In response to the Indian government's enquiry about communal violence, the political resident indicated that they were unaware of trouble between "Hindus and Pakistanis," thereby reiterating the slippage from Indians to Hindus or, in other words, reinforcing the conflation of nationality and religion.[84]

Despite this assurance, the Indian government continued to be concerned that Indian citizens, and specifically those who were Hindus, were experiencing discrimination or violence due to their religion. To substantiate their concerns, government officials pointed to common practices at oil companies. Oil companies, including AIOC, classified their Indian and Pakistani employees by religion.[85] Some oil companies also hired workers based on their nationality or religion. For example, Aramco followed the request of the Saudi Arabian government to only hire Christians and Muslims.[86] In addition, Indian citizens employed in the Arabian Peninsula argued that they faced discrimination, but they reported that Pakistani workers were treated well—notwithstanding arguments to the contrary in the Pakistani press.[87]

Indian government officials also expressed concern about relations between India and local governments in the Arabian Peninsula, and they believed local governments were developing a more favorable view of Pakistan and a less favorable view of India. For example, after India's independence in 1947, the ruler of Bahrain joined the political agent and the political resident at the national day celebrations for both India and Pakistan.[88] However, the Indian and British governments believed that sympathy was growing for Pakistan.[89] In October 1947, a Bahraini firm made collections for refugees arriving in Pakistan from India.[90] The following year, in 1948, the ruler of Bahrain and local Arabs attended Pakistan's national day celebrations but did not attend Indian celebrations.[91] Similarly, when M. K. Gandhi, a leading figure of the Indian nationalist movement, was killed in 1948, only the sheikh of Sharjah sent a condolences telegram.[92] In contrast, at the death of Muhammad Ali Jinnah, a leading figure in the founding of Pakistan, flags throughout the Arabian Peninsula were flown at half mast; and in Manama, Bahrain, there was a memorial in the *juma' masjid* (congregational mosque) and cinemas were closed throughout the city.[93]

Many Indian government officials were operating under the assumption that anti-Indian sentiments were the same as anti-Hindu sentiments. Given this assumption, Indian government officials were particularly concerned about communal violence in the Arabian Sea. However, most communal violence that we find archival evidence for was not against Hindu Indians, but against Sikh Indians. One example of this occurred in Bahrain, where the political agent reported that there was violence against Sikhs, and the British administration reported that this violence was perpetuated by Muslims from India *and* Pakistan. Following this violence, the British government reported that all Sikhs left Bahrain. This incident, in February 1948, was the first incident of Indian "communal strife" to occur in Bahrain.[94]

Violence against Sikh employees also occurred or was threatened at other job sites. For example, at Abadan, there was relatively little unrest between Indians and Pakistanis who practiced different religions until December 1947. At that time, a Muslim tradesman, "who had been discharged for bad workmanship, attacked several Sikh employees of AIOC" in the bazaar and near their living quarters. As a result, Sikh employees said they would not go back to work without security. AIOC managers refused this request, and

Sikh workers asked to be repatriated, which the company did. In total, the company reported that seventeen Hindus and Sikhs were involved.[95] At PCL (Qatar), communal tension also played out. In early 1948, managers at an oil project found that both Indian and Pakistani workers had acquired weapons.[96] It was estimated that fifty Muslims were preparing to attack nine Sikh employees. The company was able to stop the attack before it began, and no one was fired, although it was suggested that the ringleader should be fired if he could be found. Like at other job sites, Sikh personnel working at PCL (Qatar) asked to be repatriated to India.[97]

Despite Sikhs experiencing the brunt of the violence, Hindus also experienced some violence. In 1948, a fight occurred in Bahrain between a Hindu Indian and two Iranians, and this fight was attributed to anti-Hindu and anti-Indian sentiments. Following the fight, the Indian community in Bahrain said that it was threatened with violence.[98] Government officials also feared that the Muslim League, an Indian political party during the nationalist movement, was putting out propaganda against "Indians and Sikhs"—using a formulation that equated Hindus and Indians while excluding Sikhs from the Indian nation.[99] Despite some incidents involving Hindu Indians, the majority of the recorded communal violence was directed at Sikhs. One reason that Sikhs may have been a target was their visible role in the British armed forces as the British asserted imperial control in the Arabian Sea.[100] This association and the anti-imperial sentiments in the Arabian Sea at the time may have contributed to the discrimination and violence Sikhs experienced in the later 1940s.

British and US managers blamed Sikhs for the violence they experienced, and managers attributed the violence following the partition of British India to Sikhs. Indeed, some managers argued that Sikh employees were fearful because "they know so well what damage their brothers in the Punjab have done to the Muslims."[101] Therefore, these managers argued, the oil companies ought to repatriate all their Sikh employees. The push to repatriate Sikh employees neatly elided the role of Sikhs as members of the British armed forces and as anti-imperial organizers. It also obscured the role of British colonialism in the violence and chaos of partition.[102] By repatriating Sikh employees, who were often at the forefront of labor organizing, the companies were able to fire vulnerable workers while blaming the workers themselves for their circumstances.

The Indian government did not respond to these reports of violence against Sikh Indians or inquire into the experiences of Muslim Indians. This illustrates the uneven application of state intervention to protect citizens.[103] It also underscores contested understandings of who belonged to the Indian nation.[104] Thus, membership in the nation was central in determining whose rights the state protected, and not all government officials agreed on who was included in the Indian nation. Religion, class, and education level also impacted who appealed to the state to protect their rights. In this context, the Bapco chemists' invocation of human rights was effective not only because of their nationality but also due to their class and religion.

CONCLUSION

Claims for protection against racial discrimination were most commonly taken up by governments when they were made by members of a nation-state's majority group. Such calls for rights simultaneously reified and obfuscated state and corporate power, and specifically helped reinforce the racialization of nationality, which workers argued was the root of the violation of their rights.[105] The role of human rights in protecting individuals but not protecting minorities or collective rights emerged in the drafting of the UN's Universal Declaration of Human Rights and the work done by US delegates to prevent US racism from being considered a human rights violation. At the United Nations, US government representatives argued strongly against the idea of minority rights that were put forward by leading African Americans.[106] Similarly, in India, leading nationalist, Dalit activist, and author of the Indian constitution, Bhimrao Ramji Ambedkar also expressed "interest in taking the problem of untouchability to the United Nations," but he met resistance from Indian officials.[107]

As rights were (and continue to be) formulated and codified, they emphasized individuals and an individual's ability to successfully petition their own government for protection. As seen in the case of the Indian chemists, their religion, class, and citizenship informed their national belonging and ability to make claims upon the state. In addition, the chemists, who were university-educated, were offended that they were so poorly treated despite their education, their expertise, and India's status as a newly independent state. As in other international contexts, Indians fought against discrimination, while they also reinforced racist practices. For example, the chemists used discriminatory language about local workers.[108] By using stereotypes and racialized categories, the chemists did not call into question labor hierarchies; rather, they only challenged their own position within those hierarchies.

Rights were ensured by one's country of citizenship, and at oil projects in the Arabian Sea, governments had limited options for intervention. Indeed, oil company managers believed that migrant workers' rights were assured by their employers. Prior to India's and Pakistan's independence, one manager noted that an Indian or Pakistani has "no standing in the country [Saudi Arabia], except as the Company [Aramco] protects him,"[109] articulating the precarity of foreign workers compared to the position of local workers in the company. After independence, Pakistani and Indian workers were able to petition their own governments for support, but their governments had limited power to protect them. In contrast, local workers appealed directly to the local governments for protection. In response, members of the ruling family would sometimes intercede on behalf of local workers, and the oil companies would raise wages for local workers, thereby reinforcing the differential treatment of workers based on their nationality.[110]

Such interventions led to further divisions among workers, as workers found some success changing their working and living conditions when they formed solidarities based on their nationality. But, as the Indian government's actions showed, not all citizens were seen as needing equal protection of their rights. Thus, the logic of human rights, particularly when accompanied by segregation, the racialization of nationality, and the enactment of state sovereignty, made both international strikes by workers and claims for broad, collective rights decreasingly likely.

Four
SHAPING NATIONALISM OUTSIDE OF THE NATION-STATE

IN 1950, BRITISH PETROLEUM DECIDED TO BUILD A REFINERY AT Aden, a British crown colony that was located on the Arabian Peninsula between the Indian subcontinent and the Suez Canal, in today's Yemen.[1] The following year, the Iranian government under Prime Minister Mohammad Mosaddegh nationalized the country's oil in a move to defend "the nation's land and its resources."[2] The subsequent expulsion of British and other foreign companies from the city of Abadan, Iran, and the loss of the refinery there—the world's largest, and Britain's single largest investment overseas—was devastating to the Anglo-Iranian Oil Company (AIOC) and the British government.[3] Shortly after this, in 1954, AIOC changed its name to British Petroleum (BP).[4] The nationalization of the refinery at Abadan also meant many of the approximately two thousand Indians working for AIOC lost their jobs.[5] Following Iran's nationalization of oil, BP and the British government wanted to build the refinery in Aden "in the shortest possible time." To do so, at the height of construction, fourteen thousand men were working on construction of the refinery. This included ten thousand local workers as well as workers from Europe, the United States, the Middle East, India, and Pakistan.[6]

Living and working conditions at the Aden refinery construction project were far from ideal, and in 1953, 350 Indian employees at the Aden refinery construction project went on a forty-eight-hour hunger strike.[7] During this strike, workers argued that two interrelated factors made their work on the Aden refinery unbearable: workers' living conditions and racist discrimination by management.[8] Workers lived in makeshift plywood tents—these were extremely hot as a result of having no fans,[9] and they were located near the latrines, which smelled bad and were of poor quality. One visiting Indian official described them as "insufferable."[10] In addition to their miserable living quarters, workers were upset that the company charged them a significant portion of their earnings for food that was of poor quality, "unpalatable to Indian taste," and did not accommodate dietary restrictions.[11] Even a European personnel supervisor at the refinery agreed that the food served to Indians was not good. As a result of poor quality of food served, the supervisor observed that many workers lived on bread and jam. He thought that this likely led to nutritional deficits, as workers became increasingly unable to perform hard labor the longer they subsisted on this diet.[12] These conditions differed from those of US and European employees. Like the chemists employed by Bapco a few years earlier, the Indian workers at Aden argued that racism underpinned their poor working and living conditions—a claim they substantiated by pointing to Indian workers' forced segregation from white workers and the verbal abuse Indian workers experienced from white managers.

Unlike previous strikes in the Arabian Peninsula, when Indian workers at the Aden refinery construction project went on strike, they exhibited a national solidarity that cut across job categories. Notably, at Aden, the striking workers were all Indians, and they did not form alliances with workers from other countries, as they had done at Abadan and Kuwait in the mid- to late 1940s. Prior to the 1953 hunger strike at the Aden refinery construction project, Indians also went on strike without forming coalitions with workers of other nationalities. However, those earlier strikes were often ineffective due to lack of unity among the Indian employees. The division between Indian employees was most pronounced between senior and junior employees. One Indian government observer argued that senior workers were loath to join collective action. Other Indian government officials also attributed this lack of unity to a generational difference—namely, officials argued that senior workers were more submissive, whereas junior workers felt more strongly about their rights and were more emboldened by the new independence of India.[13]

Distinct from the 1946 strike at Abadan, in which Indian managers did not participate, and from the filing of complaints by the chemists at Bahrain Petroleum Company (Bapco), in which unskilled workers did not participate, the hunger strike at Aden mobilized workers at all levels, from day laborers to skilled employees. The fact that it was not just skilled, educated Indians protesting their working conditions, and that Indians across job types collectively appealed to the Indian government based on citizenship, suggests that organizing based on citizenship was gaining popularity among Indian workers abroad. During this hunger strike at Aden, workers who were of differing classes and job skill levels as well as from diverse regions of India petitioned the Indian government to secure their rights. However, despite this broad coalition of Indians, workers and Indian administrators continued to conflate Indian citizens and Hindu religious adherents.

Issues around laborers working throughout the British Empire had been central to Indian nationalist movements in the early twentieth century.[14] After India's independence, the requests of laborers working abroad show how, after 1947, Indian nationalism was imagined by workers and by government officials. The nationalism that informed the collective Indian hunger strike at Aden did not exist within a vacuum, and the increasing formation of worker solidarities by nationality was further reinforced by how labor was recruited and by oil companies' managerial practices. These practices segregated workers by nationality and housed workers in remote areas. They also gave different nationalities different benefits and pay, thereby spurring conflict between nationalities and decreasing the likelihood that workers would form class-based solidarities that had the potential to halt oil production.

THE CONSTRUCTION OF THE ADEN REFINERY

When construction on the Aden refinery began in 1952, BP managers described the Europeans who began working at the project as "pioneer constructors," and they focused on the rough conditions under which managers had to live.[15] Despite the challenges of living in Aden, BP managers thought Aden was different from other states on the Arabian Peninsula because of its "established commercial and light industrial organisations." In contrast, they saw oil companies to be "the sole industrialists" in other parts of the Arabian Peninsula.[16] Local labor was also more plentiful in Aden than in other countries on the Arabian Peninsula in which BP operated, and BP wanted to give preference to local workers.[17] BP's decision to preferentially hire local workers was in compliance with prior restrictions the government of Aden had implemented concerning companies hiring Indian workers, particularly Indian domestic workers, because the government argued that there were ample numbers of Adenese to perform such jobs.[18] However, with the arrival of almost three thousand foreigners for the refinery project, there were no longer enough local workers, and the oil companies, with the assent of Aden's government, looked to India to supply domestic staff, including cooks and skilled tradesmen.[19] The hiring process, their living conditions and working conditions, and the racism they experienced all contributed to the dissatisfaction of Indian workers and informed worker solidarities during the hunger strike.

Historically, BP (India) had overseen recruitment of Indian workers, but to expedite construction and in need of skilled tradesmen, BP contracted much of its labor through the US contractor Bechtel and the British contractor Wimpey. Bechtel spearheaded much of the recruitment in India, and initially hired over six hundred Indian tradesmen and other skilled workers.[20] BP saw benefits to contracting because it placed responsibility for working conditions on the contractors, which allowed the company to differentiate its own practices from the practices of contractors.[21] Thus, BP hoped to distance itself from labor issues. An additional benefit was that contracting legally moved the responsibility for workers onto contractors.[22] Recruitment of Indian workers by Bechtel was rocky. Bechtel was a relatively new player on the Indian recruiting scene, and this meant it lacked the connections that recruiters for BP (India) held.[23] As a result, Bechtel's recruiters faced more bureaucratic hurdles than BP (India) recruiters usually faced. Despite these drawbacks, BP continued to contract recruitment through Bechtel.

Some of the issues that Indian workers faced came from miscommunication between Bechtel and BP, with workers bearing the brunt of the negative consequences that arose. For example, Bechtel's agent had told prospective Indian workers that they would be given an allowance to cover the money deducted for eating in the mess hall. However, this was not in line with BP's policy, and when Indian workers arrived in Aden, they found they were charged for eating at the mess hall but did not receive a stipend to cover it. This charge was even more upsetting to Indian workers because their camp was far from the city, and they had little option but to eat at the mess hall.[24]

Indian workers were also unhappy with their working conditions. At the Aden refinery construction project, Indian workers were employed for a term of eighteen months.[25] They worked most Sundays, and workers reported putting in at least ten hours a day.[26] While the company claimed ten-hour workdays were stipulated in the contract, workers reported that these hours were too long and that they had not been informed of these hours before arriving in Aden.[27] Furthermore, workers were confused by the payment system for overtime hours. The company claimed that workers would be paid overtime upon completion of their contracts, but workers were unaware of this condition.[28]

In addition, Indian workers were aggrieved by the discrepancies between British and Indian accommodations. At the Aden refinery construction site, there were four camps, based on nationality: the British/American Camp, Italian Camp, Indian Camp, and National Camp, which included all noncontract employees hired locally at the site, in the Aden Protectorate, and in Yemen. These camps reflected the contracts used to employ workers.[29] The British/American Camp provided worker recreation that was not available to Indians. One British manager reflected on his time at the construction project: "Clubs and an enclosed bathing beach provided relaxation for many employees, whilst impromptu cricket and football matches against Aden clubs were enjoyed by the more energetic." In addition, while Indians lived in tents, US and British workers lived in prefabricated buildings.[30]

The discrepancies in living conditions contributed to worker dissatisfaction. In addition, the form worker action took was also impacted by the location of worker camps. The Indian labor camp was twenty miles from the site of the refinery. As a result, workers commuted a long distance every day for work, and they were not paid for this time. This isolation of the Indians' camp influenced in several ways how workers could advocate for better working and living conditions. First, the distance of the camp from the city meant that it was hard for workers to contact the Indian government and ask it to negotiate with the company on their behalf.[31] A second way the camp's isolation impacted workers was that it made it challenging for workers to form solidarities with Arabic- and Farsi-speaking workers through regular interactions and shared experiences. Indeed, the isolation helped foster discord between groups. Separate work camps were not new at this time, but with isolation, camps were becoming increasingly strict in their segregation practices. In comparison, at Abadan in 1946, workers lived near workers of other nationalities. This proximity facilitated affiliations across nationalities, whereas isolation in Aden reinforced separation between groups.

Like Indian workers at Bapco and Aramco in the 1940s, Indian workers at Aden attributed the inequalities they experienced to racism. Workers argued that discriminatory practices at the refinery meant that they were forced to work long hours, segregated from white employees, and treated disrespectfully. One worker said that he often worked twelve or fourteen hours a day and was given no credit for overtime. He described spending all day in the hot sun, and upon asking for a transfer, being refused. When he quit, he said that the European worker who replaced him was given a "fat" salary and assistants.[32] Indian workers pointed to the fact that Americans and Europeans worked shorter hours for higher wages. Americans and Europeans also had better amenities—for example, their bar was always open, whereas the Indian bar was open only part of the day. Such management practices reinforced worker division along national lines, applied racialized labor hierarchies rooted in British colonial imaginings of civilizational progress and US Jim Crow policies, and naturalized inequality through the application of economic models.

Indian employees argued that the discrimination they faced was based on skin color,[33] and they pointed to the fact that they were barred from leisure spaces. The cinema, for example, was off limits to Indian workers and designated "European only"—something Indian workers said was in breach of their contract. Indians also did not receive equal access to the cricket field.[34] Discrepancies in treatment were compounded by the verbal abuse workers faced. Multiple workers wrote that the US manager in charge of the Indian employees' mess hall reportedly abused their nationality in the most "insulting of terms." This verbal abuse was made worse by the fact that Indians were not treated as well as Europeans and Americans.

Finally, workers complained that one's nationality determined one's pay grades: Workers of different nationalities performed the same job, but they received different wages due to their nationality.[35] As a result, Indian workers were paid less than workers from the eastern Mediterranean. Indian workers particularly felt it was unfair that they were paid the same amount as local workers, whom they characterized as having fewer skills and less experience. One Indian described the situation by pointing out that the Adenese "orderly who serves the office with tea and has little or no qualifications to be called literate draws as much pay as us.... The Indian is getting a very raw deal."[36]

Compensating employees based on their nationality, segregating leisure facilities, and housing workers separately also worked to exacerbate differences between groups. Thus, despite experiencing discrimination, Indians were not above marshaling discriminatory discourse.[37] Indeed, it was deemed particularly outrageous that they, Indian workers, were not even treated as well as the Arab employees. These complaints illuminate how segregation and differential treatment helped to promote solidarities among Indian workers across job type and pay grade, while decreasing international solidarities among workers.

SOVEREIGNTY, CITIZENSHIP, AND INDIAN EMIGRATION

Indian workers' shared experiences of migration in conjunction with difficult working conditions, unresponsive employers, and racist discrimination served to foster collective action among all Indians. Collective worker action was also influenced by the history of India's struggle for independence from colonial rule and workers' citizenship in the new Indian state. It is notable that workers decided to participate in a hunger strike as opposed to a work stoppage. Building upon the popularity of trade unions in India after World War I, strikes in India were a popular method of agitating against working conditions and promoting solidarity among workers. In 1951, there were 120 registered strikes and hundreds of additional strikes in the Indian *beedi* industry alone.[38] Hunger strikes, in contrast, were infrequent in India and uncommon at oil projects in the Arabian Peninsula. Facing restrictions on labor unions and formal strikes, the hunger strike at Aden gave workers a means to address their working conditions. This method of protest, popularized by M. K. Gandhi, was especially poignant given the history of India's colonization and the contemporary discrimination workers faced.

During the hunger strike, workers appealed directly to the Indian government, insisting that the government was responsible for ensuring their rights even when they were working abroad. Before the hunger strike began, Indian workers had conveyed their grievances to the commissioner of the government of India in Aden. In their communications, they told the commissioner that they were working ten-hour days and not getting paid for overtime.[39] When the commissioner failed to instigate changes on their behalf, Indian workers intensified their actions. They began their hunger strike and sent a telegram to the Indian ambassador in Egypt alerting him to their circumstances.[40] As in the case with the Bapco chemists, appealing to the Indian government reflects the importance to workers of India's 1947 independence from British colonial rule.

As workers petitioned the Indian government, they raised questions about the ability of the Indian state to intervene on behalf of its citizens, even when those citizens were abroad. These questions of sovereignty were closely connected to the ways in which the government regulated Indian emigration. Generally, emigration policies are a key mechanism through which states demarcate citizens from noncitizens, define their borders, and assert sovereignty.[41] In India, emigration regulations built upon colonial policies, and following independence, Indian bureaucrats continued to use the emigration regulation system developed by the British government to move indentured workers to plantations and, later, workers to the oil fields. Concerning emigration to work in the Arabian Peninsula, Indian emigration regulations stipulated that the Indian government needed to approve all contracts for workers going abroad and recruiters needed permission from the Indian government before they could recruit in India.

As Bechtel and BP sought to hire Indians to build the Aden refinery, contracts became a central concern of the Indian government, and specifically, Indian government representatives were concerned about workers' rights and with jurisdiction for the arbitration of disputes.[42] In 1952 at the Aden refinery construction project, there were different contracts for tradesmen, domestic workers, and general class employees. During initial negotiations, the companies and the Indian government agreed that Aden's contract should follow the "basic principles" of the Kuwait Oil Company's contract—a contract that was first negotiated by the British colonial government. In addition, both sides agreed that when the Kuwait Oil Company's contract changed, so would the Aden contract. The contracts for workers at the Aden refinery included stipulations that workers had to take a medical test, that they acknowledged that they worked "at [their] own risk," and that their references would be checked. The protector of emigrants in Bombay looked over these contracts and insisted that they needed to contain stipulations for overtime; that the companies could not stop pay during strikes; and that companies had to give reasons for terminating employment.[43] Indian officials also argued that arbitration should be overseen jointly by the British government of Aden and the Indian Commission in Aden.[44]

As the Indian government negotiated with oil companies over the contracts for Indian workers and attempted to play a role in arbitrating workplace issues involving Indian workers in Aden, Indian bureaucrats actively debated and codified sovereignty and citizenship in the context of the new Indian state. Regulating emigration helped establish the sovereign boundaries of the new country. Through writing and negotiating contracts with oil companies, the government tried to ensure that Indians' rights were assured. When the Indian government received complaints from workers abroad, many government officials were particularly concerned about discrimination against Indians at their worksites. In their investigation of these complaints, officials were divided in their view of workers as rational actors versus workers as precarious subjects in need of protection. Overlapping with these competing notions of workers was another set of questions regarding the role and obligation of citizens abroad to represent India in a positive light and how Indian workers abroad impacted India's reputation globally.

INDIA'S REPUTATION IN THE WORLD

As Indian bureaucrats negotiated contracts with oil companies that sought to hire Indian workers and as they received complaints from Indians working abroad, they articulated a belief that Indian citizens abroad were representative of the country of India. Therefore, government officials argued, Indians working abroad should be treated with the respect due to the newly independent India. Indian government officials were particularly concerned with the numbers of Indians being hired, their treatment by the oil companies, and the types of jobs for which they were hired.

When recruitment for the Aden refinery's construction began, Indian bureaucrats were troubled by Bechtel's recruitment practices. First, the government was concerned that the company was only hiring six hundred Indians, and moreover that they were not being hired for skilled positions. They contrasted British Petroleum's plans to hire Indian cooks with the company's proposal to hire fifteen hundred skilled workers from Italy and suggested the company was discriminating against Indians and favoring Europeans.[45]

A second problem regarding recruitment for the Aden refinery was brought up by the commissioner of the government of India in Aden, A. B.

Thadani, when he heard about the recruitment plan. Thadani's critique revolved around the relationship between India's international reputation and the class of workers going abroad. After six cooks traveled to Aden, Thadani wrote to the government in New Delhi, arguing that no more Indian cooks should be allowed to migrate to Aden. He pointed out that the Indians currently living in Aden were rich and the arrival of poor Indians to work as cooks would harm the reputation of India.[46] As the commissioner put it, the cooks would "lower India in the eyes of everyone." In addition, he argued, without their families the "servant class" would "get into all sorts of trouble" and their presence "would also start economic conflict with another class of Arabs."[47] Put bluntly, cooks were seen as poor international ambassadors of India. Other Indian officials vehemently disagreed with the commissioner's assessment. The protector of emigrants in Bombay wrote to the commissioner that it was "the first time in my life that I have ever heard it suggested that the profession of a cook is a dishonourable one." He further argued that every country had cooks, and he did not believe that the profession was "degrading to the mother country."[48] In this debate, the idea that citizens working abroad served to embody and represent India was not disputed; rather, the dispute centered on the nature of the work and the class of the citizen migrating.

India's new status as an independent country provided an important framework and context for this debate. One official wrote that it was the view taken by the Indian government that "emigration from dependent British India was a source of embarrassment; emigration from free India may be a source of strength." In order to ensure that emigration was a source of strength, any proposal for Indian emigration had to be considered on its own merits and would only be permitted if emigration was sure to be on "honourable terms, consistent with the dignity of India."[49] In this perspective, the honor of India was embodied in each migrant and it was the Indian government's duty to oversee emigration in order to maintain India's reputation abroad.

Despite the Indian government's efforts, problems with the recruitment of workers for the Aden refinery continued. As clerks began to migrate to Aden in increasing numbers, accusations of racial discrimination against Indians abounded. The companies were accused of hiring only the lowest level of clerks from India. Instead of rehiring Indians who had previously worked as tradesmen at the Abadan refinery, the overwhelming majority of the Indians BP and its contractors hired were employed as laborers and domestic workers. In addition, only a couple of Indian doctors, who were to exclusively attend to workers from Asia, as well as a few clerks were employed for the Aden project.[50] Furthermore, Indian clerks were not paid enough to maintain a middle-class standard of living, and, similarly to the cooks, this was seen as blemishing both India's reputation and the reputation of all Indians living in the Arabian Peninsula. In addition, there were allegations that even though the clerks were paid only at the lowest skill level, they were actually working at a much higher level. Officials believed that the company was taking advantage of the high rates of unemployment in India.[51]

Overall, many bureaucrats in the Ministry of External Affairs were upset by the fact that Indians were not being treated the same as Europeans and Americans; instead, the bureaucrats argued, Indians were being treated similarly to or worse than Arab workers.[52] The fact that Indians were not being treated equally with Americans and Europeans caused many officials to claim that the oil companies were treating Indian citizens just as the British had treated India under colonialism.[53] Such arguments were congruent with a general rhetoric used in discussions of Indian overseas emigration that asserted that India was defined and represented by its citizens abroad.

The idea that temporary migrants were representatives of the new Indian nation made worker complaints against employers for discrimination particularly salient to Indian officials in the Ministry of External Affairs. Not wanting to perpetuate a cycle in which colonial inequalities were reinforced, Indian officials advocated that Indians should only be allowed to travel to countries where they were treated equally with locals.[54] The implementation of this policy, however, was difficult given the international managerial practices of the oil companies, the fact that many Indians did not want to be treated similarly to Arabs, and the increasing numbers of uneducated Indian workers going abroad.

RELIGIOUS DISCRIMINATION AND CITIZENSHIP

Government officials were concerned about the discrimination Indians faced as a nationality, and these concerns grew as some Indian government officials and workers argued that Indian Hindus experienced even greater discrimination than Indians of other religions, particularly those who were

Christians. Accusation of religious discrimination were effective in mobilizing action by the Indian government, and the government halted the recruitment of Indians for the Aden construction project based on these allegations. As government officials investigated claims of religious discrimination, Indian bureaucrats considered citizens not as a homogenous category, but within the specificity of India's demography. Religion was a critical category for both oil companies and the Indian government, and government responses were informed by two seemingly competing views of India as a secular state and India as a Hindu nation.

Claims of religious discrimination first emerged around who was hired for the Aden refinery construction project, and prospective employees argued that those responsible for hiring for the project were discriminating based on religion.[55] For example, a Hindu man who had moved from West Pakistan to India during the partition reported that he had applied for a clerk position at the Aden refinery project but was not hired because of his religion. In a letter to the president of India, the man reported that the hiring agent for the contractors told him, "The policy of the Company is to recruit only Indian Christians."[56] This complaint was passed to the Ministry of External Affairs, which asked the protector of emigrants to investigate. This investigation became even more pressing when the ministry received another complaint from an Indian Hindu who claimed that at the Aden refinery project, "In all cases Hindus are discriminated against." Soon after, additional complaints from Hindu workers were received, particularly because the companies were not rehiring the thousands of Indians who had been employed in Iran but who had been forced to leave their jobs and return to India when the Iranian government nationalized oil and oil infrastructure from 1951 to 1953.[57]

Managers at BP denied the Indian government's allegations of religious discrimination, putting blame for discriminatory hiring on their contractors, Bechtel and Wimpey. In response, agents for Bechtel and Wimpey said their preferential hiring of Christians was purely economic, as the companies needed to set up a cheap kitchen.[58] To illustrate their point that this was neither racial nor religious discrimination, agents for Bechtel and Wimpey noted that they were willing to take Hindus and Muslims who did not follow restrictive (and, the companies argued, expensive) dietary restrictions. Indian officials were split on the reasonableness of this explanation.

For example, the protector of emigrants based in Bombay believed it was reasonable, but the undersecretary for the Ministry of External Affairs overrode the Protector of Emigrant's decision and halted recruitment until a better explanation was given.[59] Thadani, the commissioner of the government of India in Aden, took a conciliatory tone between the two. In Thadani's opinion, the company ought to recruit "'persons of a broad mind' who can eat at one kitchen." This should be possible, he argued, because the contract period was for a short time. Thadani developed this position after speaking with a representative of the contractors who explained the need for a common mess hall for workers. Thadani's only complaint was that Arabs were given special arrangements. The contractors replied that they were required to make special provisions only for the host country and that special provisions could not extend to all nationalities. They also said that if they were building a refinery in India, then they would consider special kitchens for Hindus.[60]

Recruiters denied that they were discriminating against Hindus, but they did admit that religion played a factor in some hiring decisions, and Sikhs, in particular, were actively discriminated against during the hiring process. The head recruiter for both Bechtel and Wimpey said that he was hiring "Indians of all types," except for Sikhs. The reasoning he gave for this was that "Sikh employees are apt to be argumentative when a number of them gather together in an organization."[61] Echoing the lack of interest the Indian government showed toward the violence Sikhs experienced in the Arabian Peninsula following the 1947 partition of colonial India, in the case of the Aden refinery construction project, Indian officials made no formal or written complaints regarding this discrimination.

While the Indian government did not mobilize to protect the rights of Sikh Indians, it did act to protect the rights of Hindu Indians. In response to considerable pressure from the Indian government, including the government's halting of recruitment of Indians to work at the construction of the Aden refinery, Bechtel and Wimpey agreed to recruit Hindus, Muslims, and Parsis from India, as long as workers from these religious groups agreed to the present kitchen situation and did not need religious days off.[62] Eventually, the Indian government allowed these contractors to restart the recruitment of Indians for the Aden refinery project, and the companies immediately engaged a dozen Hindu and Parsi workers.[63]

To ensure that the companies continued to hire a diversity of Indians, the Ministry of External Affairs asked the protector of emigrants in Bombay to collect information on the religion of workers hired for the Aden refinery construction project.[64] This investigation revealed that, despite assurances from Bechtel and Wimpey, Christians continued to be hired in disproportionately higher numbers. For example, in June 1953, thirty-four Christians, five Hindus, and one Muslim were recruited. Government officials were unhappy with these numbers, and they questioned why Christians, a minority in India, were still being recruited in larger numbers than Hindus.[65]

Claims of religious discrimination against Hindus were not limited to the recruitment selection process but were also made about the treatment of workers in Aden. In particular, the discussion over diet and discrimination against Indian workers emerged again later that year when the commissioner for the government of India in Aden investigated complaints by workers regarding the food they were served. The employees at the Aden refinery claimed that 50 percent of the meals were beef, and the other 50 percent were mutton. No other choices were served, and this was particularly problematic as many Hindus generally do not eat beef and some Hindus, particularly those of higher castes, often do not eat mutton. Perhaps forgetting his position on "open-minded" Indians working for the project that he had taken a year earlier, the commissioner wrote to both the Ministry of External Affairs and the protector of emigrants to complain, saying he could not see why Indians had to eat beef and that this forcing of beef upon workers struck him as discrimination against Indians. He claimed this was especially true because the company did not serve pork to Arab Muslims.[66] The protector of emigrants disagreed with the commissioner, and he reasoned that workers were also given salad and curries, so there was no need for Indian workers in Aden to eat beef.[67]

Bureaucrats working in the Ministry of External Affairs objected to the selective hiring of religious groups, and their reasons for this may be read in two different, but not mutually exclusive, ways. The most obvious would be that in the context of the partition of India into the countries of India and Pakistan at the end of British colonialism and following a period of heightened communal violence, bureaucrats working in the Indian government were aware of possible discrimination against Hindus and wanted to actively protect against it as a way of protecting Indian citizens and India's reputation.

This was especially important in the context of the decision made by the Indian government in the late 1940s that Pakistani Hindus could come to India and become Indian citizens.[68] Similarly to the Indian government's inquiries in the late 1940s about violence against Hindus in the Arabian Peninsula, Hinduism and the Indian nation were linked.[69] Following India's independence, the Indian government debated the idea of secularism and the role of religion in Indian governance. Indeed, the term "secular" did not appear in the Constitution until 1976.[70] The question becomes, then, to what extent secularism was mobilized as principle of statecraft in the early years of India's independence.[71]

In debates over citizenship, many of the Indian officials working at the Ministry of External Affairs were mobilizing a Gandhian view of secularism that promoted pluralism and tolerance.[72] Indian government officials were informed by a definition of secularism according to which it was the government's job to protect the religious rights of citizens. This view of secularism differs from that often discussed in the United States, which emphasizes the separation of religious and state institutions.

Many bureaucrats in the Indian government were inclusive in their view of who was an Indian citizen, and this is supported by data about the population of Indians living in Aden at the time. In the early 1950s, over ten thousand Muslims were classified as Indians in Aden. When the Pakistani consul heard of this, he argued that they should "'naturally' be classified as Pakistani Muslims in view of their religion." However, when he attempted to get them to re-register to change their nationality, not a single Indian Muslim changed their nationality. Officials in the Indian Ministry of External Affairs were delighted by this, and they used it to reinforce the idea of an inclusive Indian state.[73]

In its debates with the oil companies regarding religious hiring, the Indian government was, in a sense, encouraging oil companies to interact with Indian citizens in a similar manner as the state itself did—by protecting religious practice. While this policy was by no means consistently applied, as is seen in the example of the exclusion of Sikhs from the Aden project without Indian government complaint, this vision of India as a plural nation motivated some Indian bureaucrats, particularly those working in the Ministry of External Affairs. At the same time, however, the focus on the treatment of Hindus reinforced a view of India as a Hindu nation.

INDIAN EMIGRATION REGULATIONS

As Indians of all religions and classes faced increasingly segregated and poor working and living conditions abroad, Indian government officials grappled with ways the government could help. Some protectors of emigrants pressed for the expansion of the Emigration Act and stressed that it was necessary for the government to convince citizens of the act's importance. Government officials also pushed for more Indian representatives on the ground in the Arabian Peninsula. These responses by the Indian government reflect further changes in how the British administration responded to problems raised by Indians after India's independence from colonial rule in 1947. By the early 1950s, Indian government officials believed that only Indian officials would act to safeguard Indians and that the British government could no longer be relied upon to protect Indian citizens' rights. However, as the Indian government sought to guarantee the rights of Indians working abroad, oil company practices undermined these actions.

In their efforts to protect citizens working abroad, Indian government officials pointed to the utility of the Emigration Act for Indians who complied with it.[74] One advantage of the Emigration Act, Indian government officials argued, was that it allowed for workers abroad to register complaints regarding their treatment by employers. Upon their return to India, migrants could register complaints against their employer with the local protector of emigrants. The protector of emigrants would then investigated the complaint, and if the complaint was found to be valid, the protector of emigrants would attempt to negotiate with the company on behalf of the worker. If a worker did not get permission to emigrate, however, the government felt it was unable to act on behalf of the worker if a problem arose.

The proportion of complaints received from Indians working abroad regarding oil companies was not large in comparison with the total number of workers traveling to work for the oil companies, but complaints did grow steadily in the early 1950s, and progress resolving complaints was slow. In 1951, twenty-five complaints were lodged with the protector of emigrants in Bombay, but two were found to be false.[75] By 1952, the Ministry of External Affairs in New Delhi instructed all protector of emigrants offices to ask returning workers if they had complaints against their employer. In 1952, there were thirty-one complaints pending and four additional complaints were received.[76] In 1953, the government estimated that six thousand to seven thousand Indians were traveling to the Arabian Peninsula annually and were estimated to be remitting around 2.5 million Indian rupees every year.[77] In 1954, forty-nine new complaints were received. Complaints usually involved the behavior of the employer or compensation the worker believed he was owed.[78]

In order to ensure the rights of Indians working in the Arabian Peninsula, officials proposed a plan that involved job site inspections. The first step was to ask British political agents in the Arabian Peninsula about the conditions for workers there. Next, the Indian government was to send representatives to the Arabian Peninsula as quickly as possible. An additional step, officials suggested, was to have the protector of emigrants in Bombay warn workers of the conditions at oil projects in the Arabian Peninsula so that they might choose not to go in the first place.[79] The warning was accompanied by a form signed by the worker that he was aware of the risks, understood the terms of the contract, and accepted those terms "without reservation."[80] Government officials hoped that this would decrease the number of complaints received by the protector of emigrants offices. They also hoped it would dissuade Indians who were likely to "feel disgruntled and make complaints on returning to India" from migrating. By preemptively discouraging some complaints, government officials particularly hoped to decrease the amount of what they characterized as "flimsy" complaints, thus giving the government more time to investigate legitimate complaints.[81]

An example of the difficulty the Indian government had in assessing the validity of workers' complaints is seen in the case of Mr. Diaz. Mr. Diaz was an employee at the Aden refinery construction project who was fired for not being able to perform his duties. When he was fired, Mr. Diaz was forced to pay for his own passage back to India.[82] The management at the refinery construction project argued that Mr. Diaz was a "neurotic type of man, unsuitable for a strenuous construction job." To support this assessment, the manager reported that Mr. Diaz, who worked as a clerk, had told one of his supervisors that stapling, his primary task, caused him heart palpitations and that he suffered a dislocated shoulder from excessive stapling.[83] These health problems rendered him unable to complete his work. In addition, the company said that Mr. Diaz had mostly unfavorable work reviews and a belligerent attitude.[84] Due to these complaints, BP felt it had due cause to fire Mr. Diaz without a month's pay in lieu of a termination notice. According to Mr. Diaz, BP also garnished five hundred rupees from his wages in order to cover his passage back to India, and this left him with only five rupees. Mr. Diaz was told that any additional money due to him would be sent to the Bechtel office in Bombay for him to pick up.

When Mr. Diaz was terminated, the Indian Employee Committee advised him to visit Mr. Thadani, the commissioner of the government of India in Aden, to complain. Upon meeting Mr. Diaz, the commissioner agreed that Mr. Diaz was "a neurotic person," but the commissioner also felt the company should pay a month's salary in lieu of termination notice and cover Mr. Diaz's return passage to India. These issues, the commissioner claimed, were moral ones, and he wrote to the Ministry of External Affairs for legal advice.[85] The Ministry of External Affairs replied that workers only had to pay for the type of passage for which they were entitled and were responsible for the fare only if they had quit their jobs. If a worker is fired, officials said, the worker may be responsible for his own return fare, but there should be a way for the worker to appeal.

The case of Mr. Diaz encouraged the Indian government to renew its talks with the government of Aden regarding the arbitration of complaints made by Indians against the oil companies. However, because there was nothing in place at the time, Mr. Diaz's only recourse was to file a complaint with the protector of emigrants in Bombay.[86] In order to address migrant complaints like Mr. Diaz's dismissal, the Ministry of External Affairs sent the protector of emigrants a list of questions to ask returned migrants. The goal of these questions, according to their memos, was to ascertain if workers registering complaints upon return were exaggerating their work situations at oil projects in the Arabian Peninsula.[87] In addition, the government finalized plans to send representatives to oil projects, so that they could receive direct reports on the conditions there.[88]

Even when Indian government officials believed worker complaints were legitimate and they wanted to assist workers, they found the tools at their disposal inadequate to the task. Given the large numbers of Indians traveling abroad, the Indian government had difficulty regulating emigration. For example, less than one-third of the migrants traveling to the Arabian Peninsula fell under the scope of the Emigration Act. Largely this was because the Emigration Act of 1922 did not adequately address the needs of postcolonial India and did not allow the Indian government to respond to changes, such as new methods of transport.

In the 1950s, oil companies and some workers used the limitations of the Emigration Act to avoid the drawn-out emigration process in India. One way that emigrants worked around the jurisdiction of the act was by flying out of India. The wording of the 1922 act only covered departures by sea, and companies used this loophole to fly Indian workers out of India to job sites in the Arabian Peninsula without going through the necessary steps. In 1950, 1,584 people were documented as having left India in this manner. However, this number was rapidly increasing, and rumors circulated in the Bombay protector of emigrants office and in New Delhi at the Ministry of External Affairs offices that "chartered aircraft left Bombay almost every month carrying workers who had not been registered under the Emigration Act." While not all oil companies used air travel to circumvent state restrictions, many companies participated in this practice. The American Independent Oil Company (Aminoil), for instance, regularly flew Indians to Saudi Arabia without registering them.[89] Through such practices, oil companies directly sidestepped the sovereignty of the Indian government. These practices also limited the ability of Indian government to ensure the rights of workers abroad and made government attempts to address worker complaints, through actions like halting recruitment, less effective.

PAY, NATIONALITY, AND GLOBAL WEALTH INEQUALITIES

In their response to Indian workers' complaints concerning racist discrimination and poor working and living conditions, agents for British Petroleum (India) argued that "complaints from the returning emigrants are a perfectly ordinary and normal feature of this type of business."[90] Furthermore, BP managers in Aden said that Indians were being treated fairly given the type of project for which they were employed, and they argued, "The conditions are not out of line with what one would expect in a construction job." Indeed, in September 1953, one manager pointed to the fact that 444 Indians were employed directly by BP at the project, and only twenty-five Indian workers "have left for all causes, including medical." Managers claimed that this was a low attrition rate for oil construction projects, and they asserted the Indian government was responding to unsubstantiated rumors.[91] BP also argued discrimination was not the reason they paid workers differently for the same job. Rather, they explained that pay varied by nationality because, they said, work ethics varied by nationality and due to global wealth inequalities.[92] In this logic, nationality was used to structure differential wage pyramids, with negative consequences for non-British and non-US workers. These practices and discourses mobilized economic models to obfuscate the ways in which wealth disparities were and continue to be integral to oil production.[93]

Global wealth inequalities were invoked by managers to legitimate the discrepancies among nationalities in pay and living conditions at the Aden refinery project. One manager stated that the company was "in no way responsible for the different standards of living and comparative wage scales throughout the world."[94] Through such an argument, managers claimed that the differences in treatment and pay of employees were based on the nationality of the employee, even as the companies' management simultaneously refused to deal with employees through national employee committees or unions.

Economic models impacted how pay was calculated in two key ways. First, oil companies and their contractors calculated wages based on the location of the project. Because wages in Aden were generally lower than wages at other places in the Arabian Peninsula, company officials argued that wages for the Aden construction project should also be lower.[95] Second, the contractors Bechtel and Wimpey not only argued that pay should be based on location of the project, but they also insisted that "wages must be based on the value of take home pay in each country." And this belief was used to justify paying workers of different nationalities different amounts for the same job.

These policies were applied to workers of all nationalities. For example, this logic was mobilized when negotiating with the Italian government after that government asked that Italian workers receive the same pay as British workers. By insisting that pay be calibrated to the "take-home value" in each country, Bechtel and Wimpey convinced the Italian government that it should allow differential wages. One manager reflected on their success in negotiating with the Italian government:

> To admit that there is a difference in value of these wages between Italy and Britain is to admit that there is not only a difference in the cost of living but to admit, and this is the main point, that there is a difference in the standard of living between the workmen of Britain and Italy. Such an admission would present the Italian Communist Party with ammunition the Government say they cannot afford to allow them.

Here, Bechtel and Wimpey were relying on the perceived negative political impact that the Italian government would experience by pushing for the same wages for Italian and British workers. Despite what they saw as the political power of this argument, Bechtel and Wimpey did offer a pay raise for Italian workers who learned English and mastered "technical phraseology"—an offer that was not given to Indian workers, perhaps because of Indian workers' fluency in English. Importantly, the contractors did not anticipate that they would have to pay Italian workers this amount because of the complexity of technical phraseology in English and because Bechtel and Wimpey managers were the ones who judged workers' fluency in English.[96] This example highlights how offers of possible equal pay were only given selectively (in this case, it was only offered to European workers), and for the few workers who were eligible, it was almost impossible to meet the requirements.

Due to wage calculations based on the location of project and the value of take-home pay, Indian workers who were previously employed at Abadan found the pay and benefits at Aden to be worse than those at Abadan.[97] Even though wages were low, the company was convinced that unemployment in India and the fact that there were relatively few major constructions projects happening at other oil projects in the Arabian Peninsula meant that Indians formerly employed at Abadan would agree to such poor terms. One manager described Indian labor as "a buyer's market!,"[98] pointing to how economic conditions in India meant oil companies were able to hire large numbers of Indians at low wages.[99]

During the hunger strike, company management met with the Indian Employee Committee, an informal representative body of Indian workers at the Aden project. However, management declined to keep a written record of what was discussed, arguing that it was not the policy of the company to "deal with a group or a nationality unless they returned to work and tendered their requests through the proper channels set up for them."[100] The company also argued that Indian employees got the same rice, fish, meat, and other food as all other workers at the site. They pointed out that Indian chefs cooked the food for all Indian employees. One company manager said, "The British, Americans, and Italian personnel accept the condition with understanding and tolerance; not so the Indians." Many managers felt that Indian employees simply needed to adapt and claimed that Indian employees were "reactionary" and likely to "inflect other employees with radical ideas."[101] In such cases, oil management response to workers was based on workers' nationality, yet managers refused to engage with workers collectively.

TACTICS TO CONTROL INDIAN WORKERS

Avoiding large-scale work stoppages was a key issue from the perspective of oil companies and the British government. Labor unrest was fraught as oil was necessary for the military and industry, and work stoppages were costly for oil companies. Some managers had experience with large-scale strikes, including the 1946 strikes in Iran. For example, Donald MacNeill, a former project head overseeing the Iranization of the workforce for AIOC, was directly involved with the staffing for the construction of the Aden refinery.[102] Oil company managers used segregation to control workers and global wealth inequalities to justify the different treatment of workers based on their nationality and the segregation of the workforce. With segregation, management minimized workers' ability to build broad coalitions across nationalities and, therefore, reduced both the number of strikes and strikes' impact on oil production. The large numbers of Indians looking for work also meant that strikes by Indians were less effective, as new workers could be easily found in India. Thus, in the early 1950s, India's emigration system was ambiguous in its protection of workers: It gave the government limited power to protect workers, but it also provided a strong infrastructure to send replacement workers. Companies were aware of this, and to control workers, they used spies and outright intimidation, including threatening workers that they could be easily replaced.

Given that worker committees were not recognized by the company, Indian workers were reliant on the Indian government to act on their behalf. During the strike, workers had hoped the government would exert some pressure on the oil company to improve their living and working conditions, but the government's intervention did not meet worker expectations. At the onset of the strike, the Indian government stopped all Indians from emigrating to work at the Aden refinery project, but this halt lasted for only a brief period. When emigration reopened, Indian workers at the Aden refinery construction project became fearful they would be fired,[103] because the company used a "spy system" to control workers.[104] This spy system was composed of six Indian informants who provided the company with information about other Indian workers. The result was that, on the whole, Indian workers were afraid of the informants.[105] This spy system was particularly perilous for the Indians who led the Indian Employee Committee, as they feared the company was compiling a "black list" of those suspected to have led the strike and that the employees on the list would be "sent packing."[106] Indian workers at the refinery knew there were many Indians willing to take their place, and with reopened recruitment, disgruntled workers could be easily dismissed and replaced by workers who would not complain.

In large part, companies could easily replace workers because of the recruiting system used in India. Embedded in the same migration network that British intelligence officer Thomas had blamed for the unrest among Indians at Abadan in the 1940s, recruiting agents were pivotal figures between local recruiters (or subagents) and the oil companies. These agents often held great sway with the Indian government officials. One recruiter for both Bechtel and Wimpey boasted that he could move "recruits and others in and out of India without the need of visas or travel documents,"[107] indicating that his connections with a few influential Indian government officials allowed him to bypass Indian emigration regulations.

For workers, recruiters were often a source of stress—they facilitated migration, but often at the expense of the worker, and workers reported that they felt exploited by both their employers and recruiting agents. For example, Indian workers at the Aden refinery construction project claimed that they were not told about the working conditions in Aden. In addition, they said that the agent who recruited them did not accurately portray their living conditions and that they were told that they would not be charged for food.[108]

Workers also complained that the recruiting system was trying to "mak[e] capital" off workers, thereby implying that the contractors, local recruiters, and perhaps even government officials were charging workers high fees for emigration permission, which was needed for Indians to legally travel to work in the Arabian Peninsula.[109] Even paying these fees did not guarantee jobs. For example, one worker reported that he paid a bribe of two hundred rupees to be hired for a manual labor position at Aden. However, when he arrived at the site, the company discovered that he was underage and sent him back to India.[110]

The Indian government sought, with varying efficacy, to protect the interests of Indian citizens abroad. While this at times created obstacles for companies that wanted to hire Indian workers for oil projects, Indian workers were still relatively easily to hire. As oil companies worked around Indian emigration regulations, they avoided oversight from the Indian government. Indian bureaucrats, for their part, felt unable to lend support to workers who did not move through the formal emigration channels. Company managers threatened to dismiss Indian workers, and they reminded workers of how easily they could be replaced with new workers, brought in "without going through the Emigration formalities."[111] This made Indian workers more attractive than local workers who the company could not easily deport when they went on strike.

MANAGEMENT OF LOCAL WORKERS

Not only were there large numbers of Indians looking for jobs, but there were also many local workers searching for jobs. Given high local unemployment rates, BP managers anticipated that, when the company's recruiting office opened, the office would be "besieged by numbers of persons who have made their way there independently to seek work."[112] This proved to be an accurate prediction, and some potential employees traveled from their homes to the construction project.[113]

Hiring local workers posed key challenges for managers. One challenge was that company hiring managers had to determine who qualified as a local worker. For example, Adenis, workers from the Protectorate of Aden, and workers from Yemen were all considered "locals," but each group was given different benefits, and managers feared workers would cause disruptions or go on strike if managers incorrectly categorized workers.[114] In addition, local workers also required training, unlike Indian workers who were hired only if they had the requisite skills.[115] Managers also found recruiting local workers to be difficult, particularly given the large number of laborers the company needed to hire, and that to hire these workers managers were required to go on recruiting trips.

In their reports, managers described that the recruitment of local workers in Aden involved copious amounts of paperwork, rough travel, subterfuge, and physical danger. These issues with recruitment were exemplified in a BP manager's description of a recruiting trip to Dhala, in the British Aden Protectorate, which he undertook with a manager from the contractor Wimpey, a doctor, a photographer, and additional support staff. In his record of the trip, the BP manager detailed the "considerable amount of staff work" required before they could even begin recruitment. In order to receive a pass to enter an area for recruitment, management was required to coordinate between British government offices, receive permission from the Political Officer, and receive permission from the local government of the area. The manager then described their travel through areas he characterized as politically unstable and dangerous, with high rates of "highway robbery, murder and general nuisance." When the BP team arrived at the recruiting site, they were given assistance by local and British officials.[116] However, managers saw their task as to require constant vigilance because prospective employees used "tricks" to be hired. These "tricks" included "short men standing on stones, rejected men moving behind the ranks and appearing again further up, and even selected men, by this method getting selected twice, and obtaining two tickets, one of which would be sold to a less fortunate friend."[117] On the whole, managers found the recruitment process for local workers was much more labor intensive than the recruitment process for Indian workers.

From the perspective of managers, local workers were harder to hire than Indian workers, and they were also more disruptive than Indian workers when they went on strike. For example, in April 1956, after five carpenters were fired, a coalition of local workers, including all the carpenters, dock workers, and taxi workers at the Aden refinery, went on strike.[118] During the strike, local workers made three demands.[119] The first was that during Ramadan, working hours be cut from eight hours to seven, but that workers still receive pay for eight hours of work. The managers at Wimpey agreed to this. The second was that every worker, "no matter who, or what they were or where they lived" received transportation to the job site. Wimpey managers put this under discussion.[120] The final demand was increased pay. To resolve the strike, Wimpey waited on the results of government discussions.[121] Throughout the strike, BP managers blamed the strike on the practices of their contractors, Bechtel and Wimpey.[122] However, the practices of the contractors and BP were interrelated. As managers at Wimpey attempted to placate workers, they also sought to reassure BP that they would make no additional concessions to worker demands, as these would impact BP.[123]

The fact that local workers had some of their demands met, in contrast to the companies' response to Indian workers' hunger strike, demonstrates that local workers had some, albeit limited, power to organize and change their working and living conditions. Local workers continued to advocate for changes. As Abdalla Burja describes, local labor migration to oil projects and subsidiary industries helped spread "revolutionary nationalist ideas" throughout Aden and Yemen.[124] The circulation of these ideas helped to shape the armed revolution against British rule in 1963, and they contributed to the end of British rule in Southern Arabia in 1967.[125]

CONCLUSION

While local workers were able to strike and make some changes to their working conditions, Indian workers faced challenges negotiating directly with their employers, and their only recourse was to appeal to the Indian government. By doing so, workers built solidarities based on their nationality, and their choice to mobilize with a hunger strike situated their actions within the country's own nationalist movement. Evoking India's struggle for independence conveyed the outrage Indians felt when facing racial discrimination. Through appealing to national identity, the striking Indian employees drew the attention of both the company and Indian government officials, but they saw few changes. After the strike, cold water became available to Indians and workers eventually moved into a new camp. However, there were still no fans in workers' sleeping areas; the food quality continued to deteriorate, but beef was served less often; and the number of hours worked remained the same.[126]

During their hunger strike, Indian workers defined themselves as a discrete community by emphasizing their differences from European and Arabic-speaking employees. Workers saw their position, as Indians, to be unique and unequal to the position of Americans, Europeans, and Arabic-speaking workers. Divisions between groups were heightened by managerial practices and economic models that were used to justify differential pay and benefits based on nationality. Indians were not alone in their critiques of management. There were multiple common complaints by many workers, and, for example, Arabic-speaking and Farsi-speaking workers also complained of living in deplorable conditions and being subjected to racist treatment. But there were no large-scale, international worker agitations in response to these issues. Oil company practices made it challenging for workers to form broad, intergroup solidarities, and, as will be discussed in the next chapter, oil company officials, local governments, and British administrators also wrote labor laws that limited workers' ability to strike.

Five
WRITING LABOR LAWS

IN 1954, LOCAL WORKERS AT THE BAHRAIN PETROLEUM COMPANY (Bapco) refinery in Bahrain went on strike demanding their rights. According to Bapco managers, this strike was influenced by people from outside Bahrain and directed toward the government, not the company. A Bapco manager, Leigh Josephson, recalled the strike:

> They got to the students, the younger group of people. Yes, there was a lot of unrest among the young people. They not only went on strike.... well, they never did go on strike against the company. They tried to, but they were not successful. They did a lot of damage in town—broke windows, set service stations on fire, set a bunch of our busses on fire at our bus depot. Just malicious. It was opposition—a group of young people. A lot of them were our trainees—our young student trainees that we had sent off to England for training and then coming back to Bahrain. All they would say is, "We want our rights!" That's all I ever got out of them.[1]

Josephson described the strike as a violent outburst. He also reported that workers were organized and demanding rights, but he characterized these demands as nonsensical:

> This group was so militant in the refinery, and they came marching up and tried to come through [the] hall in a group. I just went out and

confronted them. I said, "What is your beef? Why?" "Well, we want our rights." "Well, what rights do you want?" They wouldn't tell me. They just wanted "our rights." ... In my view, they had no reason to complain about their rights. They were getting a free education. I told these boys, "We're paying for your education; the government gives you free hospital, free schools; you don't have to pay any taxes. What more do you want? You're being treated very well." I couldn't get them to agree, so I just alerted our security to bring in the government security people. They were still pretty radical, so the local security came in, plus our security, and just loaded them on the busses and sent them home.

Josephson reported that he told the striking workers to come back to work when they were "ready to talk sense."[2] The strike then continued for several weeks, and according to another Bapco manager, the strikes ended after the population felt "suffering from lack of wages as well as of gasoline and kerosene."[3] Following the strike, about 50 percent of the employees were rehired.[4]

Josephson's and other Bapco managers' engagement with this strike in 1954 illuminates three themes that emerge around worker strikes in the Arabian Peninsula in the 1950s and the response of oil companies and governments to these strikes. First, Bapco managers identified the leaders of strikes as young men who oil companies had sent to England for additional education. This resonates with descriptions of strike leaders at other oil projects in the early 1950s. For example, in 1953, Arabian American Oil Company (Aramco) managers noted that the leaders of a large strike were workers that the company had sent to the United States or Lebanon for training.[5] Second, managers characterized workers' call for rights as misguided or incomprehensible. As managers described their response, they pointed to benefits such as free education or hospitals. This response depoliticized the claims made by striking workers—managers interpreted workers' claims to be about personal benefits and ignored workers' claims for political or workplace changes. Such responses also articulate a paternalism that was often used by managers in regard to calls for self-determination or development.[6] Third, managers used local security forces to end the strike after attempts to "talk sense" failed. This militarized response reflects the potential dangers strikes posed to the local government, the British administration, and oil companies and draws attention to how local governments, the British administration, and oil companies collaborated to end strikes.

The 1954 strike described by Josephson was just one of multiple large strikes that occurred in Bahrain between 1954 and 1956.[7] At that time, nationalism, along with anti-imperialism and pan-Arab movements, mobilized large numbers of Bahrainis, including those employed in the oil industry.[8] In addition, the magazine *Sawt al-Bahrain* (Voice of Bahrain) spread an anticolonial message, criticized Bapco, and argued for better working conditions for employees at the oil refinery.[9]

The strikes that occurred in Bahrain from 1954 to 1956 built upon unrest that occurred during Moharram in 1953 and the subsequent formation of the High Executive Committee, later renamed the National Union Committee.[10] The committee drew upon pan-Arab nationalism, religious rituals, anti-imperial sentiments, class inequalities, antagonism with non-khalijis, and solidarity with Palestine.[11] The committee's popularity was seen to be a response to dissatisfaction with increasing government control over commerce, increasing numbers of migrant workers in Bahrain, that Bahrain was experiencing a slower pace of development than in Kuwait, and that locals were being promoted at a slower rate than in Saudi Arabia.[12] The success of the movement was seen in its ability to bridge sectarian and class divisions within Bahrain.[13] The resulting organization, the General Trade Union, was able to attract thousands of members in its first few months.[14]

Low-levels of worker unrest continued in Bahrain, and in late 1956, there was a large strike. Bapco managers described this strike as indicative of an emerging nationalism and characterized the strike as the "first serious friction" between Bapco and its employees.[15] Particularly influential at that time was Egypt's nationalization of the Suez Canal Company on July 26, 1956. People living and working on the Arabian Peninsula, including Indian and Pakistani workers,[16] participated in demonstrations in support of Egypt. After Israeli, British, and French forces invaded Egypt in late October and early November 1956, these demonstrations intensified—there were calls to boycott English companies, worker strikes, and sabotage at oil projects.[17] During these strikes, popular sentiment was believed to be with Egypt, and massive public support limited the local governments' ability to respond. Finally, British troops entered Manama in November 1956, the committee was disbanded, and its leaders were jailed.[18]

In the 1950s, worker actions were shaped by historic labor relations at oil companies, anticolonial discourse, and pan-Arab nationalism. As pan-Arab nationalism gained strength and facilitated some worker solidarities, other workers, particularly non-Arab workers, were decreasingly likely to participate in broad-based worker actions. As the Bahraini government, British government, and oil companies tried to mitigate the impact of worker strikes, they wrote labor laws that limited workers' rights and supported the rights of employers. These labor laws, implemented in 1958, differentiated citizens from noncitizens and drew heavily from restrictive labor laws written in the United States. As British government officials, oil company managers, local government officials, and labor leaders drafted and discussed these laws, the process overcame tensions and coordinated the interests of these groups. In the end, these laws discouraged strikes and made collective worker action challenging. In doing so, they disallowed tactics that workers could use to change to working, living, and political conditions, and they provided a rationalization for local police forces and imperial militaries to respond with violence to strikes.

LABOR RELATIONS AT BAPCO AND UNREST IN BAHRAIN

In the High Executive Committee's publications and pamphlets, they outlined a number of key issues that resonated widely in Bahrain.[19] Many of these issues were long standing, and they centered on labor relations at Bapco and pan-Arab nationalism.[20] These issues were informed by anticolonial sentiments, with both the American-owned Bapco and the British administration based in Bahrain described negatively as colonizers. To understand a broader context for the strikes that occurred from 1954 to 1956, this section will explore labor relations at Bapco in the 1940s and 1950s, and the following section will look at pan-Arab nationalism.

Questions over the number of Bahrainis employed in the oil industry and the positions that these workers held were key issues since the beginning of oil production in Bahrain, and they continued to be issues in the mid-1950s.[21] After assuming the throne in 1942 following the death of his father, the ruler of Bahrain, Sheikh Salman bin Hamad al Khalifa, strove to increase the number of Bahrainis employed by Bapco. This was challenging, however, because most Bahrainis worked as laborers, and large numbers of laborers were not consistently needed by the company. As a result, many Bahrainis were hired as laborers when Bapco was undergoing construction projects, but they lost their jobs once construction projects were complete and they were no longer needed. One example of this is when, in January 1945, Bapco was preparing to slow its construction phase, and the company expected to "set free" 4,500 laborers over the coming six months.[22] When new construction began, however, many of these same workers were rehired. Due to the pace of construction projects, from 1940 to 1950, the overall number of Bahrainis employed by Bapco appears relatively stable, but workers experienced little job stability. In contrast, the number of foreign workers increased. The numbers of Indians and Pakistanis employed by the company more than doubled, growing from 1,424 workers to 3,043 workers. Similarly, the number of European and US employees at Bapco also increased from 190 in 1941 to 670 in 1947 to over 1,000 in 1951.[23]

Aware of the growing number of foreigners employed by Bapco, in the late 1940s, Sheikh Salman complained to British administrators about number of Indians, Iranians, Omanis, and Qataris entering Bahrain. Specifically, Sheikh Salman was upset that people from these countries were holding jobs he believed should be held by Bahrainis.[24] Indeed, while Article 17 of Bapco's 1934 concession with the Bahraini government stipulated that employees should either be British subjects or Bahrainis, this was not implemented.[25] As a US employee of Aramco who visited Bapco in the late 1940s reported, "There are no restrictions on the engagement of Indians and foreigners versus Bahrainis which enables Bapco to obtain a good quality of non-American and non-British labor."[26] In addition, while some managers believed that Indian workers were supposed to train Bahraini workers, this training never played out in practice.[27]

Also in the 1940s, many Bahrainis, both laborers and office workers, traveled to work in Saudi Arabia and Qatar, where oil companies were hiring workers at higher pay rates than in Bahrain.[28] This migration upset the ruler, who articulated the importance of Bahraini workers for the future of the country by saying these migrants "should be working in Bahrain for the benefit of their own country."[29] The ruler also asked the political agent that no more visas be issued to Indians and Pakistanis. The reason the ruler gave was that many Indians and Pakistanis had recently arrived in Bahrain. The ruler expressed the belief that restricting visas for Indians and Pakistanis would serve to ensure jobs for Bahrainis.[30] While hoping to curtail the number of Indians and Pakistanis working in Bahrain, the Bahraini government had "no wish to restrict Arabs from other parts of the Gulf from coming to Bahrain."[31]

In the late 1940s, Bahrainis were also concerned that they were not being hired in the oil industry, and they expressed displeasure at the large numbers of Indian and Pakistani workers employed by Bapco. In 1947, a group of Bahraini workers complained about wages at Bapco and the restrictions Bahrainis faced on travel to other countries for work. These workers also made claims for self-governance.[32] Criticism of Bapco and calls for rights continued in Bahrain, and in 1950 an anonymous letter, signed by "the youth of Bahrain," was sent to the ruler. In this letter, complaints were made about the treatment of Bahraini laborers at Bapco. In particular, they pointed to the low salaries paid to Bahrainis working at Bapco, the power of Bapco to detain or jail Bahraini employees, and that the company gave inadequate compensation when workers were injured or killed on the job.[33]

In the mid-1950s, workers at Bapco continued to be unhappy with Bapco's training efforts, and they were frustrated that Bahrainis did not have better positions in the company. At that time, approximately 41 percent of the total labor force in Bahrain were categorized as foreigners.[34] The oil industry was the largest employer in Bahrain: 34 percent of all employed Bahrainis and 24 percent of all employed foreigners worked in it.[35] It also had the lowest percentage of foreign workers, employing one foreigner for every three Bahrainis.[36] When contractors in the oil industry were included, British officials estimated that at least 40 percent of Bahrain's employed population worked directly or indirectly for the oil industry.[37]

Despite the emphasis Bapco managers recalled the company put on training, in the oil industry, 53 percent of skilled workers were foreigners. Foreigners held the most prestigious jobs, and the "all-important administrative and clerical grades contain four foreigners for every [one] Bahraini." British officials argued that the reason there were still large numbers of foreigners working as general laborers was due to the low population of Bahrain.[38] They further pointed out that outside of the oil industry, 91 percent of all establishments employed less than five persons and 98 percent had fewer than twenty-five employees.[39] The proportion of foreigners was highest in manufacturing, comprising "mainly small scale handicraft type establishments," and it was also high in wholesale trading and banking.[40] In sum, Bahrainis accounted for 74 percent of workers classified as semiskilled labor, and 23 percent of all foreign workers were classified as unskilled laborers.[41] Bahraini workers continued to be dissatisfied with their positions in the company, and at the High Executive Committee's meetings, Bahrainis asked, "Why so many foreigners?"[42]

PAN-ARAB NATIONALISM

Bahraini workers were mobilized by their dissatisfaction with labor relations in the oil industry, and their actions were also informed by pan-Arab nationalism. Pan-Arabism, a nationalist movement based on claims of shared culture and politics in Arab countries, was spurred by the partition of Palestine into the states of Palestine and Israel in 1948 as well as through increasing national and Arab identification among residents in the Arabian Peninsula.

Formerly part of the Ottoman Empire, Palestine became a Mandated Territory under British control after World War I, when the League of Nations tasked the British with providing administrative "advice and assistance."[43] In 1917, the British government supported the claim that Palestine was a "national home for the Jewish people,"[44] and while other mandated territories became independent states, the British continued to administer Palestine with the goal to create this homeland. In the 1930s, the British Royal Commission proposed a plan to partition Palestine. This plan was rejected by Palestinians, many of whom "called for self-governance and democratic representation,"[45] and by Zionist leaders, who rejected cantonization. Palestinian opposition to British imperialism also grew in the 1930s, and many Palestinian leaders were arrested and at least one thousand Palestinians were killed by the British military. Throughout this decade, the plight of the Palestinian people served as a rallying point for pan-Arab activism, nationalism, and anti-imperial activities.[46]

Post–World War II, plans to partition Palestine intensified, and the British turned the matter over to the United Nations. The UN formed the Special Committee on Palestine, which drew a boundary line to demarcate the borders of Israel and Palestine.[47] In August 1947, the UN voted in favor of the partition of Palestine, and Israel made a declaration of statehood in May 1948. Pan-Arab organizing around the issue of Palestine grew even stronger when, from 1947 to 1949, the first war between Israel and Palestine occurred. During this time, referred to as the *Nakba* (meaning the catastrophe or the disaster), Palestinian towns and villages were destroyed, and approximately 750,000 Palestinians were forced to leave their homes. Witnessing Palestinians' dispossession and the injustices they experienced at the hands of imperial powers galvanized people across social divides. In Egypt, activism around Palestine in the 1940s increased feelings of national belonging and reduced class antagonism.[48]

The partition of Palestine was publicly protested throughout the Arabian Peninsula. In Bahrain, public and elite support for Palestine was strong and grew rapidly. In October 1947 in Manama, Bahrain, most shops were closed to due to protests that occurred after the release of the UN Special Committee's report that recommended the partition of Palestine. During these protests, speeches were made by Arab leaders and one Egyptian teacher.[49] A few months later, in December 1947, there were three days of demonstrations in Manama. During the protests, British officials reported that protestors chanted "Down with America, Zionists, Russians and Communists" and threw mud at the houses of Jews and Iraqi Christians. In addition, a bank, which British officials noted employed Jewish workers, had its windows broken. By the third day of protests, the numbers of protestors had swelled, and the police had trouble controlling them. A synagogue was looted, as were twelve houses and three shops that were run by Jews. After these protests, seventy people were arrested, a curfew was declared, and the ruler of Bahrain issued a notice prohibiting gatherings.[50] British administrators described these activities to be part of a nationalist movement that had the potential for political and social upheaval. For example, in Bahrain, the British administration reported that at the forefront of the demonstrations was a group of young men who were members of the "National League" or "Popular Front."[51]

In response to these popular protests in support of the Palestinian people, the British administration and local governments mobilized the police and armed forces. In Bahrain, this response included sending special police officers who operated under the general supervision and control of the British political agent.[52] Security was also increased at Bapco, as both government officials and oil company managers feared that the protests in support of Palestine would lead workers at oil companies to strike or sabotage company operations.[53] As people protested on the streets of Manama and met at public meetings, local leaders throughout the Arabian Peninsula also supported the Palestinian cause. In the Trucial Coast, the sheikh of Sharjah's son read a poem in support of Palestine and an imam in Dubai repeatedly urged people to provide financial assistance to the Arabs of Palestine.[54]

Anti-imperial and pan-Arab sentiments continued to grow in the late 1940s and early 1950s. During this time, pan-Arab nationalism, unified under the cause of the liberation of Palestine, spurred regime changes and served to rally workers at oil companies during strikes. Regime changes included the assassination of King Abdullah I in Jordan by a Palestinian nationalist in 1951, and in 1952, Egypt's King Farouq was overthrown. Following the 1952 revolution in Egypt, Gamal Abdel Nasser, one of the revolution's leaders and a proponent for pan-Arab nationalism, grew in popularity, and Nasser's "personal charisma and political daring captured the enthusiasm of the Arab masses." The result was that, during the 1950s, pan-Arab nationalism became "the leading anti-imperialist force in the Middle East [and] redrew the political and strategic map of the region, just as the creation of the state of Israel had done nearly a decade earlier."[55]

Oil company managers and researchers also observed growing nationalism and pan-Arab sympathies throughout the Arabian Peninsula. At Aramco, company managers recorded a "development of Saudi nationality," even as religion and kinship networks impacted who was hired at Aramco.[56] Interviews with Saudi workers showed that workers increasingly identified more with their nationality as Saudis than they did with their natal region or religious sect. In addition, workers believed that regional and religious identities would continue to diminish as a national Saudi identity grew. One young Aramco worker reflected:

> I feel that regional differences will diminish. I feel I am a Saudi Arab, not a Nejdi [a person from the Najd region]. Before, we differentiated between Sunni and Shia. Now when people my age (25) get together, we talk about this. We are the more educated people and we don't think these differences very important. I consider myself a Saudi. Our king gave his family name to this country and we have no choice but to use it. I call myself a Saudi Arab.[57]

Saudi national identity was understood to be growing with younger generations, and another Aramco employee reflected, "Children do not think of region, only of being Saudi Arabs. I myself feel Saudi rather than Hejazi [a person from the Hejaz region]. But I still have an attachment to my own place." Another worker expressed similar sentiments:

> A strong sense of regionalism is bad. Many think of themselves, for example, as Nejdis. But this feeling is disappearing and will disappear in a few years. Now it divides the country. I think of myself as a Saudi rather than a Nejdi. I have lent money to friends who were not from Nejd.[58]

Here, the worker points to the importance of exchange and reciprocity for shaping national identity. Aramco researchers noted that as national identity grew so, too, did pan-Arab sentiments.

At Aramco, company researchers found that Saudi workers "felt that the Arabs were one nation and were entirely sympathetic to Arab nationalism. They also expressed hostile or at least unfavorable attitudes towards Israel." Many Saudis who were interviewed by Aramco researchers said Palestine was an important issue, and Aramco researchers reported that recent events in Palestine motivated Saudis' engagement in pan-Arab movements. In addition, researchers noted that Saudi workers believed that the Americans and English were at fault for the crisis in Palestine. Workers also told Aramco researchers that the plight of the Palestinian people was a reason they participated in revolutionary activity and supported Arab unity.[59] In a context in which the futures of the countries of the Arabian Peninsula were actively debated by residents,[60] pan-Arabism and nationalism, along with outrage over the Nakba, brought some workers together while simultaneously limiting other forms of solidarity building.

RELATIONS BETWEEN ARAB AND NON-ARAB WORKERS

As pan-Arab nationalism fostered solidarity among some oil company employees, other solidarities were precluded. In Bahrain, Nelida Fuccaro writes, "By the early 1950s, 'foreigner' had become synonymous with non-Arab and non-national, and the symbol of the new face assumed by British imperialism in the oil era as the agent of the economic exploitation of the national population."[61] In this context, non-Arabs were increasingly excluded from labor organizing in Bahrain, and we see this in a speech by High Executive Committee leader Abdur Rahman al Bakir that was later published as a booklet in Cairo and a supplement in a Bahraini newspaper. In this speech, al Bakir stated that 8,700 workers had joined the Bahraini Labour Federation, but that "foreign workers," who he clarified meant "non-Arabic workers," were not allowed to join.[62] To understand how the line between Arab and non-Arab was drawn, this section considers Indian government representatives' observations on how pan-Arab nationalism impacted the standing of Indians in the Arabian Peninsula, how laws differentiated the rights of foreigners versus nonforeigners, and how oil company practices reinforced the Arab and non-Arab divide.

Indian government officials understood pan-Arab identity to be a leading source of tension between Indian workers and local workers in the Arabian Peninsula. In 1954, an Indian delegation, including Dr. Jagdish Chand, visited Kuwait and Bahrain and spoke with officials regarding Indian workers and merchants there. In particular, Dr. Chand met with the British political agent about the difficulty faced by Indian businessmen trying to get the "No Objection Certificates" required for Indians to travel in the countries of the Arabian Peninsula. The political agent replied that he would like for Indians to cultivate more joint business with the locals, but that some issues stood in the way. In Kuwait, the ruler said it was not possible to allow more Indian businessmen, and he blamed this on the behavior of Indians already in Kuwait, especially while consuming alcohol. The ruler said that in Kuwait alcohol is allowed to foreigners, but Indians are "misbehaving in public places when drunk." Despite these issues, Indian businessmen operating in Kuwait were given credit without guarantee. Overall, Dr. Chand found that "there [was] a large number of Indians living in Bahrain and Kuwait, flourishing in all walks of life. Generally their relations with locals are cordial."[63] In addition, in both countries, Indian currency was the official currency.

In Bahrain, in particular, Dr. Chand thought Indian influence was perceptible and the people in Bahrain were pro-Indian. This was due, in part, to the large number of Indian films shown in Bahraini cinemas and the fact that Hindi or Urdu was understood by one in ten Bahrainis. At local stores, Indian goods were sold. There was active trade, and Bahraini merchants regularly visited India.

Unfortunately, Dr. Chand feared the situation for Indians in the Arabian Peninsula was worsening due to economic development and the influx of Arabs from other parts of the Middle East. Dr. Chand believed that growing numbers of Arabs in the Arabian Peninsula were hurting the Indian community because, he wrote, all Arabs "inherit a common culture." Therefore, Dr. Chand argued, they were "homogenous." Dr. Chand also thought that, while orthodox locals sometimes disliked these new Arabs, most of the

Arabs arriving from other parts of the Middle East were intimate with locals and were jealous of Indians. Though clearly collapsing differences among Arabic-speaking people, Dr. Chand pointed to new and growing problems that Indians in the area were facing.[64]

According to Dr. Chand, the influx of Arabs led to nationalist feelings in the Arabian Peninsula. Oil companies were hiring local Arabs for jobs for which they used to employ Indians. Locals, however, were not yet displacing Indians because the former did not have sufficient training for skilled or semiskilled positions in oil companies. Dr. Chand described the situation:

> Indians are efficient enough to hold their jobs. Their work is appreciated—they have proved to be more trustworthy than other Arab outsiders. However, due to increasing competition, Indians have to put up with all conditions. And this competition is not only with Arabs, but also because the POE [protector of emigrants] in Bombay is ever ready to send replacements. The biggest problem facing Indians was their own attitude. Indians were "not change[ing] with the times."[65]

Dr. Chand observed Indian workers had sought-after skills, but he believed problems arose because Indians were not socializing with locals and the Indian community was divided. For example, in Kuwait, the Indian community was full of "bickering" among Indians to the point that the police had to get involved.[66] These conflicts made it hard for Indian workers to act in solidarity, and Dr. Chand specified, this issue was compounded by the fact that the protector of emigrants continued to facilitate emigration permissions even after Indians abroad complained of working conditions.[67]

In addition to pan-Arab nationalism and labor hierarchies on jobsites, tensions between Arab and non-Arab workers were informed by laws that differentiated the rights of citizens vis-à-vis noncitizens and oil company practices that separated workers and organized them hierarchically. For example, in the 1940s, Sheikh Salman "issued a proclamation forbidding the sale of movable property by Bahrain subjects to foreigners except by the permission in writing of the Bahrain Government."[68] Such laws helped create the conditions that contributed to the precarity of foreign workers. Specifically, Indian and Pakistani workers at Bapco reported that their main issues revolved around housing. Landlords had a lot of power over workers because housing was not supplied by the company, and Indians and Pakistanis could not buy land in Bahrain. This was further compounded by the fact that Indian and Pakistani workers had little job security. Indian laborers were hired on a daily contract, and these contracts did not provide Indian laborers with the same stability in income or job security as monthly wage employment.[69]

Given their precarious employment, Indian and Pakistani workers were increasingly disinclined to participate in large-scale work stoppages. In hopes of further curtailing worker actions, Bapco also implemented new practices for recruiting and hiring Indian and Pakistani workers. This included requiring that prospective Indian and Pakistani employees first have a police check completed before they were hired. The goal of this check was to allow the company to avoid hiring Indian and Pakistani workers who had previously participated in collective actions or union organizing.[70]

In addition to hiring practices, job hierarchies and living accommodations also impacted solidarities. Indians lived separately from Bahrainis and, in general, held more-prestigious jobs than Bahrainis. According to some observers, this led to Bahrainis seeing Indians with "resentment."[71] This was compounded by the fact that Indians were given allotments (like alcohol) that Bahrainis were not given. In contrast, khalijis, or Arabs from countries of the Arabian Peninsula, also worked in Bahrain, but they were mostly laborers. Khaliji laborers lived similarly to Bahrainis, and they were reportedly thought of as "cousins" by Bahrainis. Arabs from outside the Arabian Peninsula mostly worked as skilled professionals, lived second best after Europeans and Americans, and Bahrainis reportedly "looked up to" these professionals.[72]

Bapco managers also believed that the training and promotion of Bahrainis created friction with other groups. Managers observed, "Some Brits and Indians felt they were being forced out of a job by the Bahrainis coming along." However, managers thought this "wasn't a very reasonable complaint. Obviously, the company was going to bring along the local people as far and as fast as possible,"[73] thereby dismissing worker complaints and underscoring the centrality of citizenship as a conceptual category that facilitated cooperation between the local government and the oil company.

While there were barriers to worker solidarities, in the late 1940s and early 1950s, Indians did act in solidarity with Bahrainis. At times, anti-imperialism motivated workers' actions, and in the mid-1940s, Indian anti-imperialist songs were popular in Bahrain.[74] We also see solidarities among Indians, Pakistanis, and locals during the protests in Manama over the partition of Palestine in 1948. During those protests, Arabs, Pakistanis, and Indians came together to mobilize around this issue, and Indians gave speeches in support of the Palestinian people.[75] In addition, in the early 1950s, Indian workers at Bapco sought to form broad coalitions with other workers to strike over their working conditions.[76]

Despite these solidarities, overall, pan-Arab nationalism, laws that differentiated citizens from noncitizens, and oil company practices helped foster collective action among Bahrainis, while excluding Indian, Pakistani, and other non-Arab workers. In contrast, pan-Arab sentiments may have helped to ease these same tensions when they occurred with non-khaliji Arabs. The focus by the government and oil company officials on hiring and training nationals helped cultivate nationalist and pan-Arab sentiments within Bahrain, which in turn fostered the strikes in the 1950s.[77]

OIL AND IMPERIALISM IN BAHRAIN

In 1954 and 1955, the British administration in the Arabian Peninsula, Bapco management, and the local Bahraini government tried to coordinate their responses to social unrest in Bahrain despite growing tensions among these groups. These responses were informed by the role Bahrain played in oil production, Bahrain's importance for the British administration in the Arabian Peninsula, and the recent nationalization of oil in Iran.

Bahrain was the administrative center of the Persian Gulf Residency and central to British governance in the region. The British government also saw Bapco's refinery as an important component of Middle Eastern oil production.[78] Oil had been discovered in Bahrain 1932, the refinery at Awali began construction in 1936, and it officially opened in 1937. In 1945, the pipeline in Bahrain was extended to Saudi Arabia so that the refinery at Awali could refine Saudi oil. Oil extraction rose rapidly from 1946 to 1948 in Bahrain, but then leveled off after 1948.[79] By 1954, roughly 85 percent of the oil refined in Bahrain came from Saudi Arabia, and it was the refinery's role in oil production that gave Bahrain a prominent place in Middle Eastern oil production.[80]

In the mid-1950s, Bahrain's oil extraction was already past "its peak and entering a comparatively rapid decline." This decline, the growing oil industry in neighboring states, and the fact that offshore fields were not being developed contributed to tensions between Bapco and the ruler of

Bahrain. The ruler wanted Bapco to increase oil extraction and explore offshore production sites. Increased income from oil production was necessary, the ruler said, because "the country was in great need of money to finance its necessary projects of public works and welfare," and to supplement the state's budget.[81] Reportedly, the ruler did not trust Bapco's reasons for why oil production could not increase, and he questioned why Bapco planned to decrease the rate of production in the coming years.[82] As the ruler pressed for expanded production and development of offshore fields,[83] the British government sought proposals that would increase Bahraini's revenue from the refinery,[84] and in May 1955, rates at Bapco refinery came in line with those of Saudi Arabia.[85]

The British government supported the ruler of Bahrain by helping him receive increased revenue from Bapco's refinery, and the government rationalized this intervention between the company and the local ruler by pointing to the United Kingdom's increasing reliance on oil. In the mid 1950s, oil consumption in the UK was rising and expected to grow rapidly, largely due to industrial consumption. This anticipated increase in consumption meant that the Middle East, with an estimated 64 percent of the world's oil resources at the time, was seen as central to daily life and industrial growth in the UK. Given the growing demand for oil, British government officials believed that the British government would have few options if a country in the Middle East nationalized oil. This is different from the experience of the British government only a few years earlier, when oil was nationalized in Iran in 1951 to 1953. In response to that nationalization, the Anglo-Iranian Oil Company (AIOC) organized an almost worldwide embargo of Iranian oil. However, by 1955, the UK's need for oil was seen to preclude an embargo in the face of nationalization.[86]

Drawing on the British experience in Iran, British government officials believed that "enemies may play on the indigenous forces of nationalism and cupidity in order to disrupt the commercial operations of our oil companies."[87] And the British government believed there were three clear enemies acting against British interests: Russians spreading communism, Egyptians using pan-Arab nationalism, and Saudis who sought influence in the Middle East.[88] To respond to these threats, some government officials suggested the British reallocate the money the British government received from direct taxation of oil companies' profits and BP dividends. This money, they argued, should be put into spreading British influence through better communications, offering technical assistance and education, and, significantly, supplying arms on credit.[89] In addition, to ensure political stability and continued access to oil, British government officials argued that US and British oil companies needed to coordinate their policies.[90]

As British government sought to shore up its position in Bahrain and the Middle East more generally, both the ruler of Bahrain and Bapco responded to requests made by the High Executive Committee. In 1954 and 1955, the ruler agreed to elective representative participation in committees that supervise education and health, appointing an Egyptian jurist to revise the penal code, and improvements to the police force.[91] Some attempts were also made to improve labor relations. For example, in the mid-1950s, Bapco and the Bahraini government raised wages in response to a raise given to workers at Aramco in Saudi Arabia.[92] In addition, Bapco provided some training for Bahrainis. However, the number of Bahrainis employed at Bapco did not see a significant increase.[93] Finally, the Labour Law Advisory Committee was created in order to draft a labor law and address workers' right to strike. This committee included representatives from the government, employers, and employees. Representation for the government included two members of the royal family and a British employee of the Bahraini government. Employers were represented by a manager from Bapco,[94] an influential Arab merchant, and a contractor. Workers also had three representatives—one for government employees, one from Bapco, and a third representing commercial employees.[95] Worker representatives were elected, and these elections were held on April 24, 1955.[96]

Despite these changes, the British government's and Bapco's overall response to the High Executive Committee was to argue for slow development while maintaining the status quo. This policy was conveyed in British Foreign Secretary Anthony Eden's March 1955 response to the leaders of the committee after they requested support from the British administration: "You can't run before you can walk." In addition, the British administration asserted that the Bahraini government had the full support of the British government.[97] As we will see in the next sections, these responses were not considered adequate by many Bahrainis. As workers continued to strike, Bapco, the British government, and the local government turned to military intervention and restrictive labor legislation to control worker action.

1956 STRIKES AND CONCERNS OVER SECURITY

In 1956, issues in Bahrain came to a head, beginning in March and culminating in November 1956, when the British military entered Manama. First, in March 1956, five or six demonstrators were killed by the police.[98] In their analysis of this event, the British administration characterized the "underlying political tension" in Bahrain as "serious and prolonged."[99] After these demonstration in March 1956, the ruler agreed to make additional changes. These included recognizing the High Executive Committee under the new name of the National Union Committee; setting up an administrative council to assist in state administration and to serve as a means of contact between government and public; and holding an enquiry into the disturbances early in March. In return, Abdur Rahman al Bakir, a leader of the committee, agreed to leave Bahrain for six months.[100]

Following these negotiations, the British government remained concerned about popular support for the National Union Committee, and they noted that an open meeting of the committee on June 15, 1956, drew two thousand people.[101] In circulars, the committee continued to press for political rights.[102] In July 1956, a circular called attention to multiple problems in Bahrain, including wealth inequality, lack of education, and the influence of foreign companies. A second July circular listed additional worker complaints at Bapco, including the dismissal of local labor, the import of foreign labor, the bad treatment of local employees, the lack of annual raises, and the delay in instituting the new labor law.[103] In addition to addressing labor relations, both circulars also addressed citizens' rights. The first circular argued that it is the "birthright" of every individual "to have say in his country's affairs and administration."[104] The second circular discussed the rights of the people and argued "the peaceful strike and demonstrations are the natural right for every people by which they may express their will, wishes, and protests."[105]

Circulars advocated for the rights of citizens, demanded improved labor conditions, and connected Bahrainis' experiences to those of other colonialized peoples. One flyer specifically targeted the British. This pamphlet described the situation: "Bahrainis' brave action against this old colonist [the British government] has proved to the world that the Arabs are like other people who dislike colonialism. A boiling volcano that will burst when the opportunity comes."[106] It went on to discuss the importance of Bahrain creating alliance with Egypt, Saudi Arabia, and Syria. These alliances, the author argued, were the "right path to attain the honor of independence and restore your plundered rights"[107]—once again, centering both the rights of citizens and freedom from colonialism.

While pamphlets critiquing colonialism circulated, the Bahraini government, with support of the British administration, began a program of increasing the police force, initially to 350 police officers. Many of the new police officers were foreigners, mostly Baluchis and Muscatis, because, the British administration believed, "as foreigners in Bahrain, they were less likely to be caught up in local interests."[108] By late May 1956, the British administration reported that there were 450 police officers in Bahrain, and only 180 of these police officers were Bahraini. As the police force grew, Bapco received additional protection, and the Bahraini government added a force of approximately fifty men to guard the refinery and oil fields.[109]

Increasing the size of the police force did not fully alleviate security concerns, and British administrators were worried that the police force would be unable to handle large-scale demonstrations. This led to speculation on what possible roles the British government should play if unrest grew. Generally, the desire was to avoid British interference and continue to strengthen the police force. As one administrator wrote, "We must avoid if at all possible using British troops to put down Arab demonstration," in part because it would hurt "world opinion" about the British. However, given that the police force could not yet "be relied upon to maintain order without support," British officials argued the British government may need to step in, and they justified this by pointing out that large strikes could threaten Europeans and Indians with violence.[110]

The Bahraini ruler also looked to the British government for support, and at this time, conversations between the British administration and the ruler often focused on security and the use of British armed forces. Following one discussion, a British official reported that the ruler "knew we [the British] had troops in Bahrain but we could only use them in the very last resort in order to avert disaster. We could not use them until something had gone seriously wrong." While the ruler agreed with this, he also told the official that he felt the British administration should be "prepared to support him rather than let everything be destroyed." In response, the British government representative told the ruler: "This we would be prepared to do."[111]

Tensions in Bahrain heightened even more when Egypt nationalized the Suez Canal Company on July 26, 1956. This action was broadly supported in Bahrain, and the National Union Committee continued to agitate for political change in Bahrain as well as articulate support for Egypt. For example, on August 10, when al Bakir was asked "What is the attitude of the people of Bahrain towards the Western threat to Egypt?," he replied, "If any aggression is carried about against Egypt by anyone, we will immediately destroy the oil refinery, air and naval bases, and all other British and American establishments." He explained that this course of action had been "decided by the Bahrain Labour Federation," which he said had 8,700 members.[112] This threat to British and US establishments was all the more alarming given that the National Union Committee had been training men using military drills and providing trainees with uniforms and badges.[113]

Unrest continued in Bahrain, and issues reached a critical juncture when France, Britain, and Israel invaded Egypt on October 29, 1956. The invasion of Egypt provoked popular action, and the National Union Committee organized a strike that led to what British administrators described as "serious disturbances."[114] During the strike, the people "call[ed] for the downfall of imperialism." In addition, eight buildings housing British troops were set on fire, as were three British ships in Bapco's docks. "The demonstrators blew up the road leading to the air-fields in Muharram which is an international centre for the supply of oil to the West,"[115] thereby threatening both British governance and oil infrastructure.

In response to these actions, "British troops came down onto the streets and killed four free unarmed citizens," and British troops entered Manama in November 1956.[116] Following the strike, there was a British "crack down" on labor and nationalist organizations in the country.[117] Organizers were jailed and charges were brought against the leaders of the National Union Committee. These included allegations of attempted assassinations of the ruler and his family; intended destruction of palace, airport, and other buildings; attempts to overthrow of lawful government and deprivation of the ruler's lawful authority; and deliberately disobeying orders of government that had allowed them to have a peaceful procession.[118] Furthermore, the charges alleged that disobeying these orders led to "serious disturbances including violence, arson and great damage to the towns of Manama and Muharraq."[119]

Following the trial, five leaders were jailed, with sentences ranging from ten to fourteen years, and other leaders were deported.[120]

Throughout the military intervention and subsequent trials, British administrators worried about how the British government was seen by the Bahraini people and the international community. While the British government saw itself as separate from the trials of the labor leaders, the administration was still critiqued by many Bahrainis, as Bahrainis felt it had too much influence with the ruler and that British officials "poke their noses" into internal affairs.[121] In Britain, too, Labour Party politicians questioned if human rights standards were being followed.[122] British administrators responded that human rights standards were followed, and officials contextualized the legal proceedings within the specificities of Bahraini culture and governance. Perhaps unsurprisingly, this response did not refer to the role the British administration played historically and at the time in Bahraini governance.

Despite the distance the administration hoped to make in the eyes of both the British and the Bahraini people, the bottom line for the British government continued to be upholding the status quo. As one administrator wrote, "Broadly our political objectives in Bahrain are to maintain public order and shaikhly rule and to give the latter as broad a popular base as possible."[123] In order to do so, the British saw the benefit of enacting labor laws that would make it hard for workers to legally go on strike. Such laws were meant to discourage strikes, and they also rationalized and facilitated militarized responses to strikes by imperial and local governments.

DEBATES ON UNIONS AND STRIKES

Following the 1956 strikes, finalizing the draft labor laws provided one way for governments to protect their interests and to coordinate different stake holders. Bahrain's labor laws had been delayed multiple times, in part because the Bapco representative had objected to certain sections of it.[124] But the new labor laws gained greater urgency as labor laws were seen as a useful way to handle political action while maintaining the appearance of rights. As the local government, British government, and oil companies tried to mitigate the political possibilities of labor organizing, they wrote increasingly stringent labor laws. These laws drew upon US antiunion legislation. The result was that the Labor Ordinance was skewed in favor of employers, with a "Management Rights" section in the law (Section 38) and a right-to-work clause (Section 39.a).[125]

Overall, in Bahrain, restricting unions and strikes became easier after leading labor activists were sentenced to prison or exiled after the 1956 strikes. Following the trials of labor leaders, the labor movement seemed to have trouble garnering support, and a call for a one-day strike in protest of labor leaders' prison sentences was largely ignored.[126] Seeing participation in strikes waning, the drafters of the labor law felt emboldened to incorporate stricter policies toward both unions and strikes in the laws.

As the law was being drafted, there were debates as to whether unions should be allowed and, if allowed, what restrictions should be placed on them. Current events, particularly in Jordan and Aden, shaped how restrictions on unions were discussed.[127] British administrators reported that the ruler of Bahrain felt that his ability to restrict unions was strengthened by King Hussein's action of abolishing trade unions in Jordan. In addition, they reported that the ruler also wanted to avoid unions as sites of "extreme nationalism" as they were in Aden and cautioned that communists could penetrate labor unions. Given these risks, the ruler reported felt he was "being sufficiently liberal if he permits unions to be formed in accordance with the amendments he had proposed."[128] In debating these issues, the law's drafters expressed concerns over pan-Arab nationalism and the possibilities of political instability. However, British administrators also reflected that unions were popular in Bahrain and expressed concern about the consequences of banning unions. Thus, the drafters debated a series of ways to curtail unions' political power. Topics discussed included a union's liability during a strike, if Bahraini unions could create affiliations with international unions, the role of foreigners in unions, and if unions should be federated.[129] As they debated these issues, the drafters tried to determine the effectiveness of unions in addressing labor relations and fostering political change.[130]

Initially, labor unions received some protection from liability in the draft labor law. In the draft written by the committee, labor union leaders were exempted from "court action for tortious acts committed by or on behalf of a trade union in contemplation or furtherance of a trade dispute." This protection drew on English law and was patterned after the Indian Trade Unions Act, 1926.[131] However, a union's protection from liability was challenged by the ruler and also by Bapco's US management representative.[132] These challenges won out, and when the ordinance was published, initial protection of unions was reversed, and the heading became "Liability of Trade Unions." The new policy made unions liable for actions occurring during a trade dispute and hindered unions' ability to organize strikes.

A second key concern was whether affiliations with unions outside of Bahrain should be allowed. Such affiliations were seen as having both benefits as well as dangers. British officials believed such a policy would not be effective in limiting pan-Arab influence entering via such organizations as the Arab Federation of Trade Unions and the Arab Oil Workers Union.[133] In addition, British government officials thought some international organizations, such as the International Confederation of Free Trade Unions or the International Petroleum Workers' Federation, could be of use to Bahrain's unions.[134] Like in other areas of the Middle East, anticommunist trade unions were thought to be helpful because they worked as intermediaries between companies and workers and were often sympathetic with British or US government policies.[135] Indeed, some prominent anticommunist trade unions received backing from US government organizations, including the CIA, in hopes of replicating US labor practices globally and combatting communism. This was not a new tactic. In Egypt during World War II, the British had attempted to co-opt trade unions to spread pro-British propaganda and support British policies,[136] and as discussed in chapter 1, following the 1946 strikes in Iran, AIOC managers believed trade unions could help temper worker actions.[137] On the other hand, government officials worried pan-Arab labor movements would gain additional influence if unions were allowed outside affiliations. Therefore, they argued that affiliations should only be allowed with government approval.[138]

A third issue arose over the participation of foreigners in unions, and the 1957 draft law specifically excluded from union membership foreigners who came to Bahrain under contract. The draft law also allowed unions to opt to exclude foreigners. The drafters of the law saw such exclusions as a way to mitigate outside influences, including pan-Arab nationalism, within unions. The problem with formally excluding foreigners, a British judge pointed out, was that such an exclusion could provide leverage for local workers to pressure a company to stop hiring foreign workers. One proposed solution was to forbid foreigners from holding office in unions.[139]

A fourth large question about unions was if there should be one federated union, and there was general concern about the political impact of a federated union.[140] The British administration believed that it was better to have smaller, unfederated unions. This was because the administration argued that a smaller union was "more likely to concern itself with workers' economic interests rather than be tied to a political movement." However, they argued that the law should leave door open for smaller unions to federate at later stage, and officials echoed former Foreign Secretary (and at the time Prime Minister) Eden's adage that one must learn to walk before they can run.[141] The ruler of Bahrain argued that restrictions should be placed on unions, and particularly a single federated union because "Bahrain is not yet ready for them."[142] The administrators worried that the thousands of Bahrainis who were "members of the Bahrain Labour Federation may not be convinced of this reasoning," and they expected that this part of the labor law would be out of line with the public's expectations. In addition, British administrators expressed concern that, like with the trial of the leaders, the population would see these prohibitions as due to the British government and not stemming from the ruler.[143] This view of the political possibilities of a federated union may be contrasted with union activity in Egypt, where, following the 1952 revolution, "independent union organizing [was] banned." Later, in 1957, Nasser created the Egyptian Trade Union Federation (ETUF), and in 1959, he implemented a one-union-per-sector policy. The result was a "very hierarchical union system."[144] As Joel Beinin details, the ETUF had increasingly close connections to the government, which ultimately helped to dampen the impact of labor activism.[145]

In addition to imposing restrictions on unions, workers' right to strike was also greatly curtailed. When discussing how to deal with strikes in the labor law, the ruler wanted to remove all reference to strikes, so as to make clear that they were prohibited.[146] However, British government officials worried that this would not have the intended impact, and they feared people would think the omission of strikes was tacit permission to strike.[147] British officials also expressed concern that removing all reference to strikes could limit the rights of employees to leave their jobs and limit the rights of employers to dismiss workers. These rights, British government officials argued, were "one of the basic freedoms in democratic society and it is denied only in Communist states and other totalitarian countries, and if the Ruler were to abolish it then he, or rather H.M.G., would be arraigned at the United Nations and the I.L.O.," as several International Labor Organization conventions supported the right of workers to collectively bargain and to go on strike.[148]

In order to evaluate possible precedent for and effectiveness of prohibiting political strikes, British government officials referred back to previous British labor legislation: the 1927 Trade Disputes and Trade Unions Act.

> [This act] declared illegal strikes and lock-outs which in their purpose went beyond the furtherance of trade dispute within the trade or industry in which the workers or employers were engaged and which were designed to coerce the Government either directly or by inflicting hardship upon the community.[149]

However, they were unable to ascertain the efficacy of the 1927 act's "unequivocal banning of strikes"—particularly in preventing political strikes. This was because British administrators believed British trade movements had shifted tactics, moving from politics to direct "industrial agitation."[150] Rather than ban strikes, a better alternative, British government officials argued, was to include a provision in the labor law that "requir[ed] prior compliance with conciliation or arbitration procedures."[151] This, they felt, was already present in the law with the section that required a "complicated cooling off procedure of twenty-one days before a strike or lock out could be considered legal."[152]

As restrictions on strikes were debated in Bahrain, the California Texas Oil Company (Caltex), the parent company of Bapco, actively petitioned the British government to make strikes illegal in Bahrain, and the company's legal advisors provided language for doing so. In May 1956, Caltex's legal advisers met with British government officials in London. In that meeting, Caltex lawyers specifically requested that "legislation be introduced to make it illegal to call a strike which was not in furtherance of a trade dispute with a particular company on whose premise the strike took place." Government officials saw benefits to this request, particularly because the provision "would deal equally with sympathy strikes and political strikes."[153] Officials thought such legislation would maintain production, reduce the efficacy of strikes, and ensure political stability.

British officials also believed that Caltex's own policies would help curtail strikes. British administrators described the American-owned company as "a single rich and tough employer." Due to Caltex's attitudes toward unions and the Bahraini government not being "well disposed towards" unions, British government officials suspected unions in Bahrain would face "perpetual financial difficulties" and lawsuits.[154] British officials also assumed that Caltex would seek to legally curtail workers' ability to strike. This insight drew from Caltex's active efforts to undermine employee strikes at the company's operations globally. For example, in India in 1954, Caltex sued their workers because the company wanted to fire twenty-one workers and suspend one worker for an illegal strike. While the Industrial Tribunal in India found that the strike was illegal, it also found that Caltex could not dismiss the striking workers. Caltex repeatedly appealed this ruling until the case reached the Indian Supreme Court, where the court agreed with the Industrial Tribunal and did not allow Caltex to fire the workers.[155] While not winning the case, the length of time the company pursued the lawsuit, the cost of the trial for workers, and Caltex's continued legal actions against unions were thought to hamper future strikes.[156]

Not only did Caltex directly petition the British government concerning Bahrain's labor law, but the company also had a representative on the Labour Law Advisory Committee. As legal restrictions on strikes were discussed, the oil company representative and the British administration were often in disagreement. And British administrators attributed these disagreements to differences between the British and US views on political strikes.[157] Specifically, British government officials believed that the British regard political strikes as "legitimate in principle" whereas in the United States, the view was the opposite. To substantiate this claim, British officials cited the Taft-Hartley Act, 1947, and its restrictions on union activities.[158]

In the end, the Bahraini labor law had key similarities with the Taft-Hartley Act. For example, the complicated twenty-one-day cooling-off period proposed in the Bahraini labor law was similar to the sixty-day advanced notification of a strike required by the US Taft-Hartley Act.[159] Additional similarities included the liability of unions and the restrictions on which industries could go on strike. In the United States, the "Taft-Hartley Act imposes considerable restraints upon the right of employees to organize to bargain collectively and to utilize instruments of self help. Employers are accorded increased legal rights."[160] It was constraints such as these that were echoed in the Bahraini Labor Ordinance.

Given the differing attitudes toward strikes, the similarities between the Bahraini Labor Ordinance and the Taft-Hartley Act demonstrates the power of oil companies to shape local laws. In October 1957, the ruler approved the industrial compensation law and, after making several major changes, he approved a draft labor law in November. Both laws, the Compensation Ordinance and the Bahrain Labor Ordinance, were put into effect in 1958.[161] The restrictions in these laws on unions and strikes curtailed the rights of workers and depoliticized worker actions. These laws also differentiated workers by citizenship, thereby undermining collective solidarity by workers. For example, multiple groups were not covered in the industrial compensation law, including domestic workers and those who were entitled to repatriation to their home country at the end of their employment.[162]

Even after the labor laws were implemented, the Labour Advisory Committee (with the same membership structure as the Labour Law Advisory Committee) continued to meet. British officials thought having an oil company representative on this standing committee was beneficial because it provided oil companies a way to avoid the introduction of legislation that they found undesirable, and officials suggested that other countries on the Arabian Peninsula also create labor committees that included oil company representatives.[163]

RESTRICTIONS ON WORKER ACTIONS THROUGHOUT THE ARABIAN PENINSULA

It was not only in Bahrain that workers experienced restrictions on their ability to agitate for better working conditions. Throughout the 1950s, workers' rights were increasingly curtailed in the Arabian Peninsula. Some restrictions on worker organizing came from staffing choices made by oil company managers. In addition, changing societal views on citizenship and the ease of firing foreign workers versus the power of local workers to pressure their governments all contributed to changing responses to worker actions.

In Saudi Arabia, Aramco managers believed Palestinians were good employees because they did not have a state to protect their rights. When discussing Palestinians who worked at Aramco's refinery in Saudi Arabia and who had previously worked at the Haifa refinery, US managers reflected on how Palestinians' statelessness impacted their organizing:

[Palestinians] carry out plan operation work and craft work as well as clerical, and they give some trouble regarding wages and conditions. So far, they are not organized into labour unions, and some of them now hold senior operating posts, a fear was expressed that if they were organized, they could cause serious dislocation of operations. In the meantime, **they seem too scared to take too drastic action in their protests as most of them are displaced persons from Israel, and they have not forgotten where they came from and what may await them on their return.**[164]

According to Aramco managers, Palestinians' status as refugees meant they were less likely to form unions or have large-scale work stoppages.

In Kuwait, nationals continued to have some ability to change their working conditions and influence government policies. Restrictions on strikes were implemented as attitudes toward foreigners shifted in Kuwait during the 1950s due to increasing oil wealth, the growing popularity of pan-Arab nationalism, and rapid modernization.[165] While the ruler until 1950, Sheikh Ahmed al Jaber al Sabah "was always keen that foreigners should be allowed to acquire Kuwaiti nationality easily,"[166] attitudes were changing, and in 1959, the Kuwaiti government passed a new nationality law that was much more restrictive in who could become a Kuwaiti citizen.

In the 1950s, we also see that Indian and Pakistani workers were less successful in building broad solidarities to address their labor and living conditions, and the worker actions that they did organize were decreasingly effective. At this time, there were large numbers of non-Kuwaitis working in the country, and by November of 1953, KOC managers estimated that twenty thousand men from neighboring countries and India had arrived in the past couple of years for work.[167] The government was not "inclined" toward unions, and KOC managers worried about labor difficulties with Indian and Pakistani workers.[168]

In December 1953, the Indian and Pakistani tradesmen living at Jewan Camp and employed by the Kuwaiti government went on strike. Indians and Pakistanis composed 63 percent of the close to 1,800 tradesmen living at the camp. British government officials speculated that the recent death of an Indian worker and the lack of transport for the funeral were the cause of the strike.[169] In the list of demands given by workers, they asked for transportation for funerals, better medical facilities, consistency in job requirements across departments, and improved medical conditions. In addition, workers stated that they were unhappy with their wages and that they had been misled as to their wages in terms of Kuwait's cost of living. To substantiate this, the tradesmen provided evidence that British Petroleum recruiters in India and Pakistan had misinformed them of the cost of living in Kuwait, thereby lowering their potential savings from their salary while working in Kuwait.[170]

During this strike, Sheikh Abdullah al Mubarak al Sabah, the head of public security in Kuwait, visited the camp and negotiated some of the terms set by the striking workers. In addition, British government officials agreed to provide daily doctor visits, and the political agent agreed to investigate workers' claims, provided the striking workers returned to work. The government also circulated a notice, in Urdu, that complaints would only be listened to once workers returned to work.[171] Seven days after the strike began, government officials dismissed and then deported thirty-nine Indian and Pakistani workers who had still not returned to work.[172]

The ease by which managers could fire Indians and Pakistanis in Kuwait may be contrasted with the impact local workers had on government policies. The power of local workers to make claims on their government and the ability of pan-Arabism to shape solidarities was particularly clear in 1956, when there was an attempt to unionize Arab workers.[173] This became even more evident a few months later, in late October and early November 1956, when there was unrest following the invasion of Egypt by Israeli, British, and French forces.

At that time, both Kuwait Oil Company (KOC) managers and Kuwaiti government officials were keenly aware of the power of popular opinion and how it limited possible responses to strikes. One manager wrote, "Obviously the sympathy with Egypt over the Suez affair makes it difficult for the authorities to take action against Arabs who profess to be doing their bit for the Arab cause."[174] This was also observed by Sheikh Jabir, a son of Kuwait's ruler, Sheikh Abdullah al-Salem, who pointed out the power of these movements in structuring governance.[175] When asked if Iraq and Saudi Arabia would withhold oil from the United States, France, and Britain following the armed response to Egypt's nationalization of the Suez Canal Company, Sheikh Jabir predicted that those countries "would be forced to do so by the labouring classes, who would go on strike rather than produce oil for the Western Powers, and who might also indulge in sabotage to fulfill their purposes." Sheikh Jabir added that he feared a similar situation could arise in Kuwait.[176]

Sheikh Jabir's words proved prescient. In Kuwait, strikes and protests following the invasion of Egypt were banned by the government, but they occurred anyway.[177] These popular displays of support for Egypt were violently repressed and led to the eventual banning of clubs and newspapers by Ruler Abdullah al-Salem.[178] Unrest was not limited to strikes and protests, but also extended to physical sabotage of KOC facilities, and in December there were eight explosions at KOC's oil operations.[179] In Saudi Arabia, while workers did not hold large strikes, the country did stop selling to French and British interests, including the supply of oil sent to Bahrain.[180] In these cases, khaliji workers were effective in influencing government officials, even as their ability to strike was actively curtailed.

CONCLUSION

In a 1960 report about pan-Arab movements and labor, Willard A. Beling argued that the "large foreign element" in the Arabian Peninsula states had grave consequences for labor organizing. He wrote:

> The large foreign element, of course, has produced innumerable problems of labor relations. In addition, from the workers' point of view, the heterogeneous character of the labor forces precludes united action. Consequently, in these states, labor strikes which are often labeled "general" strikes, are general strikes only so far as the local Arab employees are concerned. The other nationalities usually remain on the job.[181]

However, as the events in this chapter demonstrate, Beling's analysis misses much of the work done by oil companies to segregate workers, the impact of militarized responses to worker actions, and the writing of increasingly strict local labor laws.

In Bahrain, workers continued to agitate for better working conditions despite restrictive laws and armed response to strikes. In 1965, there were disturbances in Bahrain that lasted a fortnight. Like many strikes at Bapco historically, the issue of redundancy was a pressing issue for the workers. In addition, the British administration understood these 1965 strikes to be representative of dissatisfaction of the population under the ruler, and the

British administration once again feared growing pan-Arab nationalism.[182] One British official wrote:

> [The] pretext was redundancy of some BaPCo workers but the affairs rapidly developed into a trial of strength between the regime and those elements—mainly the youth—who chafe at the anachronism inherent in Shaikhly regime under British protection and long for national assemblies, trade unions, election, political newspapers and all other paraphernalia of independence and progress.... Strikers and demonstrators stressed the slim resources of the Bahrain State Police to their limit and it was touch and go if British troops would have to intervene. The life of the country was seriously disrupted.

This description is strikingly similar to the description of strikes in Bahrain from 1954 to 1956. For example, in both the 1950s and 1960s strikes, generational differences were important, and the youth of the country were thought to be a pressing problem. In Bahrain, there was an annual population increase of just over 3 percent, and 75 percent of the population was under thirty years of age. There were also tensions over jobs for Bahrainis, and nearly 50 percent of all jobs were occupied by foreigners.[183] Also as in earlier strikes, the police were called to intervene. As we will see in the following two chapters, in the 1960s, the dominant perspective that strikes at oil projects were threats to imperial, national, and corporate security led to increasingly militarized responses to strikes and stringent restrictions on labor organizing.

Six
CURTAILING COOPERATION

IN QATAR IN 1963, LOCAL WORKERS AT SHELL COMPANY, QATAR, (SCQ) and Qatar Petroleum Company (QPC) went on strike in the weeks before Eid al-Adha (May 4, 1963).[1] Prior to these strikes, large celebrations were planned in Doha in honor of the upcoming unification of Egypt, Syria, and Iraq into the United Arab Republic. Local workers were eager to participate in this celebration of pan-Arab unity, and they asked QPC for time off work to attend the celebrations. Managers approved this request to attend what they described as "pro-Arab demonstrations."[2] According to QPC managers, after the celebrations, most local workers went home, but some people continued to demonstrate. Finally, out of reported frustration, the nephew of the ruler of Qatar fired a machine gun into the crowd, injuring five people.

This violence by the nephew of the ruler elicited indignation by Qatari workers, and in response, an overwhelming majority of local employees at QPC and SCQ called for a twenty-four-hour general strike. The strike began on April 21, and most Qataris did not go to work at the oil companies that day. Expatriate employees continued to work, and they were not impeded by striking workers. During the strike, a group called the National Unity Front made thirty-five demands, and leaders said they would continue to strike until their demands were met. In the days after the initial strike, the Qatari government arrested the strike leaders. Following these arrests, local workers slowly returned to work.

In QPC managers' description of the 1963 strike, they characterize it as "an attempt to coerce the Ruler by force and to challenge the established order in Qatar and amounted almost to an attempted revolution."[3] Many of the demands put forward by the worker committee emphasized the rights of nationals while limiting the roles of non-Qataris in governance and other prominent positions. These demands included that the government should restrict who may claim Qatari citizenship, recruit Qataris for the police force, ensure the head of all government departments were Qataris, promote Qataris working at the oil companies and give them a raise of 50 percent, and forbid foreign merchants from importing goods.

In addition to securing the place of Qataris vis-à-vis non-Qataris, worker demands also addressed wealth inequalities within Qatar. For example, organizers of the strike called for the "abolition of any distinction between classes and the stamping out of anarchy, recklessness and autocracy."[4] While some demands focused on the rights of Qataris and wealth inequalities, other claims reflected pan-Arab solidarities. Such demands included the termination of non-Arabs employed in public security and on the police force as well as the Arabization of leading positions in those organizations. Strike leaders also focused on more general worker rights, including calls on the government to allow workers to strike and to recognize labor unions so that they could join international unions.

As this chapter explores, throughout the 1960s Qatari workers continued to agitate for their rights, but like Bahraini workers in the 1950s, they faced obstructions as labor laws became increasingly strict. The power of workers to agitate for improved labor conditions was also negatively impacted by the fact that responses to strikes were increasingly militarized, trade unions were made illegal, workers experienced differing labor conditions based on their nationality, and international solidarities were discouraged.

OIL AND LABOR IN QATAR, 1930S–1950S

In 1935, Petroleum Development Qatar (PDQ, renamed Qatar Petroleum Company in 1953), received oil concessions in Qatar.[5] While the company initially had no plans to "embark upon a 'speedy exploitation,'" exploratory drilling began in 1938, and oil was discovered at the Dukhan Field in late 1939.[6] In 1940, oil production was paused, like in many countries of the Arabian Peninsula, due to World War II.[7] Following the war, oil exports began in 1950, and it was estimated that the ruler of Qatar received between US$1 million and US$2 million for concessions that year.[8] Following a revision of the concession in 1952, the government of Qatar and PDQ entered into a fifty-fifty profit sharing model, and by 1958, the Qatari government's profits from PDQ's oil production rose to US$61 million.[9] In addition to PDQ's operations in Qatar, in 1952, a subsidiary of Royal Dutch Shell, SCQ, acquired concessions for offshore oil exploration in Qatar, and SCQ began offshore oil production in the 1960s. Despite growing oil production and rising revenues from oil during the 1950s, labor relations at QPC were described by British officials as "unsatisfactory," and they blamed both the company's management as well as workers for this state of affairs.[10] Workers, too, were clearly unhappy with their working conditions, and during this decade there were repeated strikes by workers of all nationalities.

One set of strikes by Indian workers in 1953 focused on the continued differential treatment of Indian and non-Indian employees. Like the Indian chemists in Bahrain in the late 1940s and Indian workers at Aden in the early 1950s, Indian workers in Qatar argued that oil company managers discriminated against them on the basis of their nationality and religion. In addition, these Indian workers argued that this discrimination existed throughout the company, and laborers as well as skilled professionals complained of poor treatment. One medical doctor complained that he was treated "like an ordinary medical orderly." Given their even lower pay, day laborers felt especially vulnerable to discriminatory policies. Laborers felt that discrimination at QPC influenced everything from their daily interactions with management to their housing conditions. Anger over the latter came to a head and rig workers stopped work for a short period in 1953. Strikes by Indians, however, were becoming less effective. During the strike, the Qatari ruler, Sheikh Ali bin Abdullah al Thani, intervened. With this intervention, the men returned to work, despite the fact that the company did not comply with their demands.[11] Throughout the 1950s the ability of Indian workers to agitate for better working conditions was increasingly curtailed.

Qatari workers, too, expressed dissatisfaction with oil company practices, and these workers struck regularly in the 1950s as well. Some worker dissatisfaction was due to the fees they had to pay in order to get a job with the oil company. Through at least the early 1950s, QPC subcontracted out the hiring of local Qatari labor and some foreign labor to a local agency owned by Abdullah Darwish—this agency also had many contracts with QPC for building worker accommodations, offices, and recreational buildings as well as supplying water to the oil project.[12] The agency was also responsible for paying workers, and after employment, the agency deducted "registration fees" as well as other fees from Qatari workers' wages.[13] At times, wages were misdirected entirely.[14] In addition, the sheikh's representative to the company also charged workers fees for nationality certificates, which were needed as the company tried to fulfill its concession obligations by hiring Qatari workers.[15] Qatari government representatives also assisted in the recruitment of non-Qatari laborers residing in Doha, including Saudis, Omanis, Muscatis, and Baluchis, and they issued non-Qatari laborers work permits.[16]

In the 1950s, Qatari workers were also motivated by pan-Arab nationalism. Similarly to what occurred in Kuwait and Bahrain in November 1956, workers at QPC demonstrated and attempted to disrupt oil production following the British, French, and Israeli invasion of Egypt.[17] Unrest in Qatar continued into 1957, and there were multiple strikes that year. During these strikes, workers argued for better positions for Qatari workers—a prelude to the demands made in 1963.

Much of the efficacy of Qatari worker strikes in the late 1950s was dependent on workers' ability to gain the support of the Qatari government. When the government did not support workers, their demands were usually not met. For example, during multiple strikes in 1957, workers asked that QPC give them the same benefits given to khaliji workers at other oil companies operating on the Arabian Peninsula. During one strike, Qatari workers asked for a raise like the one given to Bapco workers in Bahrain. However, workers received little support from the Qatari government, and they did not receive a raise.[18] At other times, the Qatari government supported workers. During another strike in 1957, the Qatari government offered some support to workers and advocated that workers be paid for the days that they were on strike.

Following a strike in January 1957 over job duties during which the Qatari government was seen by the British to have sided with the workers, the British political resident suggested the drafting of labor legislation.[19] Such legislation, the political resident reasoned, could establish procedures that bypassed the intermediary role played by the sheikh or his representatives and allow the oil company to hear grievances and negotiate directly with workers.[20] Thus, a labor law would eliminate the Qatari government's role as intermediary and reduce the possibility that the Qatari government could successfully intercede with the oil company on behalf of workers.

CITIZENSHIP AND QATARIZATION

In 1960, Sheikh Ali abdicated, and his son, Sheikh Ahmad bin Ali al Thani, became the ruler of Qatar. The following year, the Citizenship Law of 1961 was passed. This law marked a change from the 1951 Nationality Regulations that were more expansive in their definition of citizens.[21] As Jill Crystal describes in her history of oil and governance in Qatar, following the 1961 law, additional laws in 1963 and 1964 gave Qataris "commercial advantages." These laws required that foreign firms place orders through Qatari merchants, granted the Chamber of Commerce the power to issue certificates of origin and nationality, banned foreign real estate purchase, and regulated the kafala system, including work visas and sponsorships. In addition, non-Qataris were required to work with Qatari partners and non-Qataris could not own more than 51 percent of existing businesses, new commercial businesses had to be wholly Qatari owned, and new industrial businesses were required to be owned 51 percent by Qataris.[22] Following the 1963 strikes, the Qatari government reminded Qataris that a new citizenship law had been implemented in 1961 in which citizens were defined as those who had settled in Qatar prior to 1930.[23] The government also promised to continue to restrict who could become a citizen of Qatar and to hire more Qataris for government positions, including the Qatarization of the post office.[24]

At this time, such moves to exclude foreigners, including non-khaliji Arabs, from jobs was also occurring at other places in the Arabian Peninsula. In Kuwait, this occurred following the restrictive nationality law passed in 1959. This law, according to Farah al-Nakib, "distanced Kuwaitis from potentially contaminating Arab expatriates—who began to outnumber Kuwaitis during this early oil period of rapid modernization and increased migration—by denying the latter the right to apply for citizenship. It also created a singular and exclusive national community to replace all other loyalties, including Arab nationalism."[25] Restrictions on who could become a citizen worked in conjunction with the Kuwaitization of government positions. For example, in the mid-1960s, 48 percent of employees in the Kuwaiti government were Palestinian, but as pressure for Kuwaitization of the government grew, Palestinians increasingly shifted to work in the private sector.[26]

In the 1960s, local merchants throughout the Trucial Coast were calling on local rulers to protect their financial interests and legally restrict the share of foreigners in the economy, and these changing laws impacted non-khaliji Arabs, Indians, and Pakistanis.[27] For example, in 1963, Mr. Bhatia, an Indian living in Dubai, was informed that he was no longer able to receive imports of Philips radios from the company. Since 1957, Mr. Bhatia had been the Philips Radio agent in Dubai. However, Philips had written to Mr. Bhatia and told him that new regulations made it necessary for all agencies to be held by Dubai citizens. As a result of this new regulation, Philips Radio would send its next shipment of radios to a firm called the United Arab Agencies (UAA)—an agency owned by two wealthy Dubai merchants. When Mr. Bhatia protested, the UAA told him he could have a quarter of the company and act as titular agent if he did the ordering. Further stipulations by the UAA included that Mr. Bhatia would not have access to the accounts and that the arrangement had to remain a secret. Displeased with this offer, Mr. Bhatia continued to protest, and the matter was referred to the British political agent. In response, the British intervened, and the final arrangement agreed upon was that Mr. Bhatia would invest 25 percent and would receive 25 percent of the profits.

In their analysis, British officials found "there are several unsavory factors about the affair." First, Mr. Bhatia had no other agencies and was dependent on Philips for his livelihood whereas the owners of agency were some of the richest men in Dubai. Second, Mr. Bhatia had lived in Dubai for his entire life, as had his father and grandfather. Third, the regulation the ruler had described in his letter to Philips did not exist, and there were dozens of agencies held by foreigners that were not touched. Finally, it was widely believed the ruler had a financial interest in United Arab Agencies.[28] Mr. Bhatia's experiences were only one of many instances of increasing restrictions on Indian merchants in the Arabian Peninsula. In the case of Mr. Bhatia, it appears that the ruler of Dubai worked with powerful merchant families in order to exclude a non-khaliji resident from the economy, even though the latter's family had lived in Dubai for generations. In mediating this dispute, the British put the blame largely on Mr. Bhatia, whom British officials argued ought to have taken a local partner earlier.

As the Qatari government responded to the 1963 strikes by restricting citizenship and hiring Qataris for government jobs, the Qatari government also announced that it would reduce the spending of the ruling family, begin to charge everyone for water and electricity, and commission a study by a British firm to "study the natural resources of Qatar and find the best means of utilising them for the country's benefit."[29] In addition, worker committees for Qatari citizens were established at the oil companies, and contractors were encouraged to hire Qatari workers.[30] The push to hire Qatari workers also impacted contracting companies, including the Qatari contracting company, Darwish Brothers. Following a law passed in Qatar a little over a month before the strikes, in March 1963, that encouraged the hiring of locals by contractors, managers at Darwish Brothers reported they needed to hire foreign workers because there were no Qataris available. Upon hearing this, the deputy ruler of Qatar, Sheikh Khalifa, sent a truck to northern villages and brought down a "truckload of tribesmen" eager to find employment.[31] The problem, from the contractor's perspective, was that these Qatari laborers demanded twenty rupees a day, while imported labor's going rate was four rupees per day. Contractors were unhappy, and, according to QPC managers, Qatari employees of contractors were also unhappy due to poor treatment by contractors.[32]

Despite the changes promised by the Qatari government, popular reception was tepid, and the ruling family continued to receive criticism.[33] Critics argued that the ruling family's expenditures continued to be too high. In addition, they said that the ruling family was guilty of "negligence in supervising oil companies and utter weakness towards them, with the result that they have not fulfilled any useful function for the country, as has happened in other countries." The ruling family was also blamed for the stagnating economy,[34] and critics pointed out that there was a shortage of money in local markets as well as larger issues with trade due to the ruling family failing to settle debts.[35]

LABOR LAWS AND SECURITIZATION

The Qatari government made some concessions to demands made during the 1963 strikes, but these concessions were seen as inadequate by most Qataris. Oil companies dismissed worker actions as either directed toward the government or spurred by outside actors. Such analyses of the strikes ignored dissatisfaction workers had with the oil company. These analyses also obfuscated the role oil companies played in directly shaping social conditions and governance practices in Qatar, particularly the role companies played in writing labor laws.

At the oil companies, managers viewed the 1963 strikes as a "Qatari affair" and characterized the demands as a push for a representative government.[36] In particular, managers saw three key themes in the workers' demands. First, the demands were written in such a way as to try to gain broad support, including of the business community. Second, the demands followed what managers described as a "Middle East pattern" of nationalist organizations attempting to control security forces. Finally, they saw these demands as "aimed at the more notorious abuses and malpractices of the Ruling family."[37] The seriousness of this strike, according to managers, was reflected in that workers would choose to strike over these issues and thereby lose two weeks of pay right before Eid al-Adha, a holiday for which workers used their salaries to buy food and presents.[38] In their analysis of the strikes, managers observed that a change had occurred among Qataris, which they blamed on outside influences, including foreign teachers from countries like Egypt and Syria: "Qataris who were hitherto free from political affiliations, apart from emotional leanings towards pan-Arabism, are tending to become more party politically conscious."[39] Not only were Qataris interested in pan-Arabism, but some young Qataris were alleged to be involved with the Ba'athist Party, which espoused pan-Arab, nationalist, socialist, and anti-imperial ideas.[40]

To guard against such outside influences, the Qatari government had passed the Labour and Labour Court Laws in 1962 and amended these laws in March 1963. As these laws were drafted, British administrators believed it was important that the laws outlawed or heavily regulated trade unions. Like in Bahrain in the 1950s, British officials in the Arabian Peninsula were particularly concerned about the connection between the development of trade unions and Arab nationalist politics.[41] Concern increased when the people of Aden began armed resistance against British imperialism in October of 1963. In Aden and other locations globally, trade unions were seen to drive anticolonialist and nationalist movements. In addition, British officials also feared that communists were increasingly attempting to infiltrate unions, and they referred to the wars against colonialism in Aden, Sudan, and Algeria as representative of the danger of trade unions.[42]

Labor laws were seen as key in curtailing the influence of unions, and the British administrator believed that the sheikh of Qatar would be amenable to implementing restrictions on unions. They sought to base the Qatari labor laws on Saudi Arabia's labor law. Given that QPC "already grants conditions of employment to its employees more favourable than those required by the Saudi Law," British officials did not believe the new laws would negatively impact the oil company's operations in Qatar. Rather, according to officials, these laws would be beneficial to the oil companies because they would restrict trade unions. In addition, they said these laws would help companies because they would change the arbitration of labor disputes, particularly by restricting the local government's ability to act on behalf of workers.[43]

After the Qatari Labour and Labour Court Laws were passed and amended in 1963, the British political agent urged the Qatari government to create a group to oversee future amendments to the law and labor legislation. This group was modeled on the Bahrain Labour Advisory Committee and, importantly, had representation from the oil companies on it. The benefit of such committees, according to one British government official, was that "the presence of an oil company representative on the committee would either nip in the bud any really undesirable legislation or provide you with enough advance warning to make political representations, if thought necessary, before it was too late."[44] Such views on a standing Labour Advisory Committee with oil company representatives exemplifies both the power of oil companies to shape governance as well as the coordination between the British government and oil companies to combat worker actions.

Over the course of the 1960s, controlling worker actions became increasingly pressing as oil production increased rapidly. During this decade, the Qatari government's oil revenue more than doubled from US$54 million in 1960 to US$122 million in 1970.[45] In Qatar in 1966, the economy was entirely dependent upon oil revenues, which were US$84 million, or £30 million, that year.[46] Also during this time, pan-Arab nationalism continued to impact worker actions. In 1967, there were further agitations among workers following the Naksa, or the defeat of Arab armies during the Third Arab-Israeli War and the subsequent seizure of additional Palestinian lands by Israel.

In Qatar, social unrest continued during and after the 1967 Arab League Summit in Khartoum, Sudan, and the British administration believed that increased pan-Arab activism and labor strikes were influenced by both the

Communist and Ba'athist Parties in Damascus.[47] British administrators described the concerns of the deputy ruler, Sheikh Khalifa bin Hamad al Thani, to include maintaining the people's support while also protecting oil revenues. On administrator wrote:

> The Deputy Ruler's concern in the Oil Industry is to ensure that industrial trouble at the oilfields does not spark off a general anti-regime movement—as occurred in 1963; to protect the oil revenue by keeping industrial discipline; to prevent contact between the workers committees and subversive movements, or even bona fide international bodies based abroad and to maintain his own popularity with urban workers for domestic reasons.

As Sheikh Khalifa attempted to ensure stability, British administrators reported that he feared workers' committees were slipping out of his "paternalistic control," and he worried his influence with workers was eroding.[48]

In this context, Sheikh Khalifa was "no longer certain" that he could "enforce a return to work in SCQ in the event of a major dispute,"[49] and both the local government and the British administration began to emphasize state security in their responses to worker actions. In January 1968 Sheikh Khalifa requested that the British administration provide a "full report on security forces in Qatar and recommendations for their development." Six months later, the British government delivered a plan that required substantive financial investment in Qatar's security apparatus by the Qatari government, including the purchase of £1 million worth of weapons and vehicles.[50] This recommendation was in line with earlier weapons sales to Qatar. For example, in the late 1940s, the ruler of Qatar wanted to purchase weapons to secure oil areas, and the British administration looked favorably upon these requests because of rapidly expanding oil activities.[51] By the 1960s, defense contracts were lucrative for the British government and, in 1969, £19.5 million in British contracts—for power, gas, and arms supplied—were signed.[52]

1968 STRIKES IN QATAR

In August 1968, strikes occurred in the offshore oil fields run by SCQ. In part, this strike was notable because it was the largest generalized industrial unrest in Qatar since 1963. It was also notable because workers defied the instructions of the deputy ruler, Sheikh Khalifa, to return to work. British officials characterized Sheikh Khalifa's inability to get the workers to return to work as an uncommon reaction to the ruler's intervention in Qatar.[53] The British administration believed that the 1968 Qatari strikes were spearheaded by a small, organized group of workers who were influenced by non-khaliji actors operating in the Arab world. The majority of workers in Qatar, the British administration believed, participated in but were not excited by the strike. To substantiate this, they pointed to the fact that worker committees were unable to get all oil workers in the country to participate, and workers at QPC, the other oil company in Qatar at the time, did not participate in the strike.[54]

Workers at SCQ first voiced their grievances on August 24, 1968. Then, on August 26, daily-rate workers at both SCQ and Shell Marketing Company went on strike. Monthly workers continued to work, and these workers maintained essential services. On August 27, workers at SCQ on Halul Island joined the strike, and workers communicated between the onshore project and the island via a radio taken from a moored tanker. When the strike began, the deputy ruler ordered replacement workers to step in. This was refused by Shell on the grounds that working on marine operations was dangerous for untrained workers and because the company feared sabotage. Despite these concerns, during the strikes, there was no violence or damage done.

By the end of the day on August 27, the British administration believed that most workers wanted to return to work but were restrained by the strike's organizers. On August 28, the workers' committee was thought to be negotiating with workers at QPC and those in government service for a general strike on August 31. It was assumed that if the strike had continued, intermediate staff would have joined, most likely stopping Shell's oil production in Qatar completely. Before this could happen, the strike leaders met with the deputy ruler and said they would return to work, but they did not actually do so until after a second meeting on August 28. In that meeting, the strike leaders saw the deputy ruler, apologized for their behavior, and instructed the men back to work, telling them the demands would be pursued by constitutional means. Although the strike was resolved relatively quickly, the deputy ruler was reportedly annoyed, angry, and suspicious of foreign influence behind the strike.

During the strikes at Shell in 1968, the workers demanded four basic things. First, they asked for a raise of 16 percent, backdated to August 1967 to compensate for an increased cost of living. Second, the workers asked for an increase in annual increments. This increase would bring SCQ in line with QPC's pay and had been promised by the deputy ruler the year before.[55] The question of wages was, according to Qatari Director of Labour Khreis, the key issue in the strike. Mr. Khreis based this belief on recent worker demands: Early in 1967, workers made a deal where they would not receive any wage increases. However, with the closing of the Suez Canal, the price of rice was increasing. Workers argued that this was an exceptional circumstance. Shell's management rejected this argument, and wages had been a source of dispute ever since. The disagreement over wages was further compounded because the company wanted to link a raise with the workers' approval of a pension scheme.[56] Without approval of the pension scheme, neither QPC nor SCQ were able to implement their redundancy schemes, and thus, the companies were stuck with an excess of local workers.[57] The result was that SCQ was holding out a raise as a bribe to workers. Workers saw through this and refused to link the two issues.[58]

The third demand by workers concerned the advancement of khaliji workers in SCQ's workforce. Workers were particularly upset by the failure of the company to upgrade laborers and to promote workshop men who had passed the trade test earlier that year. Finally, workers wanted the company to cease using contractors because, workers reported, contractors did not hire many locals, did not promote local workers, and did not pay well.[59] These last two demands addressed the fact that Qatari workers were looking for promotion opportunities in the oil companies, and they wanted training so that they could be moved into higher positions.

In addition to working with Shell to end the strikes, the deputy ruler also tried to work directly with the striking workers. When SCQ refused to pay workers for the days the workers were on strike, the deputy ruler said he would personally pay their wages if the workers agreed to give him, in writing, two weeks' notice before striking. The workers' committee refused this proposition.[60] Notably, this proposed requirement for written notice before striking was similar to the labor laws restricting worker strikes implemented in Bahrain in the 1950s. Globally, legally requiring workers to give advanced notice before holding a strike was becoming a popular tactic to temper labor movements. In the 1960s, the UK government attempted to pass a law requiring English workers to vote and then wait before striking, but in 1968, this law was refused by the UK Trade Union Congress.[61]

WORKERS' COMMITTEES AND THE 1968 STRIKE

The British administration believed the objectives of strike leaders in 1968 Qatar were to "cultivate a more aggressive attitude on the part of the Qatari people vis-à-vis the oil companies, and to encourage the workers to reject the traditional paternalism of the state in labour relations."[62] This was a change from the position that was taken in Qatar in 1963, when the state was seen to be the mediator between oil companies and the people, and the British government believed that workers' committees were the cause of this change.

During the 1968 strikes, British administrators argued that workers' committees were actively trying to undermine the position of the Qatari government, particularly the government's role in mediating labor disputes. Immediately before the strike, the leaders of the workers' committee had asked to see the deputy ruler, but the deputy ruler was busy thanks to a visit by the Iraqi ambassador. The strike leaders did not tell the workers why the deputy ruler did not meet with them, giving the workers the impression that they were refused a meeting for no reason. Not only were the workers' committee undermining the authority of the Qatari government, but British officials blamed the strike on the organization and composition of workers' committees and the relationship between workers' committees and the oil companies.

For the British administration, the 1968 strike, following upon the earlier strike that occurred at SCQ a year before, was "difficult to understand."[63] This was because "Shell was internationally known for the quality of its personnel management and the value it placed on good industrial relations."[64] In fact, both the British and the Qatari government agreed that SCQ management always properly negotiated with the workers' committee and that the working conditions at SCQ were better than at QPC, where there were no strikes. As a result, the British administration and the oil company management decided that QPC workers did not strike because the company was staffed by older, more conservative workers, and these workers took a leading role in labor relations between Qatari workers, the company, and the state.[65]

In contrast, Qatar's Director of Labour Khreis, a Jordanian, suggested that the SCQ operation was "trouble prone" for a number of reasons.[66] First, it was an offshore operation, which generally caused labor trouble. Second, there were frequent changes on the personnel side, leading to a lack of continuity in policy and lack of contact with worker representatives. Third, the trouble tended to happen when the general manager was away. Fourth, several members of the workers' committee were thought to be irresponsible and "out to make trouble."[67]

An additional key problem for SCQ, according to Mr. Khreis, was the organization of workers. At QPC, there were two workers' committees—one at the Dukhan oil field and the other at the Umm Said terminal. At each location, the committee leaders represented both Qatari daily-rate workers (i.e., unskilled workers and laborers) and Qatari monthly-rate workers (i.e., semi-skilled, skilled, and supervisory workers). Ideally, the workers' committees were supposed to represent all nationalities, but in practice they represented only Qatari workers, leaving other nationalities to raise concerns through informal channels. Workers' committees did not have a formal legal status, but they were treated as such by the company's management, and the workers' committees were decided by election. Elections were well attended, and attempts to delay elections by the government or company were met with unrest at the camps.[68] QPC provided the committees with spaces to meet. During meetings, workers took their individual grievances to the committee. From the British perspective, the efficiency of the QPC committee system was seen in the fact that there had been no large-scale strikes at QPC since 1963.

At SCQ, on the other hand, there were two different workers' committees at the same worksite. One committee represented Qatari daily-rate workers and the other Qatari monthly-rate workers. The monthly-rate committee was inactive, and the trouble stemmed from the daily-rate workers' committee. The leaders of the committees were becoming "professionalized as the same people tend to be re-elected year by year. The members are working class and illiterate, but they are becoming more experienced and this makes dealing with them somewhat easier." As the committees became more established, they were likely to refer disputes to the court or to a conciliation hearing.[69]

The difference in the treatment of worker committees by the management of SCQ and QPC reflected the differing managerial styles at each company. At SCQ, conflicts often had to be passed along to a supervisor who worked off-site. At QPC, conflicts could be solved on-site with a superintendent. The immediacy of conflict resolution and familiarity between workers and management led the British administration to suggest that QPC had implemented a model that British firms in the Arab world might want to consider mimicking in order to avoid costly strikes.[70] In addition, they pointed out that the QPC supervisors were British men who had spent their lives in the Middle East and who "have acquired special expertise dealing with the Arab personnel."[71]

The influence of worker committees was growing, but the various committees had differing attitudes toward the Qatari government and the oil companies. The tensions seen elsewhere in the Arabian Peninsula between youth and an older, more conservative generation were also at play in Qatar. In Qatar, young workers identified more with the cause of Palestine. However, measures were taken to ensure that workers who were loyal to the al Thani family were elected. These measures allowed for the older generation to win the election. As a result, "the workers' committees at both Dukhan oil field and Umm Said terminal were loyal to the al Thani family. They were very conservative in the outlook, and were bona fide representatives of the labour force, with real authority to negotiate with the Company on its behalf." In part, the loyalty was ensured by the election style. The laborers nominated ten men in order of preference to be on the executive committee. The names were then given to the deputy ruler, and the first three he found to be acceptable were given the position.[72]

Despite these policies to control the outcome of elections, the actual ability of the deputy ruler to refuse the workers' choices had limitations, and the government of Qatar, the British administration, and the oil companies worried that committees were influenced by outside groups, particularly pan-Arab nationalists. For example, in 1965, a person considered by the deputy ruler to lack respect and who was suspected of making "clandestine visits" to Cairo was reelected by the workers at SCQ. When the deputy ruler tried to block him taking the position, the workers resisted, "confirmed the election," and the deputy ruler acquiesced. SCQ's management also feared that the leaders of the workers' committees were in touch with workers at Kuwait Oil Company and with workers in Bahrain because they showed knowledge of conditions at other oil projects. Despite these beliefs, there was no evidence of workers coordinating with outside groups.[73]

ATTEMPTS TO PREVENT ADDITIONAL STRIKES

In looking for the cause of the 1968 strike, managers at both QPC and SCQ suspected that the leaders of the workers' committees were traveling to Egypt where they were exposed to pan-Arab and nationalist sentiments. Similarly, the British administration feared that there was discontent in the Arabian Peninsula due to growing nationalism, the increasing popularity of the Arab League and pan-Arab movements, and worker dissatisfaction with oil industry practices. In particular, British government officials believed the Arab Federation of Petroleum Workers to be at the heart of the 1968 strike in Qatar.[74] Indeed, many of the requests made by striking workers were similar to the platform adopted by the 1961 meeting of the Arab Federation of Petroleum Workers. This platform included nationalization of oil resources and profit sharing for workers. It also advocated for the end to differentiations between nationals and nonnationals by oil companies and opposed the practice of contract, or temporary, labor.[75]

In addition to the influence of outside groups, both the British administration and SCQ managers believed "the real cause" of the strike was worker disgruntlement with contract labor. Prior to this time, the Qatari government and the oil companies had signed a provision that limited contract labor. According to this provision, labor contracting could only occur if a few key issues were satisfied: The work had to be temporary or specialized in nature, Qatari nationals had to be hired first if they were available, and wage rates had to be the same as for equivalent jobs with the company. In the summer of 1968, these conditions had been satisfied, and SCQ hired contract labor with the permission of the Qatari government. The British administration believed that because workers had agreed to this, they were unable to strike on the issue and were, therefore, merely using the issue of wages as a reason to strike.[76]

Contract work often caused problems in the 1960s at oil companies, and this was true at both QPC and SCQ, even though the policies for and conditions of contract work varied between the two companies. At QPC, British officials provided a rosy picture of contract labor, arguing it was beneficial for workers.[77] At SCQ, the drilling rig was operated on contract. Mainly Yemenis, Adenis, and Omanis were hired for the positions because they were willing to live on dhows and the company claimed Qatari nationals were not. Like in 1963, the Labour Department insisted that nationals must be hired, but SCQ was reluctant to hire nationals as it would cause expenses to rise, and they would have to hire twice as many workers. To avoid this, the company threatened to send the rig to Dubai or Abu Dhabi for maintenance.[78]

As the British administration, local government, and oil companies tried to mitigate against worker calls to end contract labor and the influence of the Arab Federation of Petroleum Workers, they were also concerned about the political influence of non-khaliji workers in Qatar and the consequences of firing redundant Qatari laborers. In 1968, Jordanians and Palestinians were the largest minority groups in Qatar, and government officials worried that these groups would grow in size in the following years. As future industrial projects were planned, officials believed they would require additional outside workers because it would take a long time for the government training scheme to produce enough skilled workers to stop needing immigrants to fill the positions.[79] While non-khaliji workers were needed in Qatar, the British administration saw the presence of foreign workers from other areas of the Middle East to be a potential threat to political stability in Qatar. For example, British officials thought Palestinian workers, in particular, openly disliked the Qatari government due to the discrimination they faced and deportations from Qatar. However, as much as the British believed Palestinians contributed to destabilizing work sites in the Arabian Peninsula, there was no actual evidence of organizing efforts among the Palestinians working in the Qatari oil fields.[80]

By focusing so much attention on outside influences, the British failed to recognize and address the interest of workers in international labor movements as well as the tensions among Arab workers in Qatar. Arab workers were not a homogenous category, and not all non-Qataris were viewed in the same way by Qatari workers. While some Arab workers were considered outsiders to Qatar and their presence, via contract work, was one of the workers' complaints during the strike, other Arab workers were considered to be part of the worker movement. For example, one of the three strike leaders was Bahraini, showing that local workers built alliances on earlier kinship and exchange networks within the Arabian Peninsula and that these alliances did not necessarily follow formal state borders.[81]

Aware of the power of political alliances among khaliji workers, at both SCQ and QPC, managers saw firing redundant workers and, in particular, firing khaliji workers to be problematic and fraught. In the mid- to late 1960s, this was a critical issue, as the majority of Qataris employed in the oil industry were working as unskilled laborers and did not have adequate knowledge of English to work in management or skilled positions. The companies had hired laborers for construction phases of oil projects, but they did not need these laborers after construction was finished.

At QPC, management wanted to dismiss a group of redundant workers, but the Qatari government would not let them, for four main reasons. First, the government feared the workers would leave with their money to find work in Abu Dhabi. Second, the "workers wanted to force the Company to produce a permanent and generous pension scheme." Third, it was believed that the dismissal of workers had been the source of QPC's labor trouble in 1963, and neither the company nor the British administration wanted a repeat of the strike.[82] Finally, the government feared swelling the numbers of unemployed, as the government thought there was a link between high unemployment and political instability, and they referenced the strikes in Bahrain in 1965. As a result, QPC retained approximately four hundred workers whom management had already found to be redundant.

Oil companies were not alone in having large numbers of redundant workers. In government positions in Qatar, over half of the nationals employed were redundant. In addition, nationals qualified for social assistance, and "fit men expect[ed] personal aid from the sheikhs connected with their families." Students who had gone abroad for education also relied on the government to find them jobs that suited their "qualifications and prestige."[83]

While both the oil companies and the Qatari government employed large numbers of redundant workers to avoid potential labor unrest, not all nationals of Qatar received the same job protection. In 1964, QPC fired some redundant employees. These workers were all members of the Mohennedy tribe. This tribe had some disagreements with the ruling family of Qatar and migrated to Kuwait in 1963. Failing to find work there, the group returned to Qatar.[84] The tribe's uncertain political standing led to the government not protecting all nationals equally. This standing may also have influenced the fact that other workers did not feel solidarity with the workers who were dismissed and, as a result, there was no collective action following their dismissal.

INTERNATIONAL ORGANIZATIONS AND THE QUESTION OF UNIONS

While the British administration thought the most destabilizing influences on oil company workers came from other parts of the Arab world, they also feared that labor movements in Britain and the United States could adversely influence worker committees. In particular, the British administration wanted to "discourage" contact between Qatari workers and international labor organizations. And British administrators believed that Qatar joining international organizations, such as the International Labor Organization (ILO), would lead to the legalization of trade unions, and, subsequently, political upheaval.[85] In contrast, some Qatari government officials expressed the desire to join international organizations in order to improve the situation of workers and legalize unions.

In 1968, both the Qatari government officials and oil company managers were dissatisfied with the way the 1962 labor law was being interpreted, and the Qatari government felt the labor situation at oil projects was unsatisfactory.[86] In particular, Director of Labour Khreis was frustrated that workers' committees did not have legal standing. Khreis also pointed out that the labor law permitted joint consultative committees, but these had not been implemented. This meant the workers' committees in 1968 had no legal status and were not registered with the Labour Department. Instead of restricting committees' activities, however, this situation gave the committees greater leeway to "meddle" in politics. The solution, according to Khreis, was to legalize trade unions and specify their responsibilities and limits. In this way, he argued, order and discipline could be maintained in industrial relations.[87]

A judge of the Labour Court in Qatar also complained that labor relations in the country were problematic and claimed that a major problem was the court's inability to enforce its rulings. This was particularly true in cases in which defendants had influence with the ruling family. In 1968, for example, there were fifty cases in which the judgments were ineffective. According to the judge, "This was contrary to the basic conception of the rule of law and a denial of the elementary rights of the individual worker." Furthermore, the judge argued that nonnationals in Qatar were at a "great disadvantage" in the court system. The Labour Code provided indemnities and paid holidays only for Qatari nationals. Other workers could only obtain these benefits if an appropriate clause was inserted in their contracts, and the majority of nonnational workers did not have formal contracts of service.

The whole situation, the judge argued, was due to the influence of the merchants of Doha who wanted a supply of cheap foreign labor. The result was that Qatari and other workers were employed side by side on the same job, but they enjoyed different conditions of labor.

The judge noted that the situation would have to change when Qatar joined the ILO. Joining the ILO, he argued, would pressure the government to "amend its labour laws and practices to conform to internationally accepted standards."[88] The suggestion that Qatar join the ILO was not unexpected by the British administration. In the early 1960s, the Qatari government joined a number of international organizations. For example, in 1961, Qatar joined OPEC, and in 1964, Qatar joined UNESCO and the WHO.[89] Furthermore, the judge was not alone in his desire to join the ILO, and other members of the Qatari government also wished to join the ILO in order to cement labor relations and improve labor conditions.[90]

As a first step in joining the ILO, the deputy ruler sent a letter to the British political resident in Doha indicating the Qatari government's desire to join the organization. In reply, the political resident wrote that the British administration was against Qatar joining the ILO.[91] When pressed on this issue, the British government initially tried to defer the conversation, but after additional inquiries, British administrators told the director of labor that if all Qatar wanted from joining the ILO was technical assistance, then they could receive such assistance without becoming a member. Officials pointed to the example of Saudi Arabia, whose lead the British administration felt Qatar should follow in all matters relating to international labor politics.[92]

This reply, however, did not satisfy Director of Labor Khreis, and he indicated that technical assistance was "irrelevant." Instead, he argued, "the object of joining would be to take part in the widespread international activities of this United Nations organization." To which the political resident's office replied that if Qatar joined the ILO, it would have to follow the rules set by the organization. This meant Qatar would need to send a tripartite committee to the annual conference and include a worker representative in this committee. The British argued this would be hard to do, especially considering that workers' committees did not have legal status. Therefore, the British argued, "It would be unwise for Qatar to join the ILO unless it was prepared to give full legal recognition to labour unions in the internationally accepted sense."[93] This reasoning, however, did not discourage the Qatari government as much as the British administration hoped. While the British administration was not eager for Qatar's government to recognize trade unions, the director of labor and the Arab Federation of Petroleum Workers were eager to formalize the government's recognition of unions.[94]

Aware that the Qatari government still wanted to join the ILO despite British officials' recommendations against it, British government officials reached out to the ILO about the issue, and they were relieved to find that the ILO would be reluctant to accept Qatar as a member. The ILO's deputy director general and deputy legal adviser reported that the organization "would be most reluctant to see a fresh wave of new members or indeed observer delegations from the tiny Gulf States with their negligible populations." In addition, ILO administrators argued, "There are already problems of balance and influence within the Organisation which the onset of raw new members reinforcing one of the several racial groupings would only accentuate."[95] Thus, the ILO responded negatively to Qatar's interest. The "several racial groupings" referred to by ILO officials may be an allusion to the fact that, as of December 1968, approximately 38 percent of the states who were members of the ILO had participated as full members of the Non-Aligned Movement's Second Summit in Egypt held in October 1964. This conference called for the end of colonialism, imperialism, and neocolonialism; the end of racial discrimination and apartheid; respect for self-determination; and a "new international division of labour."[96]

In their arguments against Qatar joining the ILO, the British administration also pointed to the labor situation in Kuwait, which they described negatively. In the late 1960s, Kuwait was the only country of the Arabian Peninsula to have joined the ILO. According to the British, joining the ILO led to all three oil companies operating in Kuwait to have registered trade unions, and Kuwaiti government ministries were also unionized.[97] The British understood Kuwait's participation in the ILO to have spurred increased Arab nationalist actions in the country, and they claimed, this was to the detriment of Kuwaiti workers.

While the British administration did not want Qatar to join the ILO, they were more ambivalent about the country strengthening ties with the Arab League. The British administration believed that such an association was likely to bring into question state labor policies that the British also found problematic—in particular, the discriminatory treatment between Qataris and other Arabs and the permissive attitude adopted toward Iranian immigration. While the British administration wished for a stricter view by the Qatari government on Iranian migration, they were wary of the danger that closer association with the Arab League would lead to increased demand for workers' associations, and specifically, of the legal recognition of trade unions in place of the de facto recognition by the government of existing oil company committees. This, British officials feared, would allow Qatari workers to organize themselves more effectively and would bring the union leaders into closer contact with pan-Arab and international labor movements.

As they discussed the benefits and drawbacks of Qatar participating in international organizations like the ILO and the Arab League, the British administration anticipated that the labor question was likely to become very important in Qatar in the coming years. In particular, they believed the legalization of trade unions would become an increasingly serious issue, and they contended that this issue was political, not industrial. Formalizing unions was dangerous, according to British officials, because three groups were interested in influencing khaliji workers. First, unions were a potential target to nationalist groups in Qatar and Bahrain who were frustrated by the lack of devolution of power by ruling families. Second, unions could also be used by other Arabs working in the Arabian Peninsula—Arabs who suffered from discrimination and lack of political expression. Finally, unions could provide a way for pan-Arab political groups to exert pressure and garner support of pan-Arab policies. The British argued that these groups would use unions to influence khaliji workers, with dire consequences for political stability and oil production.

Despite these dangers, some British administrators cautioned that a negative stance regarding trade unionism was not necessarily the wisest course. They saw the trend in Arab countries toward the development of trade unions. While there was the danger of subversion, these government administrators argued that unions could also be a major factor in a gradual political revolution of the Arab world, allowing for slow internal social reform while also providing a bulwark against communism. Therefore, these British administrators suggested that the deputy ruler delegate this aspect of government administration to a member of the ruling family; importantly, that person should have sufficient control over the Labour Department and be able to maintain relations with both the oil companies and with international labor groups.[98]

CONCLUSION

While members of Qatar's government wanted to implement stronger labor laws and strengthen the position of unions in the country, in the late 1960s and early 1970s fewer and fewer Qataris were actually working in vulnerable positions in the oil industry. By 1969, in Qatar, local people no longer did the lowest-level jobs—this position had been assumed instead by migrants. Increasingly, the majority of Qataris had shifted away from performing manual labor. This did not mean all Qataris were rich; indeed, a "minority of indigenous Qataris [were] still living in poorer circumstances." These poor Qataris, British officials explained, were "too proud to beg assistance from the Ruler, and either too lazy, or too backward in education and training, to find themselves a better niche in society."[99] In this explanation, British administrators both mobilized stereotypes about khalijis and also articulated their understanding of how the Qatari state's relations with citizens was shaped by the distribution of oil wealth. Overall, these changes led to a stark situation in the late 1960s, where one could literally see the contrast between the "very large palaces and grandiose villas" of the native Qataris and the "shanties and sheds in which the mainly expatriate labour-force live."[100]

The discrepancies between living and working conditions for national and foreign workers were due, in part, to the reallocation of oil money. The huge amounts of oil revenue were beneficial in distributing wealth across Qatari families. According to one Qatari government official, 53 percent of the oil revenue went to the ruling family. Of that, £10 million went to the ruler and his immediate family, and £3 million went to the deputy ruler.[101] From the ruler, wealth was then redistributed through tribal networks. However, the reallocation of resources was not the only factor in the decreasing numbers of Qataris working in the oil fields. The British administration and companies' resistance to recognizing unions and the increased pressure on the state to respond militarily to strikes meant that the stability of the state was best assured by hiring foreign workers—workers who could be easily fired and deported from the country.

At oil projects, workers from India and Pakistan were the easiest to fire when their positions became redundant. Indeed, oil company managers argued that Indians and Pakistanis could be fired without any problems.[102] In addition, workers from India were thought to be largely apolitical and, therefore, as posing little danger of destabilizing the state government or even being able to foment large-scale work stoppages.[103] This was particularly true because Indian workers showed no interest in the pan-Arab movements that the British administration, oil companies, and local governments suspected of influencing khaliji and other Arab workers. In contrast, firing khaliji workers had a greater chance of causing local worker unrest and, potentially, destabilizing the British administration, oil companies, and local governments. Resolving labor disputes between oil companies and local workers was challenging because the authority of the ruler was not always absolute, police were often ineffective, and workers did not listen when told to return to work. The consequences of strikes meant the loss of money for oil companies. Managing the workforce required increasing investments in policing and the armed forces. The situation in Qatar was not unique, and we will see in the next chapter that in Abu Dhabi, too, the securitization of oil along with changing oil company practices led to the depoliticization of labor at oil projects.

Seven

SECURING OIL PROJECTS

IN LATE MAY AND EARLY JUNE 1963, THE KHALIJI WORKERS AT OIL projects in Abu Dhabi held a series of strikes. These strikes began at the onshore projects of Abu Dhabi Petroleum Company (ADPC)[1] and ADPC's subcontractors.[2] Located over one hundred kilometers west of Abu Dhabi City, the strikes were centered at Jebel Dhanna, Tarif, and Murban. On May 21, at Jebel Dhanna, workers guarded the gates to the camps and did not allow company officials to enter. The strike was well organized and nonviolent, and the order to strike was "passed around quickly and obeyed absolutely."[3] At other oil projects in Abu Dhabi, the strikes were more volatile. In Tarif, the oil company office was "besieged" by around one hundred workers with sticks, and when a British agent visited the Tarif offices, he and his companions faced a crowd of thirty workers "armed with stones and iron bars." The unrest radiated out to smaller camps, and at a nearby camp, called Santa Fe, the expatriate staff, mostly Americans, were "besieged in the offices and mess-hall" and property was destroyed or stolen.[4] Beginning on May 31, the strikes spread offshore and the workers at Abu Dhabi Marine Areas (ADMA) at Das Island also began to participate in the strikes.[5] Here, too, violence erupted: Two British managers were beaten, and two Indian clerical staff were injured.[6] Criticizing oil companies' lack of training and promotion for local workers and angry about the firing of redundant workers, during these strikes workers defined their community and advocated for the removal of the British from Abu Dhabi.

Oil company managers and British government officials in the Arabian Peninsula feared these strikes were influenced by pan-Arab movements, and they worried about the future nationalization of oil in Abu Dhabi if the strikes were successful. Informed by these fears and finding it difficult to control the striking workers, British government officials and oil company managers responded by characterizing the strikes as security risks to the Abu Dhabi government, to the British government, and to oil companies' property. In Abu Dhabi, the characterization of these strikes as security risks facilitated a militarized response, in which authorities attempted to mobilize both the state's police force and imperial military infrastructure.

Following these strikes, oil companies operating in Abu Dhabi continued to be concerned about the security of oil projects, and they sought solutions to mitigate their risk in the event that oil was nationalized. These concerns over nationalization resulted in increased contracting within the oil industry in the Arabian Peninsula. From 1963 to 1968, militarized responses to strikes along with changing oil company practices impacted state sovereignty and workers' rights, including the role the government played in protecting the rights of workers.

LOCAL LABOR RELATIONS AT OIL PROJECTS

In 1960, commercial quantities of oil were found in Abu Dhabi. Following this discovery, oil work shifted from exploration to construction, which required a large expansion of the workforce. Strikes such as those in 1963 were highly disruptive, and a central concern shared by the British administration, the oil companies, and the ruler of Abu Dhabi, Sheikh Shakhbut ibn Sultan al Nahyan, was how to best manage workers, including workers who were citizens of Abu Dhabi. In the early 1960s, worker action was informed by class differences, living conditions, and changing practices in the oil industry, particularly the increase in contracting. Contracting negatively impacted labor relations, because managers employed by contractors were often insensitive to or unaware of local workers' cultural or religious practices. In addition, contractors were less likely to retain redundant workers to maintain positive labor relations. This was particularly an issue as oil projects in

Abu Dhabi moved from construction phases, in which many workers were required, to maintenance phases, which required thousands fewer workers.

In keeping with the parameters of their oil concession with Abu Dhabi, British companies were required to hire Abu Dhabi nationals, when possible, for positions. As oil projects began to hire more workers for construction projects, in 1961, Sheikh Shakhbut implemented a temporary Labour and Worker's Law,[7] which classified two types of workers: daily and monthly. For daily workers, the workday was eight hours; wages were to be deducted on days workers were absent; transportation was made available to workers to and from work; companies provided free water and rest facilities; after the first month, the daily wage was paid for a day of rest each week; and after two weeks of employment, workers were paid for religious and official holidays. For monthly workers, such as drivers, watchmen, foremen, and skilled workers, the workday was also eight hours, but overtime was two times workers' normal pay; nationals had to be hired first, and foreigners were required to get permission from the municipality; the companies were required to supply water; and for absences, workers were to be warned three times and the municipality told before action was taken by the company. The municipality would then investigate the absence and advise the worker. Finally, companies were required to submit a list of all workers showing names, nationalities, and occupations.[8]

The labor law created different working conditions for daily and monthly pay workers, and these differences, along with the emphasis the Abu Dhabi government placed on oil companies hiring nationals, influenced the contours of worker actions during the 1963 strikes. These were marked by the high levels of participation by less-skilled khaliji workers and the lack of participation by management. Living conditions also influenced who participated in the strikes and worker actions during the strike. For example, at Jebel Dhanna there were eight hundred Arab workers, who worked mainly as laborers and drivers; about six hundred Indian and Pakistani workers; and about four hundred European workers. The workers were housed separately according to region of origin: Indian and Pakistani workers did not share a camp with the local workers, and European workers had their own camp.[9] Separate living conditions may have dissuaded solidarities among workers of differing nationalities. However, because the worker camps were located far apart, the camps' distances from each other may also have discouraged violence among groups during the strikes at Jebel Dhanna.

Oil company managers, for their part, were also unhappy with their own working conditions, and this exacerbated already poor labor relations. One British administrator observed, "The companies are working under great difficulties, far greater than they had probably anticipated, both in regard to the nature of labour, its extraordinary ineffectualness and its apparently inimical demands on them." British government officials believed that worker demands, the hot climate, and long work hours wore on managers and made them more irritable with workers.

Despite these hostile conditions, British government officials cautioned companies to remember that strikes were costly and that it was better to avoid them. The solution, administrators offered, was that local workers should be treated "with a tolerant and a certain liberal attitude toward a primitive people." Furthermore, management should try to understand that these "primitive people" see foreigners as "intruders" in their land. The British administrators suggested that companies adapt to cultural norms when possible. For example, they praised the Lebanese Contracting and Trading Company (CAT) for giving workers a large enough food allowance to feed not only themselves but also "quite a number of hangers on" who lived in the camp with them, and British officials pointed out it was cheaper to feed extra people than lose thousands of pounds a day during a strike.[10]

Such strategies sought to improve day-to-day operations, but industry-level changes were creating new problems and contributing to growing worker dissatisfaction. One industry-wide practice that was increasing rapidly was contracting out the maintenance of oil projects to smaller companies. Oil companies contracted out jobs in order to distance themselves from labor issues and to save money. For example, oil companies hoped that contracting would alleviate some of the pressure the companies felt while navigating the economic and political risks associated with firing workers. This was particularly the case in Abu Dhabi as oil projects changed. Initially ADPC itself carried out exploration and production, including drilling. However, the exploration phase was winding down in the early 1960s, and the company was contracting out most of the drilling.

Many of the contractors working in Abu Dhabi in 1963 operated differently from the seismic party contractors used by the companies in the past.

Previously, ADPC had maintained all relations with labor onshore and with the local government, such that contractors appeared, to many people, to be a part of the company. In contrast, the new drilling contractors hired and fired employees themselves. While ADPC said it would do its best to ensure that labor conditions at contractors were to the company's own standards, British officials and ADPC managers feared problems, because they believed contractors were tougher on laborers, quicker to fire employees, and only looking for a quick profit on projects. In anticipation of these changes, large oil companies were anxious for locals to understand that contractors were separate from the main companies and that the latter were no longer responsible for labor relations.[11]

The British administrators and oil company managers believed some contracting companies, like Bechtel, had adequate experience to manage workers, but new contractors were not seen to have sufficient knowledge of local cultural practices—repeating a theme that arose in the 1940s as oil projects developed in the Arabian Peninsula. Both ADPC managers and the British administration feared that new contractors lacked the experience and knowledge necessary to "handle" local labor. When ADPC was in charge of operations, for example, it saw it as part of its long-term interest to train rig crews to operate rigs. There was concern that contractors did not feel the same way and would not consider local crews sufficient. In addition, contractors were less likely to retain redundant employees.

The pace of changes further aggravated operating conditions and labor relations. Previous contractors had learned how to interact with local workers through the company's camp bosses. New company contractors did not have this experience, and there had already been at least one incident involving one of the new contractor's managers. A seismic team was returning and stopped the truck for one of the men. When the contractor's manager saw that the worker had stopped to say his prayers, the manager said he would not wait and drove off, abandoning the worker miles out in the desert.[12] In response to this incident, ADPC removed the contractors involved.[13] Both company managers and the British administration worried that workers would not be patient with a second round of cultural offenses.

An additional problem was labor redundancy following the completion of construction projects, and by 1963, many projects were focused on maintenance. Construction projects had required thousands of workers, but only for the duration of the construction project. After construction ended at oil projects, the number of workers needed to maintain the oil projects decreased significantly and resulted in the dismissal of most workers from their jobs. However, firing local workers was problematic and managers and government officials feared that local workers, upon the termination of their colleagues, would cause trouble and stop oil production.[14]

PERSPECTIVES ON THE 1963 STRIKES

In seeking to understand the cause of the strikes in May and June 1963, British government administrators in the Arabian Peninsula emphasized the influence of outsiders, changing practices within the oil industry, and the inefficiency of the ruler of Abu Dhabi, Sheikh Shakhbut. British administrators also argued that either the workers were copying each other or, more probably from the British perspective, the strike was coordinated from the outside. While British government officials and oil project managers preferred the latter theory, they had trouble finding evidence to corroborate it.[15] When one looks at the strikes from the perspective of the workers, we see multiple motivations behind the strikes, including the desire to improve labor conditions, local networks, rumors, and a questioning of the oil companies' and British administration's authority in Abu Dhabi.

Rumors and speculation fueled the British administration's and oil companies' perspectives on both the strikes and the strikes' potential consequences. Believing the strike in Tarif was completely unexpected and "without any real cause," one British government official wrote, "Everyone in the management of the oil company seems convinced that trouble is being deliberately stirred up by agitators from outside but no one seems to know what the motives for this are."[16] While there was no direct evidence that the strike was instigated by external forces, some Abu Dhabi workers had been employed elsewhere in the Arabian Peninsula, and this lent weight to the fear that these workers "may well have come under hostile influence."[17] In the months after the strikes, rumors of additional potential strikes abounded. For the British, these rumors were spurred by fears that the radio broadcast Sawt al-Arab (Voice of the Arabs), which discussed worker salaries and conditions, was instigating workers to strike. The main problem, according to this radio broadcast, was that foreigners were being given better jobs and higher pay than nationals.[18]

At Jebel Dhanna, the management of both ADPC and the contractor Bechtel, for their part, also believed that the strikes had no cause and were instigated by outside troublemakers.[19] Echoing these sentiments, a British government administrator wrote:

> Although the workers may have had some genuine grievances, the strikes were worked up by a group of agitators and a degree of co-ordination and organization was displayed which is totally foreign to Abu Dhabi nature. Most of the companies had a small group of trouble-makers, usually men from outside Abu Dhabi, amongst their employees, but hitherto they had not been allowed by Abu Dhabi authorities to sack them. It is not yet clear whether these trouble-makers were acting on their own initiative or whether they were receiving instructions from outside.[20]

As managers and British administrators blamed outside influences for the strike, at both Jebel Dhanna and Das Island, British managers and administrators also believed that the workers were striking out of sympathy for their compatriots at other sites. They offered the lack of violence at Jebel Dhanna as the basis for this claim.[21] Another reason the British administration feared that the offshore and onshore strikes were connected was because the workers at ADMA and at ADPC made a similar series of demands.[22]

Onshore, at Jebel Dhanna, worker demands included a wage increase. They also demanded that locals be paid the same as other Arab employees, arguing for "equal pay for equal work." In addition, they said the oil company should hire local men for work currently done by expatriates.[23] At Das Island, worker demands were almost exactly the same as the demands at Jebel Dhanna, with a few key differences. First, at Das Island, there were more Indians and Pakistanis working in technical and managerial positions and, thus, the foreigners identified by the striking khaliji workers included not only Arabs from outside of the Arabian Peninsula but also Indians and Pakistanis.[24] The workers at Das Island, like Jebel Dhanna, also requested that all jobs be given to nationals and, going a step further, asked for educational programs in order to make this possible. Furthermore, they requested that three men be taken from the island, including an Indian doctor.

While workers demanded that local men be hired for jobs, their definition of local was informed by khaliji networks that moved across state boundaries and were not confined to the geographic boundaries established to facilitate oil concessions.²⁵ As Matthew MacLean demonstrates, in the 1950s and 1960s, subjects of the Trucial States moved on the scales of "trans-Gulf and Indian Ocean merchants, labor migration within the Gulf, and seasonal migration within the Trucial States."²⁶ These scales influenced events at Jebel Dhanna, where the strikes were attributed to the company's proposal to fire seven workers. However, only two of these workers were from Abu Dhabi. The most influential of the men the company wanted to fire were three Awamir from Hadhramaut, part of the Aden Protectorate.

Rumors were also circulating among workers, and these rumors spurred collective action perhaps as effectively as a coordinated effort by labor leaders.²⁷ For example, the precipitating event at Das Island may also have been the arrest of an Awamir employee who was stealing cars and joyriding them around the camp at night. A British manager apprehended the man, but as the manager spoke no Arabic, the employee was taken to the Arab affairs officer. Upon his release, the employee told his colleagues that, while in the UK camp, he was beaten by the Arab affairs officer, who was Lebanese.²⁸

As workers participated in collective action to protest management's actions and improve their working conditions, they invoked the sovereignty of the ruler of Abu Dhabi and questioned oil companies' control over oil projects. This was seen in negotiations, and initially, workers did not want to give their demands to company officials. At Tarif, workers refused to discuss their demands with company officials there and insisted that they would only speak with Sheikh Sultan, the son of Sheikh Shakhbut. Workers demanded to speak directly with the ruler or one of his sons was repeated at the other sites, and the workers at Das Island wanted to negotiate directly with another of the ruler's sons, Sheikh Said. Such appeals revealed the workers' understanding of the ruler as an advocate for their rights as well as the authoritative figure with regard to work negotiations. The prestige workers assigned to the ruler and members of the royal family was such that even representatives of the sheikh, if not actually related to the sheikh, were not always accepted as authorities. For example, a representative for Sheikh Sultan was unable to prevent the workers from striking at the Santa Fe camp.²⁹

Even after work at Jebel Dhanna resumed, workers remained resistant to the British government and oil companies, and they threatened management with violence. Workers also told managers that they would tell on the management to the sheikh, and Sheikh Shakhbut would then throw the managers out of the country. At times, workers conflated the British administration and the oil companies. During the strike at Jebel Dhanna, one worker told an Austrian manager, "You are not the boss now, we are the government here."[30] This statement draws attention to the ways workers saw oil companies to be connected to the British administration in Abu Dhabi while simultaneously refusing the legitimacy of the British administration as well as the oil company's authority.

TENSIONS AMONG THE LOCAL GOVERNMENT, THE BRITISH ADMINISTRATION, AND OIL COMPANIES

As they sought to resolve the 1963 strikes and anticipated future strikes, British administrators identified two different but interconnected problems that they believed hindered the quick ending of current strikes and opened the door to future of worker actions. First, it was hard for the government and company managers to control local workers, as workers did not recognize the authority of the British administration or companies. The British administration worried that the workers were overly susceptible to outside influences, such as pan-Arab movements, and oil companies feared these influences would destabilize the region and lead to a loss of oil revenues. The second problem, according to British officials, was the ineffective control of the ruler, Sheikh Shakhbut, over the population due to the ruler's unpopularity with the local workers in Abu Dhabi. As we will see, this perspective on the ruler's unpopularity allowed oil company managers and British officials to depoliticize workers' calls for political change. They did this by characterizing worker complaints as simply indicating dissatisfaction with the ruler and ignoring larger worker critiques of the political system and the British and oil companies' roles in that system. Laying the blame on Sheikh Shakhbut was particularly useful to oil company managers and British officials because they were unhappy with the ruler and his attitudes toward oil development, but they did not want to destabilize the monarchical rule as a political structure in Abu Dhabi and, more broadly, the Arabian Peninsula.

In the eyes of the British administration, the interconnected problems of outside influences and the ineffectiveness of Sheikh Shakhbut were illustrated by the strikes on Das Island. When laborers were leaving the island after the strike, British government officials reported that some of the men were going through the crowd disparaging the ruler and praising President Gamal Abdel Nasser of Egypt. The praise of Nasser was seen to critically undermine British control of Abu Dhabi as well as threaten British control of Abu Dhabi's oil. This was because of Nasser's close association, politically as well as in popular imagination, with pan-Arabism.[31] In addition, British administrators saw worker invocations of Nasser as undermining the power of Sheikh Shakhbut. One of the European managers rode on the boat back with the four hundred men and reported that "many of the men felt a genuine sense of grievance about their pay, but almost all were highly critical of Shakhbut, who, they said, was receiving a vast income from the oil and was doing nothing for them." These workers argued that a "new republic" should be established in Abu Dhabi.[32]

Instead of interpreting workers' request that a republic be established as a claim for democratic or representative governance, British officials and oil company managers used workers' requests for a republic as evidence that Sheikh Shakhbut lacked authority and legitimacy with the population, and therefore, he was unable to effectively rule Abu Dhabi. This interpretation elided questions concerning the form of governance raised by the striking workers and, instead, laid the issues specifically on the person of Sheikh Shakhbut. In reading the issues this way, both oil companies and the British administration insisted on seeing the strikes as a symptom of the ruler's unpopularity rather than as a broader critique of the managerial practices of the oil companies and British colonial governance. In addition, British officials and managers continued to see labor issues as specifically related to Sheikh Shakhbut, even though not all workers were thought to be unhappy with him. Indeed, according to company reports, many workers went along with the strike in order to voice grievances about labor conditions, treatment by oil management, or out of fear of being "beaten up" if they did not participate.

The British administration's characterization of Sheikh Shakhbut and, specifically, the ruler's lack of popularity must be situated within a larger context of relations among the ruler, the oil companies, and the British administration. Sheikh Shakhbut's relationships with the oil companies and the British administration had been fraught for decades prior to the 1963 strikes. When oil exploration first began in Abu Dhabi in 1939, Sheikh Shakhbut had been reluctant to participate and only entered into concession agreements after threats from the British administration.[33] As oil exploration continued,

Sheikh Shakhbut had also refused to take payment from Petroleum Development (Trucial Coast) for prospecting.[34] According to the British Residency, Sheikh Shakhbut had an "unreasonable attitude" toward oil companies, and the Trucial Coast's political agent regularly had to arbitrate disputes between the companies and the ruler.[35] Throughout his rule, Sheikh Shakhbut continued to challenge oil company operations. By the early 1960s, the relationship between Sheikh Shakhbut and the oil companies was in tatters, and from 1962 to 1964, the British government repeatedly attempted to remove Sheikh Shakhbut from power and put in place his brother, Sheikh Zayed bin Sultan al Nahyan.[36]

One key issue in the early 1960s was that Sheikh Shakhbut did not want to change the terms of Abu Dhabi's concession with British Petroleum (BP), much to the disappointment of the company. In particular, Sheikh Shakhbut was unwilling to enter into a fifty-fifty profit sharing agreement with the company. While, from 1949 to 1951, fifty-fifty profit sharing was a contentious issue between the Iranian government and the Anglo-Iranian Oil Company (AIOC),[37] these agreements were increasingly becoming the norm: The ruler of Saudi Arabia signed a fifty-fifty agreement with the Arabian American Oil Company (Aramco) in 1950, the ruler of Kuwait signed a fifty-fifty agreement with the Kuwait Oil Company (KOC) in 1951, and the ruler of Qatar signed a fifty-fifty agreement with Petroleum Development (Qatar) in 1952.[38] In contrast, Sheikh Shakhbut could not be persuaded to enter into such an agreement, even in the face of threats. For example, he was told that he must sign a fifty-fifty agreement so before receiving a much-needed loan.[39] As Abu Dhabi's oil production grew exponentially beginning in 1962,[40] fifty-fifty profit sharing would have provided six to seven times more income to Sheikh Shakhbut than the current agreement,[41] yet Sheikh Shakhbut continued to refuse such an arrangement.

Sheikh Shakhbut's refusal to accept a fifty-fifty profit sharing agreement was often seen by British officials and oil company managers as representative of his provincialism and misunderstanding of economics.[42] However, as seen in the critiques of Shakhbut recorded on the boat from Das Island after the strikes, Sheikh Shakhbut's reasons for refusing a fifty-fifty agreement most likely related to pressure from Abu Dhabi nationals over the income he received from oil companies. This issue came to a head when a BBC Arabic broadcast gave the impression that Sheikh Shakhbut's signing of a fifty-fifty profit-sharing agreement was a fait accompli. This radio report outraged

Sheikh Shakhbut. He was particularly upset by the part of the broadcast that described how wealthy he would become as oil production intensified:

> [Current plans for oil exports] would give the ruler of this Trucial state oil royalties of some 10 million pounds a year under the existing terms of the concessions, which provide effectively for the ruler to be paid one pound a ton. Once production has really got under way a renegotiation of the concessions to provide for the usual 50–50 profit-sharing agreement would increase the ruler's income still more.[43]

Sheikh Shakhbut was reportedly so distressed by this news story that he refused to have payments put into his accounts until the company corrected this reporting.[44] The reason for this distress, oil company managers believed, was that the ruler did not want his subjects reminded that under a fifty-fifty agreement his personal wealth would increase.[45]

Left unsaid in managers' analysis were the reasons the company would want to increase their payments to the ruler. While it may be thought that fifty-fifty profit sharing would reduce an oil company's profits, in reality the loss was offset by relief for overseas tax given by the US and British governments to oil companies.[46] Because of this tax break, it cost nothing to the oil companies, and in the 1950s and 1960s, they used profit sharing as a way to try to align the interests of local governments with their own. Oil company officials also believed that fifty-fifty agreements provided some protection against the growing movements for the nationalization of oil globally.[47]

THE IMPLEMENTATION OF SECURITY MEASURES

British administrators undermined Sheikh Shakhbut's leadership by arguing he was unpopular among the people and characterizing the ruler's response to the strikes as ineffective.[48] They also described the ruler as overly sympathetic with the striking workers and pointed to his reluctance to punish those who used violence during the strike.[49] As the strikes continued, the police were first used to try to control workers, and then British military action was taken. Following the strikes in May and June 1963, both the British administration and Sheikh Shakhbut agreed to invest in policing in hopes of ensuring that future strikes could be ended quickly and effectively.

Early in the days of the strikes at ADPC, Sir William Luce, the British political resident in Bahrain, met with the ruler to impress upon him that "his primary responsibility [was] to enforce law and order." Sir Luce attempted to clarify to the ruler the British government's position on the strikes. He told Sheikh Shakhbut that the "British were not concerned with industrial disputes between workers and their employers or with breaking strikes, but we were concerned with the security of lives and property of people under our jurisdiction who were working in his State." He continued that if the ruler was unable to maintain order, and British government officials "saw that the lives and property of those to whom we have an obligation were thereby imperiled, I should not hesitate to take such steps necessary to protect them." Sir Luce said that he was confident that Sheikh Shakhbut would take the appropriate action, and he believed having the British interfere in the matter would hurt the ruler's reputation and standing among the populace.[50]

Despite Sir Luce's report that his meeting had effectively galvanized Sheikh Shakhbut, after a few days of strikes, British officials were still dissatisfied with the ruler's response. Sheikh Shakhbut had been using his sons, Sheikh Sultan and Sheikh Said, to act as intermediaries with the workers, but British administrators believed these sons had little influence.[51] At Jebel Dhanna, officials claimed that Sheikh Sultan drank heavily during the strikes. The result was that workers, company managers, and British officials had to postpone meetings to discuss the workers' terms. For his part, the ruler's son was also displeased with the companies and accused them of blatantly ignoring laws established by the ruler.[52]

At the strikes on Das Island, Sheikh Said may have been more effective than his brother was at Jebel Dhanna. Sheikh Said arrived at Das Island after the ruler's representative there admitted he could not control the situation because the workers "regarded him as a company stooge."[53] Immediately upon arrival, Sheikh Said agreed to throw out the troublemakers. He also "mixed extensively with the workers during his stay on Das [Island]."[54] In order to resolve the strike on Das Island, Sheikh Said tried to send forty troublemakers back to Abu Dhabi City by ship. However, a number of other workers also wished to go, and when the ship eventually sailed, about four hundred workers, or two-thirds of the Arab workforce, left the island.[55] The result was a "wholesale withdrawal of local labor."[56] After the ship sailed, the island was quiet.[57] When the ship arrived in Abu Dhabi, the forty troublemakers were arrested and the remainder of the men returned quietly to their homes.⁵⁸ Over the course of the following few weeks, the majority of the workers returned to work on Das Island.⁵⁹

The ruler's response to the strikes on Das Island surprised the British administration because they thought Sheikh Shakhbut should deal strongly with the troublemakers. Instead, Sheikh Shakhbut released the forty men arrested for the strike, including those known to have committed violence. He also dismissed the strike as a minor affair and said that the company could have avoided the strike had it paid its workers more. Further surprising British officials, the ruler declined to arrest the troublemakers in Tarif.⁶⁰ When Sheikh Shakhbut encouraged the companies to raise wages, the British interpreted this as a simplistic and ineffective response, designed primarily to maintain his own popularity.⁶¹

According to the British administration and management of oil companies, the ineffectiveness of Sheikh Shakhbut was compounded by the inability and reluctance of the Abu Dhabi police to restore order.⁶² In part, the British claimed the Abu Dhabi police were ineffective because they lacked training and leadership.⁶³ They were also seen as identifying with the workers and supporting the workers' cause. At the Tarif strikes, the police "fraternised with the strikers, shaking hands and rubbing noses with them."⁶⁴ At Das Island, the police were completely absent during the strike, something the British attributed to police solidarity with the strikers.⁶⁵

Sheikh Shakhbut was reportedly "disturbed" by accounts of the unsatisfactory performance of his police force during the strikes; he had hoped the police would be more effective in controlling workers. As a result, in early July, Sheikh Shakhbut agreed to hire a Bahraini police officer to train Abu Dhabi's police force for three months, with particular attention to be paid to security duties.⁶⁶ In October 1963, in order to further improve the police force, the British administration proposed that a riot squad be trained and stationed near Jebel Dhanna. They also suggested that the police force's salaries and conditions of service be regularized.⁶⁷

Security measures were not limited to police intervention, and the military was also mobilized during the strike. In order to ensure effective protection of British property and persons, British administrators sent to the area two units of the Trucial Oman Scouts (TOS), a paramilitary security force under British government control.⁶⁸ The TOS were instructed to interfere only if the

Abu Dhabi police force "failed and the Europeans and other foreign nationals' lives are threatened." Specifically, the TOS were told not to stop the strikes, but rather "to guard each installation and to form a defended centre in each area, where European and other foreign national staff can take shelter if the police are overwhelmed."[69] The TOS also provided cover for planes to land at Tarif and Jebel Dhanna after striking workers blocked the roads to those sites.[70]

In addition to mobilizing the TOS, the British administration sent the HMS *Striker*, a ship in the British Royal Navy's Amphibious Warfare Squadron, to the vicinity of Das Island, but "out of sight of the Island." The *Striker* was to act as a backup in case the TOS lost control of the onshore situation. In anticipation of such an event, plans were drawn up for Sir Luce to order a landing party from the *Striker* onto the island.[71] Finally, company managers reported that a Scots Greys regiment of the British Army were waiting in reserve in case the strikes intensified.[72]

Through the mobilization of military and police forces, the British administration sought to develop a security apparatus to respond to strikes. This security apparatus circumvented the ruler's sovereignty over affairs internal to Abu Dhabi by arguing for the need to protect individuals under British jurisdiction and oil company property. The increased regularity with which strikes were characterized as threats to people and property points to the growing association between security and oil.

PROPOSED REFORMS AT OIL COMPANIES

In the early 1960s, reforms were suggested by the Abu Dhabi government, the British administration, and the oil companies. As they sought to improve labor relations, tensions continued among Sheikh Shakhbut, the oil companies were at odds with each other over some reforms, including training workers and pay. These issues show that oil companies were not monolithic actors, even when they were partially owned by the same parent company. Despite some differences, the oil companies did agree that the ruler should be discouraged from intervening in labor affairs and that the government should have more restrictive policies on strikes, similar to those put in place in Bahrain in the late 1950s. The result was that the power of the government to protect the rights of citizens was actively undermined through the logics of corporate efficiency and national security.

As oil companies suggested reforms, they were not always in agreement, and the different solutions put forward by ADPC and ADMA demonstrate the tensions between the two oil companies. Even though BP had an ownership stake in each of the companies, managers at each company actively sought to differentiate their company from the other. Disagreements between the companies increased as labor troubles continued into the late summer and early fall of 1963.[73] In response to continued worker unrest, ADPC announced a plan to give workers a second raise. The reason, according to ADPC managers was:

> The whole attitude of national labor had changed following the May strike. Discipline had deteriorated; the grievance procedure agreed with the authorities and published to all was completely ignored; contractors' employees were frequently refusing to work until their complaints, however minor, were remedied; and the general temper of labour was now very uncertain.

In this context, a raise to mitigate worker unrest was particularly needed, ADPC managers said, because oil operations were entering a "peak and vital phase" during which they required the maximum number of men on-site. Managers admitted there was "no positive information available to support the view that industrial unrest was imminent." Despite this, they feared that, "in view of the general atmosphere which now prevailed it was considered by all concerned that the probability of such unrest could no longer be ignored." Therefore, managers argued that "lack of immediate action on their part would almost inevitably lead to strike action on the mainland."[74]

While ADMA managers reported experiencing the same issues with their workers, ADMA managers were skeptical of ADPC's reasoning for giving workers a raise. Most importantly, they believed a raise for ADPC employees would cause unrest among ADMA employees.[75] In addition, ADMA managers feared ADPC plans to improve living conditions for workers and to provide training would also cause unrest among ADMA workers. For example, ADPC wanted to introduce air conditioning for all staff and labor, including Indian, Pakistani, and khaliji workers. ADMA believed that if ADPC implemented these changes, then ADMA would be forced to provide the same for its employees, and these changes, ADMA managers argued, would be enormously costly.[76]

Training was also important for both ADMA and ADPC, and both companies expressed a desire to "avoid the company developing into the usual pyramid with European technologists at the top, a broad band of Indian/Pakistani technicians and tradesmen in the supervisory and middle layers, and a large body of unskilled local labourers at the bottom."[77] However, attempts to coordinate training created further friction between the two companies. Given recent international events, including growing pan-Arab movements and movements to nationalize natural resources, ADMA managers argued that ADPC's proposed training scheme came from an earlier moment in oil operations. Reflecting on the changes in the oil industry from the 1930s to the 1960s, specifically, they argued ADPC managers were "living in the 'late [nineteen-] thirties' and that the sooner they come down to earth the better for all Persian Gulf Operators."[78] Such a perspective drew on BP's recent experiences with the nationalization of oil in Iran in the early 1950s and tensions at oil projects throughout the Arabian Peninsula in 1956 after Egypt was invaded by the British, French, and Israeli armies.

ADMA managers, therefore, argued against long-term training programs, and they explained this position was "partly in view of the unknown potential of the trainees and partly because of other factors—some of them political—which influenced Company's operations over the years."[79] Furthermore, ADMA managers characterized ADPC's proposed training scheme, which involved hundreds of workers participating in staged training for multiple years, as "grandiose," "unrealistic," and "uneconomic."[80] As the companies attempted to come to an agreement over worker training, tensions increased, and ADMA managers accused ADPC managers of not being open to joint consultation.[81]

Despite quarrels over wages and training, oil company managers agreed on multiple topics, including the importance of increased contracting for each company's operations, the need for restrictive labor laws, and that the ruler should play less of a role in labor relations. Contracting was also a focus of local merchant interest, and merchants put pressure on the ruler to encourage contracting with local companies. In response, in 1964, Sheikh Shakhbut issued a decree encouraging companies use local contractors for transportation. For their part, oil companies were happy to increase local contracting, because the companies saw contracting as advantageous to their operations, both providing cheaper services and helping improve relations between the oil companies and the local population.[82]

Given their agreement on the need for labor policies in Abu Dhabi that discouraged strikes, oil company managers met with the Abu Dhabi government and suggested restrictive policies about strikes that were similar to those put in place in Bahrain in the late 1950s. These policies included that employees must first give their complaints to the company and the ruler's representatives before going on strike, the police force should be bolstered so as to be more effective during strikes, striking workers should not be paid for the duration of their work stoppage, and the present warning system should be maintained.[83] The ruler agreed to all of these suggestions, but later reconsidered his agreement regarding the written warnings and asked the companies, only a few days later, to cease giving written warnings because they upset workers. The largest point of friction came when the companies said that they did not want to take back the men thought to be the leaders of the 1963 strikes. The ruler disagreed with the company position and argued these men should be taken back as a gesture of forgiveness. Finally, after much discussion, the ruler conceded that the companies must do what they thought was right, but that he remained convinced the companies should rehire the strike leaders.[84]

Importantly, the oil companies wanted the ruler to play a smaller role in arbitrating labor disputes. When representatives from ADPC and ADMA met with the ruler to discuss how to avoid future strikes, they wanted to be sure that security measures would be implemented, but they did not want to encourage Abu Dhabi government representatives, including Sheikh Said and Sheikh Sultan, to interfere in labor matters. Company managers believed that such interference was increasing and that this interference would adversely impact the ability of companies to discipline workers. Specifically, managers worried they would "lose the right of discharging personnel for misconduct or breaking company regulations as a result of such interference."[85] They were particularly concerned with not being able to fire local workers, who were mostly employed as laborers. By restricting the role of the ruler in strikes, companies reduced some of the efficacy of strikes by local workers, as the government had fewer legal resources to use to intervene in company practices and to protect citizens' rights.

NEW LABOR LAWS AND MIGRATION REGULATIONS

In 1966, two significant changes for labor relations occurred in Abu Dhabi: New labor laws were passed, and Sheikh Zayed, with support from the British government, including the British RAF and the TOS, removed Sheikh Shakhbut from power and became the ruler of Abu Dhabi.[86] Abdel Razzaq Takriti describes this change as a "colonial coup," or a change in the head of a government that was instigated by the colonial power with the goal of structural continuity and with little popular engagement.[87] In Abu Dhabi, it was not only the British administration who welcomed Sheikh Zayed; the oil companies were pleased as well. This was particularly the case because Sheikh Shakhbut had recently withdrawn his representative at ADMA. This meant that the company had to deal with labor issues by appeasement. However, "with the succession of Shaikh Zaid [Zayed] the Company was able to tighten up discipline and has henceforth refused to pay for days lost through strike action. Since Nov[ember] 1966 there has been no trouble."[88] Specifically, in the late 1960s, oil companies were able to, as they characterized it, "tighten discipline" as new labor laws were passed, the Labour Department opened in 1967, and migration regulations and work permits led to increased surveillance of foreign laborers.

Abu Dhabi's labor law was similar to the laws passed in other parts of the Arabian Peninsula. The law applied not only to nationals of the Trucial Coast or Muslims but to all workers in Abu Dhabi. However, the working conditions laid out in the law were basic, so much so, in fact, that the ADPC happily viewed them as "reasonable and simple," noting that "the Company's own regulations are more advanced" and that the new law lacked even provisions to ensure that workers had access to shade and drinking water.[89] The law also sided heavily with companies. It prohibited strikes and lockouts prior to the hearing of the case by a reconciliation committee, forbade violence to persons and property, and forbade workers in public utilities from striking "if such action will endanger public health, endanger life, or cause serious damage to property."[90] Having many similar provisions as the labor laws written in Bahrain in the late 1950s, these laws greatly reduced the power of collective worker action.

Not all Abu Dhabi government officials were pleased with the new labor laws, and they argued for additional protections for workers and unions. Some of these issues had been debated since the early 1960s. For example, following the strikes in 1963, Director of Labour Sayyid A. Hijazi had proposed changes to labor practices in Abu Dhabi. He advocated that Abu Dhabi join the International Labor Organization and for the government to provide labor education to inform workers of their rights, recognize trade unions, open more labor offices in the oil fields, and set up a Department of Social Affairs.[91] The British administration objected to these reforms. In particular, the British administration argued that these reforms would open Abu Dhabi to disruptive outside influences, such as pan-Arab groups.

In 1967, unions continued to be a topic of debate between the Abu Dhabi government and the British administration. In conversations with Sayid Hassan Jumaa, a high-ranking Abu Dhabi government employee, a British administrator elaborated what he understood to be the problems with trade unions and the reasons that Arab nations "had never had the ability" to develop industrial movements. First, the British official argued, trade unions had become the only civilian institution with political significance. This was because, according to British administrators, Arab countries were unable to "evolve" adequate political institutions. Second, he argued, "in the traditional evolutionary Arab states, it was difficult for trade unions to develop on Western European lines because industry was either relatively unimportant to national security or it was all-important." Third, Arab nations were "paternalist in nature," meaning that they protected the rights of workers without workers themselves having to agitate for changes. Finally, given the "the lack of developed political institutions and the banning in many countries of political groups opposed to the ruling regime, the trade unions became a target for infiltration by political forces seeking some form of expression." When asked if the Abu Dhabi government should try to help develop unions, the administrator insisted that the change must happen slowly. The administrator argued that "there was certainly no case for formation of trade unions in a primitive society such as existed in Abu Dhabi." A better solution, according to this administrator, was a system of joint consultative committees for the oil industry, such as the ones in Qatar, where the oil companies and the government could influence the leadership of committees.[92]

An additional site of disagreement between British administers and the Abu Dhabi government was around wage levels. The new labor law allowed the Department of Labour to regulate minimum wages, but a year after the law's drafting, this still had not happened. An even larger problem regarding wages was that the government had recently issued a schedule of grades and salaries for government employment. The oil companies, in particular, feared that this would cause all wages in the country to rise. Instead of the government raising wages, British officials recommended the government focus on the distribution of oil wealth to nationals, and specifically, officials suggested that the Abu Dhabi government adopt a family allowances scheme.[93] Abu Dhabi government officials disagreed with this advice, insisting that "the worker in Abu Dhabi should benefit through increased wages in the growing prosperity of the town" and that, as the town developed, the average worker would need more money to enjoy these new amenities.[94] Abu Dhabi government officials also objected to the family allowances scheme on the grounds that it would improve the working conditions of nationals but would do nothing to help the large foreign workforce in the country.

Two areas the Abu Dhabi government and the British cooperated on were how to handle illegal immigration and the regulation of work permits. Given Abu Dhabi's rapidly growing economy, British officials believed that these two issues were critical. The British feared that as wages increased, so too would illegal immigration, and they worried that illegal immigration would lead to political instability.[95] Abu Dhabians did not want to take jobs as unskilled workers and preferred more prestigious jobs, such as truck driving and working on the oil rigs. Large contractors were thus forced to hire foreigners to take these jobs and would even send "a truck to the town with the foreman" to get extra laborers if needed. The ruler drew up a law concerning foreigners, but they had to wait to implement it until the political resident in Bahrain offered his suggestions.

Closely related to the issue of illegal immigration, according to British officials, was the need to better regulate work permits. The regulation of work permits points to differing engagements with labor and citizenship. The director of labor issued permits to nationals regardless of skill (red permits) and to all foreigners working in skilled or executive posts (blue permits), but no permits were issued to unskilled foreigners. For the British administrators, not giving permits to unskilled foreigners was a potential source of trouble, because it meant that unskilled laborers could evade government surveillance and control. Increased oversight of unskilled foreigners, according to British government officials, diminished the risks of internal political subversion. British officials tried to encourage the issuing of work permits to all workers by arguing that doing so would be beneficial to nationals. Permits, according to the British, ensured nationals "benefitted as much as possible from the development at hand" by not losing jobs to unskilled foreigners.[96] However, considering most nationals increasingly refused unskilled labor positions, this seems largely incongruous.

OIL NATIONALIZATION AND INCREASED CONTRACTING

In the late 1960s, oil production was rapidly growing, and in 1967, Abu Dhabi joined OPEC. By 1968, Abu Dhabi became the fourth largest producer of oil in the Middle East after Saudi Arabia, Iran, and Kuwait, and oil income in Abu Dhabi was £68.6 million.[97] As oil company managers watched the growing trend internationally toward nationalization, they believed it was only a matter of time before almost all oil projects globally were nationalized.[98] Oil companies responded to threats of nationalization through increasing the practice of contracting. The benefits of contracting, for oil companies, was that it displaced risks associated with nationalization onto multiple companies. However, contracting had negative consequences for workers, and the process of depoliticizing the oil fields was further advanced as contracting accelerated.

As increasing numbers of countries nationalized natural resources, oil company boards sought to maximize profits while minimizing financial investment. Regarding expropriation, one manager reflected, "All you can do is to try and make a deal that permits you to do business in the country on a different scale, a different basis of operation. There's not much you can do that's permissible. All you can hope for is a reasonable recompense."[99] In some areas, oil companies had trouble receiving compensation for nationalized oil projects and infrastructure. For example, when Sri Lanka nationalized all oil projects in 1961, California Texas Oil Company (Caltex) only received compensation for its refineries and other investments after "outside governments brought pressure on the Ceylonese." However, in Bahrain, Qatar, and the Trucial States, oil company managers believed that local governments would compensate them when this occurred. One manager said, "If a government is reasonable—and many of the Middle East governments are—they will compensate the company in a fairly reasonable way when they expropriate."[100] Many managers believed that this was because Middle Eastern governments wanted to continue working with international oil companies. The US government took a similar perspective on OPEC, and according to Nathan Citino, in the late 1950s, the US government saw OPEC as a way member states attempted to get better terms and more money from the oil companies, not stop the export of oil. In addition, "the desire for increased revenue and competition for markets also gave OPEC members strong incentives to exceed production ceilings and to renege on prorating agreements."[101] Ultimately, concerning nationalization, companies said they found it easiest to "simply meet these crises as they occurred," which managers argued was the "most realistic way to handle" such events.[102] At the same time, companies implemented practices, like increased contracting, to mitigate potential loses.

Fearing the nationalization of oil in Abu Dhabi, in 1967 ADMA began a reorganization in which the bulk of its activities, including the management of labor, would be performed by contractors. To explain this shift, one manager wrote:

> For reasons well known to all it is now commonplace of the oil industry, in the Middle East as elsewhere, for companies themselves to carry out only those parts of their operations which are central to the business of finding, producing, processing and exporting oil; all other services are sought from contractors specializing in different spheres of support activity. How far this process can be pushed depends strictly on the variety and performance standards of contractors able and willing to put in economic bids in the geographical areas concerned. It is to be noted that the contractability of a particular activity has no necessary connection with its "importance," or its "basic" or "non-basic" nature; for example, drilling is "basic" enough, but is now contracted out to a degree which would have been regarded as impossible in the Middle East twenty years ago.... At present time, about 80% of the 1,233 operating personnel of ADMA are engaged in spheres in which contractors in the Arabian Gulf are prepared to bid.[103]

The benefits of this change, managers argued, was "simplification, leading to a widening of responsibilities at all levels, to the minimization of unnecessary demarcation between jobs and to the creation of unimpeded career lines."[104] Furthermore, ADMA would retain "firm control and a power of veto over all structures erected on the Island, and all service facilities (shops, travel agents, social amenities) set up by contractors."[105] Thus, ADMA would retain control, but contracting would simultaneously decrease company responsibility. As one manager wrote, "too great a degree of control by the company would defeat the aims of the method, while too little would render it vulnerable to Government pressure in the event of a dispute."[106] Finally, contracting would lower costs, as contractors paid less, on average, than oil companies did for daily paid employees.[107]

The British government characterized ADMA's shift as "a major policy change in going over to contracting, as opposed to the present system of direct labour." And British officials assumed that ADMA, "like other oil companies . . . is worried about the political situation and the possibility of increasing nationalist pressure." For labor, the benefit of the proposed contracting scheme, from the British government's perspective, was that the company "will insist on identical conditions between their employees and contractors, who will often be working side by side." However, British officials did admit that contracting had some negative consequences for workers. For example, ADMA would no longer train workers and would close its current training operations. In addition, ADMA would not ensure that nationals would be hired by contractors—a potential issue from the government's perspective since "a pool of unemployed Bedouin labour is said to be building up gradually at Tarif."[108]

Ultimately, British government officials expected ADMA would "squeeze out redundant men and unproductive elements during the operation," and they believed the company preferred contractors to do this because of recent "hard experiences" by BP and Iraq Petroleum Company in Syria and Iraq.[109] In the end, the reorganized ADMA would have only a small headquarters based in Abu Dhabi City, with twenty-four British senior staff and thirty-three training and clerical staff, plus a handful of tradesmen, all from India and Pakistan.[110] This reorganization was seen as cost effective because Indian and Pakistani workers were paid less than khalijis.[111] This also helped reduce the efficacy of strikes because, like we saw at oil projects in Aden and Kuwait in the 1950s, if Indian and Pakistani workers went on strike, then they could be fired, deported quickly, and easily replaced.

CONCLUSION

Avoiding strikes was a central concern of the British administration, particularly as contracting created additional tensions with workers. In the mid-1960s, some British commentators complained that the British only controlled 35 percent of the Middle East's oil but paid for 100 percent of the defense forces in the region. Moreover, critics argued, paying for these defense forces contributed a significant amount to the British balance of payments deficit.[112] Despite these arguments, in the late 1960s, the British administration took an increasingly militarized approach to strikes, but there were divisions within the government concerning this stance. In one note, the political agent in the Trucial States wrote that things currently were calm, but "looking at our file, however, I am alarmed to see the immense amount of correspondence on military networks suggesting almost a major campaign. It is of course always possible that trouble will blow up again but at present all is quiet, largely through our policy of 'playing it cool.'"[113]

"Playing it cool" was not agreed upon politically, particularly by members of the British Conservative Party. When Conservative Party politician Alexander Lloyd visited the Trucial Coast, the commander of the Abu Dhabi Defense Force met with him and painted a "gloomy picture" that the Trucial States would soon face a similar situation to that in Aden, where nationalist forces fought for independence from British colonialism from 1963 until the British withdrawal in 1967. Lloyd took these concerns seriously, and he explicitly connected worker strikes to political revolutions in his conversation with the political agent. In this conversation, Lloyd argued that there was "too much leniency towards wage claims etc. . . . On internal security he said the Trucial States were wide open and there was only one good policeman in all of the Trucial States."[114] In response to those who wanted to build the British military presence in the region, the political agent replied that he did not think it would be effective: "There must be a clear distinction between matters within our control and matters outside of it. If Nasser or another trouble-maker was determined to start terrorism in the Trucial States he could and would certainly do so whether or not we had a military presence in Sharjah to serve as an excuse."[115] Thus, labor relations and statecraft were contested and debated among British administrators, Abu Dhabi governmental employees, and oil company managers. However, as security and oil became increasingly associated, responses to strikes increasingly used military or police intervention. Militarization, in conjunction with contracting, labor laws, and employment policies that removed workers' ability to make effective claims, dealt severe blows to the political possibilities that oil worker strikes held.

Conclusion
DEPOLITICIZING LABOR

IN 1971, THE BRITISH GOVERNMENT ENDED ITS FORMAL ROLE IN governance in the Arabian Peninsula. At that same time, however, oil was increasingly seen by government administrators as critical to the British economy. With the Americans in Saudi Arabia, many British administrators saw the benefits of maintaining a relationship with regional rulers, but they cautioned that the relationship would be difficult to continue without Britain offering help to the countries of Arabian Peninsula. Many British administrators urged their government to do so. They specified that the importance of the Arabian Peninsula was not limited to its production of oil. Using newfound oil wealth, merchants imported large amounts of British goods.[1] In the late 1960s and early 1970s, British market share in the Arabian Peninsula fluctuated between 25 percent and 35 percent. Military goods were a particularly lucrative area of trade. For example, in 1968, British exports to Qatar were estimated to be £7.1 million and in 1969 they were £5.5 million, excluding defense contracts. Defense contracts were lucrative for the British government and, in 1969, £19.5 million in British contracts—in power and gas, and arms supplied—were signed with the Qatari government.[2]

These contracts, along with the increasing consistency of responding to strikes with military force, reflect what Michael Watts calls the "economization of security" or the "control of strategic natural resources as an explicit part of security policy."[3] As oil was discursively tied to security for the US and British governments, work stoppages were understood to have global consequences for both the nation-state and industry. One place we see this is in Bahrain. While Bahrain had relatively small oil reserves, interruptions in Bahrain Petroleum Company's (Bapco) operations were seen to have an impact on local politics in the Arabian Sea and globally.[4] Not only would interruptions harm the Bahraini government, but places in Asia, including India, were large markets for refined petroleum from the Bapco refinery, which refined oil from Saudi Arabia, Bahrain, and (after the coup that removed Mosaddegh from power) Iran.[5] Even after refineries were built in Asia, ports in Bahrain continued to be place from where Saudi crude was shipped.[6] According to oil company directors, refineries were also the key to maintaining a foothold in various areas as countries nationalized oil.[7]

In addition, oil refined at Bapco's refinery in Bahrain became increasingly central to the US military, particularly during the Vietnam War, when the refinery was a key source of jet fuel. The fact that Bapco's refinery produced jet fuel was critically important for the United States and, particularly, US military activity in Asia. During World War II, California Texas Oil Company (Caltex) had taken a loan from the Reconstruction Finance Corporation, a US government agency, to restructure the refinery to produce jet fuel.[8] After the war, there was no buyer for jet fuel from the Bapco refinery, and the company was forced to renegotiate the contract.[9] A market for jet fuel subsequently opened with the Vietnam War, when the Bapco refinery began to supply the US armed forces.[10] However, in 1967 and in 1973, US support for Israel meant that "the image of America in the Arab countries had reached a new low."[11] Bapco's refinery almost shut down as workers protested supplying oil to US and British interests. At that time, it was only through coordination between the ruler of Bahrain and Bapco managers that oil continued to be supplied to the US armed forces.[12]

The British administration assumed that the failure or success of the postcolonial countries on the Arabian Peninsula would impact the British, but that this fate was largely out of British hands. Still, there was disagreement in the British administration regarding the best path for the new countries of the Arabian Peninsula. Some felt the success of these countries would be dependent upon their moving toward a new, representative form of government, with educated khaliji Arabs taking roles in government administration. From the British perspective, the problem with moving toward a more representative form of government was that the families of the local rulers were drawing considerable allowances from oil revenues, and thus ruling families were loath to accept the need for shifting governmental forms.

Not all British officials agreed on the need for a more representative government, however; indeed, many British officials argued that a sheikhly government would be most amicable to post-1971 British interests.[13] Maintaining a good environment for British economic interests was uncertain given the rising number of foreigners in the region and the growing number of foreigners staffing the government. For example, in Qatar, the bulk of the ministries and departments of government were staffed by expatriates from other countries of the Arab world, with Palestinians being the most prevalent nationality in the government. These Arab expatriates were seen to be destabilizing and potentially subversive to the governments of the Arabian Peninsula.[14] Tied up with the question of government staffing and expatriates were strikes and other worker actions oil projects. As managers and government officials sought to manage competing pressures and maintain stability, the rights of workers were limited; nationals were employed mainly in government positions; and the ability of foreigners to own companies and property was constricted.

THE NATIONALIZATION OF OIL

In 1960, Iran, Iraq, Kuwait, Saudi Arabia, and Venezuela founded OPEC. Qatar joined OPEC in 1961 and Abu Dhabi in 1967. OPEC's goals were to coordinate oil policy among member states and the "determination of the best means for safeguarding the interests of member countries individually and collectively."[15] In 1974, many countries on the Arabian Peninsula nationalized part or all of the oil industry: Kuwait and Qatar took 60 percent participation in 1974 and full participation in 1975; the United Arab Emirates (of which Abu Dhabi was now a part) took 60 percent participation in 1974; and Saudi Arabia took 60 percent participation in 1974 and "settled the terms of full nationalization" in 1976.[16] Building upon recent trends in contracting, the major oil companies, themselves, became contractors, hired by states for their services.[17] As we saw, both in oral histories with California Texas Oil Company (Caltex) managers and in letters written by managers at British Petroleum (BP), the oil companies had foreseen this change and had, in turn, increased contracting themselves so as to minimize risk and ensure continued profits.

Oil companies were also able to recover much of the profits lost during nationalization through tax credits in the US and UK.[18]

These changes led to greater profits for the oil-producing countries of the Arabian Peninsula. For example, in Qatar in 1969, three oil companies had concessions. Two of these companies produced approximately nineteen million tons of crude, and oil revenues were approximately £50 million per year.[19] The third company, Qatar Oil Company (Japan), was granted a concession that included a fifty-fifty profit-sharing agreement in 1969, and the company discovered oil in 1971 offshore at Sharwa Island. However, the government was extending its control of the oil industry, and in 1968, the National Oil Development Company acquired the plant and local marketing. It was succeeded by Qatar National Petroleum Company, which the government established in April 1972 to carry out operations in all phases of the petroleum industry. The Tehran Agreement, an agreement between oil companies and the governments of the oil producing countries of the Persian Gulf signed on February 17, 1971, increased the consolidated tax rate for crude exports. Instead of fifty-fifty profit sharing, this agreement meant countries were to receive 55 percent of the profits and oil companies 45 percent. As a result, the Qatari government's revenue was US$198 million in 1971, an increase of 62 percent over 1970. In 1972, taxes again increased, and the Qatari government's profit was estimated at US$242 million. Finally, following a tax increase in 1973, the Qatari government took in revenues of US$2 billion in 1974.[20] Qatar was not unique, and all of the oil-producing countries of the Arabian Peninsula made record profits.

PRECARIOUS LABOR

As oil generated astronomical profits for companies and governments, oil projects grew, and additional manpower was needed. As a result, increasing numbers of Indians and Pakistanis moved to work in the Arabian Peninsula. By 1975, few khaliji workers were employed as laborers, and most laboring positions in the Arabian Peninsula were held by workers from India and Pakistan. Looking to the future, employers and government officials believed that businesses would continue to rely on workers from the subcontinent to staff projects.[21]

By encouraging local governments to hire citizens for positions in government and by hiring more foreign employees for oil projects, oil companies were better able to control their workforces. Furthermore, by encouraging the development of the *kafala* or sponsorship system, oil companies increased workers' dependency on companies and disenfranchisement in terms of their ability to mobilize for better worker conditions. In addition, the British administration, oil companies, and local governments sought to keep the countries of the Arabian Peninsula stable by ensuring the rest of the population was content. This included making sure that politically influential merchants were happy and that the rulers made concessions to them in order to legitimate and secure their authority within the territory.[22]

The practices that began in the 1940s and were codified in the 1950s and 1960s are still used today in the Arabian Peninsula. Almost all manual labor at oil projects is performed by people from South Asia or the Philippines. Indian and Pakistani men who wish to legally emigrate must receive permission from their governments, and the same system used to move indentured workers in the nineteenth century and to replace unruly workers at oil projects in the mid-twentieth century is still used. For many migrant laborers, the emigration process requires that they take out large loans at high interest rates. While working in the Arabian Peninsula, workers continue to live in camps organized by their nationality, and these camps are far from city centers. Labor laws also continue to favor employers, and strikes and unions are illegal.

Oil companies and the British administration thus worked together to create the so-called traditional labor practices of the Arabian Peninsula. Rather than unchanging traditions, contemporary labor practices are made to appear traditional through powerful narratives about the region and a complex set of historical relationships. Through military force, contracts, the setting of geographic boundaries, writing labor laws, and responses to worker actions, the Arabian Peninsula was fashioned to facilitate oil production. In this book, we have seen that the Arabian Peninsula was a central site where governance, labor management, and imperialism met. In a context of anticolonial activism and Cold War politics, oil extraction was structured by companies and governments as they tried to manage potential disruptions. Citizenship became a key factor in the effectiveness of strikes. The forms of governance and management practices that were implemented at oil projects during the twentieth century were best suited to working with foreigners whose recourse to government support was tenuous. This merging of managerial practice, growing nationalism, and governmental style provided the foundation for the current labor hierarchies prevalent in the Arabian Sea's oil industry, and the rights of individuals were made secondary to the security of the nation-state.

Notes

Oil Companies and Major Contractors

1. The American Oil Company was formerly Standard Oil of Indiana and later became part of BP.

2. Conoco later merged with Phillips Petroleum Company to form ConocoPhillips.

3. A subsidiary of Superior Oil, IMOC was given the first offshore oil concession in Qatar in 1949, but the company withdrew in 1952.

4. In 1932, PAT sold its foreign holdings to Jersey Standard.

Introduction

1. Ferrier, *History of the British Petroleum Company*, Vol. 1, 323; Jacks, "Purchase of the British Government's Shares," 139; Sampson, *Seven Sisters*, 56; UNT OH 0668: Interview with Murdo MacIver by Dr. Ronald Marcello, (Ridgefield Connecticut: November 9, 1985).

2. Today, all of Bahrain's onshore oil reserves, 125 million barrels, is located in the Awali field. Bahrain's offshore oil is located in the Abu Safah field, which is jointly shared with Saudi Arabia.

3. Bapco was "incorporated in Ontario, Canada, on the 11th January 1929 by the Standard Oil Company of California to carry on 'oil business' in the Persian Gulf. Its authorized capital is $500,000 in 5,000 shares of a par value of $100, and its Head Office is at Ottawa." BP ARC123142: APOC and Bahrain Petro Company 1925–1933. Initially, Gulf Oil (Gulf) held the Bahrain concession, but Gulf found out that holding the concession violated the terms of the Red Line Agreement, which Gulf had

signed. Gulf then sold the concession to SoCal. UNT OH 0659: Interview with Leslie A. Smith by Dr. Ronald E. Marcello (Greenville, South Carolina: August 1, 1985).

4. In 1937, Standard Oil Company of California (SoCal) and the Texas Company (today Texaco), jointly created the California Texas Oil Company (Caltex). Bapco was a wholly owned subsidiary of Caltex until 1981, when 60 percent of the company was acquired by the Bahraini government. In 1997, the Bahraini government assumed total ownership of Bapco. Later, SoCal became Chevron, then Chevron Texaco, and then Chevron.

5. UNT OH 0659: Interview with Smith.

6. Kinninmont, "Bahrain," 35.

7. HIA McConnell, Box 1, Folder 6: Journal Entry, February 16, 1939.

8. Fuccaro, *Histories of the City and State in the Persian Gulf*, 151–52.

9. Beinin, *Workers and Peasants*, 96.

10. Bradley, "Indian Workers' Great One Day Strike." For more on strikes in India in the 1930s, see Chakrabarty, "Conditions for Knowledge of Working-Class Conditions." Note that British India, or simply "India" prior to 1947, refers to much of the area today known as India, Pakistan, and Bangladesh. Prior to 1937, British India also included Myanmar, which the British called Burma.

11. Crowther, *Analysis of Strikes in 1938*.

12. Office for National Statistics, "History of Strikes in the UK."

13. NAI, MEA, Near East Branch, 1941, F 360-N/41: Annual Report of the Bahrain Petroleum Co. Ltd. 1940.

14. Seccombe and Lawless, "Foreign Worker Dependence in the Gulf," 564–65.

15. Kinninmont, "Bahrain," 35.

16. Kinninmont, "Bahrain," 36–37.

17. Gupta and Ferguson, "Beyond 'Culture,'" 16–17; Lowe, *Intimacies of Four Continents*, 7.

18. For a discussion of indentured labor from India, see Bates, "Coerced and Migrant Labourers in India"; Carter, *Servants, Sirdars, and Settlers*; Kale, *Fragments of Empire*; Metcalf, *Ideologies of the Raj*, 136–44; Yang, *Limited Raj*.

19. Report by J. B. Howes, Assistant Political Agent Bahrain, 21 December 1938, FO 1016–56, in RE (8), 642.

20. Lorimer, *Gazetteer of the Persian Gulf*.

21. Confidential dispatch No. 1/41 from Sir S. Crawford, Political Resident, Bahrain, to Mr. D. J. McCarthy, Arabian Department, Foreign and Commonwealth Office, 14 April 1969, FCO8/1146, in RQ (3), 9; Board of Trade, 28 June 1928, Oil Interests in the Persian Gulf, IOR:L/PS/18/B413, in RE (7), 769.

22. Note, *tradesmen* is used in this book to describe the category of work that was historically called "artisan" or "artisanal." In addition, *tradesmen* calls attention to

the fact that all of the workers discussed in this book were men. Indian women did migrate during this time, but usually with family members. For a discussion of women's migration to the Arabian Peninsula in the 1950s and 1960s, see Wright, "'The Immoral Traffic in Women.'"

23. Letter to British Political Agency, Doha, from RHM Boyle, 7 April 1969, FCO8/1146, in RQ (3), 7–11.

24. Review of Events in Qatar, 29 December 1969, in RQ (3), 23–33.

25. Coronil and Skurski, "Dismembering and Remembering," 289.

26. Guha, "Prose of Counter-Insurgency"; Guha, "Small Voice of History." See also Prakash, "Subaltern Studies as Postcolonial Criticism."

27. Amin, *Event, Metaphor, Memory*; Amin, "Gandhi as Mahatma"; Chakrabarty, "Conditions for Knowledge of Working-Class Conditions," 229; Chakrabarty, *Rethinking Working-Class History*.

28. Stephan Palmié points out that the writing of history is an exercise in power. Western modernity "ultimately rests on a fortiori logic that unfolded—and continues to unfold—not on the basis of any transhistorical first principles, but through the global realities of power that it both reflects and reproduces into its own narrative structures or dispelling them into the realm of the irrelevant, mistaken, unreal, or fictitious." Palmié, *Wizards and Scientists*, 16. See also Coronil, *Fernando Coronil Reader*; Trouillot, *Silencing the Past*.

29. Cohen and Odhiambo, *Risks of Knowledge*, xi. This book is also informed by Chandra Bhimull's anthro/historical approach and the multiple ways she engages with short-lived or scarce moments in the archive. Bhimull, *Empire in the Air*, 84–90.

30. Amin, *Event, Metaphor, Memory*; Eley, "Transnational Labour History"; Eley, *A Crooked Line*; Guha, "Small Voice of History," 1, 8; Trouillot, *Silencing the Past*.

31. For a discussion of contemporary connections among the countries of the Arabian Peninsula, Middle Eastern economics, and global capitalism, see Hanieh, *Money, Markets, and Monarchies*.

32. As Nicos Poulantzas stresses, "Social class is defined by its place in the ensemble of social practices, i.e., by its place in the ensemble of the division of labour which includes political and ideological relations." In addition, classes only exist as part of class struggle. However, Poulantzas cautions, we should avoid "the 'voluntarist' error of reducing class determination to class position." Poulantzas, *Poulantzas Reader*, 186.

33. For examinations of ideas and practices circulating throughout the Arabian Sea, see Alam, *Languages of Political Islam*; Bishara, *Sea of Debt*; Cole, *Sacred Space and Holy War*; Cole, *Roots of North Indian Shī'ism*; Ghosh, *In an Antique Land*; Hegland, "Shi'a Women's Rituals"; Jalal, *Partisans of Allah*; Majchrowicz, *World in*

Words; Metcalf, *Islamic Revival in British India*; Metcalf, *Islamic Contestations*; Minault, *Khilafat Movement*; Zaman, *Ulama in Contemporary Islam*.

34. Mir, *Social Space of Language*, 139.

35. Such changes are not unique to the Arabian Peninsula, and in Iraq we see these interactions to shape urban space and understandings of ethnicity. Bet-Shlimon, *City of Black Gold*.

36. See, for example, Karl, "Creating Asia."

37. Balibar and Wallerstein, *Race, Nation, Class*, 54; Tilly, "States and Nationalism in Europe"133, 142–43.

38. Ehsani, "Disappearing the Workers," 18, 25.

39. Watts, "Resource Curse?," 53; Watts, "Righteous Oil?," 375–77.

40. Martin-Amouroux, "World Energy Consumption."

41. Our World in Data, Energy Institute, https://ourworldindata.org/grapher/oil-production-by-country.

42. Watts, "A Tale of Two Gulfs," 439.

43. Vitalis, *Oilcraft*; Mitchell, "Ten Propositions on Oil."

44. Mitchell, *Rule of Experts*, 74.

45. Rose, *Powers of Freedom*, 102.

46. HIA McConnell, Box 1, Folder 6: Journal Entry, February 16, 1939.

47. For example, see Davidson, *Abu Dhabi*, 2.

48. For example, in 1965, oil made up 97 percent of the Saudi Arabia's, Kuwait's, and Qatar's total exports. Rouhani, *History of O.P.E.C.*, 107.

49. Mahdavy, "Patterns and Problems," 432, 437.

50. Mitchell, "Carbon Democracy," 408; Mitchell, *Carbon Democracy*, 5–8, 21. See also Daniel Yergin's discussion of pipeline development in the 1860s in the United States as a way of moving oil that was not be easily interrupted by striking workers. Yergin, *The Prize*, 16–18.

51. Mitchell, *Carbon Democracy*, 35–36, 105–8.

52. Vitalis, *America's Kingdom*.

53. For example, Das Gupta shows that racism in colonial industrial projects informed working conditions and management policies. Das Gupta, *Labour and Working Class*, 63–64.

54. Robinson, *Black Marxism*, 24; Coronil, *Magical State*.

55. Pandey, "Racialization of Subaltern Populations," 89.

56. Naoroji, *Poverty and Un-British Rule*; Dutt, *Economic History of India*; Patnaik, "Revisiting the 'Drain.'"

57. Rodney, *How Europe Underdeveloped Africa*.

58. Coronil, *Magical State*, 33–35, 45; Mitchell, *Rule of Experts*, 16; Wang, *End of the Revolution*, 62.

59. Coronil, *Magical State*, 34, 45, 388; See also Tsing, "What Is Emerging?," 335.

60. Mongia, "Race, Nationality, Mobility," 535.

61. Pandey, "Racialization of Subaltern Populations." According to Benedict Anderson, one of the paradoxes of the nation is "the objective modernity of nations to the historian's eye vs. their subjective antiquity in the eyes of nationalists." Anderson, *Imagined Communities*, 5.

62. Malkki, "National Geographic"; Sanjek, "Rethinking Migration, Ancient to Future."

63. NAI, MEA, Emigration Section, 1953, F.6–6/53-Emi: Oil Companies in the Persian-Gulf and Mid-East—Recruit of Indian workers from India.

64. NAI, MEA, Emigration, F. 22–8/48-Emi: Skilled workers engaged by the Bahrein [sic] Petroleum Co., Bahrein.

65. Hall, *Fateful Triangle*, 98.

66. Brown, *States of Injury*, 52–76.

Chapter 1

1. Abrahamian, "Strengths and Weaknesses of the Labor Movement in Iran," 181, 186, 197.

2. Eventually, the Iranian military and Tudeh Party leaders ended the strike. IOR/L/PS/12/3769A: Coll 20/52(3) Persian Gulf Diaries: Bahrain Intelligence Summaries 1946: No. 24 of 1947; BP ARC118823: Lessons of 1946: An essay on the Personnel Problems of the Oil Industry in South Iran, by Donald MacNeill, 1949.

3. Mitchell, *Carbon Democracy*; Ladjevardi, *Labor Unions and Autocracy in Iran*.

4. Abrahamian, *Iran Between Two Revolutions*.

5. NAI, MEA, Middle East Branch [ME], 1946, 10-(91)-ME/46: Thomas letter to General Headquarters, 10 July 1946.

6. Petersen, *Middle East between the Great Powers*, 19.

7. Abrahamian, "1953 Coup in Iran," 185.

8. See, for example, Anderson, *Imagined Communities*; Eley and Suny, "Introduction." In the case of places under imperial or colonial control, nationalist leaders often used the notion that a place was different from the West as a way of defining national identity. Chatterjee, *Nation and Its Fragments*, 3–13.

9. Lerner, *Passing of Traditional Society*, 19–42.

10. Khalidi, *Resurrecting Empire*, 83; Yergin, *The Prize*, 139–40.

11. A notable example of this was the battle between business magnate John D. Rockefeller and President Theodore Roosevelt. This led to a Supreme Court decision in 1911 that forced Rockefeller's company, Standard Oil, to dissolve into thirty-four separate companies. See Nersesian, *Energy for the 21st Century*, 133.

12. Ferrier, *History of the British Petroleum Company*, Vol. 1, 165, 190.

13. This argument was not compelling to the government of India, which declined to undertake a long-term contract with the British government for APOC's oil. Jacks, "Purchase of the British Government's Shares," 143, 156.

14. Jacks, "Purchase of the British Government's Shares," 141–43, 161; Sampson, *Seven Sisters*, 54–55.

15. Ferrier, *History of the British Petroleum Company*, Vol. 1, 179. Shell was formed in 1907 through the merger of Royal Dutch Petroleum Company of the Netherlands and the "Shell" Transport and Trading Company of the United Kingdom.

16. Royal Dutch Shell was owned 60 percent by the Dutch and 40 percent by the British, but the company was registered and domiciled in London and considered itself a British company. The British government considered Shell a Dutch one. Nersesian, *Energy for the 21st Century*, 147.

17. Ferrier, *History of the British Petroleum Company*, Vol. 1, 195–202, 289; Jacks, "Purchase of the British Government's Shares," 162; Sampson, *Seven Sisters*, 56. This acquisition has impacted how the company has been seen since, with many believing the company's actions were on behalf of the British government. However, we will see that the relationship between the two was varied, ranging everywhere from cooperative to actively hostile.

18. Ferrier, *History of British Petroleum Company*, Vol. 1, 199.

19. Jacks, "Purchase of the British Government's Shares," 143, 156.

20. BP ARC68731: T Wynne (India Office), 1914–1922: "Notes of Refinery Activities from 1906 to 1916," written in Abadan on April 20, 1936 re 1909–1916.

21. Keddie, *Roots of Revolution*, 79–85, 90.

22. Ehsani, "Oil, State and Society in Iran," 193, 212.

23. Ehsani, "Pipeline Politics in Iran," 433.

24. Ehsani and Elling, "Abadan: The Rise and Demise of an Oil Metropolis," 30.

25. Over six thousand Indians worked at Burmah Oil in 1904. Corley, *A History of the Burmah Oil Company*. In addition, India and Iran had centuries-long cultural and political exchanges. See Cole, "Iranian Culture and South Asia."

26. Seccombe and Lawless, "Foreign Worker Dependence in the Gulf," 558.

27. Metcalf, *Imperial Connections*, 136–44. This network moved Indian workers to the oil fields and continued after India's independence in 1947. For a discussion of Indian labor recruitment and emigration policies in the present, see Wright, *Between Dreams and Ghosts*, 30–36.

28. BP ARC68731: T Wynne (India Office), 1914–1922.

29. BP ARC68731: Letter to Secretary, Government of India, Foreign and Political Department, Delhi, from Chairman APOC, 21 December 1920. For a discussion of Indians working in Iraq, see Tetzlaff, "Turn of the Gulf Tide."

30. NAI, MEA, Emigration, 1953, 17–6/53-Emi: Indian Emigration Act—Proposal for an amendment of.

31. Minault, *Khilafat Movement*; Metcalf, *Islamic Contestations*.

32. BP ARC68731: Letter to the Chairman of the Board of APOC from the Secretary to the Government of India, Foreign and Political Department, 25 November 1920.

33. Atabaki, "Indian Migrant Workers in the Iranian Oil Industry," 208.

34. BP ARC68731: Letter to Secretary, Government of India, Foreign and Political Department, Delhi, from Chairman APOC, 21 December 1920.

35. NAI, MEA, Emigration, 1953, 17–6/53-Emi: Indian Emigration Act—Proposal for an amendment of.

36. BP ARC5484: General Manager's Monthly Reports, Abadan, August 1926.

37. Atabaki, "Time, Labour-Discipline and Modernization in Turkey and Iran," 13–14.

38. Ferrier, *History of the British Petroleum Company*, Vol. 1, 623–29.

39. HIA McConnell, Box 1, Folder 7: Journal Entry, January 28, 1942.

40. Keddie, *Roots of Revolution*, 92, 107–9, 113; Bamberg, *History of the British Petroleum Company*, Vol. 2, 88; Rouhani, *A History of O.P.E.C.*, 88.

41. Keddie, *Roots of Revolution*, 110.

42. Kashani-Sabet, "Cultures of Iranianness," 171.

43. Ferrier, *History of the British Petroleum Company*, Vol. 1, 623–29.

44. Kashani-Sabet, "Cultures of Iranianness," 167.

45. Vejdani, *Making History in Iran*, 82.

46. Kashani-Sabet, "Cultures of Iranianness," 174–75.

47. Metcalf, *Islamic Contestations*, 143–44, 180–87. See also Boyk, "Nationality and Fashionality."

48. Chatterjee, *Nationalist Thought and the Colonial World*, 36–39.

49. Production grew from 4.4 million tons of crude oil in 1930, to 6.8 million tons in 1935, to 9.25 million tons in 1939, and to 16.82 million tons in 1945. Bamberg, *History of the British Petroleum Company*, Vol. 2, 71, 242.

50. While there was an increase in the number of Indians working in Iran, the percentage of foreigners in AIOC's total workforce remained relatively stable. Bamberg, *History of the British Petroleum Company*, Vol. 2, 247.

51. Seccombe and Lawless, "Foreign Worker Dependence in the Gulf," 563.

52. The numbers of Indians skilled tradesmen varied by year. In 1946, Indian recruitment was at a standstill, but in 1947, AIOC needed to hire 170 new Indian recruits because the requirement for skilled tradesmen could not be met by local labor or by the training department.

53. BP ARC112467: Abadan Labour Department, Indian Section, Annual Report 1947, Sections A and B.

54. Farmanfarmaian was influential in the development of Iran's oil industry. He worked in the military, then in 1943–1949 was in the Ministry of Finance; in 1949–1958 he was director general of petroleum, concessions, and mines; in 1958 he was director of sales for National Iranian Oil Company; and later he was Iran's first ambassador to Venezuela.

55. Farmanfarmaian and Farmanfarmaian, *Blood and Oil*, 184–85.

56. Farmanfarmaian and Farmanfarmaian, *Blood and Oil*, 187.

57. IOR/L/PS/12/3769A: Coll 20/52(3) Persian Gulf Diaries: Bahrain Intelligence Summaries 1946: No. 24 of 1947; BP ARC118823: Lessons of 1946 by MacNeill.

58. Bamberg, *History of the British Petroleum Company*, Vol. 2, 93.

59. BP ARC118823: Lessons of 1946.

60. BP ARC118823: Lessons of 1946.

61. See Said, *Orientalism*; Hall, "West and the Rest."

62. Mehta, *Liberalism and Empire*, 18, 31, 198–99; Metcalf, *Ideologies of the Raj*, 24.

63. Chakrabarty, *Provincializing Europe*; Lowe, *Intimacies of Four Continents*, 7; Mitchell, *Carbon Democracy*, 83; Pomeranz, "Empire & 'Civilizing' Missions." Discourses about development and modernization often justified colonialism by arguing that colonial powers were "helping" the colonized break free of practices (real or imagined), including *sati*, child marriage, and slavery. See, for example, Arnold, "Touching the Body"; Chakravarti, "Whatever Happened to the Vedic Dasi?"; and Prakash, *Bonded Histories*. Such narratives also often justified military conquest through mobilizing the trope of invaders as liberators. See Abu Lughod, "Do Muslim Women Really Need Saving?"; Cole, *Napoleon's Egypt*; Eley, "Historicizing the Global."

64. See Robins, *Corporation that Changed the World*, 160–61. See also Marx, "British Rule in India."

65. Minute by the Hon'ble T. B. Macaulay, 2nd February 1835.

66. Eley, "Liberalism, Europe, and the Bourgeoisie," 300.

67. BP ARC118823: Lessons of 1946.

68. BP ARC118823: Lessons of 1946.

69. Pletsch, "Three Worlds." Matthew Hull demonstrates that as development projects, particularly those focused on democracy, were implemented in India, they "aggressively attacked existing forms of sociality." Hull, "Democratic Technologies of Speech," 257.

70. Jayal, *Citizenship and Its Discontents*, 15.

71. BP ARC118823: Lessons of 1946.

72. Beinin and Lockman, *Workers on the Nile*, 304–9, 361.

73. BP ARC118823: Lessons of 1946.

74. War Manpower Commission, *Training Within Industry Report*, x. TWI faced a backlash, particularly from unions, in the 1950s. Despite this backlash, the program was pivotal in shaping contemporary human resources practices. Breen, "Social Science and State Policy in World War II," 265; Ruona, "Foundational Impact of the Training Within Industry Project."

75. War Manpower Commission, *Training Within Industry Report, 1940–1945*, xii (emphasis in original).

76. War Manpower Commission, *Training Within Industry Report, 1940–1945*, 210.

77. War Manpower Commission, *Training Within Industry Report, 1940–1945*, 214.

78. Pomeranz, "Empire & 'Civilizing' Missions," 37; Lowe, *Intimacies of Four Continents*, 23–24.

79. IOR/R/15/2/856: "File 36/7 Sabotage of American Petroleum Establishment in the Middle East," Letter from Lewis Jones, American Embassy, London, to Lance Pyman, Assistant Head, Eastern Department, Foreign Office, 11 May 1948.

80. NAI, MEA, Middle East Branch [ME], 1946, 10-(91)-ME/46: Thomas letter to General Headquarters, 10 July 1946.

81. NAI, MEA, ME, 1946, 10-(91)-ME/46: Thomas letter to General Staff Branch, 10 July 1946.

82. IOR/R/15/2/912: Thomas letter to General Headquarters, 31 July 1946.

83. NAI, MEA, ME, 1946. 10-(91)-ME/46: Thomas letter to General Headquarters, 31 August 1946.

84. IOR/L/PS/12/3751B: Coll 30/5(3) "Bahrein [sic] Residency Monthly Letter—Summary of Events," No. 81 (13/298), 8 June 1948.

85. Prakash, *Mumbai Fables*, 164–65.

86. IOR/R/15/2/912: Letter from Political Resident, Persian Gulf, to Foreign, New Delhi, 21 November 1946.

87. IOR/R/15/2/319: File 8/16 Bahrain Intelligence Summary 1948, No. 12 of 1948, 1–31 July.

88. Matthiesen, "Migration, Minorities, and Radical Networks," 479.

89. Karl, "Creating Asia."

90. Bose, "Taraknath Das," 163–65.

91. Ramnath, "Two Revolutions"; Oberoi, "Ghadar Movement."

92. Sohi, *Echoes of Mutiny*, 76–81.

93. Ramnath, *Art for Life*, 22.

94. Eley, *Forging Democracy*, 264–65. See also Zhou, "Nationalism and Communism," 330–31.

95. Beinin, *Was the Red Flag Flying There?*, 18–19.

96. IOR/R/15/2/912: File 43/1 Activitie [sic] of the Tudeh Party in the Persian Gulf: Note by Confidential Clerk, 22 March 1948.

97. Abrahamian, "Strengths and Weaknesses of the Labor Movement in Iran," 186.

98. NAI, MEA, ME, 1946, 10-(91)-ME/46: Note by Sd. H.C. Beaumont, 5 September 1946.

99. BP ARC118823: Lessons of 1946.

100. Mitchell, *Carbon Democracy*, 107.

101. BP ARC14706: The Kuwait Report, 1949.

102. Atabaki, "Indian Migrant Workers," 191, 204.

103. HIA Snyder, Box 19, Folder 2: Notes on Anglo-Iranian Oil Company, Personnel Planning Committee, April 3 to 7, 1949.

104. Glover, *Making Lahore Modern*.

105. IOR/R/15/2/912: Note by Confidential Clerk 22 March 1948; Keddie, *Roots of Revolution*, 122–23.

106. Farmanfarmaian and Farmanfarmaian, *Blood and Oil*, 186.

107. Keddie, *Roots of Revolution*, 121–22.

108. Mitchell, *Carbon Democracy*, 107.

109. Abrahamian, "Strengths and Weaknesses," 186–88.

110. NAI, MEA, ME, 1946, 10-(91)-ME/46: Thomas letter to General Headquarters, 24 August 1946.

Chapter 2

1. BP ARC106992: Memorandum: Excessive Overtime, 26 May 1948.

2. BP ARC106992: Demands by Junior Staff, 10 February 1948.

3. BP ARC106992: Letter to W. J. Shute from Artisan Welfare Society.

4. IOR/L/PS/12/3751B: (97/1/48), 16 September 1948.

5. BP ARC106992: Letter to W. J. Shute from Artisan Welfare Society.

6. These were different political situations than in Iran, where the British had wanted to create a protectorate in the late 1910s but stopped due to pressure both externally, from the United States and Russia, and internally by the Iranian people. Keddie, *Roots of Revolution*, 81–85; Katouzian, "Campaign Against the Anglo-Iranian Agreement of 1919."

7. HIA Snyder, Box 19: Personnel Planning Committee visit to Kuwait Oil Company, June 6–7, 1949.

8. Mitchell, "Society, Economy, and the State Effect," 77.

9. Trouillot, "Anthropology of the State," 126.

10. Cohn, *Colonialism and Its Forms of Knowledge*, 3; Scott, *Seeing Like a State*.

11. Singha, *A Despotism of Law*, xvi, 33–36, 287.

12. Ferguson, "Seeing Like an Oil Company"; McClintock, *Imperial Leather*, 16; Stoler, *Carnal Knowledge and Imperial Power*, 206.

13. Onley, "Raj Reconsidered," 50.

14. Onley, *Arabian Frontier of the British Raj*.

15. Anscombe, *Ottoman Gulf*; Haller, "Selective Recognition as an Imperial Instrument."

16. Onley, "Raj Reconsidered"; Onley, *Arabian Frontier of the British Raj*.

17. Before 1946, the Persian Gulf Residency was overseen by the British colonial government of India.

18. Bradshaw, *End of Empire in the Gulf*, 2–3.

19. Saleh, "Labor, Nationalism and Imperialism in Eastern Arabia," 3; Onley, "Raj Reconsidered"; Onley and Khalaf, "Shaikhly Authority in the Pre-Oil Gulf."

20. Letter from Shaikh Khaled bin Ahmad, Sharjah, to Political Resident, Persian Gulf, Bushire, 19 Jamada ath-Thaniya 1340 (17 February 1922), 189-S Of/922, in RE (7), 773. For a discussion of efforts by the British to keep Americans out of the Trucial Coast in the 1930s, see Said, "Preliminary Oil Concessions in Trucial Oman," 116.

21. TPC was originally formed in 1914. NEDC was a US oil syndicate that included Standard Oil Company of New Jersey (Jersey Standard or Esso, later Exxon), Standard Oil Company of New York (Socony, later Mobil), Gulf Oil, the Pan-American Petroleum and Transport Company, and the Atlantic Refining Company (later Arco). Jersey Standard and Socony later assumed total control over the NEDC after they bought out their partners in the 1930s. Socony-Vaccum was a company that was the product of the 1932 merger of two former Standard Oil Companies: Socony Vacuum Company and Standard Oil of New York. Socony-Vacuum was later renamed Mobil. After merging with Standard Oil of New Jersey, the company then became ExxonMobil in 1999. Federal Trade Commission, "Joint Control Through Common Ownership."

22. Calouste Gulbenkian, an Armenian businessman who was a partial stakeholder of TPC, received the remaining 5 percent share.

23. According to an employee of SoCal, originally Gulf Oil negotiated the concession for oil exploration in Bahrain. However, when Gulf realized this was in violation of the Red Line Agreement, the company sold its concession to SoCal. UNT OH 0659: Interview with Smith.

24. Later, in 1946, Jersey Standard and SoCal wanted to invest in Aramco, but were unable to do so due to the terms of the Red Line Agreement. "Consequently, Jersey Standard and Socony joined the U.S. Government in pressuring the other members of the IPC to abrogate the terms of the Red Line Agreement. Although the French Government and Gulbenkian protested, both had withdrawn their objections by November 1948, in exchange for a greater share of the output of the IPC, whose boundaries were now redrawn to exclude Saudi Arabia, Yemen, Bahrain, Egypt, Israel, and the western-half of Jordan." See Office of the Historian, Foreign Service Institute, "1928 Red Line Agreement."

25. Bamberg, *History of the British Petroleum Company*, Vol. 2, 150.

26. PCL had the same ownership as IPC, but did not have a representative from the government of Iraq on the board of directors. Said, "Preliminary Oil Concessions," 117.

27. Said, "Preliminary Oil Concessions," 118–22.

28. IOR/R/15/2/865: File 38/3 II P.C.L. Qatar Concession: Letter from PDQ to Political Agent, Bahrain, 22 January 1949.

29. Boundary debates could also lead to violent conflicts. For example, the state that is today known as Oman experienced three wars from the 1950s to the 1970s, all concerning the drawing of boundaries and oil concessions. Limbert, *In the Time of Oil*.

30. IOR/L/PS/12/3751B: (95/14/49), 2 December 1949. Aminoil was a consortium of US oil companies.

31. IOR/R/15/2/319: File 8/16 Bahrain Intelligence Summary 1948: Bahrain Intelligence Summary for Period 1st to 15th June 1948; IOR/L/PS/12/3751B: (95/11/49), 8 September 1949. The same arbiter was also used to decide a boundary despite in Bahrain. Seabeds were increasingly a pressing issue. In July 1949, the rulers of Bahrain, Kuwait, Qatar, and Trucial Coast sheikhdoms (excluding Kalbah) issued proclamations claiming jurisdiction over the seabeds. These issues were particularly salient after 1945 when the President Harry Truman issued two proclamations extending US governmental control of "the natural resources of the subsoil and seabed of the continental shelf beneath the high seas but contiguous to the coasts of the United States as appertaining to the United States, subject to its jurisdiction and control." This proclamation by the US had a mixed reception by British officials. Some in the British administration thought there could be benefits for their own access oil production, particularly in the Caribbean, but they were also worried about the impact of such claims and how they would complicate boundary disputes. IOR/L/PS/12/3751B: (95/8/49), 5 July 1949; Office of Public Affairs, Department of State Bulletin, 485.

32. CAB 134-1086: Middle East Committee: Kuwait, Sea-bed Concession, Note by the Joint Secretaries, 29 December 1955.

33. IOR/R/15/5/251: "File 5/1 XVI Kuwait Oil Company" [147r] (293/856): Secret, W.R.H., Persian Gulf Residency, Bahrain, 18 May 1948.

34. IOR/R/15/2/865: File 38/3 II P.C.L. Qatar Concession.

35. IOR/L/PS/12/371B: Letter from Persian Gulf Residency, Bahrain, 8 March 1948.

36. IOR/R/15/2/1453: File 15/11 Rules and Regulations Reports on working of the Bahrain Order in Council, Annual report on the working of the Bahrain Order in Council 1949, for the year 1949.

37. Seccombe and Lawless, "Foreign Worker Dependence in the Gulf," 551.

38. Takriti, *Monsoon Revolution*, 10–24; Samin, *Of Sand or Soil*, 172.

39. Bamberg, *History of British Petroleum Company*, Vol. 2, 147–48.

40. This had been a worry since the early 1930s, when oil was discovered in commercial qualities by Bapco. Anticipating an influx of Americans, the British government in Bahrain worried that additional Americans would be beyond the powers of the local Arab police—and this was an issue that the British felt continued to be a problem throughout the 1940s and 1950s. BP ARC123142: APOC and Bahrain Petro Company 1925–1933, Bapco Report, 9 June 1932; HIA McConnell, Box 1, Folder 8: Journal Entry, August 28, 1944.

41. Gornall, "Some Memories of Bapco," 33.

42. IOR/L/PS/12/1301: Ext 574/48 "Roster of Employees of Petroleum concessions, Ltd, Bahrain, Petroleum Development (Qatar) Ltd. and Petroleum Development (Trucial Coast) Ltd": PCL (Bahrain): Roster of Employees as on 31st December 1947: Nationalities on Payroll.

43. Here, the category "Indian" was inclusive of workers from British India as well as Goa. IOR/L/PS/12/1301: PDQ: Dukhan-Qatar: Employees Roster as at [sic] 31st December 1947: General Summary. At Petroleum Development (Trucial Coast) Ltd., staff were exclusively British and American, and only one subject of the Trucial Coast held a skilled position. IOR/L/PS/12/1301: Petroleum Development (Trucial Coast) Ltd., Roster of Employees as on 31st December 1947: Nationalities on Payroll.

44. IOR/R/15/5/268: File 5/16 Chief Local Representative for KOC and Aminco, relations between companies and Shaikh: Letter to Political Resident, Persian Gulf, from Political Agency, Kuwait, December 1, 1949.

45. IOR/L/PS/12/3715B: Letter from the Political Gulf Residency, Bahrain, 31 January 1949.

46. KOC was a joint venture by the Anglo-Persian Oil Company (APOC) and Gulf Oil formed in 1934. The agreement categorized KOC as a British company and gave the British administration significant power in the company. Bamberg, *History of British Petroleum Company*, Vol. 2, 150.

47. Bamberg, *History of British Petroleum Company*, Vol. 2, 341–44.

48. IOR/R/15/5/268: Memorandum: The Bahrain Petroleum Company's local relations.

49. The American Independent Oil Company (Aminoil) was a consortium of the independent oil companies Philips, Ashland, and Sinclair. It was created to bid on the Kuwait Neutral Zone concession. Yergin, *The Prize*, 438.

50. IOR/R/15/5/268: Memorandum: The Bahrain Petroleum Company's local relations.

51. IOR/R/15/5/268: Letter to Sir Rupert Hay from B. A. B. Burrows, Foreign Office, London, 18 June 1949.

52. IOR/R/15/5/268: Letter to Sir Rupert Hay, Political Resident, Persian Gulf, from H. G. Jakins, Political Agency, Kuwait, 1 December 1949. Despite the British describing the Kuwaiti ruling family as politically unified, there were divisions within it. Crystal, *Kuwait*, 93–94.

53. IOR/R/15/5/268: Memorandum: The Kuwait Oil Company's Local Relations at Kuwait, 19 October 1949.

54. BP ARC106992: Letter to L. T. Jordan from C. A. P. Southwell, 18 November 1949. This did not need to be decided by the government for nonnationals. BP ARC106992: Letter to Colonel A. Galloway, H.M. Political Agent, Kuwait, from L. T. Jordan, 15 December 1948.

55. IOR/R/15/5/268: Letter to B. A. B. Burrows, Foreign Office, London, from W. R. Hay, Persian Gulf Residency, Bahrain, 2 May 1949.

56. IOR/R/15/5/268: Letter to Sir Rupert Hay from Political Agency, Kuwait, 8 February 1949.

57. IOR/R/15/5/251: File 5/1 XVI Kuwait Oil Company: Indian Labour Positions as of 30 September 1948.

58. BP ARC106992: Cable Figures to London June–September 1949.

59. IOR/L/PS/12/3751B: Letter to Burrows from Persian Gulf Residency, Bahrain, 9 December 1948.

60. Seccombe and Lawless, "Gulf Labour Market and Early Oil," 109.

61. Seccombe and Lawless, "Gulf Labour Market and Early Oil"; BP ARC106992: Aide Memoire: Iraqi Labour, 22 March 1948.

62. IOR/R/15/5/268: Letter to Sir Rupert Hay, Bahrain, from J. E. Chadwick on behalf of B. A. B. Burrows, Foreign Office, 18 June 1949.

63. IOR/R/15/5/268: Letter to H. G. Jakins, Political Resident, Persian Gulf, from Political Agency, Kuwait, 25 July 1949.

64. IOR/R/15/5/268: Letter to H. G. Jakins, Political Resident, Persian Gulf, from Political Agency, Kuwait, 25 July 1949.

65. BP ARC106992: Letter to General Manager, KOC, from Motherwell Bridge and Engineering Co., Ltd., 26 April 1948.

66. IOR/L/PS/12/3751B: (95/7/49), 6 June 1949.

67. IOR/L/PS/12/3751B: (95/11/49), 8 September 1949.

68. IOR/R/15/5/251: File 5/1 XVI Kuwait Oil Co: Monthly Progress Report to the Managing Directors, August 1948, Part VIII—Personnel and Welfare.

69. BP ARC106992: Letter to Southwell from L. T. Jordan, 20 June 1948.

70. BP ARC106992: Letter, Artizan [*sic*] Rates of Pay, from J. W. Lowdon, 26 May 1948. PDQ was a subsidiary of Petroleum Concessions, Ltd. PDQ's name changed to Qatar Petroleum Company (QPC) in 1953. Rouhani, *A History of O.P.E.C.*, 95.

71. BP ARC106992: Letter to Southwell from L. T. Jordan, 10 August 1948; BP ARC106992: Memorandum: Bulk Labour, 29 May 1949.

72. BP ARC106992: Note to Jordan, 28 April 1948.

73. BP ARC106992: Letter to Manager, KOC, from AIOC (India) Manager, Bombay, India, 19 April 1948.

74. BP ARC106992: Letter, Indian Welfare, 9 May 1948.

75. BP ARC106992: Memorandum: Recommendation for Obtaining a Balanced Labour Force, from Labour Superintendent to General Manager, 12 September 1948.

76. BP ARC106992: Letter to Manager, KOC, from AIOC (India) Manager, Bombay, India, 19 April 1948.

77. BP ARC106992: Memorandum: Recommendation for Obtaining a Balanced Labour Force, from Labour Superintendent to General Manager, 12 September 1948.

78. IOR/R/15/5/251: Letter to W. R. Hay, Political Resident, Persian Gulf, from the Political Agency, Kuwait, Outside Labour for the Kuwait Oil Company, Limited, 24 July 1946; IOR/R/15/5/251: Notes on a Visit to Kuwait, March 1947; IOR/R/15/5/251: Memorandum, Future Constitution and Activities of the Kuwait Oil Co, from Political Agency, Kuwait, 21 July 1946; IOR/R/15/5/251: Letter to Tandy, Political Agent, Kuwait, from Office of the Political Resident, Persian Gulf, 7 July 1946.

79. BP ARC106992: Letter to C. A. P. Southwell from L. T. Jordan, 22 May 1948; BP ARC106992: Aide Memoire: Iraqi Labour, 22 March 1948.

80. BP ARC106992: Letter to C. A. P. Southwell from L. T. Jordan, 20 June 1948.

81. IOR/R/15/5/268: Letter to H. G. Jakins, Political Resident, Persian Gulf, from Political Agency, Kuwait, 25 July 1949.

82. IOR/R/15/5/251: Letter to W. R. Hay from Political Agency, Kuwait, Outside Labour for the Kuwait Oil Company, 24 July 1946.

83. BP ARC106992: Letter to Bourne from M. W. Sinclair, Indian Rates of Pay.

84. BP ARC106992: Cable Figures to London, June to September 1949.

85. BP ARC106992: Letter to C. A. P. Southwell from L. T. Jordan, 17 September 1949.

86. IOR/L/PS/12/3751B: (95/11/49), 8 September 1949; (95/8/49), 5 July 1949.

87. BP ARC106992: Letter to C. A. P. Southwell from L. T. Jordan, 5 November 1949; BP ARC106992: Letter to C. A. P. Southwell from L. T. Jordan, 7 November 1949; BP ARC106992: Letter to L. T. Jordan from C. A. P. Southwell, 27 October 1949; IOR/R/15/5/268: Letter to Sir Rupert Hay from Political Agency, Kuwait, 1 December 1949.

88. BP ARC106992: Letter to C. A. P. Southwell from L. T. Jordan, 5 November 1949.

89. BP ARC106992: Memorandum: Employment of Local Labor, 29 December 1949.

90. FO 1016–126: Nationality: Kuwait: Decree of Law No. 2 of 1948. This changed with the 1959 Law No. (15), which began the "legal distinction between Kuwaiti nationals and others. Prior to that loyalty to the Amir was the primary requisite for de facto citizenship and those who wished to travel were issued papers identifying their bearers as associates of the Amir." Alhajeri, "Citizenship and Political Participation in the State of Kuwait," 70–71.

91. BP ARC106992: Letter to the Manager, KOC, from Abdulla Mulla Saleh, Unskilled Bulk Labour, 23 August 1948. KOC's records show that during the late 1940s, most khaliji migrant laborers were Omani. Seccombe and Lawless, "Gulf Labour Market and the Early Oil Industry," 108–9.

92. BP ARC106992: Letter to C. A. P. Southwell from L. T. Jordan, 7 November 1949.

93. Seccombe and Lawless, "Gulf Labour Market and the Early Oil Industry," 106–7.

94. HIA Snyder, Box 19, Folder 1: Personnel Planning Committee visit to Kuwait Oil Company, Labor force of KOC, June 1, 1949.

95. BP ARC106992: Letter to C. A. P. Southwell from L. T. Jordan, 24 October 1949; BP ARC106992: Memorandum: Local Labour Employed by Seismograph Services, Ltd., April 11, 1949; BP ARC106992: Letter to C. A. P. Southwell from L. T. Jordan, Progress Report of the Seismic Services, Ltd., 22 February 1949.

96. BP ARC106992: Letter to C. A. P. Southwell from L. T. Jordan, 6 November 1949.

97. BP ARC106992: Extract from a letter to General Pyron (Ex 455) from Mr. Hamilton, 18 October 1949.

98. BP ARC106992: Extract from a letter to General Pyron (Ex 455) from Mr. Hamilton, 18 October 1949; BP ARC106992: Memorandum: Redundant Labour, 17 September 1949.

99. BP ARC106992: Letter to C. A. P. Southwell from L. T. Jordan, 7 November 1949.

100. BP ARC106992: Letter to the Manager, KOC, from Abdulla Mulla Saleh, Unskilled Bulk Labour, 23 August 1948.

101. BP ARC106992: Letter to C. A. P. Southwell from L. T. Jordan, 5 September 1948.

102. BP ARC106992: Letter to General Manager from Marine Superintendent, 5 December 1948.

103. BP ARC106992: Letter to D. M. Corbett, Labour Superintendent, from L. T. Jordan, 29 November 1948.

104. BP ARC 106992: Letter to C. A. P. Southwell from L. T. Jordan, 5 September 1948; BP ARC106992: Letter to the Manager, KOC, from Abdulla Mulla Saleh, Unskilled Bulk Labour, 23 August 1948; BP ARC106992: Letter to C. A. P. Southwell from L. T. Jordan, 18 October 1948.

105. BP ARC106992: Letter to Heads of Departments from L. T. Jordan, General Manager, 16 June 1949; BP ARC 106992: Note, 18 April 1948.

106. BP ARC106992: Letter to C. A. P. Southwell from L. T. Jordan, 24 October 1949.

107. BP ARC106992: Letter to C. A. P. Southwell from L. T. Jordan, 31 August 1949; BP ARC 106992: Memorandum: Warning Slips, 3 March 1949.

108. This is part of a larger trend in the twentieth century for corporate and state responsibility to become increasingly placed onto the most vulnerable individuals. See Wright, *Between Dreams and Ghosts*, 168–79; Rose, *Powers of Freedom*, 80–84, 154.

109. BP ARC106992: Letter to C. A. P. Southwell from L. T. Jordan, 31 August 1949.

110. BP ARC106992: Note to J. W. Lowdon from L. T. Jordan, 21 March 1949.

111. BP ARC106992: Letter to R. J. Ross, Bechtel, from L. T. Jordan, 12 September 1948.

112. IOR/R/15/5/268: Letter to Sir Rupert Hay, Political Resident, Persian Gulf, from H. G. Jakins, Political Agency, Kuwait, 1 December 1948. They also noted that individual contractors may feel the "draught, but they have done well and will doubtless launch out elsewhere."

113. Following the strike, worker discontent grew because they were not paid for the time they were on strike. BP ARC106992: Report on the incident at Wara on 15th–16th November 1949, by Considine, Dy. Labour Superintendent, 16 November 1949.

114. BP ARC106992: Letter to C. A. P. Southwell from L. T. Jordan, 7 November 1949.

115. Rose, *Powers of Freedom*, 34–35; Watts, "Resource Curse?," 53; Watts, "Righteous Oil?," 375–77.

116. Mitchell, *Language, Emotion, and Politics in South India*; Pandey "Racialization of Subaltern Populations." To destabilize the territorialization of culture, Gupta and Ferguson argue, one must explore how the "identity of a place emerges by the intersection of its specific involvement in a system of hierarchically organized spaces with its cultural construction as a community or locality." Gupta and Ferguson, "Beyond 'Culture,'" 8.

Chapter 3

1. NAI, MEA, Emigration, F. 22-8/48-Emi: Skilled workers engaged by the Bahrein [*sic*] Petroleum Co., Bahrein.

2. NAI, MEA, Emigration, F. 22–8/48-Emi: Memorandum to the Minister-in-charge, External Affairs Department, Government of India, Submitted by the Ex-Employees of the Bahrein [sic] Petroleum Company, Limited, Bahrein, Regarding the intolerable conditions in which the Indian employees are forced to work in Bahrein; NAI, MEA, Emigration, F. 22–8/48-Emi: Letter to the Protector of Emigrants, Bombay, July 9, 1948.

3. See Raman, "Being Indian the South African Way"; Martin, "Who Is Asiatic?," 143.

4. For a discussion of these debates in India, see Chatterji, "South Asian Histories of Citizenship," 1050–51; Cooper, *Citizenship, Inequality, and Difference*, 100; Jayal, *Citizenship and Its Discontents*; Zamindar, *Long Partition*.

5. Fields and Fields, *Racecraft*, 34–35, 43–44, 195–96. See also Pandey, "Racialization of Subaltern Populations Across the Globe."

6. Fields and Fields, *Racecraft*, 19–20.

7. Fields and Fields, *Racecraft*, 243.

8. NAI, MEA, Emigration, F. 22–8/48-Emi: Skilled workers engaged by Bahrain Petro Co.

9. IOR/R/15/2/419: Raghu, "Colour Bar in Bahrain: American Oil Kings Treat Indians as Chattels," *Free Press Journal*, 9 July 1948.

10. NAI, MEA, Emigration, F. 22–8/48-Emi: Letter to K. P. S. Menon, Foreign Secretary, Ministry of External Affairs, from Mohammed Yunus, Legation of India, Baghdad, February 28, 1952; NAI, MEA, Emigration, F. 22–8/48-Emi: Extract from report on "Bahrein" prepared by Mr. Raja Gopalan, received along with letter No. 27 dated 27-7-48 from the Embassy of India, Tehran; NAI, MEA, Emigration, F. 22–8/48-Emi: Extract from a note on "Bahrain" submitted to the Ambassador at Teheran [sic] by Mr. K.V. Vaidyanathan, an Indian national employed in the Political Agency, Bahrain.

11. UNT OH 0659: Interview with Smith; UNT OH 0661: Interview with John D. Fosque by Dr. Ronald E. Marcello, (Onancock, Virginia: August 2, 1985).

12. Due to the stipulation in the concession that British subjects staff oil projects in Bahrain, there were more British and other Europeans were working for Bapco in 1949 than at Aramco. UNT OH 0659: Interview with Smith; HIA McConnell, Box 1, Folder 8: Journal Entry, June 11, 1944; UNT OH 0675: Interview with Frederick W. Dittus by Dr. Ronald E. Marcello, (Escondido, California: September 13, 1985).

13. One example was the creation of a separate and unequal education system in the late 1940s for Saudi employees, see Vitalis, *America's Kingdom*, 114–15.

14. Das Gupta, *Labour and Working Class*; Santiago, *Ecology of Oil*.

15. In addition, there were four principal contractors, and these companies were managed by Americans: IBI employed 57 Americans, Brown Drilling employed

12 Americans, CBI employed 15 Americans, and United Geophysical employed 17 Americans. HIA Snyder, Box 19: Personnel Planning Committee, Visit to Bahrein Petroleum Company Operations, June 4, 1949. A few years later, one manager estimated that there were 9,000 workers: 5,000 were Arabs, 2,000 to 3,000 were Indians and Pakistanis, and 1,000 were from England, Canada, Australia, New Zealand, and the United States. UNT OH 0659: Interview with Smith.

16. When contractors were included in the employment numbers, there were close to 28,163 employees at Aramco projects in Saudi Arabia. This included about 4,000 Americans, 3,700 foreigners (including Indian, Italian, and Pakistani workers), and 20,000 Saudi Arabian employees. HIA Snyder, Box 19: Composition of the Aramco Field Labor Force, Field Management Committee Meeting with Personnel Planning Committee, Dharan, Saudi Arabia, April 19, 1949.

17. NAI, MEA, Emigration, F. 22-8/48-Emi: Memorandum to the Minister-in-charge; NAI, MEA, Emigration, F. 22-8/48-Emi: Letter to the Protector of Emigrants, Bombay, July 9, 1948.

18. Hall, *Fateful Triangle*.

19. HIA McConnell, Box 1, Folder 6: Journal Entries: February 24, 1939, May 11, 1939. Saudi workers were also addressed in this manner, and they expressed that they actively resented being called "boy," see HIA Snyder, Box 15: A Report Prepared from Research Conducted by the Special Study Group by Thomas F. O'Dea, February–August 1963.

20. HIA Snyder, Box 15: Special Labor Relations Report, "Boys in the Back Room," December 30, 1958; HIA McConnell, Box 1, Folder 6: Journal Entry, December 10, 1938.

21. HIA Snyder, Box 15: Labor Relations Report, September 1958.

22. NAI, MEA, Emigration, 1953, F.6-6/53-Emi: Letter to POE, Bombay, from E.E. Evans, Recruiting Agent, Arabian American Oil Co, 30 March 1954.

23. HIA McConnell, Box 1, Folder 6: Journal Entry, December 10, 1940.

24. UNT OH 0659: Interview with Smith; Vitalis, *America's Kingdom*.

25. HIA Snyder, Box 19: Personnel Planning Committee, Visit to Bahrein Petroleum Company Operations, June 4, 1949.

26. HIA Snyder, Box 19: Personnel Planning Committee, Visit to Bahrein Petroleum Company Operations, June 4, 1949.

27. Gornall, "Some Memories of BAPCO," 19, 23–25, 45.

28. NAI, MEA, Emigration, 1953, F.6-6/53-Emi: Letter to POE, Bombay, from E.E. Evans, Recruiting Agent, Arabian American Oil Co, 30 March 1954.

29. The issue of feeding workers was recurrent, and one Aramco manager reflected, "The whole thing carries dynamite, as we must show no discrimination against the Arabs. This is apt to appear in the food problem. The answer seems to be: Arab food for Arabs, Italian food for Italians, American food for Americans, even

if some of it comes from the same box." HIA McConnell, Box 1, Folder 8: Notes from Operations Meeting, November 29, 1944.

30. HIA Snyder Papers, Box 15, Folder 1: Social Change in Saudi Arabia: Problems and Prospects: A Report by Thomas O'Dea, Prepared from Research Conducted by the Special Study Group, February–August 1963.

31. HIA McConnell, Box 1, Folder 8: Journal Entry, April 7, 1944. Following World War II, Bechtel "had a lot of work going on" in the Middle East, and over the second half of the twentieth century, Bechtel rapidly became one of the largest contractors globally. In 1960, the company had a nonmanual staff of 3,900, and its revenue was US$460 million. By 1982, Bechtel's nonmanual staff had increased to 44,500, and its revenue in 1983 was US$14.3 billion. Bechtel, "Reflections on Success," 150, 153.

32. HIA McConnell, Box 1, Folder 8: Notes from Operating Meeting, November 1, 1944.

33. HIA McConnell, Box 1, Folder 8: Journal Entry, July 14, 1945; HIA McConnell, Box 1, Folder 8: Journal Entry, July 1953.

34. Cooper, *Citizenship, Inequality, and Difference*, 97.

35. See also, Banerjee, *Becoming Imperial Citizens*; Mongia, *Indian Migration and Empire*.

36. Jayal, *Citizenship and Its Discontents*, 15, 28–29.

37. Saleh, "Labor, Nationalism and Imperialism in Eastern Arabia," 64–69.

38. Seccombe and Lawless, "Foreign Worker Dependence in the Gulf." In 1941 and 1943, the British government in Indian considered revising the contracts for the Indian employees at Bapco. The matter was dropped both times without substantive revisions, but debates over these revisions set precedents that were used in subsequent contract negotiations. NAI, MEA, Emigration, 1952, D5853/52-Emi.: Letter to Sampath from POE, Bombay, 11 October 1952.

39. HIA McConnell, Box 1, Folder 8: Journal Entry, October 24, 1944.

40. IOR/L/PS/12/958: Ext 5034/44 "Discontent among Indian Personnel of Arabian American Oil Co. at al Khobar and Dhahran": Note, T. Hickinbotham, November 9, 1944; HIA McConnell, Box 1, Folder 8: Journal Entry, June 11, 1944; HIA McConnell, Box 1, Folder 8: Journal Entry, October 24, 1944. While there were shortages in some places during the war, other places, such as Dubai, experienced a "war trade boom." IOR/L/PS/12/3769A: Bahrain Intelligence Summary No. 8 for Period 16th to 30th April 1947. Janam Mukherjee finds in India that the British colonial government "used World War II instrumentally and at times extremely cynically to justify—and indeed amplify—the brutality and rapacity with which it clung to power in India. World War II, in this context, represented only a somewhat frenzied accentuation of the injustices that marked daily life under British rule since

its inception. For the population of Bengal, moreover, it meant famine." Mukherjee, *Hungry Bengal*, 10.

41. HIA McConnell, Box 1, Folder 8: Journal Entry, October 24, 1944.

42. HIA McConnell, Box 1, Folder 8: Journal Entry, October 26, 1944.

43. This appeal to the political agent is not surprising. Before signing their contracts, Indian employees had hoped the British political agent would be the arbiters of their contracts, because they said that they could not trust the company. IOR/L/PS/12/958: Telegram to H.M. Minister, Jedda, from Political Resident at Bahrain, November 13, 1944.

44. HIA McConnell, Box 1, Folder 8: Journal Entry, October 8, 1944.

45. HIA McConnell, Box 1, Folder 8: Journal Entry, October 29, 1944.

46. IOR/L/PS/12/958: Memorandum from Political Agency, Bahrain, to Mr. C. A. Rodstrom, the Bahrain Representative, Aramco, Bahrain, November 9, 1944.

47. IOR/L/PS/12/958: Telegram from the Protector of Emigrants, Bombay, to the Political Agent, Bahrain.

48. They were able to do this because there was help from the US armed forces to move US workers. In addition, the ruler of Saudi Arabia approved the hiring of Italians from Eritrea. HIA McConnell, Box 1, Folder 8: Journal Entry, October 8, 1944. Italians from Eritrea were precarious because of the Allies' conquest during World War II and the subsequent mass unemployment in Eritrea. Until 1951, Eritrea was a British Protectorate. See Beyan, "Unemployment and Social Disorder during the British Colonial Period in Eritrea."

49. The public and ruling officials in the Arabian Sea were aware of the partition of British India and were critical of the British role in creating the situation. Indeed, the sheikh of Ras al Khaimah questioned the British political agent on the partition of India and subsequent chaos and violence with the goal of embarrassing the British administrator. IOR/L/PS/12/3769A: Bahrain Intelligence summary No. 8 for Period 16 to 30 April 1947.

50. Cohn, *Colonialism and Its Forms*, 26–27.

51. Cohn, *Colonialism and Its Forms*. See also Pandey, *Construction of Communalism*, 6, 21, 45. In addition, communal identities were taken up by Indian nationalists. See Jalal, *Sole Spokesman*, 5; Pandey, *Construction of Communalism*, 11–12; Thapar, "Imagined Religious Communities?," 229–30. This colonial form of knowledge production, which considered religion to be a primary, fixed category, was also mobilized in the partition of Palestine. The partition of India has parallels with the partition of Palestine—both partitions occurred in the late 1940s in areas that had previously been under British administrative control. In addition, the logics of both partitions were informed by colonial governance based on communal identities, in which groups are separated by their religion and nationality is conflated

with religion. See chapter 5 for a longer discussion of how the partition of Palestine impacted worker actions in the Arabian Peninsula.

52. See also: Mongia, *Indian Migration and Empire*; Banerjee, *Becoming Imperial Citizens*.

53. IOR/R/15/5/251: Telegram, from India Office, London, to Political Resident, Bushire, May 19, 1945; IOR/R/15/5/251: Commonwealth Relations Office, August 27, 1947. In contrast, for companies operating within British Protectorates, contracts for Iraqis, Syrians, and Egyptians who were hired for "positions of importance" needed approval from the British political agent. IOR/R/15/2/912, File 43/1 Activite [sic] of the Tudeh Party in the Persian Gulf: Marginalia, April 27, 1949.

54. IOR/R/15/5/251: Memorandum from British Residency, Bushire, to the Political Agent, Kuwait, April 28, 1945; IOR/R/15/5/251: Telegram from India Office, London, to Political Resident, Bushire, May 19, 1945.

55. It was not only the chemists who had trouble receiving cooperation from the British authorities in the Arabian Peninsula. The British political agent was also uncooperative when the Indian government asked for the number of Indian employees at AIOC and Aramco. NAI, MEA, Emigration, 1948, F. 22–8/48-Emi: Letter to Ministry of External Affairs, New Delhi, from Persian Gulf Residency, Bahrain, 16 January 1950; NAI, MEA, Emigration, 1948, F. 22–8/48-Emi: Letter to Ministry of External Affairs from Embassy of India, Tehran, 15 March 1950.

56. NAI, MEA, Emigration, 1948, F. 22–8/48-Emi: Letter to Political Agent, Bahrein [sic] from Indian Employees Association Bahrein, 24 June 1948; NAI, MEA, Emigration, 1948, F. 22–8/48-Emi: Express Letter to New Delhi from Assistant Political Agent, Bahrein, 16 August 1948; NAI, MEA, Emigration, 1948, F. 22–8/48-Emi: Letter to Political Agent, Bahrein [sic] from Indian Employees Association Bahrein, 20 March 1948.

57. Following Indian government debates and the circulation of documents provides us with an analytic to understand how state power functioned. Matthew Hull's work on bureaucracy in Pakistan follows files to understand "its ability to support the formation of an authoritative voice of government, to allow individuals to escape responsibility, and to facilitate individual and small group enterprise within the larger organization." Hull, *Government of Paper*, 160.

58. NAI, MEA, Emigration, 1948, F. 22–8/48-Emi: Skilled workers engaged by the Bahrein Petroleum Co., Bahrein and Revision of Form of agreement entered into between Bahrein Petroleum Co.; NAI, MEA, WANA section, 1960, 6-C(34)/60WANA: Iraq's Request for helping them in their Oil Industry—Note from the Ministry of Mines and Fuel.

59. NAI, MEA, Emigration, 1953, F.6–6/53-Emi: Letter to Ghatge from Sinclair, 14 January 1954.

60. NAI, MEA, Emigration, 1948, F. 22–8/48-Emi: Skilled workers engaged by the Bahrein Petroleum Co., Bahrein.

61. NAI, MEA, Emigration, 1953, F.6–6/53-Emi: Marginalia. This debate continues into the present; see Wright, *Between Dreams and Ghosts*, 21–42.

62. The Indian ambassador to Iran argued that the condition of workers in Bahrain was much worse than the condition of workers in Iran. NAI, MEA, Emigration, 1948, 22–8/48: Extract from note on "Bahrain," (Original in AWT. Branch F. No. 3(9)-AWT/50).

63. NAI, MEA, Emigration, 1948, F 22–8/48-Emi: Skilled workers engaged by the Bahrain Petroleum Company; NAI, MEA, Emigration, 1948, F. 22–8/48-Emi: Letter to Yunus, Undersecretary to the Government of India, from R.B. Ghatge, 1 July 1953.

64. NAI, MEA, Emigration, 1948, F 22–8/48-Emi: Skilled workers engaged by the Bahrain Petroleum Company.

65. NAI, MEA, Emigration, F. 22–8/48-Emi: Skilled workers engaged by the Bahrein [sic] Petroleum Co., Bahrein.

66. IOR/R/15/2/419: "Colour Bar in Bahrain."

67. Liu, "Shadows of Universalism."

68. Arendt, *Origins of Totalitarianism*; Quataert, *Advocating Dignity*, 20–22.

69. Pakistani workers in Saudi Arabia made similar claims, and this was discussed in the Pakistani press in the 1940s and early 1950s. In the Pakistani paper *Freedom*, Pakistani workers drew direct connections to their treatment at Aramco and the treatment of African Americans in the United States. Furthermore, they argued that this racialization and racism was due to US prejudice against Muslims. Vitalis, *America's Kingdom*, 98–105.

70. HIA Snyder Papers, Box 15: A Report Prepared from Research Conducted by the Special Study Group by Thomas F. O'Dea, February–August 1963.

71. Maul, "International Labour Organization and the Globalization of Human Rights."

72. Bhagavan, "A New Hope"; Prashad, *Darker Nations*, 11, 34–47.

73. See Mazower, *No Enchanted Palace*; Pearson, "Defending Empire at the United Nations."

74. Terretta, "'We Had Been Fooled into Thinking,'" 332.

75. NAI, MEA, Emigration, 1953, F6–6/53-Emi: Oil Companies in the Persian-Gulf and Mid-East.

76. Access to newspapers may have been especially important in galvanizing government officials, particularly given that some Indian officials felt the chemists had not been good employees and were, furthermore, making "a mountain out of a mole [sic]." NAI, MEA, Emigration, F. 22–8/48-Emi: Skilled workers engaged by the Bahrein [sic] Petroleum Co., Bahrein.

77. As Lisa Mitchell writes, by 1913 "languages were no longer primarily associated with places but were increasingly imagined as inalienable attributes of people." Mitchell, *Language, Emotion, and Politics*, 35.

78. IOR/L/PS/12/3769A: Bahrain Intelligence Summary for Period 1st to 15th July 1947.

79. NAI, MEA, Emigration, 1948, F. 22–8/48-Emi: Memorandum to the Minister-in-charge.

80. NAI, MEA, Emigration, 1948, F. 22–8/48-Emi: Telegram to Indian delegation, Paris, from Foreign, New Delhi, 8 December 1948; NAI, MEA, Emigration, 1948, F. 22–8/48-Emi: Serial No. 14.

81. Butalia, *Other Side of Silence*, 44–45. At times, Indian politicians fomented communal tensions and violence for electoral politics. For example, Paul Brass demonstrates that communal riots were not spontaneous eruptions of primordial hatreds but "dramatic productions, creations of specific persons, groups, and parties operating through institutionalized riot networks within a discursive framework of Hindu-Muslim communal opposition and antagonism that in turn produces specific forms of political practice that makes riots integral to the political process." Brass, *Production of Hindu-Muslim Violence*, 369.

82. Constituent Assembly Debates, India, Volume VII, 6 December 1948, speech by Lakshmi Kanta Maitra; Constituent Assembly Debates, India, Volume IX, 11 August 1949, Speech by P. S. Deshmukh; Constituent Assembly Debates, India, Volume IX, 12 August 1949, Speech by Jawaharlal Nehru.

83. For example, see Constituent Assembly Debates, India, Volume VII, 6 December 1948, speech by Lokanath Misra; Citizenship Amendment Bill, 2019.

84. IOR/L/PS/12/3751B: D.O. No. 540-S, 8 March 1948.

85. BP ARC112467: Abadan Labour Department, Indian Section, Annual Report 1947: Table XIII: Total Strength by Rates of Pay, 31 December 1948.

86. HIA McConnell, Box 1, Folder 9: Minutes of Planning Committee, Meeting of January 5, 1944.

87. Vitalis, *America's Kingdom*, 103. Pakistanis and the Pakistani government also accused the British government and oil companies of discrimination against Pakistanis after the devaluation of the Pakistani rupee. IOR/L/PS/12/3715B: Coll 30/5(3) "Bahrein [sic] Residency Monthly Letter—Summary of Events: Letter to Burrows from W. R. Hay, July 1, 1948; IOR/L/PS/12/3715B: Letter to Burrows from W. R. Hay, June 6, 1949; Letter to Burrows from W. R. Hay, October 29, 1948.

88. IOR/L/PS/12/3769A: Bahrain Intelligence Summary for Period August 1–15, 1947.

89. IOR/L/PS/12/3769A: Bahrain Intelligence Summary for Period August 16–31, 1947.

90. IOR/L/PS/12/3769A: Bahrain Intelligence Summary for Period October 16–31, 1947.

91. IOR/R/15/2/319: Bahrain Intelligence Summary for Period August 1–15, 1948.

92. IOR/R/15/2/319: Bahrain Intelligence Summary for Period February 16–March 15, 1948.

93. IOR/R/15/2/319: Bahrain Intelligence Summary for Period September 1–15, 1948.

94. IOR/L/PS/12/3751B: D.O. NO. 350-S, 9 February 1948.

95. BP ARC112467: Abadan Labour Department, Indian Section, Annual Report 1947, Section A: Employment.

96. IOR/R/15/2/613: Letter to Pelly, Political Agency, Bahrain, 22 January 1948.

97. IOR/R/15/2/613: Letter to Sir Rupert Hay, Political Resident, Persian Gulf, from the Political Agency, Bahrain, 4 February 1948.

98. IOR/R/15/2/319: Bahrain Intelligence Summary for Period January 16–31, 1948.

99. IOR/L/PS/12/3751B: D.O. No. 350-S, February 9, 1948.

100. BP ARC: 118823: Lessons of 1946.

101. IOR/R/15/2/613: Letter to Sir Rupert Hay, 22nd January 1948.

102. Jalal, *Sole Spokesman*, 293.

103. See also: Metcalf, "Too Little and Too Much"; Pandey, "Can a Muslim be an Indian?"

104. For example, in the 1920s, V. D. Sarvarkar, a leading a proponent of Hindutva ideology, argued that India was a Hindu nation defined by geographic unity, racial features, and a common culture, and he considered Sikhs to be Hindus. Savarkar, *Hindutva*, 125–29. However, government officials who were proponents of Hindutva were not concerned about the treatment of Sikh Indians.

105. Brown, *States of Injury*, 107–14; Brown, "'Most We Can Hope'"; Marx, "Jewish Question."

106. DuBois, "An Appeal to the World." See also Das, *Critical Events*, 84–90; Quataert, *Advocating Dignity*, 38, 55.

107. Mehta, "Diaspora as Spokesperson and Watchdog," 79. See also Ambedkar, *States and Minorities*.

108. NAI, MEA, Emigration, F. 22–8/48-Emi: Memorandum Submitted by the Ex-Employees of the Bahrein Petroleum Company, Ltd., Bahrain, 1948.

109. HIA McConnell, Box 1, Folder 8: Journal Entry, July 14, 1945.

110. UNT OH 0659: Interview with Smith.

Chapter 4

1. BP ARC100081: BP in Little Aden; Bamberg, *History of British Petroleum Company*, Vol. 3, 74–75.

2. Mosaddegh was an Iranian politician who served as prime minister from 1951 to 1953 and who led efforts to nationalize oil in Iran. He was removed from power in 1953 following a coup fomented by the US ambassador and the CIA. See Abrahamian, "1953 Coup in Iran"; Kashani-Sabet, "Cultures of Iranianness," 178.

3. Bamberg, *History of British Petroleum Company*, Vol. 2, 513; Coxon, *Oil Industry in 1951*.

4. Prior to 1954, BP was subsidiary of AIOC.

5. Seccombe and Lawless, "Foreign Worker Dependence in the Gulf," 563; NAI, MEA, Emigration, 1952, F 23–9/52-Emi: Letter to Minister Home Affairs from K. Appunni Menon, 10 December 1952.

6. BP ARC100081: BP in Little Aden.

7. NAI, MEA, Emigration, 1953, F.23–9/52-Emi: Telegram to Embassy of India, Cairo.

8. NAI, MEA, Emigration, 1953, G/16307: Letter to POE, Bombay, from BP, 10 June 1953.

9. NAI, MEA, Emigration, 1953, 2954/53-Emi: Letter to the Secretary, MEA, from Thadani, 10 June 1953.

10. NAI, MEA, Emigration, 1953, 2954/53-Emi: Letter to the Secretary, MEA, from Thadani, 10 June 1953; NAI, MEA, Emigration, 1953, F.23–9/52-Emi: Extract from Monthly Report No. 5 of 1953.

11. NAI, MEA, Emigration, 1953, F.23–9/52-Emi: Aden—Recruitment of 600 skilled workers from India.

12. NAI, MEA, Emigration, 1953, F. 23–9/52-Emi: Extract from Monthly Report No. 5 of 1953.

13. NAI, MEA, Emigration, F. 22–8/48-Emi: Skilled workers engaged by the Bahrein [sic] Petroleum Co., Bahrein.

14. Bose, "Taraknath Das," 168–71.

15. BP ARC100081: BP in Little Aden.

16. BP ARC24486: Letter to Sinclair from MacNeill, 14 November 1952.

17. BP ARC24486: Suggested Procedure for Local Recruitment, Aden, by Baxter, 1 August 1952; BP ARC100081: BP in Little Aden.

18. Despite previous government prohibitions, there were already large numbers of Indians living in Aden, and there was evidence of Indian influence in Adenese social practices. BP ARC106992: Letter to Jordan, KOC, from Gidney Jr., American Consulate, 29 September 1948.

19. Aware of the vastly different labor needs of the oil refinery during the construction phase versus during the refinery's maintenance, Indian government representatives assumed that only a few Indians would be kept at the refinery once construction was finished. NAI, MEA, Emigration, 1952, F 23–9/52-Emi: Letter to

POE Bombay Regarding Aden Refinery Construction, 26 March 1953; NAI, MEA, Emigration, 6637/52-Emi: Express Letter to All Passport Issuing Authorities in India, 24 November 1952; NAI, MEA, Emigration, 1953, F.23–9/52-Emi: Aden—Recruitment of 600 skilled workers from India; BP ARC24486: Letter to Sinclair from MacNeill, 6 November 1952; BP ARC24486: Letter to Taylor from Mullay, 27 June 1952.

20. BP ARC24486: Letter to Adey, 24th June 1952; NAI, MEA, Emigration, D5080/52-Emi: Letter to Sampath from Ghatge, 13 October 1952; NAI, MEA, Emigration, 1953, F.23–9/52-Emi: Aden—Recruitment of 600 skilled workers from India.

21. BP ARC24486: Letter to MacNeill from Baxter, 10 September 1953.

22. In Aden, Bechtel was forced to sponsor and guarantee workers, releasing BP from this responsibility. BP ARC24486: Aden: Administration: Project: Foreign Labor: Aden Refinery, Immigration Regulations, 19 August 1952.

23. BP ARC24486: Letter to MacNeill from Sinclair, 14 July 1952.

24. BP ARC24486: Letter to Sinclair from MacNeill, 14 November 1952.

25. NAI, MEA, Emigration, 1953, F.23–9/52-Emi: Aden—Recruitment of 600 skilled workers from India.

26. NAI, MEA, Emigration, 1953, F.23–9/52-Emi: Letter to Ghatge from Thadani, 19 March 1953.

27. NAI, MEA, Emigration, 1953, F.23–9/52-Emi: Aden—Recruitment of 600 skilled workers from India.

28. NAI, MEA, Emigration, 1953, F.23–9/52-Emi: Letter to Thadani from Ghatge, 26 March 1953.

29. Designations included Contract Americans, Contract British, Contract British/Americans, Contract Italians, Contract Indians, Contract Palestinians, Lebanese, etc. (if used). BP ARC24486: Letter from McAuliffe, 25th June 1952; BP ARC24486: Letter to Sinclair from MacNeill, 6th November 1952. For a discussion of how oil companies reshaped urban spaces in Iraq and these spaces became sites of labor unrest, see Fuccaro, "Reading Oil as Urban Violence."

30. BP ARC100081: BP in Little Aden.

31. NAI, MEA, Emigration, 1953, F.23–9/52-Emi: Aden—Recruitment of 600 skilled workers from India.

32. NAI, MEA, Emigration, 1953, F.23–9/52-Emi: Extract from Monthly Report No. 5 of 1953; NAI, MEA, Emigration, 1953, 2954/53-Emi: Letter to the Trade Commissioner, Aden, from Bechtel and Wimpey, 20 May 1953; NAI, MEA, Emigration, F. 22–8/48-Emi: Skilled workers engaged by the Bahrein [sic] Petroleum Co., Bahrein.

33. NAI, MEA, Emigration, 1953, 2954/53-Emi: Letter to the Trade Commissioner, Aden, from Bechtel and Wimpey, 20 May 1953.

34. NAI, MEA, Emigration, 1953, 2954/53-Emi: Letter to the Secretary, MEA, from Thadani, 10 June 1953; NAI, MEA, Emigration, 1953, F.23–9/52-Emi: Letter to Indian

Trade Commission from Indian Employees Committee, 4 July 1953; NAI, MEA, Emigration, 1953, G/16307: Letter to POE, Bombay, from BP, 10 June 1953.

35. Indians received better pay than local labor for the same job. For example, when hiring Indian domestics, the company increased the rate of category C & D to differentiate between Indian and local Arab labor. BP ARC24486: Aden: Administration: Project: Foreign Labor (1951–58): Letter to Sinclair from MacNeill, 14 November 1952.

36. NAI, MEA, Emigration, 1953, F.23–9/52-Emi: Letter to Indian Trade Commission from Indian Employees Committee, 4 July 1953.

37. NAI, MEA, Emigration, 1953, G/16307: Letter to POE, Bombay, from BP, 10 June 1953; NAI, MEA, Emigration, 1953, 2954/53-Emi: Extract from Monthly Report No. 4 of 1953.

38. A beedi is a tobacco product that is smoked, similar to a cigarette or mini-cigar. Agarwala, "From Work to Welfare," 430.

39. NAI, MEA, Emigration, 11(5)CA/53: Letter to the Secretary, MEA, from Commissioner, 22 May 1953.

40. NAI, MEA, Emigration, 1953, F.23–9/52-Emi: Telegram to Embassy of India, Cairo.

41. Gabaccia, Hoerder, and Walaszek, "Emigration and Nation Building"; Torpey, "Leaving."

42. NAI, MEA, Emigration, 1948, F. 22–8/48-Emi: Skilled workers engaged by the Bahrein Petroleum Co., Bahrein.

43. NAI, MEA, Emigration, 1952, 6261/52-Emi: Letter to Sampath from Ghatge, 3 November 1952; NAI, MEA, Emigration, 1952, 6378/52-Emi: Letter to Sampath from Ghatge, 10 November 1952; NAI, MEA, Emigration, 1952, F 23–9/52-Emi: George Wimpey and Company Limited, Preliminary Agreement and Form of Agreement.

44. In practice, however, arbitration was not consistently available, and workers had trouble appealing their cases once they lost their positions with the company. Other contracts asked that the company remit a portion of the workers' pay for employees through company representatives based in India. This provision may have been included because some countries, such as Ceylon and Burma, limited the amount of money Indians living there were able to remit back to India. NAI, MEA, Emigration, 1952, 6378/52-Emi: Letter to Sampath from Ghatge, 10 November 1952; NAI, MEA, Emigration, 1952, 23–9/52-Emi: Letter to POE, Bombay from Deputy Secretary, MEA, 8 December 1952; NAI, MEA, Emigration, 1952, 7027/52-Emi: Letter to Deputy Secretary, MEA, 22 December 1952; NAI, MEA, Emigration, F. 22–8/48-Emi: Skilled workers engaged by the Bahrein [sic] Petroleum Co., Bahrein; NAI, MEA, Emigration, 1954, F. 13-9/54-Emi: Material required by Sri Lanka Sundaram M.P. for a paper on the "Effect of Emigration."

45. NAI, MEA, Emigration, 1952, D 7061/52-Emi: Extract from monthly report No. 12 of 1952 from Indian Government Commission, Aden, 17 December 1952.

46. The concern over poor citizens migrating and hurting a country's reputation has colonial antecedents. During the colonial period, the British government did not want poor English people in India so as not to tarnish the image of the empire. See, for example, Ballhatchet, *Race, Sex, and Class*; Mills, *Gender and Colonial Space*.

47. NAI, MEA, Emigration, 1952, D 7061/52-Emi: Extract from monthly report no. 12 of 1952 from Indian Government Commission, Aden, 17 December 1952.

48. NAI, MEA, Emigration, 1952, F 23-9/52-Emi: Letter POE Bombay Regarding Aden Refinery Construction, 26 March 1953.

49. NAI, MEA, Emigration, 1954, F. 13-9/54-Emi: Material required by Sri Lanka Sundaram M.P. for a paper on the "Effect of Emigration."

50. Indian cooks were categorized as semiskilled workers by the Indian government.

51. NAI, MEA, Emigration, 1953, D. 3206/53Emi: Letter to the Secretary of the Government of India from A. B. Thadani, 18 July 1953.

52. NAI, MEA, Emigration, 1952, D 7061/52-Emi: Extract from Monthly Report No. 4 of 1953; NAI, MEA, Emigration, 1953, F. 6-6/53-Emi: Report from Qatar Petroleum Company, 10 July 1953.

53. NAI, MEA, Emigration, 1953, F. 6-6/53-Emi: Action taken on the report of the Good-will Mission to the Persian Gulf in 1948.

54. NAI, MEA, Emigration, Section D 3798/54-Emi: Letter to Undersecretary, MEA, from Seshan, 22 October 1954.

55. NAI, MEA, Emigration, 1952, D 752-AWI/5342: Letter to the Secretary for the Government of India, MEA, from Commissioner for the Government of India, 29 January 1953.

56. NAI, MEA, Emigration, 1952, D 1110-AW5/B47: Letter to the Indian Consulate, Aden, from Bhagwanji Virji Satikuvar, 28 January 1953.

57. NAI, MEA, Emigration, 1952, 1101/53-Emi: Letter to Minister of Home Affairs from Appunni Menon, 10 December 1952.

58. It was not only at Aden that Christians were preferentially hired. At Bapco and Aramco, Christians were also preferentially hired, and this practice impacted other nationalities, as well. For example, Palestinians—who the Saudi government required that the company hire in the proportions of 70 percent Muslims and 30 percent Christians—were in practice hired at a fifty-fifty ratio of Muslims to Christians. UNT OH 0659: Interview with Smith; BP ARC24486: Aden: Administration: Project: Foreign Labor, Memorandum, 31 July 1952.

59. NAI, MEA, Emigration, 1952, 1112/53-Emi: Letter to the Under-Secretary, MEA, from the POE, Bombay, 14 March 1953.

60. NAI, MEA, Emigration Bureau, 1952, F 23-9/52-Emi: Note for Office Record from Thadani.

61. NAI, MEA, Emigration Bureau, 1952, F 23-9/52-Emi: Letter to Mr. Ghatge from A. B. Thadani, 19 March 1953.

62. NAI, MEA, Emigration, 1952, F 23-9/52-Emi: Letter to Thadani from Ghatge, 26 March 1953.

63. NAI, MEA, R&I, 1956, 3(24) R&I/56: Annual Report of Aden, 1955; NAI, MEA, Emigration, 1952, F 23-9/52-Emi: Letter to POE Bombay Regarding Aden Refinery Construction, 26 March 1953.

64. NAI, MEA, Emigration, 1952, F 23-9/52-Emi: Letter to POE, Bombay, from Undersecretary MEA, 16 May 1953.

65. NAI, MEA, Emigration, 1953, F 23-9/52-Emi: Letter to the POE, Bombay, from Undersecretary, MEA, 9 October 1953.

66. NAI, MEA, Emigration, 1953, 12(1)CA/53: Letter to Ghatge from Thadani, 28 April 1953.

67. NAI, MEA, Emigration, 1953, F 23-9/52-Emi: Letter to Ghatge from Thadani, 5 June 1953.

68. Zamindar, *Long Partition*.

69. The connection between India and Hinduism has been written about at length. For examples, see Banerjee, *Make Me a Man*; Ghassem-Fachandi, *Pogrom in Gujarat*; Gupta, *Sexuality, Obscenity, Community*; Jones, *Socio-Religious Reform Movements*; Malhotra, *Gender, Caste, and Religious Identities;* Minault, *Secluded Scholars*; Oberoi, *Construction of Religious Boundaries*; Pandey, "Can a Muslim Be an Indian?"; Sarkar, *Hindu Wife, Hindu Nation*; van der Veer, *Religious Nationalism*. Today, Indian workers in the Arabian Peninsula continue to critically engage with this association between Hinduism and India; see Wright, *Between Dreams and Ghosts*, 113–36.

70. Sunder Rajan and Needham, "Introduction."

71. I draw the distinction between secularism as a "value" and secularism as a "principle of statecraft" from Menon, "Living with Secularism."

72. For a longer discussion of Mahatma Gandhi's view of secularism and how Nehru's view differed, see Sunder Rajan and Needham, "Introduction," 15–16; Khilnani, "Nehru's Faith," 89–103.

73. NAI, MEA, R&I, 1956, 3(24): Annual Report of Aden, 1955.

74. NAI, MEA, Emigration, 1953, 17-6/53-Emi: Indian Emigration Act—Proposal for an amendment of.

75. NAI, MEA, SEA section, 2/54/6551/10003: Report on the working the Indian Emigration Act (VII of 1922) for the year 1951.

76. NAI, MEA, Emigration, 1953, F. 17-6/54-Emi: Annual Report on the Working of the Indian Emigration Act VII of 1922 and the Rules Issued Thereunder during the Year Ending 31st December 1952, of the Ports of Bombay, Porbandar, Bedi Bunder and Port Okha.

77. NAI, MEA, Emigration, 1953, F. 17-6/54-Emi: Report on the Working of the Indian Emigration Act (No. VII of 1922) for the Year 1952; NAI, MEA, Emigration, 1954, F. 13-9/54-Emi: Material required by Sri Lanka Sundaram M.P. for a paper on the "Effect of Emigration."

78. NAI, MEA, Emigration, 1955, F20-2/55-Emi: Annual Report on the Working of the Emigration Act; NAI, MEA, SEA section, 1952, 2/54/6551/10003: Report on the working the Indian Emigration Act (VII of 1922) for the year 1951.

79. NAI, MEA, Emigration, 1948, F. 22-8/48-Emi: Skilled workers engaged by the Bahrein Petroleum Co., Bahrein.

80. NAI, MEA, Emigration, 1953, F. 17-6/54-Emi: Annual Report on the Working of the Indian Emigration Act VII of 1922 and the Rules Issued Thereunder during the Year Ending 31st December 1952, of the Ports of Bombay, Porbandar, Bedi Bunder and Port Okha.

81. NAI, MEA, Emigration, 1948, F. 22-8/48-Emi: Skilled workers engaged by the Bahrein Petroleum Co., Bahrein.

82. NAI, MEA, Emigration, 1953, D2956/53-Emi: Letter to the Ministry of External Affairs from the Commissioner of the Government of India, Aden, 3 July 1953.

83. NAI, MEA, Emigration, 1953, T.J. Dias, Badge No. 7180: J. F. Williams, 30 June 1953.

84. NAI, MEA, Emigration, 1953, F23-9/52-Emi: Letter to Administration from W. H. Jones.

85. NAI, MEA, Emigration, 1953. D2956/53-Emi: Letter to the Ministry of External Affairs from the Commissioner of the Government of India, Aden, 3 July 1953.

86. NAI, MEA, Emigration, F. 23-9/52-Emi: Letter to the Commission from the Ministry of External Affairs, 11 August 1953.

87. NAI, MEA, Emigration, 1948, F. 22-8/48-Emi: Skilled workers engaged by the Bahrein Petroleum Co., Bahrein.

88. NAI, MEA, Emigration, 1952, F 23-9/52-Emi: Letter to Thadani from Ghatge, 3 March 1953.

89. NAI, MEA, Emigration Section, D3091/54-Emi: Letter to the Controller General of Emigration from the Protector of Emigrants, Bombay, 24 August 1954; NAI, MEA, Emigration Section, D2721/53-Emi: Letter to Yunus from POE, Bombay, 4 June 1953.

90. BP ARC24486: Letter to MacNeill from Sinclair, 14 July 1952.

91. BP ARC24486: Letter to MacNeill from Baxter, 10 September 1953.

92. For example, managers argued that Italians "slack-off." BP ARC24486: Aden Refinery Project, Italian Wage Rates by H. S. Mullay, 13 November 1952.

93. Chomsky, *Linked Labor Histories,* 3; Wright, *Between Dreams and Ghosts,* 4–5.

94. NAI, MEA, Emigration, 1953, F.6-6/53-Emi: Report Dated 30 July 1953 from Messrs. Middle East Bechtel Corporation and George Wimpey & Co., Ltd., Aden.

95. BP ARC24486: Letter to Sinclair from MacNeill, 6 November 1952.

96. BP ARC24486: Italian Wage Rates.

97. BP ARC24486: Letter to Sinclair from MacNeill, 14 November 1952.

98. BP ARC24486: Letter to Sinclair from MacNeill, 6 November 1952.

99. Such a position ignored that the economic conditions in India were largely shaped by extractive British colonialism, which impoverished the subcontinent and funded the growth of British infrastructure and industry. See Mukherjee, *Hungry Bengal*; Patnaik, "Revisiting the 'Drain.'"

100. NAI, MEA, Emigration, 1953, F.6-6/53-Emi: Minutes of Meeting with Two Representatives of Indian Employees, 3 June 1953.

101. NAI, MEA, Emigration (originally in AWT section), 1953, F.6-6/53-Emi/D.2049/AWT/54: Report of Dr. Chand, Embassy of India, Baghdad, 22 April 1954.

102. BP ARC24486: Letter from Baxter to MacNeill, 10 September 1953. Note, also at Aden, Training Within Industry (TWI) was still being used to train managers. BP ARC143434: Staff Relations Matters, 1947–1971: Industrial Relations for Staff, 1953; BP ARC143434: Circular to Certain Members of Staff from Gibson.

103. NAI, MEA, Emigration, 1953, 27321/53-Emi: Telegram to Foreign Office, New Delhi, 8 July 1953.

104. NAI, MEA, Emigration, 1953, 2954/53-Emi: Extract from Monthly Report No. 4 of 1953; NAI, MEA, Emigration, 1953, 2779/53-Emi: Letter to Secretary, MEA, from Commissioner, 27 June 1953.

105. When told about the spies, the commissioner "gave [the Indian employee] a short lecture on building national character, for communicating to his colleagues [at the refinery]." NAI, MEA, Emigration, 1953, 2954/53-Emi: Extract from Monthly Report No. 4 of 1953.

106. NAI, MEA, Emigration, 1953, 2779/53-Emi: Letter to Secretary, MEA, from Commissioner, 27 June 1953.

107. NAI, MEA, Emigration, 1953, F.23-9/52-Emi: Letter to Ghatge from Thadani, 19 March 1953. The central role recruiters play in staffing oil projects continues into the present, see Wright, *Between Dreams and Ghosts.*

108. BP ARC24486: Letter to Sinclair from MacNeill, 14 November 1952.

109. NAI, MEA, Emigration, 1953, F.23-9/52-Emi: Letter to Indian Trade Commission from Indian Employees Committee, 4 July 1953.

110. NAI, MEA, Emigration, 1953, F6-4/53-Emi: Report on the Service Conditions etc. of Indian employees in the Oil Refinery Project at Aden.

111. NAI, MEA, Emigration, 1953, 17-6/53-Emi: Indian Emigration Act—Proposal for an amendment of.

112. BP ARC24486: Requested Procedure for Local Recruitment by Baxter, 1 August 1952.

113. BP ARC24486: Telegram to L. H. Baxter Aden Refinery from MacNeill, 7 November 1952. Abdalla S. Burja's ethnography describes how migration impacted social organization and hierarchies in Hadhramaut. Burja, *Politics of Stratification*, 54–88.

114. For example, while workers from colonial Aden were recruited and their travel was covered, the company did not want to give workers from the Protectorate and Yemen travel allowances, for fear that it would negatively impact local Aden employers. BP ARC24486: Telegram to L. H. Baxter Aden Refinery from MacNeill, 7 November 1952.

115. BP ARC100081: BP in Little Aden.

116. BP ARC100081: BP in Little Aden. Oil company practices of hiring local labor through local sheikhs had a large impact on social structures in these areas. See Burja, *Politics of Stratification*; Seccombe and Lawless, "Gulf Labour Market and the Early Oil Industry," 103–4.

117. BP ARC100081: BP in Little Aden.

118. BP ARC24486: Extract of Letter from BP (Aden), 16 April 1956; BP ARC24486: Letter from Heron to Johnston, 14 October 1956.

119. When the demands were put forward, a "proper Union spokesman was not present." BP ARC35938B: Payment, Accounts Etc.

120. These were interesting demands because the contract between BP and Wimpey stated that Wimpey needed observe local holidays and to transport its employees. BP ARC35938B: Aden Refinery Project: Construction of Staff and Labour Housing at Little Aden: Agreement between Anglo-Iranian Oil Company Limited and George Wimpey and Company Limited, 10 March 1953: Conditions of Contract: Labor.

121. BP ARC24486: Extract of Letter from BP (Aden), 16 April 1956.

122. BP ARC24486: Note from Superintending Engineer Construction to Staff Department Labor Relations, 26 April 1956.

123. BP ARC24486: Letter from Heron to Johnston, 14 October 1956.

124. Burja, *Politics of Stratification*, 169.

125. Halliday, *Revolution and Foreign Policy*, 8.

126. NAI, MEA, Emigration, 1953, 3496/53-Emi: Letter to Das Gupta from Ghatge, 1 August 1953; NAI, MEA, Emigration, 1953, F 6-6/53-Emi: Report Dated 30 July 1953 from Messrs. Middle East Bechtel Corporation and George Wimpey & Co., Ltd., Aden.

Chapter 5

1. UNT OH 0688: Interview with Leigh D. Josephson by Dr. Ronald E. Marcello, (Medford, Oregon: May 27, 1986).
2. UNT OH 0688: Interview with Josephson.
3. UNT OH 0659: Interview with Smith.
4. UNT OH 0688: Interview with Josephson.
5. HIA McConnell, Box 1, Folder 7: Journal Entry, October 24, 1953.
6. Fuccaro, "Shaping the Urban Life of Oil," 71; Vitalis, *America's Kingdom,* 40.
7. See also: Lawson, *Bahrain,* 62–67.
8. According to one academic who visited Bahrain in the 1950s, people did not distinguish between pan-Arab or pan-Islamic unity. Qubain, "Social Classes and Tensions in Bahrain," 272–73.
9. Wafa Alsayed has conducted significant research on this publication. Alsayed, "*Sawt al-Bahrain.*"
10. While the organization's name changed on March 23, 1956, the organization's aims did not. FO 371–126895: Internal Political Situation in Bahrain: Resume of the Proceedings Against Five Members of the "Committee of National Union."
11. Fuccaro, *Histories of the City and State in the Persian Gulf,* 152, 176, 180; Qubain, "Social Classes and Tensions in Bahrain," 270.
12. Lawson, *Bahrain,* 58; Qubain, "Social Classes and Tensions in Bahrain," 277–78.
13. Fuccaro, *Histories of the City and State in the Persian Gulf,* 152; Qubain, "Social Classes and Tensions in Bahrain," 271–73.
14. Khalaf, "Labor Movements in Bahrain."
15. UNT OH 0659: Interview with Smith.
16. BP ARC106831: The Suez Canal: Diary of Events.
17. BP ARC106831: Letter to Southwell 16 August 1956; BP ARC106962: Letter to Jordan from Southwell, 5 November 1956; BP ARC106962: Telegram (Q1238) to Jordan from Southwell, 21 December 1956; BP ARC106962: Telegram (199) to Southwell from Jordan, 11 December 1956; BP ARC106962: Letter (ITJ/CAPS/577) to Southwell form Jordan, 20 December 1956; BP ARC106962: Letter (ITJ/CAPS/581) from Jordan, 20 December 1956.
18. Fuccaro, *Histories of the City and State in the Persian Gulf,* 186.
19. FO 1016–440: Bahrain Movement for Representational Government: Letter from G. A. Gault, Political Agent, 30 March 1955.
20. The British government saw the key issues somewhat differently, and a British government report identified three key reasons behind the tensions. First, they argued that there were sectarian tensions, despite the cooperation between Shia and Sunni Muslims in the group. Second, they believed that educated Bahrainis

were frustrated with the ruler and his British advisor. Finally, they attributed the cause to Arab nationalist feelings that came from Nasser's Egypt. FO 371–126895: Notes for the Adjournment of Debate, March 7; FO 1016–440: Letter from G. A. Gault, Political Agent, 30 March 1955.

21. FO 1016–468: Text of Speech Delivered by al Bakir in Kuwaiti Union Club in Cairo.

22. IOR/R/15/2/419: File 10/3 Bapco Labour: Letter, Political Resident, 6 January 1945.

23. Gornall, "Some Memories of Bapco," 44.

24. IOR/R/15/2/319: Bahrain Intelligence Summary for Period 1st to 15th January 1948.

25. HIA Stevens, Box 1: Bahrain Concession with Bahrein Petroleum Company Ltd., Canada, December 1934; HIA McConnell, Box 1, Folder 5: James Terry Duce, History of Oil Concessions in the Middle East, reprinted from Bulletin of the Near East Society.

26. HIA Snyder, Box 19, Folder 1: Personnel Planning Committee, Visit to Bahrain Petroleum Company Operations, June 4, 1949.

27. HIA McConnell, Box 1, Folder 9: Journal Entry, May 3, 1944.

28. IOR/R/15/2/319: Bahrain Intelligence Summary for Period 16th to 31st August 1948; IOR/R/15/2/319: Bahrain Intelligence Summary for Period 1st to 15th September 1948.

29. IOR/R/15/2/319: Bahrain Intelligence Summary for Period 16th to 31st January 1948.

30. IOR/L/PS/12/3715B: Letter to Burrows from W. R. Hay, Persian Gulf Residency, 6 June 1949; IOR/R/15/2/319: Bahrain Intelligence Summary for Period 16th to 31st January 1948; IOR/R/15/2/319: Bahrain Intelligence Summary for Period 16th to 31st August 1948; IOR/R/15/2/319: Bahrain Intelligence Summary for Period 1st to 15th September 1948.

31. Government of Bahrain, *Annual Report*, 37, cited in Finnie, "Recruitment and Training of Labor," 130.

32. IOR/R/15/2/419: Translation of Leaflet Distributed by "Home Front."

33. IOR/R/15/2/419: Anonymous Letter, 14 January 1950.

34. In 1957, there were approximately 42,000 males in Bahrain between the ages of 15 and 65. Of the 30,000 of these included in a census, 59 percent were Bahrainis and 41 percent foreigners. FO 371–127014: Marginalia, The Census in Bahrain.

35. FO 371–127014: The Census of Employment in Bahrain, S. Rose, May 8, 1957. The oil industry had the lowest percentage of foreigners.

36. FO 371–127014: Letter from W. F. Crawford, May 1, 1957; FO 371–127014: Draft Letter to E. F. Given, British Residency, Bahrain, from A. R. Walmsley, June 4, 1957.

37. FO 371–127014: Letter from W. F. Crawford, May 1, 1957.

38. FO 371–127014: The Census of Employment in Bahrain, Note by S. Rose, May 8, 1957; FO 371–127014: Letter from Walmsley, June 5, 1957.

39. FO 371–127014: Letter from W. F. Crawford, May 1, 1957.

40. FO 371–127014: The Census of Employment in Bahrain, Table 45: Range of Mean Daily Wages.

41. FO 371–127014: Letter from W. F. Crawford, May 1, 1957; FO 371–127014: The Census of Employment in Bahrain. Note, the British administrative category of "Bahraini" continued to be vague, and in the census, a Bahraini subject was defined as a person who was born in Bahrain or who held a Bahraini passport. FO 371–127014: Report on the Census of Employment in Bahrain, 1956, Chapter One, Industrial Classification of Establishment and Workers.

42. CAB 134–1086: Middle East Oil Committee: Meeting 1–16 (1955); Papers 1–32 (1955–1956); Meeting 1 (1956); Papers 1–3 (1956): Annex: Middle East Oil after the Persian Agreement.

43. Supreme Council of the Principal Allied Powers' San Remo Resolution of 25 April 1920.

44. Balfour Declaration, 1917.

45. Allen, *A History of False Hope*, 74.

46. Woolbert, "Pan-Arabism and the Palestine Problem," 309–10; Haller, "A Call for Solidarity."

47. Chester, "A 'High Iron Railing'"; Sinanoglou, *Partitioning Palestine*.

48. Beinin and Lockman, *Workers on the Nile*, 361–62.

49. IOR/L/PS/12/3769A: Bahrain Intelligence Summary No. 19 for Period 1st to 15th October 1947.

50. IOR/L/PS/12/3769A: Bahrain Intelligence Summary No. 23 for Period 1st to 15th December 1947.

51. IOR/L/PS/12/3769A: Bahrain Intelligence Summary No. 23 for Period 1st to 15th December 1947; IOR/L/PS/12/3769A: Bahrain Intelligence Summary No. 22 for Period 16th to 30th November 1947.

52. IOR/R/15/2/613: Notes on the Duties of a Special Police Officer; IOR/R/15/2/613: Notice: King's Regulation under Article 83 of the Qatar Order-in-Council, 1939, February 3, 1948.

53. IOR/L/PS/12/3769A: Bahrain Intelligence Summary No. 23 for Period 1st to 15th December 1947.

54. IOR/L/PS/12/3769A: Bahrain Intelligence Summary No. 20 for Period 16th to 31st October 1947. The Nakba was a catalyst for pan-Arab nationalism and anti-imperial activism, but the lines of solidarity between Arabs and non-Arabs

and between khalijis and non-khalijis were not clearly demarcated. For example, during some protests in opposition to Palestine's partition, protestors drew parallels between the partition of Palestine with the partition of India. In March 1948, there were both anti-Jewish and anti-Sikh protests in Bahrain. At this time, rumors circulated Manama in which Hindus were described as "brothers of Jews." The British government believed Muslims from the Indian subcontinent were behind these rumors and that they were using the solidarity Bahrainis felt with Palestinians to leverage sympathy for Pakistan. IOR/L/PS/12/3751B: D.O. No. 540-S, 8 March 1948; IOR/R/15/2/319: File 8/16 Bahrain Intelligence Summary 1948: Bahrain Intelligence Summary No. 1 for Period 1st to 15th January 1948.

55. Beinin, *Was the Red Flag*, 100, 204.

56. HIA Snyder Papers, Box 15, File 1: Social Change in Saudi Arabia: Problems and Prospects: A Report by Thomas O'Dea, Prepared from Research Conducted by the Special Study Group, February–August 1963; Citino, *From Arab Nationalism to OPEC*, 100; Hertog, *Princes, Brokers, and Bureaucrats*, 50.

57. HIA Snyder Papers, Box 15: A Report Prepared from Research Conducted by the Special Study Group by Thomas F. O'Dea, February–August 1963.

58. HIA Snyder Papers, Box 15: A Report Prepared from Research Conducted by the Special Study Group by Thomas F. O'Dea, February–August 1963.

59. HIA Snyder, Box 15, File 1: Social Change in Saudi Arabia: Problems and Prospects: A Report by Thomas O'Dea, Prepared from Research Conducted by the Special Study Group, February–August 1963.

60. For these debates in Saudi Arabia, see Bsheer, *Archive Wars*, 55; Bsheer, "A Counter Revolutionary State."

61. Fuccaro, *Histories of the City and State in the Persian Gulf*, 190. Similarly, in Oman, pan-Arab movements also influenced national identity. In addition, Mandana Limbert tells us that over the course of the twentieth century, as "Oman became tied to the politics of the Arab world, 'Arabness' increasingly became understood as an ethnic or racial category." Limbert, *In the Time of Oil*, 135, 143.

62. FO 1016–468: Text of Speech Delivered by al Bakir in Kuwaiti Union Club in Cairo.

63. NAI, MEA, 1954, F. 14(1)-Pol54: Embassy of India, Baghdad, 3 July 1954, Letter Oil Companies in the Persian Gulf and adjacent areas—Living and working conditions of Indian Employers, to Ministry of External Affairs, New Delhi; NAI, MEA, Emigration (originally in AWT section), 1953, F.6-6/53-Emi/ D.2049/AWT/54: Report of Dr. Chand, Embassy of India, Baghdad, 22 April 1954

64. NAI, MEA, 1954, F. 14(1)-Pol54: Embassy of India, Baghdad, 3 July 1954, Letter Oil Companies in the Persian Gulf and adjacent areas—Living and working

conditions of Indian Employers, to Ministry of External Affairs, New Delhi; NAI, MEA, Emigration (originally in AWT section), 1953, F.6-6/53-Emi/ D.2049/AWT/54: Report of Dr. Chand, Embassy of India, Baghdad, 22 April 1954.

65. NAI, MEA, 1954, F. 14(1)-Pol54: Embassy of India, Baghdad, 3 July 1954, Letter Oil Companies in the Persian Gulf and adjacent areas—Living and working conditions of Indian Employers, to Ministry of External Affairs, New Delhi; NAI, MEA, Emigration (originally in AWT section), 1953, F.6-6/53-Emi/ D.2049/AWT/54: Report of Dr. Chand, Embassy of India, Baghdad, 22 April 1954.

66. NAI, MEA, 1954, F. 14(1)-Pol54: Embassy of India, Baghdad, 3 July 1954, Letter Oil Companies in the Persian Gulf and adjacent areas—Living and working conditions of Indian Employers, to Ministry of External Affairs, New Delhi; NAI, MEA, Emigration (originally in AWT section), 1953, F.6-6/53-Emi/ D.2049/AWT/54: Report of Dr. Chand, Embassy of India, Baghdad, 22 April 1954.

67. This may be contrasted to when the Indian government temporarily halted emigration in response to the hunger strikes by Indians working in Aden.

68. IOR/L/PS/12/3715B: Letter to Burrows from W. R. Hays, Persian Gulf Residency, Bahrain, 6 May 1949.

69. NAI, MEA, Emigration, 1953. F6-6/53-Emi: Oil Companies in the Persian-Gulf and Mid-east.

70. FO 371–109945: Letter from C. Costley White, 11 January 1954.

71. Not only were Indians seen with resentment by Bahrainis, but they were also seen as subordinates by the British. Qubain, "Social Classes and Tensions in Bahrain," 276; Beling, "Recent Developments in Labor Relations," 159.

72. Qubain, "Social Classes and Tensions in Bahrain," 277–78.

73. UNT OH 0659: Interview with Smith.

74. For example, one of the most popular films shown in Bahrain in the late 1940s was the Indian film *Kismet*, with the hit song, "Aaj Himalay ki Choti se," which contains the refrain, "door hato ai duniya vaalon, hindustaan hamaara hai [Get away! O foreigners (literally: world)! Hindustan (India) is ours!]." This song quickly became so popular in India with anti-imperial and nationalist groups that the British issued arrest warrants for the song's author, Kavi Pradeep. IOR/R/15/2/319: File 8/16 Bahrain Intelligence Summary: Bahrain Intelligence Summary for Period 16th to 30th September 1948; Bahrain Intelligence Summary for Period 1st to 31st October 1948; Rangoonwalla, "1931–1946," 55; Gulzar, "Lyrics 1903–1960," 282.

75. IOR/L/PS/12/3769A: Bahrain Intelligence Summary No. 21 for the Period 1st to 15th November 1947.

76. FO 371–109945: Letter from C. Costley White, 11 January 1954.

77. See also: Fuccaro, *Histories of the City and State in the Persian Gulf,* 177–79.

78. CAB 134–1086: Annex: Middle East Oil after the Persian Agreement; CAB 134–1086: Bahrain Oil, 21 March 1955.

79. FO 371–109899: Operations of the Bahrain Petroleum Company, 1954: Bapco Annual Report, 1953.

80. FO 371–109899: Bahrain Refinery, June 1954.

81. FO 371–109899: Minute, 28 February 1954.

82. In response, the ruler requested an independent check on Bapco's data, and Bapco readily agreed. FO 371–109899: From Bahrain to Foreign Office, 31 December 1953; FO 371–109899: Letter to Shaikh Salman from Bapco Political Representative, 31 December 1953.

83. FO 371–109899: Letter from Foreign Office, 13 March 1954.

84. CAB 134–1086: Bahrain Oil, 21 March 1955.

85. CAB 134–1086: Note by Joint Secretaries, 7 May 1955.

86. CAB 134–1086: Oil Policy in the Middle East, 24 August 1955.

87. CAB 134–1086: Note by the Joint Secretaries, 13 October 1955.

88. CAB 134–1086: Note by the Joint Secretaries, 7 January 1956.

89. CAB 134–1086: Note by the Joint Secretaries, 13 October 1955.

90. CAB 134–1086: Annex: Middle East Oil after the Persian Agreement; CAB 134–1086: Minutes of a Meeting of the Committee, 6 January 1955.

91. FO 371–126895: Notes for the Adjournment of Debate, March 7; FO 1016–440: Letter from C. A. Gault, Political Agent, 28 April 1955.

92. FO 371–109945: Employees of Bahrain Petroleum Company: Large increase in rates of pay and salaries ordered by King Saud: Memorandum: Aramco Wage Increases and Bapco's reactions; FO 371–109945: Letter from Residency, Bahrain, 27 March 1954; FO 371–109945: Extract from Minute by Political Agent; FO 371–109945: Bapco General Notice, No. 161; FO 371–109945: Letter from Residency, Bahrain, 31 May 1954; FO 371–109945: Memorandum: Aramco Wage Increases and Bapco's reactions; FO 371–109945: Extract from Minute by Political Agent; FO 1016–468: Text of Speech Delivered by al Bakir in Kuwaiti Union Club in Cairo.

93. UNT OH 0688: Interview with Josephson.

94. FO 371–127015: Labour Ordinances and Labour Affairs in Bahrain, 1957: Minutes, Labour Law Advisory Committee, 7 April 1957. Eventually, Bapco's management representative was Leslie Smith.

95. Overall, they held fifty-eight meetings from 1954 to 1956. UNT OH 0659: Interview with Smith; Beling, "Recent Developments in Labor Relations in Bahrayn," 162.

96. FO 1016–440: Letter from C. A. Gault, Political Agent, 28 April 1955.

97. FO 1016–440: Letter from High Executive Committee, Bahrain, 29 March 1955; FO 1016–440: Reply from the Secretary of State for Foreign Affairs.

238 NOTES TO CHAPTER 5

98. FO 371–126895: Notes for the Adjournment of Debate, March 7; FO 1016–467: From Foreign Office to Certain of Her Majesty's Representatives, 23 May 1956.

99. FO 1016–467: Bahrain: Internal Political Situation: Commonwealth Relations Office Memorandum, 24 May 1956.

100. FO 371–126895: Notes for the Adjournment of Debate, March 7; FO 1016–467: Letter from British Embassy, Cairo, 9 June 1956.

101. FO 1016–467: Report on a Meeting held 15 June 1956 by National Union Committee.

102. FO 1016–467: Pamphlet No. 59.

103. FO 1016–468: Our Labour Demands are a Single Unit.

104. FO 1016–468: Proclamation no. 64.

105. FO 1016–468: Circular no. 64, 24 July 1956.

106. FO 1016–467: Pamphlet No. 59.

107. FO 1016–467: Pamphlet No. 59.

108. FO 1016–440: Letter from C. A. Gault, Political Agent, 30 March 1955.

109. FO 1016–467: Letter from Political Agency, Bahrain, 31 May 1956.

110. FO 1016–467: Foreign Office Telegram No. 99, 23 May 1956; FO 1016–467: Letter from Political Agency, Bahrain, 31 May 1956; FO 1016–468: Telegram to Foreign Office, 10 July 1956.

111. FO 1016–468: Letter from Gault, 9 July 1956.

112. FO 1016–468: al Ahran, Cairo, 10 August 1956.

113. FO 371–126895: Statement Read on Bahrain Broadcasting Station, 20 August 1956; FO 1016–468: Telegram, 13 August 1956; FO 1016–468: Extract from al Mizan, August 17; FO 1016–468: Telegram, 16 July 1956; FO 1016–467: Telegram from Foreign Office to Bahrain, 20 June 1956; FO 1016–468: Circular No. 71, 15 August 1956.

114. FO 371–126895: Notes for the Adjournment of Debate, March 7.

115. FO 371–126895: Local Press Extracts.

116. FO 371–126895: Local Press Extracts.

117. Khalaf, "Labor Movements in Bahrain"; Fuccaro, *Histories of the City and State in the Persian Gulf*, 186.

118. FO 371–126895: Resume of the Proceedings Against Five Members of the "Committee of National Union."

119. FO 371–126895: Marginalia.

120. Three of the leaders were held in St. Helena under the Colonial Prisoners Removal Act, 1869, which was applied to Bahrain by Order in Council on December 18, 1956. FO 371–126895: Marginalia; FO 371–126895: Parliamentary Question, 27 February 1957; FO 371–126895: Draft Reply, No. 90; FO 371–127014: Letter to K. J. Hird,

Beirut, from C. Marshall, British Residency, Bahrain, December 28, 1956; UNT OH 0659: Interview with Smith.

121. FO 371–127014: Letter to K. J. Hird, Beirut, from C. Marshall, British Residency, Bahrain, December 28, 1956.

122. FO 371–126895: Draft Reply, P. Q. No. 125.

123. FO 371–126895: Bahrain Constitutional and Administrative Reform.

124. FO 1016–468: Marginalia, 19 July 1956.

125. Beling, "Recent Developments in Labor Relations in Bahrayn," 164–65.

126. FO 371–127014: Letter to K. J. Hind, British Embassy, Beirut, from C. Marshall, British Residency, Bahrain, February 14, 1957; FO 371–127014: Letter to K. J. Hird, British Embassy, Beirut, from C. Marshall, British Residency, Bahrain, January 11, 1957.

127. FO 371–127015: Minutes, The Bahrain Labour Law.

128. FO 371–127015: Letter from E. F. Given, 10 May 1957.

129. FO 371–127014: From Bahrain to Foreign Office, January 9, 1957.

130. Beling, "Recent Developments in Labor Relations in Bahrayn," 166–67.

131. FO 371–127014: Draft letter and marginalia, G. F. Blum, Labour Adviser, April 8, 1957; FO 371–127014: Letter to K. J. Hird, British Embassy, Beirut, from C. Marshall, British Residency, Bahrain, March 15, 1957; FO 371–127015: Minutes, The Bahrain Labour Law.

132. FO 371–127014: Draft letter and marginalia, G. F. Blum, Labour Adviser, April 8, 1957; FO 371–127014: Letter to K. J. Hird, British Embassy, Beirut, from C. Marshall, British Residency, Bahrain, March 15, 1957; FO 371–127015: Minutes, The Bahrain Labour Law; Indian Trade Unions Act, 1926.

133. FO 371–127014: Draft letter to Sir B. Burrows, Bahrain, from A. R. Walmsley, 22 February 1957; FO 371–127014: Letter to K. J. Hird, British Embassy, Beirut, from C. Marshall, British Residency, Bahrain, January 11, 1957.

134. FO 371–127014: Draft letter from G. G. Blumer, Labour Adviser, February 14, 1957.

135. BP ARC143434: Constitution of the Oilfield Workers' Trade Union; Bini, "From Colony to Oil Producer"; Jafari, "Labour in the Making of the International Relations of Oil," 213; Matthews, "Kennedy Administration."

136. Beinin and Lockman, *Workers on the Nile*, 304–9.

137. BP ARC118823: Lessons of 1946.

138. FO 371–127014: Labour Ordinance and Labour Affairs in Bahrain, 1957: From Bahrain to Foreign Office, 9 January 1957.

139. FO 371–127015: Letter from Foreign Office, 12 July 1957.

140. FO 371–127015: Letter from E. F. Given, 10 May 1957.

141. FO 371–127015: Minutes, The Bahrain Labour Law.

142. FO 371–127014: Letter to K. J. Hind, British Embassy, Beirut, from C. Marshall, British Residency, Bahrain, February 14, 1957.

143. FO 371–127014: Draft letter and marginalia, G. F. Blum, Labour Adviser, April 8, 1957.

144. Said, *Revolution Squared*, 132–34.

145. Beinin, *Workers and Thieves*, 43. In contrast, in Brazil following World War II, trade unions were also seen as antagonistic to the state and industry. Colistete, "Productivity, Wages, and Labor Politics," 95.

146. FO 371–127014: Letter to K. J. Hird, British Embassy, Beirut, from C. Marshall, British Residency, Bahrain, March 15, 1957; UNT OH 0659: Interview with Smith.

147. FO 371–127014: Letter to E. F. Given, Esq., Bahrain, from A. R. Walmsley, Foreign Office, April 19, 1957.

148. FO 371–127014: Draft letter and marginalia, G. F. Blum, Labour Adviser, April 8, 1957; FO 371–127014: Letter to E. F. Given, Esq., Bahrain, from A. R. Walmsley, Foreign Office, April 19, 1957; Liukkuen, "ILO and the Transformation of Labour Law."

149. FO 371–127014: Letter to G. C. Wilson, Ministry of Labour and National Service, from G. F. Blumer, February 5, 1957.

150. FO 371–127014: Letter to G. F. Blumer, Foreign Office, from G. C. Wilson, Ministry of Labour and National Service, 12 February 1957.

151. FO 371–127014: Draft letter and marginalia, G. F. Blum, Labour Adviser, April 8, 1957.

152. FO 371–127014: Draft letter to Sir B. Burrows from A. R. Walmsley, February 22, 1957.

153. FO 371–127014: Draft letter to Sir B. Burrows from A. R. Walmsley, February 22, 1957.

154. FO 371–127014: Marginalia regarding Paragraph 2 (a) of Mr. Marshall's Letter, Section 51.

155. In the court's decision, they blamed Caltex for the strike, because the company had not given the usual advance of Rs 5–7 for the Tamil New Year's Day holiday. This action by Caltex, according to the Court, was "tactless and showed a lack of human and sympathetic approach." Supreme Court of India, Caltex (India) Ltd. vs Their Workmen, 11 February 1960.

156. For example, see Kerala High Court, M/S. Caltex (India) Ltd. Vs. Industrial Tribunal No. 2, Ernakulam & Others, 18 October 1960.

157. FO 371–127014: Draft Letter to Sir B. Burrows, Bahrain, from Mr. A. R. Walmsey, 22 February 1957.

158. FO 371–127014: Letter to Blumer from Wilson, the Ministry of Labour and National Service, 12 February 1957.

159. US Labor Management Relations Act, 1947, section 209(b); FO 371–127014: Draft Letter to Sir B. Burrows, Bahrain, from Mr. A. R. Walmsey, 22 February 1957.

160. Wohlmuth and Krupka, "Taft-Hartley Act and Collective Bargaining," 565–66; Beling, "Recent Developments in Labor Relations in Bahrayn," 168.

161. Beling, "Recent Developments in Labor Relations in Bahrayn," 163.

162. BP ARC106991: The Bahrain Employed Persons Compensation Ordinance, 1957; FO 371–127014: An Ordinance to Provide for Compensation to Employed Persons for Injuries Suffered in the Course of their Employment. Concerning the administration of the law, the ruler proposed it be administered by separate courts, not the joint court that was in the draft of the labor law. Similarly to debates in Kuwait in the late 1940s, British administrators saw this proposal regarding the courts as problematic, and the British insisted on retaining their jurisdiction over all expatriate labor. FO 371–127014: Letter to E. F. Given, Bahrain, from A. R. Walmsley, Foreign Office, May 10, 1957.

163. FO 371–168866: Labour Legislation, 1963: Letter from Political Embassy, Beirut, to Political Agent, Bahrain, 22 June 1963.

164. BP ARC24486: Aden Refinery, Discussions with Aramco, July 30, 1952 (my emphasis).

165. Crystal, *Oil and Politics*, 79; al-Nakib, "Revisiting 'Hadar' and 'Badū' in Kuwait."

166. In Kuwait, it was easier for foreigners to become citizens than in Bahrain. FO 1016–126: Minutes, 18 October 1950.

167. BP ARC106831: Inter-Departmental Memorandum from W. P. Doyle, 6 May 1956.

168. BP ARC106831: Letter to C. W. Hamilton from L. T. Jordan, 25 November 1953.

169. FO 371–109947: Formation of Trade Unions in Persian Gulf: Strikes in Kuwait: Report on the Strike of Indian and Pakistani Artisans at Jewan Camp, Kuwait.

170. Specifically, the recruiter informed workers that the cost of living was between 70 and 80 rupees per day when, in reality, it cost them 110 rupees a day to feed themselves—an assertion with which British government officials agreed. FO 371–109947: Report on the Strike of Indian and Pakistani Artisans at Jewan Camp, Kuwait, Appendix A.

171. FO 371–109947: Report on the Strike of Indian and Pakistani Artisans at Jewan Camp, Kuwait, Appendix B.

172. FO 371–109947: Report on the Strike of Indian and Pakistani Artisans at Jewan Camp, Kuwait.

173. BP ARC106831: Memorandum to General Manager from de Candole, 16 May 1956.

174. BP ARC106962: Situation Report, December 11 to December 22, 1956.

175. Sheikh Jabir al Ahmad al Sabah was appointed Kuwait's minister of finance in 1962 and then served as the ruler of Kuwait from 1977 to 2006.

176. BP ARC106906: Notes on a Conversation with Shaikh Jabir al Ahmad by J. G. Considine, 13 September 1956.

177. The government's call for no strikes was contentious, and in protest, the director general of police, Colonel Jassim al Qattami, resigned from his post along with twelve young Kuwaiti officers. BP ARC106962: Situation Report, 5th to 9th November 1956, Inclusive.

178. Farah al-Nakib describes the seriousness with which the security forces intervened in two strikes and that two workers were killed. From the Kuwaiti government's perspective, these events demonstrated the power of the clubs. The speech given by Colonel Jassim al Qattami, in which he called for "democratic rule by the people," was subsequently used by Ruler Abdullah al-Salem as a reason to ban clubs, newspapers, and other organizations. al-Nakib, *Kuwait Transformed*, 166–68.

179. Most of these explosions did not cause significant damage beyond the loss of oil. BP ARC106962: Telegram (199) to Southwell from Jordan, 11 December 1956; BP ARC106962: Letter (ITJ/CAPS/577) to Southwell form Jordan, 20 December 1956; BP ARC106962: Letter (ITJ/CAPS/581) from Jordan, 20 December 1956.

180. BP ARC106962: Letter to Southwell from de Candole, 8 November 1956; see also Citino, *From Arab Nationalism to OPEC*, 107. A strike on June 17, 1956, was, according to Robert Vitalis, the last strike in Saudi Arabian history. Vitalis, *America's Kingdom*, 159.

181. Beling, *Pan-Arabism and Labor*, 68.

182. Confidential Dispatch No. 1 (1011/66), A. D. Parsons to British Political Agency, Bahrain, 2 January 1966, in PDAW:PG (24), 470–77; NAI, WANA, 1960, File No. 6-C(34)/60: Iraq's Request for helping them in their Oil Industry—Note from Ministry of Mines and Fuel (India).

183. Confidential Dispatch No. 1 (1011/66), A. D. Parsons to British Political Agency, Bahrain, 2 January 1966.

Chapter 6

1. BP ARC39618: Qatar Petroleum Company, General: Letter to G. G. Stockwell from W. V. Fuller, 1 May 1963. These strikes followed after demonstrations in February 1963 in Doha over the execution of Abdul Karim Jassim, the nationalist prime minister of Iraq, "who was overthrown by the Ba'ath party and with the probably

assistance of the CIA that year. Footage of his execution was broadcast. Mostly Yemini and Iraqi workers, the demonstrators carried pictures of the Egyptian President and nationalist Gamal Abdel Nasser. They had been encouraged to rise up by the Egyptian nationalist radio station Sawt al-Arab." Fromherz, *Qatar*, 149.

2. BP ARC39618: Appendix B: 35 Demands made by the National Unity Front Committee.

3. BP ARC39618: General Strike in Qatar, 21 April to 7 May 1963. For a more detailed discussion of this strike and internal Qatari politics, see Crystal, *Oil and Politics*, 153–54.

4. BP ARC39618: Appendix B: 35 Demands made by the National Unity Front Committee. According to Allen Fromherz, two of the leaders of the movement were members of the al Thani family, and they were not complaining of the lack of liberal democracy but at the way "the government had 'usurped' their 'historical' roles." Fromherz, *Qatar*, 150.

5. Petroleum Development Qatar was a subsidiary of IPC. APOC acquired concessions in 1935 for Qatar. This concession transferred to IPC, which created the subsidiary Petroleum Development (Qatar). In 1953, the company changed name to QPC. Rouhani, *A History of O.P.E.C.*, 95.

6. BP ARC123142: APOC and Bahrain Petro Company 1925–1933: Personal Memo HE/32 to Elkington (APOC at Abadan) from AC Hearn (APOC London), 8/11/33.

7. Bamberg, *History of the British Petroleum Company*, Vol. 2, 172.

8. IOR/L/PS/12/3715B: Persian Gulf Residency Letter, 31 January 1949; IOR/R/15/865: Minutes, 10 September 1949.

9. Toth, "Qatar."

10. FO 371-127012: Labour Affairs, Representation of workers and strikes in Qatar.

11. NAI, MEA, Emigration (originally AWT section), 1953, F.6-6/53-Emi. D892/54: Extract from the report submitted by Mr. Mahboob Ahmed, 5th August 1953.

12. Field, *The Merchants*.

13. Seccombe and Lawless, "Gulf Labour Market and the Early Oil Industry" 100–101.

14. IOR/R/15/2/865: Letter to the Political Agent, Bahrain, 31 August 1949; IOR/R/15/2/865: Letter to the Political Agency, 3 September 1949.

15. Seccombe and Lawless, "Gulf Labour Market and the Early Oil Industry," 100–101.

16. IOR/R/15/2/865: Letter from PDQ to Political Agent, Bahrain, 4 November 1967.

17. BP ARC106962: Letter to Jordan, 5 November 1956; BP ARC106962: Telegram, 21 December 1956.

18. Shahdad, "Alharak Alshaebiu fi Qatar," 616–17.

244   NOTES TO CHAPTER 6

19. FO 371–127012: Labour Affairs, Representation of Workers and Strikes in Qatar.

20. FO 371–127012: Workers' Representation and Labour Legislation in Qatar.

21. FO 371–114728: Nationality Regulations issued by the Ruler of Qatar in 1951.

22. Crystal, *Oil and Politics in the Gulf*, 150; P. McKearney, British Political Agent, Qatar, 2 January 1965, Review of Events in Qatar in 1964, in PDAW:PG (24), 360.

23. BP ARC39618: Letter to G. G. Stockwell from W. V. Fuller, 16 January 1962.

24. BP ARC39618: Government of Qatar Gazette No. 3 for 1963, 3 June 1963.

25. al-Nakib, "Revisiting 'Hadar' and 'Badū' in Kuwait," 13.

26. Ghabra, *Palestinians in Kuwait*, 41, 43.

27. P. McKearney, British Political Agent, Qatar, 2 January 1965, Review of Events in Qatar in 1964, in PDAW:PG (24), 360.

28. A. J. M. Craig, H.M. Political Agent, 2 December 1963, Confidential Annex to the Trucial States for the Period November 1–30, 1963, in PDAW:PG (24), 219–20.

29. BP ARC39618: Government of Qatar Gazette No. 3 for 1963, 3 June 1963.

30. Shahdad, "Alharak Alshaebiu fi Qatar," 629.

31. In 1972, after deposing his cousin Sheikh Ahmad bin Ali al Thani, Sheikh Khalifa bin Hamad al Thani became the ruler of Qatar. Sheikh Ahmad had come to power after his father, Sheikh Ali, abdicated in 1960. Similarly to Sheikh Zayed in Abu Dhabi, when Sheikh Khalifa took the throne, he cut family spending and increased spending on social programs. Also like Sheikh Zayed, Sheikh Khalifa is considered by many to be the first modernizing ruler of Qatar. Wright, "Qatar," 117.

32. BP ARC39618: Letter to G. G. Stockwell from W. V. Fuller, 22 April 1963.

33. BP ARC39618: Reactions to the new Government Gazette, 3 June 1963.

34. BP ARC39618: Circular No. 1 by the Educated Youth of Qatar.

35. BP ARC39618: Letter to G. G. Stockwell from J. F. Epps, 19 April 1963.

36. BP ARC39618: General Strike in Qatar, 21 April to 7 May 1963.

37. BP ARC39618: Footnotes on List of Demands.

38. BP ARC39618: General Strike in Qatar, 21 April to 7 May 1963.

39. BP ARC39618: Report, 18 September 1963.

40. BP ARC39618: Letter to G. G. Stockwell from W. V. Fuller, 25 September 1963.

41. FO 371–127012: Labour Affairs, Representation of Workers and Strikes in Qatar, marginalia.

42. FCO 8–70: Note of a discussion on Arab labour matters, 5 September 1968.

43. FO 371–127012: Workers' Representation and Labour Legislation in Qatar.

44. FO 371–168866: Letter to Political Agent, Qatar, from British Embassy, Beirut, 22 June 1963.

45. WBGA: WB IBRD/IDA 03/EXC-10-4540S: Folder: 1772671: Travel Briefings: Middle East, and Europe: Qatar: Contribution of Petroleum to the Economy, 26 January 1973.

46. "Qatar," 7054, 4/05 530/66 in RQ (2), 709–13.

47. FCO 8–70: R. L. Morris to British Embassy Beirut, "Abu Dhabi: Report on Labour, Social and Industrial Developments," 5 December 1967 (also in: RE (2), 287–300).

48. FCO 8–70: Note of a discussion on Arab labour affairs at the US Embassy, Beirut, 5 February 1968.

49. FCO 8–70: Note of a discussion on Arab labour affairs at the US Embassy, Beirut, 5 February 1968.

50. FCO 8–740: Qatar Security Forces, British Political Agency, Doha, 31 January 1968; FCO 8–740: Qatar Security Forces, British Political Agency, Doha, 29 June 1968.

51. IOR/L/PS/12/3715B: Persian Gulf Residency, Bahrain, Letter, 9 February 1948.

52. Confidential dispatch No. 1/41 from Sir S. Crawford, Political Resident, Bahrain.

53. FCO 8–1155: Report on Labour, Industrial and Social Developments: Labour Strike at Shell Company, August 1968.

54. "Qatar," 7054, 4/05 530/66; Report on Labour, Industrial and Social Developments: Assessment and Recommendations, 6 December 1968, LAB13/2164, in RQ (2), 675–78.

55. Report on Labour, Industrial and Social Developments: Labour Strike at Shell Company: August 1968, 6 December 1968, LAB13/2164, in RQ (2), 679–80.

56. Both QPC and Shell had developed the same pension scheme. The main difference was that QPC's scheme would only apply to Qatari workers, whereas Shell's would also apply to other Arab workers and workers from India and Pakistan. Report on Labour, Industrial and Social Developments: Record of discussions: Shell Company of Qatar; Report on Labour, Industrial and Social Developments: Appendix III: Shell Company of Qatar: proposed pension scheme, 6 December 1968, LAB 13/2164, in RQ (2), 698–707; Report on Labour, Industrial and Social Developments: Record of discussions: Government of Qatar.

57. Report on Labour, Industrial and Social Developments: Assessment and Recommendations.

58. Report on Labour, Industrial and Social Developments: Record of discussions: Government of Qatar.

59. Report on Labour, Industrial and Social Developments: Labour Strike at Shell Company: August 1968.

60. FCO 8–1155: Confidential Records of Discussion: Shell Company of Qatar; "Report on Labour, Industrial and Social Developments: Record of discussions: Shell Company of Qatar," R. Morris, 6 December 1968, LAB13/2164, in RQ (2), 690–91.

61. National Archives, "Cabinet Papers."

62. Report on Labour, Industrial and Social Developments: Assessment and Recommendations.

63. This earlier strike ended due to the mediation of the QPC workers' committee. Report on Labour, Industrial and Social Developments: Record of discussions: Government of Qatar, R. Morris, 6 December 1968, LAB13/2164, in RQ (2), 681–86.

64. Report on Labour, Industrial and Social Developments: Record of discussions: Government of Qatar, R. Morris, 6 December 1968, LAB13/2164, in RQ (2), 681–86.

65. Report on Labour, Industrial and Social Developments: Assessment and Recommendations.

66. Opinions of Mr. Khreis varied between QPC and SCQ. SCQ considered him unhelpful and a source of many of their labor problems. QPC found him to be "uncorruptable" and helpful. Report on Labour, Industrial and Social Developments: Record of discussions: Shell Company of Qatar; Report on Labour, Industrial and Social Developments: Record of discussions: Qatar Petroleum Company (Q.P.C.).

67. Report on Labour, Industrial and Social Developments: Record of discussions: Shell Company of Qatar; Report on Labour, Industrial and Social Developments: Record of discussions: Qatar Petroleum Company (Q.P.C.); Report on Labour, Industrial and Social Developments: Record of discussions: Government of Qatar.

68. This happened in 1967, when committee elections coincided with Ramadan and the government decided to postpone them until after the holiday. Suspecting this was a tactic to postpone elections indefinitely, there was unrest at the camps. When the elections finally took place in March 1968, they were well attended and orderly.

69. Report on Labour, Industrial and Social Developments: Record of discussions: Qatar Petroleum Company (Q.P.C.).

70. Report on Labour, Industrial and Social Developments: Appendix II: Note on the organisation of personnel management and industrial relations at Q.P.C. and Shell. 6 December 1968, LAB 13/2164, in RQ 2, 695–97.

71. FCO 8–1155: Report on Labour, Industrial and Social Developments: Records of Discussions: Shell Company of Qatar.

72. Report on Labour, Industrial and Social Developments: Record of discussions: Qatar Petroleum Company (Q.P.C.), R. Morris, 6 December 1968, LAB13/2164, in RQ (2), 687–89.

73. "Qatar," 7054, 4/05 530/66; Report on Labour, Industrial and Social Developments: Record of discussions: Shell Company of Qatar.

74. "Qatar," 7054, 4/05 530/66.

75. "Employers' and Workers' Organisations," 651.

76. Report on Labour, Industrial and Social Developments: Record of discussions: Government of Qatar.

77. Report on Labour, Industrial and Social Developments: Record of discussions: Qatar Petroleum Company (Q.P.C.).

78. Report on Labour, Industrial and Social Developments: Record of Discussions: Shell Company of Qatar.

79. Report on Labour, Industrial and Social Developments: Record of discussions: Government of Qatar.

80. FCO 8–1155: Report on Labour, Industrial and Social Developments: Records of Discussions: Shell Company of Qatar.

81. Report on Labour, Industrial and Social Developments: Labour Strike at Shell Company, August 1968.

82. Report on Labour, Industrial and Social Developments: Record of discussions: Qatar Petroleum Company (Q.P.C.).

83. "Qatar," 7054, 4/05 530/66.

84. Report on Labour, Industrial and Social Developments: Record of discussions: Qatar Petroleum Company (Q.P.C.).

85. "Qatar," 7054, 4/05 530/66.

86. Confidential Annex to Qatar Diary No. 1 of 1963, in PG (24), 80; F 0371/185470: R. H. M. Boyle Letter to G.P. Wall, Bahrain, 17 August 1966, in RQ (1), 417; R. H. M. Boyle to Letter to G.P. Wall, Bahrain, 7 September 1966, in RQ (1), 419.

87. Workers' committees were only present at the oil companies. In cases where a labor problem arose with other private companies, the government's position was to "encourage the workers to select a delegate to represent their case. With personal complaints, individuals could always go and complain at the majlis of the Deputy Ruler." Report on Labour, Industrial and Social Developments: Record of discussions: Government of Qatar.

88. Report on Labour, Industrial and Social Developments: Record of discussions: Government of Qatar.

89. Review of Events in Qatar in 1964, P. McKearney, 2 January 1965, in PDAW:PG (24), 358–68.

90. According to the British administration, the Jordanian directors of labor in Qatar, Bahrain, and Abu Dhabi were all interested in their sheikhdoms joining the ILO. FCO 8–70: Record of a discussion on Arab labour affairs at the British Embassy, Amman, 18 July 1968; Rouhani, *History of O.P.E.C.*, 95.

91. Report on Labour, Industrial and Social Developments: Record of discussions: Government of Qatar.

92. Report on Labour, Industrial and Social Developments: Assessment and Recommendations.

93. Report on Labour, Industrial and Social Developments: Record of discussions: Government of Qatar.

94. Report on Labour, Industrial and Social Developments: Assessment and Recommendations.

95. FCO 8–70: International Labour Organization, to R. H. M. Boyle from R. H. Smith, Foreign Office, 3 July 1968.

96. Bandyopadhyaya, "Non-Aligned Movement and International Relations," 145–46.

97. FCO 8–70: Kuwait Labour Movement: Registered Unions, January 1968.

98. Report on Labour, Industrial and Social Developments: Assessment and Recommendations.

99. E. F. Hendersen Letter to British Residency, Bahrain, 13 July 1969, in RQ (3), 15–21.

100. E. F. Hendersen Letter to British Residency, Bahrain, 13 July 1969, in RQ (3), 15–21.

101. E. F. Hendersen Letter to British Residency, Bahrain, 13 July 1969, in RQ (3), 15–21.

102. "Review of the Events in Qatar in 1964," British Political Agency, Doha, 2 January 1965, in PDAW:PG (24), 359–68.

103. As one British administrator noted, over half of the population were foreigners who "have continued to devote their energies into making money and have not greatly troubled themselves with thoughts of politics." "Review of the Events in Qatar in 1964," British Political Agency, Doha, 2 January 1965; "Review of Events in Qatar in 1970," FCO 8–1472, in RQ (3), 566–73.

Chapter 7

1. ADPC was a subsidiary of Iraq Petroleum Company (IPC) established in 1939 to hold Abu Dhabi's onshore oil concessions.

2. BP ARC39612: Labour Troubles in Abu Dhabi from Pattinson to Stockwell, 4 June 1963; J. E. H. Boustead, Memo to H.M. Political Residency, Bahrain, 28 May 1963, in RE (1963), 568.

3. The main players at Jebel Dhanna were ADPC and Bechtel. J. E. H. Boustead, Record of a visit to Jebel Dhanna, 29 May 1963, in RE (1963), 573–76.

4. BP ARC39612: Strike at Tarif, May 29, 1963; BP ARC39612: Letter to Trendell, 29 May 1963; J. E. H. Boustead, Report of Visit to Tarif, 28 May 1963, in RE (1963), 569–70.

5. BP owned two-thirds of ADMA, and Compagnie Française des Pétroles (CFP) owned one-third of the company. Today this company is ADMA-OPCO (Abu Dhabi

Marine Operating Company). It is a subsidiary of the Abu Dhabi National Oil Company (ADNOC). Oil company boards were reportedly upset when oil was discovered in Abu Dhabi because the supply of oil was growing so rapidly, and they feared that prices would decrease. Bamberg, *History of the British Petroleum Company*, Vol. 3, 207.

6. Report of Strike on Das Island, 3 June 1963, in RE (1963), 578–80; Telegram No. 324 From Bahrain to Foreign Office, 1 June 1963, in RE (1963), 564.

7. This law did not apply to those under the jurisdiction of the British administration. P. C. D. Archer to British Embassy, Beirut, 26 September 1961, in RE (1961), 669.

8. Labour Law, Abu Dhabi State, 28 August 1961, in RE (1961), 670–71.

9. J. E. H. Boustead, Record of a visit to Jebel Dhanna, 29 May 1963, in RE (1963), 573–76.

10. J. E. H. Boustead, Confidential Letter to Political Residency, Bahrain, 11 October 1963, in RE (1963), 614–17.

11. FO 371–149084: E. F. Henderson, Political Agency, Abu Dhabi, Letter to D. F. Hawley, Political Agency, Dubai, 1 September 1961, in RE (12), 319–21.

12. *Salat* (prayer) times in Islam occur five times a day. They have fixed start and end times that are set based on geography and sun position.

13. FO 371–149084: E. F. Henderson, Political Agency, Abu Dhabi, Letter to D. F. Hawley, Political Agency, Dubai, 1 September 1961.

14. D. Slater to Political Residency, Bahrain, 15 September 1963, in RE (1963), 589–90.

15. J. E. H. Boustead, Confidential Memo to H.M. Political Residency, Bahrain, 3 June 1963, in RE (1963), 577.

16. J. E. H. Boustead, Memo to H.M. Political Residency, Bahrain, 28 May 1963; BP ARC39612: Telegram from Das Island to Stevens, May 29, 1963.

17. Confidential Memo from Bahrain to Foreign Office, 30 May 1963 in RE (1963), 561.

18. D. Slater to P. W. Summerscale, Political Residency Bahrain, 29 July 1963, in RE (1963), 586–87; D. Slater to F. D. W. Brown, Political Residency Bahrain, 12 August 1963, in RE (1963), 588.

19. J. E. H. Boustead, Record of a visit to Jebel Dhanna, 29 May 1963.

20. Confidential Annex to Abu Dhabi Monthly, Diary No. 5 of 1963, May 1–May 31, in PDAW:PG (24), 148–50.

21. Report of Strike on Das Island, 3 June 1963; J. E. H. Boustead, Record of a visit to Jebel Dhanna, 29 May 1963.

22. Report of Strike on Das Island, 3 June 1963.

23. Report of Strike on Das Island, 3 June 1963; Confidential Memo from Bahrain to Foreign Office, 30 May 1963, in RE (1963), 561.

24. Report of Strike on Das Island, 3 June 1963.

25. For a discussion about cultural connections among the Gulf States, see Dresch, "Introduction."

26. These movements had a lasting impact on present-day understandings of belonging, and "contemporary sub-national or trans-national identities are synonymous with pre-state patterns of mobility." MacLean, "Suburbanization, National Space and Place," 159.

27. For a discussion of how rumors helped shape large political protests in India during World War I, see Pandey, "Peasant Revolt and Indian Nationalism," 254.

28. Report of Strike on Das Island, 3 June 1963. For a discussion of joyriding as a contemporary form of sociality in Saudi Arabia, see Menoret, *Joyriding in Riyadh*.

29. J. E. H. Boustead, Report of Visit to Tarif, 28 May 1963.

30. J. E. H. Boustead, Record of a visit to Jebel Dhanna, 29 May 1963.

31. This concern over nationalization was prescient given that Nasser nationalized Egypt's oil in March 1964. "U.A.R Nationalizes Oil: Two Oil Companies," *New York Times*, March 25, 1964.

32. Report of Strike on Das Island, 3 June 1963.

33. Said, "Preliminary Oil Concessions," 127–30.

34. IOR/L/PS/12/3715B: Persian Gulf Residency Letter, 9 February 1948.

35. IOR/L/PS/12/3715B: Persian Gulf Residency Letter, 5th July 1949; Persian Gulf Residency Letter, 6 June 1949; IOR/L/PS/12/3715B: Persian Gulf Residency Letter, 5 January 1950; IOR/L/PS/12/3715B: Persian Gulf Residency Letter, 8 September 1949; IOR/L/PS/12/3715B: Persian Gulf Residency Letter, 5 January 1950.

36. von Bismarck, *British Policy in the Persian Gulf*, 170–85; Bradshaw, *End of Empire in the Gulf*, 82–84.

37. When Iran tried to negotiate a 50/50 agreement in the late 1940s, AIOC replied it would be "impractical because it was 'extremely difficult to calculate profits' but privately told the British cabinet that such a division would be 'uneconomic, absurd, and astronomical.'" Abrahamian, "1953 Coup in Iran," 186.

38. Ross, "Saudi Arabia Gets Half U.S. Oil Profit"; Bamberg, *History of the British Petroleum Company*, Vol. 2, 341–44; Rouhani, *History of O.P.E.C.*, 91.

39. BP ARC39612: Iraq Petroleum Company, Abu Dhabi Petroleum Company Limited, General, 10/07/1962 to 08/07/1963: Letter from L. F. Murphy, 1 July 1963.

40. Rouhani, *History of O.P.E.C.*, 109.

41. BP ARC39613: Iraq Petroleum Company, Abu Dhabi Petroleum Company Limited, General, 6/8/1963 to 31/8/1964: Letter from C. M. Dalley, 21 October 1963.

42. Takriti, "Colonial Coups," 897–98.

43. BP ARC39613: Extract from Arab Affairs in the British Press, 15 August 1963.

44. BP ARC39613: Letter from W. V. Fuller, 26 September 1963.

45. BP ARC39613: Letter from N. M. Eserdjian, 21st August 1963.

46. Bamberg, *History of the British Petroleum Company,* Vol. 3, 38; UNT OH 0680: Interview with James Voss by Dr. Ronald E. Marcello, (Cedar Creek, Texas: January 9, 1986; January 10, 1986; April 4, 1986; June 20, 1986).

47. Fifty-fifty profit sharing brought the local government and oil companies into closer alignment. For example, in 1953, three years after the ruler of Saudi Arabia signed a fifty-fifty sharing, Aramco managers wrote that worker actions described the fates of the oil company and the government as interconnected, and workers conflated them, too, "preaching not only the downfall of the Company, but also the government." HIA McConnell, Box 1, Folder 8: Journal Entry, October 24, 1953. Note, managers attributed this to communist influences from Lebanon and India, McConnell, October 24, 1953. But Vitalis notes there is no evidence of this. Vitalis, *America's Kingdom,* 152.

48. Confidential Memo from Bahrain to Foreign Office, 30 May 1963.

49. J. E. H. Boustead, Report of Visit to Tarif, 28 May 1963; J. E. H. Boustead, Record of a visit to Jebel Dhanna, 29 May 1963.

50. W. H. Luce to Foreign Office, 5 June 1963, in RE (1963), 567.

51. Confidential Memo from Bahrain to Foreign Office, 30 May 1963.

52. J. E. H. Boustead, Record of a visit to Jebel Dhanna, 29 May 1963.

53. Report of Strike on Das Island, 3 June 1963.

54. Confidential Memo to H.M. Political Residency, Bahrain, 3 June 1963.

55. Telegram No. 328, From Bahrain to Foreign Office, 3 June 1963, in RE (1963), 565.

56. Economic Annex to Abu Dhabi Monthly, Diary No. 6. June 1–June 30, 1963, in PDAW:PG (24), 156–57.

57. Telegram No. 328, From Bahrain to Foreign Office, 3 June 1963.

58. J. E. H. Boustead Letter to Political Residency, Bahrain, 17 June 1963, in RE (1963), 584–85.

59. Abu Dhabi Monthly Diary No. 6 of 1963, June 1–June 30, in PDAW:PG (24), 152–53.

60. In addition, Sheikh Shakhbut used rumor as a tool to attack company management practices. He accused the company of causing the strike because the company allowed the general manager of ADMA to beat an Arab for trying to steal a car. The British accepted the validity of this story, but insisted that the assailant was the Lebanese manager, not the British general manager. J. E. H. Boustead Letter to Political Residency, Bahrain, 17 June 1963.

61. J. E. H. Boustead, Memo to H.M. Political Residency, Bahrain, 28 May 1963.

62. Confidential Memo from Bahrain to Foreign Office, 30 May 1963.

63. J. E. H. Boustead, Memo to H.M. Political Residency, Bahrain, 28 May 1963.

64. J. E. H. Boustead, Report of Visit to Tarif, 28 May 1963.

65. Report of Strike on Das Island, 3 June 1963.

66. Confidential Annex to Abu Dhabi Monthly Diary, No. 7 of 1963, July 1–July 31, in PDAW:PG (24), 159.

67. F. D. W. Brown Letter to Political Residency, Bahrain, 16 October 1963, in RE (1963), 613.

68. Confidential Memo from Bahrain to Foreign Office, 30 May 1963; Telegraph No. 322, From Bahrain to Foreign Office, 31 May 1963, in RE (1963), 563. The Trucial Oman Levies were founded in 1951 and renamed the Trucial Oman Scouts in 1955; TOS was "a security force under direct British control designed to preserve law and order in the seven Trucial States and protect their borders." von Bismarck, *British Policy in the Persian Gulf*, 18.

69. J. E. H. Boustead letter to Political Residency, Bahrain, 30 May 1963, in RE (1963), 571.

70. BP ARC39612: Telegram to Stephens, 31 May 1963; BP ARC39612: Telegram to Stephens, 29 May 1963.

71. Telegram No. 324 From Bahrain to Foreign Office, 1 June 1963; "Drafting Forecast—Your Next Ship," 2.

72. BP ARC39612: Telegram to Stephens, 31st May 1963; BP ARC39612: Telegram to Stephens, 29th May 1963.

73. BP ARC39613: Letter from Fuller, 28 August 1963.

74. BP ARC39613: Meeting in IPC Offices, 27th August 1963.

75. BP ARC39613: Meeting in IPC Offices, 27th August 1963.

76. BP ARC39612: Report on Visit to Das and Abu Dhabi, 1st–10th December 1962, by Savile, December 1962.

77. BP ARC39612: Training in Abu Dhabi, An Informal Meeting to Continue Discussing Training in Abu Dhabi by A.D.M.A. and A.D.P.C., 10 October 1962.

78. BP ARC39612: Report on Visit to Das and Abu Dhabi, 1st–10th December 1962, by Savile, December 1962.

79. BP ARC39612: Minutes of a Meeting held in Bahrain on 3rd November 1962 to discuss Training Policy in Abu Dhabi.

80. BP ARC39612: Report on Visit to Das and Abu Dhabi, 1st–10th December 1962, by Savile, December 1962; BP ARC39612: Draft: ADPC—Training.

81. BP ARC39612: Report on Visit to Das and Abu Dhabi, 1st–10th December 1962, by Savile, December 1962.

82. BP ARC39613: Letter to Grove from Dalley, 31 July 1964. The year before the strikes, merchants called on the ruler to complain that foreign firms were taking greater part of trade and contracting business. Shortly thereafter, the government of Abu Dhabi made a decree that all foreign firms operating in Abu Dhabi needed go to into a partnership with a Abu Dhabi national. However, actual implementation

of the decree was challenging because oil company representatives and British officials believed that there were few potential Abu Dhabi partners. BP ARC39612: Training in Abu Dhabi, An Informal Meeting to Continue Discussing Training in Abu Dhabi by A.D.M.A. and A.D.P.C., 10 October 1962; BP ARC39612: Letter from W. V. Fuller, 16 January 1963.

83. In this system, employees were reprimanded, or warned, three times before talks of dismissal.

84. J. E. H. Boustead Letter to Political Residency, Bahrain, 17 June 1963.

85. BP ARC39613: Letter from Fuller, 26 September 1963.

86. This was after repeated attempts from 1962 through 1964 by the British administration to remove Sheikh Shakhbut and put in place Sheikh Zayed. Bradshaw, *End of Empire in the Gulf*, 82–84; von Bismarck, *British Policy in the Persian Gulf*, 170–85.

87. Takriti, "Colonial Coups," 882–83, 899–901.

88. Sheikh Shakhbut reportedly withdrew his representative because he was upset that the pace of oil development in Dubai was outpacing Abu Dhabi's oil development. FCO 8–70: Industrial Relations: Abu Dhabi Marine Areas.

89. R. L. Morris to British Embassy Beirut, "Abu Dhabi: Report on Labour, Social and Industrial Developments."

90. FCO 8–70: Abu Dhabi Labour Law, Appendix B to R. L. Morris to British Embassy Beirut, "Abu Dhabi: Report on Labour, Social and Industrial Developments," 5 December 1967 (also in RE [2], 305–7).

91. D. Slater to Political Residency, Bahrain, 15 September 1963, in RE (1963), 589–90. As discussed in chapter 6, the British administration voiced a similar set of objections to reforms that were proposed in Qatar after a series of strikes by local workers there.

92. FCO 8–70: "Note of a discussion with Syed Hussan Jumaa," 5 December 1967 (also in RE [2], 302–4).

93. The Lebanese Social Insurance Scheme, developed by the British Embassy in Beirut, was held up as a model for this. R. L. Morris to British Embassy Beirut, "Abu Dhabi: Report on Labour, Social and Industrial Developments."

94. FCO 8/70: "Note of a discussion with Syed Hussan Jumaa," 5 December 1967, (also in RE [2], 302–4).

95. Note of a discussion with Syed Hussan Jumaa.

96. Note of a discussion with Syed Hussan Jumaa; R. L. Morris to British Embassy Beirut, "Abu Dhabi: Report on Labour, Social and Industrial Developments."

97. By 1970, "Abu Dhabi [was], relative to its population (at present 20,000), the richest country in the world." Rouhani, *History of O.P.E.C.*, 83, 92, 109.

98. UNT OH 0667: Interview with Harold Lewis by Dr. Ronald E. Marcello, (Greenwich, Connecticut: November 8, 1985).

99. UNT OH 0668: Interview with MacIver.

100. UNT OH 0667: Interview with Lewis.

101. As President Eisenhower told the National Security Council, "anyone can break up the Organization by offering five cents more per barrel for the oil of one of the countries." In Citino, *From Arab Nationalism to OPEC*, 155.

102. UNT OH 0659: Interview with Smith.

103. BP ARC24535B: A Scheme for the Reorganization of Operational Responsibilities in Abu Dhabi Marine Areas Limited: Volume 1: Explanatory Notes, 5th June 1967: Contracting Out Certain Activities.

104. BP ARC24535B: Note on the Training of Staff.

105. BP ARC24535B: Further Work Required.

106. BP ARC49813: Development and the Oil Companies.

107. BP ARC49813: Appendix D: Basic Rates for Daily Rate: Comparison between ADPC and Certain Development contractors, December 1966.

108. FCO 8–70: Industrial Relations: Abu Dhabi Petroleum Company.

109. At these sites, labor issues arose over the discharge of redundant labor. FCO 8-70: Industrial Relations: Abu Dhabi Marine Areas; FCO 8-70: Industrial Relations: Abu Dhabi Petroleum Company.

110. BP ARC24535B: Further Work Required.

111. For example, when Pakistani workers arrived in Abu Dhabi in the late 1960s, they were unhappy because they found that local men were paid higher wages for similar work. British Embassy, Beirut, Abu Dhabi: Report on Labour, Social and Industrial Development, 5 December 1967, FCO 8/70, in RE (2), 287–300.

112. HIA Darlington, Box 13, Folder 10: "Bases: Les Dernieres Sequelles de Lawrence," *Jeune Afrique*, 23 Mai 1965.

113. FCO 8–844: Trucial States: Political Affairs (Internal): Internal Security: Letter from Roberts to Balfour, 21 May 1968.

114. FCO 8–844: Letter to Stirling from Roberts, 20 December 1967.

115. FCO 8–844: Letter to Balfour from Roberts, 30 November 1967.

Conclusion

1. Confidential dispatch No. 1/41 from Sir S. Crawford, Political Resident, Bahrain.

2. Confidential Review of Events in Qatar in 1979, FCO 8-1472, in RQ (3), 570. US weapons, too, were (and continue to be) sold. From 2017 to 2021, the United States was the world's largest major arms exporter, comprising 39 percent of the global share. Saudi Arabia was the main recipient, receiving 23 percent of US major arms exports during that period. Jones, "America, Oil, and War," 211; Mitchell, "McJihad," 16; Wezeman, Kuimova, and Wezeman, "Trends in International Arms Transfers," 2–3.

3. Watts, "Righteous Oil," 378.

4. FCO 8–70: Annex III: Notes on the position of Trade Unions in the Arab States of the Middle East.

5. UNT OH 0680: Interview with Voss; UNT OH 0669: Interview with Howard Yergin by Dr. Ronald E. Marcello, (Dallas, Texas: January 23, 1986; January 24, 1986). Prior to this time, Bapco's refinery produced lubricants that were sold throughout Asia, and one of its biggest markets was India. UNT OH 0670: Interview with Robert J. Kirchhofer by Dr. Ronald E. Marcello, (Sun City Center, Florida: January 17, 1986).

6. UNT OH 0661: Interview with Fosque; UNT OH 0664: Interview with William Tucker by Dr. Ronald E. Marcello, (New York, New York: September 25, 1985).

7. UNT OH 0664: Interview with Tucker.

8. UNT OH 0668: Interview with Murdo MacIver by Dr. Ronald Marcello, (Ridgefield Connecticut: November 9, 1985). During World War II, the Reconstruction Finance Corporation gave loans to companies in order to support with the US war effort.

9. UNT OH 0664: Interview with Tucker.

10. UNT OH 0688: Interview with Josephson.

11. HIA Mitchell, Box 30, Folder 8: Talk Given by Liston F. Hills, former Chairman and Chief Executive Officer of the Arabian American Oil Company (Aramco) to World Affairs Council, San Francisco, CA, February 15, 1974.

12. UNT OH 0688: Interview with Josephson.

13. FCO 8-1146: Confidential Dispatch No. 1/41, Mr. E. F. Henderson, Political Agency, Doha, First Impressions of Doha, 13 July 1969; FCO 8-1146: Confidential Dispatch No. NBQ1/2 from Mr. D. J. McCarthy, Arabian Department, Foreign and Commonwealth Office, regarding the first impressions of the Political Agent, Qatar, 5 August 1969.

14. FCO 8-1146: Confidential Dispatch No. 1/41, Mr. R. Boyles confidential summary and valedictory dispatch No.1/1 from Doha, 7 April 1969.

15. Rouhani, *History of O.P.E.C.*, 78.

16. Bamberg, *History of the British Petroleum Company*, Vol. 3, 485–86.

17. IMF, *Taxation of Petroleum and Minerals*, chapter 4; Coronil, *Magical State*, 56.

18. Redmiles and Wenrich, "A History of Controlled Foreign Corporations."

19. R. H. M. Boyle Letter to British Political Agency, Doha, 7 April 1969, in RQ (3), 7–11.

20. WBGA: WB IBRD/IDA 03/EXC-10–4540S: Folder: 1772671: Travel Briefings: Middle East, and Europe: Qatar: Contribution of Petroleum to the Economy, 26 January 1973; Pace, "World/Continued." See also Mitchell, *Carbon Democracy*, 174–76.

21. Anthony, *Arab States of the Lower Gulf*, 14–15.

22. al-Sayegh, "Merchants' Role in a Changing Society.'"

Bibliography

Archival Collections
British Library
    India Office Records and Private Papers (IOR)

British Petroleum Archive (BP)
    The Anglo–Iranian Oil Company, Limited
    The Anglo–Persian Oil Company, Limited
    BP Trading, Limited
    The British Petroleum Company, Limited
    Burmah Shell Oil Storage and Distributing Company of India, Limited
    Kuwait Oil Company, Limited

Hoover Institution Archives (HIA)
    Charles F. Darlington Papers (Darlington)
    Philip C. McConnell Papers (McConnell)
    Richard Paul Mitchell Papers (Mitchell)
    Harry Roscoe Snyder Papers (Snyder)
    Harley C. Stevens Papers (Stevens)

National Archives of India (NAI)
    Ministry of External Affairs (MEA)
    West Asia & North Africa (WANA)

The National Archives of the UK
    Cabinet Papers (CAB)
    Foreign and Commonwealth Office (FCO)
    Foreign Office (FO)
    Records of Departments Responsible for Labour and Employment (LAB)

Published Collections of the National Archives of the UK
    Records of the Emirates (abbreviated to RE), 1820–1960, 12 volumes, edited by P. Tuson. Cambridge: Cambridge Archival Editions, 1990.
    Records of Qatar (abbreviated to RQ), 1820–1960, 8 volumes, edited by P. Tuson. Cambridge: Cambridge University Press, 1991.

Published Collections of the Public Records Office and the British Library
    Political Diaries of the Arab World: Persian Gulf (abbreviated to PDAW:PG), 1904–1965, 24 volumes, edited by R. Jarman. Cambridge: Cambridge University Press, 1998.

University of North Texas (UNT), Oral History Collection
    Caltex Oral History Project
        Interview with Frederick W. Dittus (OH 0675)
        Interview with Harold Lewis (OH 0667)
        Interview with Howard Yergin (OH 0669)
        Interview with James Voss (OH 0680)
        Interview with John D. Fosque (OH 0661)
        Interview with Leigh D. Josephson (OH 0688)
        Interview with Leslie A. Smith (OH 0659)
        Interview with Murdo MacIver (OH 0668)
        Interview with Robert J. Kirchhofer (OH 0670)
        Interview with William Tucker (OH 0664)

World Bank Group Archives, Washington, DC, United States (WBGA)

Government Documents
Census of India. New Delhi: Government of India, 1951.
Constituent Assembly Debates, India.
Crowther, Don Q. *Analysis of Strikes in 1938*. Bureau of Labor Statistics, US Department of Labor. Serial No. 9. 939, May. Washington, DC: US Government Printing Office, 1939.
Federal Trade Commission. "Joint Control Through Common Ownership—The Iraq Petroleum Co., Ltd.," in The International Petroleum Cartel, *Staff Report to the Federal Trade Commission, released through Subcommittee on Monopoly of Select*

Committee on Small Business, 47–112. US Senate, 83d Cong., 2nd session. Washington, DC: US Government Printing Office, 1952.

Indian Emigration Act of 1921.

Indian Trade Unions Act, 1926.

Kerala High Court, India. M/S. Caltex (India) Ltd. Vs. Industrial Tribunal No. 2, Ernakulam & Others. October 18, 1960. A.S. No. 111 of 1959.

Lorimer, John Gordon. *Gazetteer of the Persian Gulf: Oman and Central Arabia*. Calcutta: Supt. Government Publishing, 1908.

Ministry of External Affairs. *Annual Report 1950–51*. New Delhi: Government of India, 1951.

Ministry of External Affairs. *Annual Report 1951–52*. New Delhi: Government of India, 1952.

Ministry of External Affairs. "History and Evolution of Non-Aligned Movement." New Delhi: Government of India, August 22, 2012.

The National Archives. "The Cabinet Papers 1915–1986: 1960s and 1970s Radicalisation." https://webarchive.nationalarchives.gov.uk/ukgwa/20150605051429/ https://www.nationalarchives.gov.uk/cabinetpapers/alevelstudies/1960-radicalisation.htm.

Office of the Historian, Foreign Service Institute. "The 1928 Red Line Agreement." US Department of State. https://history.state.gov/milestones/1921-1936/red-line.

Office for National Statistics. "The History of Strikes in the UK." September 21, 2015. https://www.ons.gov.uk/employmentandlabourmarket/peopleinwork/employmentandemployeetypes/articles/thehistoryofstrikesintheuk/2015-09-21.

Office of Public Affairs, US Department of State. Department of State Bulletin 13, no. 327 (September 30, 1945).

Supreme Court of India. Caltex (India) Ltd. Vs. Their Workmen. February 11, 1960. AIR 1960 SC 1262, (1960) IILLJ 12 SC.

United States Labor-Management Relations Act, 1947. (29 U.S.C. 141) Enacted June 23, 1947, Chapter 120 of the 80th Congress, sec. 1, 61 Stat.136.

War Manpower Commission, Bureau of Training, Training Within Industry Service. The Training Within Industry Report, 1940–1945. Washington, DC: US Government Printing Office, September 1945.

Dissertations

Alhajeri, Abdullah. "Citizenship and Political Participation in the State of Kuwait: The Case of National Assembly (1963–1996)." PhD dissertation, Durham University, 2004.

Saleh, Hassan Mohammad Abdulla. "Labor, Nationalism and Imperialism in Eastern Arabia: Britain, the Shaikhs and the Gulf Oil Workers in Bahrain, Kuwait and Qatar, 1932–1956." PhD dissertation, University of Michigan, 1991.

Unpublished Papers

Alsayed, Wafa. "Sawt al-Bahrain: A Window into the Gulf's Social and Political History." *LSE Middle East Centre Blog*, July 1, 2020. https://blogs.lse.ac.uk/mec/2020/07/01/sawt-al-bahrain-a-window-onto-the-gulfs-social-and-political-history/.

Beyan, Temesgen Tesfamariam. "Unemployment and Social Disorder during the British Colonial Period in Eritrea (1941–1951)." Paper presented at the 14th Meeting of the African Economic History Network, Barcelona, October 18–19, 2019.

Coxon, G. H. *The Oil Industry in 1951: Statistical Review*. Anglo-Iranian Oil Company, April 29, 1952. https://www.bp.com/content/dam/bp/business-sites/en/global/corporate/pdfs/energy-economics/statistical-review/bp-statistical-review-1951.pdf.

DuBois, W. E. B. "An Appeal to the World: A Statement of Denial of Human Rights to Minorities in the Case of Citizens of Negro Descent in the United States of America and an Appeal to the United Nations for Redress." 1947. https://www.aclu.org/appeal-world.

Gornall, John. "Some Memories of BAPCO," typescript. Awali, Bahrain, May 1965.

Martin-Amouroux, Jean-Marie. "World Energy Consumption 1800–2000: The Results." *Encyclopédie de l'énergie*. https://www.encyclopedie-energie.org/en/world-energy-consumption-1800-2000-results/.

Articles, Books, and Papers

Abrahamian, Ervand. *Iran Between Two Revolutions*. Princeton, NJ: Princeton University Press, 1982.

Abrahamian, Ervand. "The 1953 Coup in Iran." *Science & Society* 65, no. 2 (Summer 2001): 182–215.

Abrahamian, Ervand. "The Strengths and Weaknesses of the Labor Movement in Iran, 1941–1953." In *Continuity and Change in Modern Iran*, edited by Michael E. Bonine and Nikki Keddie, 181–202. Albany: State University of New York Press, 1981.

Abu Lughod, Lila. "Do Muslim Women Really Need Saving? Anthropological Reflections on Cultural Relativism and Its Others." *American Anthropologist* 104, no 3 (2002): 783–790.

Agarwala, Rina. "From Work to Welfare: A New Class Movement in India." *Critical Asian Studies* 38, no. 4 (December 2006): 419–44.

Alam, Muzaffar. *The Languages of Political Islam: India, 1200–1800*. London: C. Hurst, 2004.

Allen, Lori. *A History of False Hope: Investigative Commissions in Palestine*. Stanford, CA: Stanford University Press, 2021.

Al-Nakib, Farah. *Kuwait Transformed: A History of Oil and Urban Life*. Stanford, CA: Stanford University Press, 2016.

Al-Nakib, Farah. "Revisiting 'Hadar' and 'Badū' in Kuwait: Citizenship, Housing, and the Construction of a Dichotomy." *International Journal of Middle East Studies* 46, no. 1 (February 2014): 5–30.

Al-Nakib, Mai. "'The People are Missing': Palestinians in Kuwait." *Deleuze Studies* 8, no. 1 (2014): 23–44.

al-Sayegh, Fatma. "Merchants' Role in a Changing Society: The Case of Dubai, 1900–90." *Middle Eastern Studies* 34, no. 1 (January 1998): 87–102.

Ambedkar, B. R. *States and Minorities: What Are Their Rights and How to Secure Them in the Constitution of Free India*. Bombay: Thacker, 1947.

Amin, Shahid. *Event, Metaphor, Memory: Chauri Chaura, 1922–1992*. Berkeley: University of California Press, 1995.

Amin, Shahid. "Gandhi as Mahatma: Gorakhpur District, Eastern UP, 1921–1922." In *Selected Subaltern Studies*, edited by Ranajit Guha and Gayatri Chakravorty Spivak, 288–342. New York: Oxford University Press, 1988.

Anderson, Benedict. *Imagined Communities: Reflections on the Origin and Spread of Nationalism*. London: Verso, 2016.

Anscombe, Frederick F. *The Ottoman Gulf: The Creation of Kuwait, Saudi Arabia, and Qatar*. New York: Columbia University Press, 1997.

Anthony, John Duke. *Arab States of the Lower Gulf: People, Politics, Petroleum*. Washington, DC: Middle East Institute, 1975.

Arendt, Hannah. *The Origins of Totalitarianism*. New York: Meridian Books, 1958.

Arnold, David. "Touching the Body: Perspectives on the Indian Plague." In *Selected Subaltern Studies*, edited by Ranajit Guha and Gayatri Chakravorty Spivak, 391–426. New York: Oxford University Press, 1988.

Atabaki, Touraj. "Indian Migrant Workers in the Iranian Oil Industry, 1908–1951." In *Working for Oil: Comparative Histories of Labor in the Global Oil Industry*, edited by Touraj Atabaki, Elisbetta Bini, and Kaveh Ehsani, 189–226. Cham, Switzerland: Palgrave Macmillan, 2018.

Atabaki, Touraj. "Time, Labour-Discipline and Modernization in Turkey and Iran: Some Comparative Remarks." In *The State and the Subaltern: Modernization, Society and the State in Turkey and Iran*, edited by Touraj Atabaki, 1–16. London: I. B. Tauris, 2007.

Balibar, Étienne, and Immanuel Wallerstein. *Race, Nation, Class: Ambiguous Identities*. London: Verso, 1991.

Ballhatchet, Kenneth. *Race, Sex, and Class Under the Raj: Imperial Attitudes and Policies and Their Critics, 1793–1905*. London: Weidenfeld and Nicolson, 1980.

Bamberg, J. H. *The History of the British Petroleum Company*, Vol. 2, *The Anglo-Iranian Years, 1928–1954*. Cambridge: Cambridge University Press, 1994.

Bamberg, J. H. *The History of the British Petroleum Company*, Vol. 3, *British Petroleum and Global Oil, 1950–1975, The Challenges of Nationalism*. Cambridge: Cambridge University Press, 2000.

Bandyopadhyaya, Jayantanuja. "The Non-Aligned Movement and International Relations." *India Quarterly* 33, no. 2 (1977): 137–64.

Banerjee, Sikata. *Make Me a Man! Masculinity, Hinduism, and Nationalism in India*. Albany: State University of New York Press, 2012.

Banerjee, Sukanya. *Becoming Imperial Citizens: Indians in the Late-Victorian Empire*. Durham, NC: Duke University Press, 2010.

Bates, Crispin. "Coerced and Migrant Labourers in India." *Edinburgh Papers in South Asian Studies* 13 (2000): 2–33.

Beblawi, Hazem. "The Rentier State in the Arab World." In *The Arab State*, edited by Giacomo Luciani, 85–98. New York: Routledge, 1990.

Bechtel, Stephen D. Jr. "Reflections on Success." *Daedalus* 125, no. 2 (Spring 1996): 147–66.

Beinin, Joel. *Was the Red Flag Flying There? Marxist Politics and the Arab-Israeli Conflict in Egypt and Israel, 1948–1965*. Berkeley: University of California Press, 1990.

Beinin, Joel. *Workers and Peasants in the Modern Middle East*. Cambridge: Cambridge University Press, 2001.

Beinin, Joel. *Workers and Thieves: Labor Movements and Popular Uprisings in Tunisia and Egypt*. Stanford, CA: Stanford University Press, 2015.

Beinin, Joel, and Zachary Lockman. *Workers on the Nile: Nationalism, Communism, Islam, and the Egyptian Working Class, 1882–1954*. Cairo: American University in Cairo Press, 1998.

Beling, Willard A. *Pan-Arabism and Labor*. Cambridge, MA: Harvard University Press, 1960.

Beling, Willard A. "Recent Developments in Labor Relations in Bahrayn." *Middle East Journal* 13, no. 2 (1959): 156–69.

Bet-Shlimon, Arbella. *City of Black Gold: Oil, Ethnicity, and the Making of Modern Kirkuk*. Stanford, CA: Stanford University Press, 2019.

Bhagavan, Manu. "A New Hope: India, the United Nations and the Making of the Universal Declaration of Human Rights." *Modern Asian Studies* 44, no. 2 (2010): 311–47.

Bhimull, Chandra D. *Empire in the Air: Airline Travel and the African Diaspora*. New York: New York University Press, 2017.

Bini, Elisabetta. "From Colony to Oil Producer: US Oil Companies and the Reshaping of Labor Relations in Libya during the Cold War." *Labor History* 60, no. 1 (2019): 44–56.

Bishara, Fahad. *A Sea of Debt: Law and Economic Life in the Western Indian Ocean, 1780–1950*. Cambridge: Cambridge University Press, 2017.

Bose, Neilesh. "Taraknath Das: A Global Biography." In *South Asian Migrations in Global History: Labour, Law and Wayward Lives*, edited by Neilesh Bose, 157–78. London: Bloomsbury Academic, 2021.

Bose, Sugata. *A Hundred Horizons: The Indian Ocean in the Age of Global Empire*. Cambridge, MA: Harvard University Press, 2009.

Boyk, David. "Nationality and Fashionality: Hats, Lawyers and Other Important Things to Remember." *South Asia: Journal of South Asian Studies* 43, no. 5 (2020): 879–97.

Bradley, Ben. "Indian Workers' Great One Day Strike." *Labour Monthly* (January 1939).

Bradshaw, Tancred. *The End of Empire in the Gulf: From Trucial States to United Arab Emirates*. London: I. B. Tauris, 2020.

Brass, Paul. *The Production of Hindu-Muslim Violence in Contemporary India*. Seattle: University of Washington Press, 2003.

Breen, William J. "Social Science and State Policy in World War II: Human Relations, Pedagogy, and Industrial Training, 1940–1945." *Business History Review* 76, no. 2 (Summer 2002): 233–66.

Brown, Wendy. *States of Injury: Power and Freedom in Late Modernity*. Princeton, NJ: Princeton University Press, 1995.

Brown, Wendy. "'The Most We Can Hope For . . .': Human Rights and the Politics of Fatalism." *South Atlantic Quarterly* 103, no. 2/3 (Spring/Summer 2004): 451–63.

Bsheer, Rosie. *Archive Wars: The Politics of History in Saudi Arabia*. Stanford, CA: Stanford University Press, 2020.

Bsheer, Rosie. "A Counter-Revolutionary State: Popular Movements and the Making of Saudi Arabia." *Past & Present* 238, no. 1 (February 2018): 233–77.

Burja, Abdalla S. *The Politics of Stratification: A Study of Political Change in a South Arabian Town*. Oxford: Clarendon, 1971.

Butalia, Urvashi. *The Other Side of Silence: Voices from the Partition of India*. New Delhi: Penguin Books, 1998.

Carter, Marina. *Servants, Sirdars, and Settlers: Indians in Mauritius, 1834–1874*. New Delhi: Oxford University Press, 1995.

Chakrabarty, Dipesh. "Conditions for Knowledge of Working-Class Conditions: Employers, Government and the Jute Workers of Calcutta, 1890–1940." In *Selected Subaltern Studies*, edited by Ranajit Guha and Gayatri Chakravorty Spivak, 179–230. New York: Oxford University Press, 1988.

Chakrabarty, Dipesh. *Provincializing Europe: Postcolonial Thought and Historical Difference*. Princeton, NJ: Princeton University Press, 2000.

Chakrabarty, Dipesh. *Rethinking Working-Class History: Bengal 1890 to 1940*. Princeton, NJ: Princeton University Press, 1989.

Chakravarti, Uma. "Whatever Happened to the Vedic Dasi? Orientalism, Nationalism, and a Script for the Past." In *Recasting Women: Essays in Indian Colonial History*, edited by Kumkum Sangari and Sudesh Vaid, 27–87. New Brunswick, NJ: Rutgers University Press, 1999.

Chandavarkar, Rajnarayan. "Workers' Politics and the Mill Districts in Bombay Between the Wars." *Modern Asian Studies* 15, no. 3 (1981): 603–47.

Chandavarkar, Rajnarayan. *The Origins of Industrial Capitalism in India: Business Strategies and the Working Class in Bombay, 1900–1940*. Cambridge: Cambridge University Press, 1994.

Chatterjee, Partha. *Nationalist Thought and the Colonial World: A Derivative Discourse*. London: Zed Books, 1986.

Chatterjee, Partha. *The Nation and Its Fragments: Colonial and Postcolonial Histories*. Princeton, NJ: Princeton University Press, 1993.

Chatterji, Joya. "South Asian Histories of Citizenship, 1946–1970." *Historical Journal* 55, no 4 (2012): 1049–71.

Chester, Lucy. "A 'High Iron Railing': Plans to Implement Partition in the Palestine Mandate and British India." *American Diplomacy* (September 2016).

Chomsky, Aviva. *Linked Labor Histories: New England, Colombia, and the Making of a Global Working Class*. Durham, NC: Duke University Press, 2008.

Citino, Nathan J. *From Arab Nationalism to OPEC: Eisenhower, King Saʿūd, and the Making of U.S.-Saudi Relations*. Bloomington: Indiana University Press, 2002.

Cohen, David William, and E. S. Atieno Odhiambo. *The Risks of Knowledge: Investigations into the Death of the Hon. Minister John Robert Ouko in Kenya, 1990*. Athens: Ohio University Press, 2004.

Cohn, Bernard S. *Colonialism and Its Forms of Knowledge: The British in India*. Princeton, NJ: Princeton University Press, 1996.

Cole, Juan R. I. "Iranian Culture and South Asia, 1500–1900." In *Iran and the Surrounding World: Interactions in Culture and Cultural Politics*, edited by Nikki R. Keddie and Rudi Matthee, 15–35. Seattle: University of Washington Press, 2002.

Cole, Juan R. I. *Napoleon's Egypt: Invading the Middle East*. New York: Palgrave Macmillan, 2007.

Cole, Juan R. I. "Rival Empires of Trade and Imami Shiʿism in Eastern Arabia, 1300–1800." *International Journal of Middle Eastern Studies* 19, no. 2 (May 1987): 177–203.

Cole, Juan R. I. *Roots of North Indian Shīʿism in Iran and Iraq: Religion and State in Awadh, 1722–1859*. Berkeley: University of California Press, 1998.

Cole, Juan R. I. *Sacred Space and Holy War: The Politics, Culture and History of Shi'ite Islam*. London: I. B. Tauris, 2002.

Colistete, Renato P. "Productivity, Wages, and Labor Politics in Brazil, 1945–1962." *Journal of Economic History* 67, no. 1 (March 2007): 93–127.

Colgan, Jeff D. *Partial Hegemony: Oil Politics and International Order*. Oxford: Oxford University Press, 2021.

Cooper, Frederick. *Citizenship, Inequality, and Difference: Historical Perspectives*. Princeton, NJ: Princeton University Press, 2018.

Cooper, Frederick. *Colonialism in Question: Theory, Knowledge, History*. Berkeley: University of California Press, 2005.

Corley, T. A. B. *A History of the Burmah Oil Company, 1886–1924*. London: Heinemann, 1983.

Coronil, Fernando. *The Fernando Coronil Reader: The Struggle for Life Is the Matter*. Edited by Julie Skurski, Gary Wilder, Laurent Dubois, Paul Eiss, Edward Murphey, Mariana Coronil, and David Pedersen. Durham, NC: Duke University Press, 2019.

Coronil, Fernando. *The Magical State: Nature, Money, and Modernity in Venezuela*. Chicago: University of Chicago Press, 1997.

Coronil, Fernando, and Julie Skurski. "Dismembering and Remembering the Nation: The Semantics of Political Violence in Venezuela." *Comparative Studies in Society and History* 33, no. 2 (1991): 288–337.

Crystal, Jill. *Kuwait: The Transformation of an Oil State*. Boulder, CO: Westview, 1992.

Crystal, Jill. *Oil and Politics in the Gulf: Rulers and Merchants in Kuwait and Qatar*. Cambridge: Cambridge University Press, 1990.

Das, Veena. *Critical Events: An Anthropological Perspective on Contemporary India*. Oxford: Oxford University Press, 1995.

Das Gupta, Ranajit. *Labour and Working Class in Eastern India*. Calcutta: K. P. Bagchi, 1994.

Davidson, Christopher. *Abu Dhabi: Oil and Beyond*. New York: Columbia University Press, 2009.

Davidson, Christopher. *Dubai: The Vulnerability of Success*. New York: Columbia University Press, 2011.

Davidson, Christopher. "Introduction." In *Power and Politics in the Persian Gulf Monarchies*, edited by Christopher Davidson, 1–6. New York: Columbia University Press, 2011.

Davidson, Christopher. "The United Arab Emirates." In *Power and Politics in the Persian Gulf Monarchies*, edited by Christopher Davidson, 7–31. New York: Columbia University Press, 2011.

"Drafting Forecast—Your Next Ship." *Navy News* 121 (July 1964): 2, 5.

Dresch, Paul. "Introduction: Societies, Identities and Global Issues." In *Monarchies and Nations: Globalisation and Identity in the Arab States of the Gulf,* edited by Paul Dresch and James Piscatori, 1–33. London: I. B. Tauris, 2005.

Dutt, Romesh. *Economic History of India, Volumes 1 & 2.* London: Kegan Paul, 1903 and 1905.

Ehsani, Kaveh. "Disappearing the Workers: How Labor in the Oil Complex Has Been Made Invisible." In *Working for Oil: Comparative Histories of Labor in the Global Oil Industry,* edited by Touraj Atabaki, Elisbetta Bini, and Kaveh Ehsani, 11–34. London: Palgrave Macmillan, 2018.

Ehsani, Kaveh. "Oil, State and Society in Iran in the Aftermath of the First World War." In *The First World War and Its Aftermath: The Shaping of the Middle East,* edited by T. G. Fraser, 191–212. London: Gingko Library, 2015.

Ehsani, Kaveh. "Pipeline Politics in Iran: Power and Property, Dispossession and Distribution." *South Atlantic Quarterly* 116, no. 2 (April 2017): 432–39.

Ehsani, Kaveh, and Rasmus Christian Elling. "Abadan: The Rise and Demise of an Oil Metropolis." *Middle East Report,* no. 287 (2018): 29–32.

Eley, Geoff. *A Crooked Line: From Cultural History to the History of Society.* Ann Arbor: University of Michigan Press, 2005.

Eley, Geoff. *Forging Democracy: The History of the Left in Europe.* Oxford: Oxford University Press, 2002.

Eley, Geoff. "Historicizing the Global, Politicizing Capital: Giving the Present a Name." *History Workshop Journal* 63, no. 1 (January 1, 2007): 154–88.

Eley, Geoff. "Liberalism, Europe, and the Bourgeoisie." In *The German Bourgeoisie,* edited by David Blackburn and Richard Evans, 293–317. London: Routledge, 1991.

Eley, Geoff. "Transnational Labour History: Explorations." *Labor: Studies in Working-Class History of the Americas* 3, no. 1 (2006): 164–166.

Eley, Geoff, and Ronald Grigor Suny. "Introduction: From the Moment of Social History to the Work of Cultural Representation." In *Becoming National: A Reader,* edited by Geoff Eley and Ronald Grigor Suny, 3–38. Oxford: Oxford University Press, 1996.

"Employers' and Workers' Organisations." *International Labour Review* 85, no. 6 (June 1962): 648–52.

Farmanfarmaian, Manucher, and Roxane Farmanfarmaian. *Blood and Oil: Inside the Shah's Iran.* New York: Modern Library, 1999.

Ferguson, James. "Seeing Like an Oil Company: Space, Security, and Global Capital in Neoliberal Africa." *American Anthropologist* 107, no. 3 (2008): 377–82.

Ferrier, Ronald W. *The History of the British Petroleum Company,* Vol. 1, *The Developing Years, 1901–1932.* Cambridge: Cambridge University Press, 1982.

Field, Michael. *The Merchants: The Big Business Families of Saudi Arabia and the Gulf States*. Woodstock, NY: Overlook, 1985.

Fields, Karen E., and Barbara J. Fields. *Racecraft: The Soul of Inequality in American Life*. London: Verso, 2012.

Finnie, David. "Recruitment and Training of Labor: The Middle East Oil Industry." *Middle East Journal* 12, no. 2 (Spring 1958): 127–43.

Fromherz, Allen J. *Qatar: A Modern History* (Updated Edition). London: I. B. Tauris, 2017.

Fuccaro, Nelida. *Histories of the City and State in the Persian Gulf: Manama since 1800*. Cambridge: Cambridge University Press, 2009.

Fuccaro, Nelida. "Reading Oil as Urban Violence: Kirkuk and Its Oil Conurbation, 1927–58." In *Urban Violence in the Middle East: Changing Cityscapes in the Transition from Empire to Nation State*, edited by Ulrike Freitag, Nelida Fuccaro, Claudia Ghrawi, and Nora Lafi, 222–42. New York: Berghahn Books, 2015.

Fuccaro, Nelida. "Shaping the Urban Life of Oil in Bahrain." *Comparative Studies of South Asia, Africa, and the Middle East* 33, no. 1 (2013): 59–74.

Gabaccia, Donna R., Dirk Hoerder, and Adam Walaszek. "Emigration and Nation Building During the Mass Migrations from Europe." In *Citizenship and Those Who Leave: The Politics of Emigration and Expatriation*, edited by Nancy L. Green and François Weil, 63–90. Urbana: University of Illinois Press, 2007.

Ghabra, Shafeeq N. *Palestinians in Kuwait: The Family and the Politics of Survival*. Boulder, CO: Westview, 1987.

Ghassem-Fachandi, Parvis. *Pogrom in Gujarat: Hindu Nationalism and Anti-Muslim Violence in India*. Princeton, NJ: Princeton University Press, 2012.

Ghosh, Amitav. *In an Antique Land: History in the Guise of a Traveler's Tale*. New York: Vintage, 1992.

Glover, William. *Making Lahore Modern: Constructing and Imagining a Colonial City*. Minneapolis: University of Minnesota Press, 2008.

Guha, Ranajit. "The Prose of Counter-Insurgency." In *Selected Subaltern Studies*, edited by Ranajit Guha and Gayatri Chakravorty Spivak, 37–44. New York: Oxford University Press, 1988.

Guha, Ranajit. "The Small Voice of History." In *Subaltern Studies IX: Writings on South Asian History and Society*, edited by Shahid Amin and Dipesh Chakrabarty, 1–12. New Delhi: Oxford University Press, 1996.

Gulzar. "Lyrics 1903–1960: A Song Travels . . ." In *Encyclopaedia of Hindi Cinema*, edited by Gulzar, Govind Nihalani, and Saibal Chatterjee, 279–94. New Delhi: Encyclopædia Britannica (India), 2003.

Gupta, Akhil, and James Ferguson. "Beyond 'Culture': Space, Identity, and the Politics of Difference." *Cultural Anthropology* 7, no. 1 (1992): 6–23.

Gupta, Charu. *Sexuality, Obscenity, Community: Women, Muslims, and the Hindu Public in Colonial India*. New York: Palgrave, 2002.

Hall, Stuart. *The Fateful Triangle: Race, Ethnicity, Nation*. Edited by Kobena Mercer. Cambridge, MA: Harvard University Press, 2017.

Hall, Stuart. "The West and the Rest: Discourse and Power." In *Formations of Modernity*, edited by Stuart Hall and Bram Gieben, 275–332. Cambridge: Polity, 1992.

Haller, Niklas A. "A Call for Solidarity: Pro-Palestinian Activity in the Trucial States, 1936–39." *Journal of Arabian Studies* 11, no. 1 (June 2021): 18–37.

Haller, Niklas A. "Selective Recognition as an Imperial Instrument: Britain and the Trucial States, 1820–1952." *Journal of Arabian Studies* 8, no. 2 (2018): 275–92.

Halliday, Fred. *Revolution and Foreign Policy: The Case of South Yemen, 1967–1987*. Cambridge: Cambridge University Press, 1990.

Hanieh, Adam. *Money, Markets, and Monarchies: The Gulf Cooperative Council and the Political Economy of the Contemporary Middle East*. Cambridge: Cambridge University Press, 2018.

Hegland, Mary Elaine. "Shi'a Women's Rituals in Northwest Pakistan: The Shortcoming and Significance of Resistance." *Anthropological Quarterly* 73, no. 3 (2003): 411–42.

Hertog, Steffen. *Princes, Brokers, and Bureaucrats: Oil and the State in Saudi Arabia*. Ithaca, NY: Cornell University Press, 2010.

Hull, Matthew S. "Democratic Technologies of Speech: From WWII America to Postcolonial Delhi." *Linguistic Anthropology* 20, no. 2 (2010): 257–82.

Hull, Matthew S. *Government of Paper: The Materiality of Bureaucracy in Urban Pakistan*. Berkeley: University of California Press, 2012.

International Monetary Fund. *The Taxation of Petroleum and Minerals: Principles, Problems and Practice*. London: Routledge, 2010.

Jacks, Marian. "The Purchase of the British Government's Shares in the British Petroleum Company, 1912–1914." *Past & Present* 39, no. 1 (1968): 139–68.

Jafari, Peyman. "Labour in the Making of the International Relations of Oil: Resource Nationalism and Trade Unions." In *Handbook on Oil and International Relations*, edited by Roland Dannreuther and Wojciech Ostrowski, 208–22. Northampton, MA: Edward Elgar, 2022.

Jalal, Ayesha. *Partisans of Allah: Jihad in South Asia*. Cambridge, MA: Harvard University Press, 2008.

Jalal, Ayesha. *The Sole Spokesman: Jinnah, the Muslim League, and the Demand for Pakistan*. Cambridge: Cambridge University Press, 1985.

Jayal, Niraja Gopal. *Citizenship and Its Discontents: An Indian History*. Cambridge, MA: Harvard University Press, 2013.

Jones, Kenneth W. *Socio-Religious Reform Movements in British India*. Cambridge: Cambridge University Press, 1989.

Jones, Toby Craig. "America, Oil, and War in the Middle East." *Journal of American History* 99, no. 1 (2012): 208–18.

Joshi, Chitra. "Kanpur Textile Labour: Some Structural Features of Formative Years." *Economic and Political Weekly* 16, no. 44 (November 1981): 1823–38.

Kale, Mahadavi. *Fragments of Empire: Capital, Slavery, and Indentured Labor in the British Caribbean*. Philadelphia: University of Pennsylvania Press, 2010.

Karl, Rebecca E. "Creating Asia: China in the World at the Beginning of the Twentieth Century." *American Historical Review* 103, no. 4 (October 1998): 1096–18.

Kashani-Sabet, Firoozeh. "Cultures of Iranianness: The Evolving Polemic of Iranian Nationalism." In *Iran and the Surrounding World: Interactions in Culture and Cultural Politics*, edited by Nikki R. Keddie and Rudi Matthee, 162–81. Seattle: University of Washington Press, 2002.

Katouzian, Homa. "The Campaign Against the Anglo-Iranian Agreement of 1919." *British Journal of Middle Eastern Studies* 25, no. 1 (1998): 5–46.

Keddie, Nikki R. *Roots of Revolution: An Interpretive History of Modern Iran*. New Haven, CT: Yale University Press, 1981.

Khalaf, 'Abd al-Hadi. "Labor Movements in Bahrain." *Middle East Report* 132 (May/June 1985).

Khalidi, Rashid. *Resurrecting Empire: Western Footprints and America's Perilous Path in the Middle East*. Boston: Beacon, 2010.

Khilnani, Sunil. "Nehru's Faith." In *The Crisis of Secularism in India*, edited by Anuradha Dingwaney Needham and Rajeswari Sunder Rajan, 89–103. Durham, NC: Duke University Press, 2007.

Kinninmont, Jane. "Bahrain." In *Power and Politics in the Persian Gulf Monarchies*, edited by Christopher Davidson. New York: Columbia University Press, 2011.

Ladjevardi, Habib. *Labor Unions and Autocracy in Iran*. Syracuse, NY: Syracuse University Press, 1985.

Lawson, Fred H. *Bahrain: The Modernization of Autocracy*. Boulder, CO: Westview, 1989.

Lerner, Daniel. *The Passing of Traditional Society: Modernizing the Middle East*. New York: Free Press, 1958.

Lesch, Ann M. "Palestinians in Kuwait." *Journal of Palestinian Studies* 20, no. 4 (Summer 1991): 42–54.

Limbert, Mandana. *In the Time of Oil: Piety, Memory, and Social Life in an Omani Town*. Stanford, CA: Stanford University Press, 2010.

Liu, Lydia H. "Shadows of Universalism: The Untold Story of Human Rights around 1948." *Critical Inquiry* 40 (Summer 2014): 385–417.

Liukkuen, Ulla. "The ILO and the Transformation of Labour Law." In *International Labour Organization and Global Society Governance*, edited by T. Halonen and U. Liukkunen. Cham, Switzerland: Springer, 2021.

Lockman, Zachary. *Comrades and Enemies: Arab and Jewish Workers in Palestine, 1906–1948*. Berkeley: University of California Press, 1996.

Longva, Anh Nga. *Walls Built on Sand: Migration, Exclusion, and Society in Kuwait*. New York: Routledge, 1997.

Lowe, Lisa. *The Intimacies of Four Continents*. Durham, NC: Duke University Press, 2015.

Luciani, Giacomo. "Allocation vs Production States: A Theoretical Framework." In *The Arab State*, edited by Giacomo Luciani, 65–84. New York: Routledge, 1990.

MacLean, Matthew. "Suburbanization, National Space and Place, and the Geography of Heritage in the UAE." *Journal of Arabian Studies* 7, no 2 (2017): 157–78.

Mahdavy, Hossein. "The Patterns and Problems of Economic Development in Rentier States: The Case of Iran." In *Studies in the Economic History of the Middle East: From the Rise of Islam to the Present Day*, edited by Michael Cook, 428–67. London: Oxford University Press, 1970.

Majchrowicz, Daniel Joseph. *The World in Words: Travel Writing and the Global Imagination in Muslim South Asia*. Cambridge: Cambridge University Press, 2023.

Malhotra, Anshu. *Gender, Caste, and Religious Identities: Restructuring Class in Colonial Punjab*. New Delhi: Oxford University Press, 2002.

Malkki, Liisa. "National Geographic: The Rooting of Peoples and the Territorialization of National Identity Among Scholars and Refugees." *Cultural Anthropology* 7, no. 1 (1992): 24–44.

Marshall, T. H. *Citizenship and Social Class*. Cambridge: University of Cambridge Press, 1950.

Martin, Marina. "Who Is Asiatic? Drawing the Boundary in the Legal and Political Framing of Indian South Africans, 1860–1960." In *South Asian Migrations in Global History: Labour, Law and Wayward Lives*, edited by Neilesh Bose, 139–56. London: Bloomsbury Academic, 2021.

Marx, Karl. "The British Rule in India." *New-York Daily Tribune*, June 25, 1853. https://www.marxists.org/archive/marx/works/1853/06/25.htm.

Marx, Karl. "On the Jewish Question." *Deutsch-Französishe Jahrbücher*, February 1844. https://www.marxists.org/archive/marx/works/1844/jewish-question/.

Mathew, Johan. *Margins of the Market: Trafficking and Capitalism across the Arabian Sea*. Berkeley: University of California Press, 2016.

Mattar, Philip. "The PLO and the Gulf Crisis." *Middle East Journal* 48, no. 1 (Winter 1994): 31–46.

Matthews, Weldon C. "The Kennedy Administration, the International Federation of Petroleum Workers, and Iraqi Labor under the Ba'thist Regime." *Journal of Cold War Studies* 17, no. 1 (Winter 2015): 97–128.

Matthiesen, Toby. "Migration, Minorities, and Radical Networks: Labour Movements and Opposition Groups in Saudi Arabia, 1950–1975." *International Review of Social History* 59, no. 3 (2014): 473–504.

Maul, Daniel R. "The International Labour Organization and the Globalization of Human Rights, 1944–1970." In *Human Rights in the Twentieth Century*, edited by Stefan-Ludwig Hoffman, 301–20. New York: Cambridge University Press, 2011.

Mazower, Mark. *No Enchanted Palace: The End of Empire and the Ideological Origins of the United Nations*. Princeton, NJ: Princeton University Press, 2009.

McClintock, Anne. *Imperial Leather: Race, Gender and Sexuality in the Colonial Contest*. New York: Routledge, 1995.

Mehta, Purvi. "Diaspora as Spokesperson and Watchdog: Laxmi Berwa, VISION, and Anti-Caste Activism by Dalits in the United States." *Diaspora: A Journal of Transnational Studies* 21 (Spring 2021): 64–86.

Mehta, Uday Singh. *Liberalism and Empire: A Study in Nineteenth-Century British Liberal Thought*. Chicago: University of Chicago Press, 1999.

Menon, Nivedita. "Living with Secularism." In *The Crisis of Secularism in India*, edited by Anuradha Dingwaney Needham and Rajeswari Sunder Rajan, 118–40. Durham, NC: Duke University Press, 2007.

Menoret, Pascal. *Joyriding in Riyadh: Oil, Urbanism, and Road Revolt*. Cambridge: Cambridge University Press, 2014.

Metcalf, Barbara D. *Islamic Contestations: Essays on Muslims in India and Pakistan*. Oxford: Oxford University Press, 2006.

Metcalf, Barbara D. *Islamic Revival in British India: Deoband, 1860–1900*. Princeton, NJ: Princeton University Press, 2014.

Metcalf, Barbara. "Too Little and Too Much: Reflections on Muslims in the History of India." *Asian Studies* 54, no. 4 (November 1995): 951–967.

Metcalf, Thomas R. *Ideologies of the Raj*. The New Cambridge History of India 3, 4. New York: Cambridge University Press, 1995.

Metcalf, Thomas R. *Imperial Connections: India in the Indian Ocean Arena*. Berkeley: University of California Press, 2008.

Mills, Sara. *Gender and Colonial Space*. Manchester, UK: Manchester University Press, 2005.

Minault, Gail. *The Khilafat Movement: Religion and Political Mobilization in India*. New York: Columbia University Press, 1982.

Minault, Gail. *Secluded Scholars: Women's Education and Muslim Social Reform in Colonial India*. New Delhi: Oxford University Press, 1998.

Mir, Farina. *The Social Space of Language: Vernacular Culture in British Colonial Punjab*. Berkeley: University of California Press, 2010.

Mitchell, Lisa. *Language, Emotion, and Politics in South India: The Making of a Mother Tongue*. Bloomington: Indiana University Press, 2009.

Mitchell, Timothy. "Carbon Democracy." *Economy and Society* 38, no. 3 (2009): 399–432.

Mitchell, Timothy. *Carbon Democracy: Political Power in the Age of Oil*. New York: Verso, 2011.

Mitchell, Timothy. "McJihad: Islam in the U.S. Global Order." *Social Text* 20, no. 4 (Winter 2002): 1–18.

Mitchell, Timothy. *Rule of Experts: Egypt, Techno-Politics, Modernity*. Berkeley: University of California Press, 2002.

Mitchell, Timothy. "Society, Economy, and the State Effect." In *State/Culture: State-Formation after the Cultural Turn*, edited by George Steinmetz, 76–97. Ithaca, NY: Cornell University Press, 1999.

Mitchell, Timothy. "Ten Propositions on Oil." In *A Critical Political Economy of the Middle East and North Africa*, edited by Joel Beinin, Bassam Haddad, and Sherene Seikaly, 68–84. Stanford, CA: Stanford University Press, 2020.

Mongia, Radhika Viyas. *Indian Migration and Empire: A Colonial Genealogy of the Modern State*. Durham, NC: Duke University Press, 2018.

Mongia, Radhika Viyas. "Race, Nationality, Mobility: A History of the Passport." *Public Culture* 11, no. 3 (1999): 527–56.

Mukherjee, Janam. *Hungry Bengal: War, Famine and the End of Empire*. Oxford: Oxford University Press, 2015.

Naoroji, Dadabhai. *Poverty and Un-British Rule in India*. London: Swan Sonnenschein, 1901.

Nersesian, Roy. *Energy for the 21st Century: A Comprehensive Guide to Conventional and Alternative Sources*. New York: Routledge, 2010.

Oberoi, Harjot. *The Construction of Religious Boundaries: Culture, Identity, and Diversity in the Sikh Tradition*. Chicago: University of Chicago Press, 1994.

Oberoi, Harjot. "Ghadar Movement and Its Anarchist Genealogy." *Economic and Political Weekly* 44, no. 50 (December 12–18, 2009): 40–46.

Okruhlik, Gwenn. "Rentier Wealth, Unruly Law, and the Rise of Opposition: The Political Economy of Oil States." *Comparative Politics* 31, no. 3 (April 1999): 295–315.

Onley, James. *The Arabian Frontier of the British Raj: Merchants, Rulers, and the British in the Nineteenth-Century Gulf*. New York: Oxford University Press, 2007.

Onley, James. "The Raj Reconsidered: British India's Informal Empire and Spheres of Influence in Asia and Africa." *Asian Affairs* 40, no. 1 (March 2009): 44–62.

Onley, James, and Sulayman Khalaf. "Shaikhly Authority in the Pre-Oil Gulf: An Historical-Anthropological Study." *History and Anthropology* 17, no. 3 (September 2006): 189–208.

Pace, Eric. "The World/Continued." *New York Times*, March 16, 1975.

Palmié, Stephan. *Wizards and Scientists: Explorations in Afro-Cuban Modernity and Tradition*. Durham, NC: Duke University Press, 2002.

Pandey, Gyandendra. "Can a Muslim Be an Indian?" *Comparative Studies in Society and History* 41, no. 4 (1999): 608–29.

Pandey, Gyandendra. *The Construction of Communalism in Colonial North India*. Delhi: Oxford University Press, 1990.

Pandey, Gyandendra. "Peasant Revolt and Indian Nationalism: The Peasant Movement in Awadh, 1919–1920." In *Selected Subaltern Studies*, edited by Ranajit Guha and Gayatri Chakravorty Spivak, 233–81. New York: Oxford University Press, 1988.

Pandey, Gyandendra. "Racialization of Subaltern Populations Across the Globe: The Politics of Difference." *Review of Black Political Economy* 43, no. 2 (2016): 87–99.

Patnaik, Utsa. "Revisiting the 'Drain,' or Transfer from India to Britain in the Context of Global Diffusion of Capitalism." In *Agrarian and Other Histories: Essays for Binay Bhushan Chaudhuri*, edited by Shubhra Chakrabarti and Utsa Patnaik, 277–318. New York: Columbia University Press, 2019.

Pearson, Jessica Lynne. "Defending Empire at the United Nations: The Politics of International Colonial Oversight in the Era of Decolonisation." *Journal of Imperial and Commonwealth History* 45, no. 3 (2017): 525–49.

Peevers, Charlotte. "Altering International Law: Nasser, Bandung, and the Suez Crisis." In *Bandung, Global History, and International Law: Critical Pasts and Pending Futures*, edited by Luis Eslava, Michael Fakhri, and Vasuki Nesiah, 574–95. Cambridge: Cambridge University Press, 2017.

Petersen, Tore T. *The Middle East between the Great Powers*. London: Palgrave Macmillan, 2000.

Pletsch, Carl. "The Three Worlds, or the Division of Social Science Labor." *Comparative Studies in Society and History* 23, no. 4 (October 1981): 565–90.

Pomeranz, Kenneth. "Empire & 'Civilizing' Missions, Past & Present." *Daedalus* 134, no. 2 (Spring 2005): 34–45.

Poulantzas, Nicos. *The Poulantzas Reader: Marxism, Law, and the State*. Edited by James Martin. London: Verso, 2008.

Prakash, Gyan. *Bonded Histories: Genealogies of Labor Servitude in Colonial India*. Cambridge: Cambridge University Press, 2003.

Prakash, Gyan. *Mumbai Fables: A History of an Enchanted City*. Princeton, NJ: Princeton University Press, 2010.

Prakash, Gyan. "Subaltern Studies as Postcolonial Criticism." *American Historical Review* 99, no. 5 (1994): 1475–90.

Prashad, Vijay. *The Darker Nations: A People's History of the Third World*. New York: New Press, 2007.

Quataert, Donald. *Miners and the State in the Ottoman Empire: The Zonguldak Coalfield, 1822–1920.* New York: Berghahn Books, 2006.

Quataert, Jean H. *Advocating Dignity: Human Rights Mobilizations in Global Politics.* Philadelphia: University of Pennsylvania Press, 2009.

Qubain, Fahim I. "Social Classes and Tensions in Bahrain." *Middle East Journal* 9, no. 3 (Summer 1955): 269–80.

Raman, Parvathi. "Being Indian the South African Way: The Development of Indian Identity in 1940s' Durban." In *Rethinking Settler Colonialism: History and Memory in Australia, Canada, Aotearoa New Zealand and South Africa*, edited by Annie Coombes, 193–208. Manchester, UK: Manchester University Press, 2006.

Ramnath, Maia. *Art for Life: Conversations with the Progressive Writers Movement.* Self-published, Barnes and Noble Press, 2020.

Ramnath, Maia. *Haj to Utopia: How the Ghadar Movement Charted Global Radicalism and Attempted to Overthrow the British Empire.* Berkeley: University of California Press, 2011.

Ramnath, Maia. "Two Revolutions: The Ghadar Movement and India's Radical Diaspora, 1913–1918." *Radical History Review* 92 (Spring 2005): 7–30.

Rangoonwalla, Firoze. "1931–1946: The Emergence of Talkies." In *Encyclopaedia of Hindi Cinema*, edited by Gulzar, Govind Nihalani, and Saibal Chatterjee, 43–60. New Delhi: Encyclopaedia Britannica (India), 2003.

Redmiles, Melissa, and Jason Wenrich. "A History of Controlled Foreign Corporations and the Foreign Tax Credit." *Statistics of Income Bulletin*, Summer 2007. US Internal Revenue Service. https://www.irs.gov/pub/irs-soi/historycfcftc.pdf.

Robins, Nick. *The Corporation that Changed the World: How the East India Company Shaped the Modern Multinational.* London: Pluto, 2006.

Robinson, Cedric. *Black Marxism: The Making of the Black Radical Tradition.* Chapel Hill: University of North Carolina Press, 2020.

Rodney, Walter. *How Europe Underdeveloped Africa.* Washington, DC: Howard University Press, 1981.

Rose, Nikolas. *Powers of Freedom: Reframing Political Thought.* Cambridge: Cambridge University Press, 1995.

Rosenthal, Robert J. "Exclusions of Employees under the Taft-Hartley Act." *Industrial and Labor Relations Review* 4, no. 4 (July 1951): 556–70.

Ross, Albion. "Saudi Arabia Gets Half U.S. Oil Profit: Ibn Saud and Aramco Agree to 50–50 Sharing Plan from Jan. 1, 1950." *New York Times*, January 3, 1951.

Rouhani, Fuad. *A History of O.P.E.C.* New York: Praeger, 1971.

Ruona, Wendy E. A. "The Foundational Impact of the Training Within Industry Project on the Human Resource Development Profession." *Advances in Developing Human Resources* 3, no. 2 (May 2001): 119–26.

Said, Atef Shahat. *Revolution Squared: Tahrir, Political Possibilities, and Counterrevolution in Egypt.* Durham, NC: Duke University Press, 2023.

Said, Edward. *Orientalism.* New York: Random House, 1978.

Said, Rosemarie J. "The Preliminary Oil Concessions in Trucial Oman, 1922–1939." *International Interactions* 3, no. 2 (1977): 112–34.

Samin, Nadav. *Of Sand or Soil: Genealogy and Tribal Belongings in Saudi Arabia.* Princeton, NJ: Princeton University Press, 2015.

Sampson, Anthony. *The Seven Sisters: The Great Oil Companies and the World They Made.* New York: Viking, 1975.

Sanjek, Roger. "Rethinking Migration, Ancient to Future." *Global Networks* 3, no. 3 (2003): 315–36.

Santiago, Myrna I. *The Ecology of Oil: Environment, Labor, and the Mexican Revolution, 1900–1938.* Cambridge: Cambridge University Press, 2006.

Sarkar, Tanika. *Hindu Wife, Hindu Nation: Community, Religion, and Cultural Nationalism.* Bloomington: Indiana University Press, 2001.

Satia, Priya. *Spies in Arabia: The Great War and the Cultural Foundations of Britain's Covert Empire in the Middle East.* Oxford: Oxford University Press, 2008.

Savarkar, V. D. *Hindutva: Who Is a Hindu?* New Delhi: Hindi Sahitya Sadan, 1928.

Scott, James. *Seeing Like a State: How Certain Schemes to Improve the Human Condition Have Failed.* New Haven, CT: Yale University Press, 1998.

Scott, Joan W. "The Evidence of Experience." *Critical Inquiry* 17, no. 4 (Summer 1991): 773–97.

Seccombe, I. J., and R. I. Lawless. "Foreign Worker Dependence in the Gulf, and the International Oil Companies: 1910–50." *International Migration Review* 20, no. 3 (September 1986): 548–74.

Seccombe, I. J., and R. I. Lawless. "The Gulf Labour Market and the Early Oil Industry: Traditional Structures and New Forms of Organisation." In *The Gulf in the Early 20th Century: Foreign Institutions and Local Responses,* edited by R. I. Lawless, 91–124. Occasional Papers Series No. 31. Durham, UK: Centre for Middle Eastern & Islamic Studies, University of Durham, 1986.

Shahdad, Ibrahim. "Alharak Alshaebiu fi Qatar, 1963–1950" (Popular movements in Qatar, 1950–1963). *Ruznama* 10 (2012): 603–33.

Sinanoglou, Penny. *Partitioning Palestine: British Policymaking at the End of Empire.* Chicago: University of Chicago Press, 2019.

Singha, Radhika. *A Despotism of Law: Crime and Justice in Early Colonial India.* Oxford: Oxford University Press, 1998.

Sohi, Seema. *Echoes of Mutiny: Race, Surveillance, and Indian Anticolonialism in North America.* Oxford: Oxford University Press, 2014.

Stoler, Ann Laura. *Carnal Knowledge and Imperial Power: Race and the Intimate in Colonial Rule.* Berkeley: University of California Press, 2002.

Stoler, Ann Laura. *Race and the Education of Desire: Foucault's History of Sexuality and the Colonial Order of Things*. Durham, NC: Duke University Press, 1995.

Sunder Rajan, Rajeswari, and Anuradha Dingwaney Needham. "Introduction." In *The Crisis of Secularism in India*, edited by Anuradha Dingwaney Needham and Rajeswari Sunder Rajan, 1–44. Durham, NC: Duke University Press, 2007.

Takriti, Abdel Razzaq. "Colonial Coups and the War on Popular Sovereignty." *American Historical Review* 124, no. 3 (June 2019): 878–909.

Takriti, Abdel Razzaq. *Monsoon Revolution: Republicans, Sultans, and Empires in Oman, 1965–1976*. Oxford: Oxford University Press, 2013.

Terretta, Meredith. "'We Had Been Fooled into Thinking that the UN Watches Over the Entire World': Human Rights, UN Trust Territories, and Africa's Decolonization." *Human Rights Quarterly* 34, no. 2 (May 2012): 329–60.

Tetzlaff, Stefan. "The Turn of the Gulf Tide: Empire, Nationalism, and South Asian Labor Migration to Iraq, c. 1900–1935." *International Labor and Working-Class History* 79 (Spring 2011): 7–27.

Thapar, Romila. "Imagined Religious Communities? Ancient History and the Modern Search for a Hindu Identity." *Modern Asian Studies* 23, no. 2 (1989): 209–31.

Tilly, Charles. "States and Nationalism in Europe, 1492–1992." *Theory and Society* 23, no. 1 (1994): 131–46.

Torpey, John. "Leaving: A Comparative View." In *Citizenship and Those Who Leave: The Politics of Emigration and Expatriation*, edited by Nancy L. Green and François Weil, 13–32. Urbana: University of Illinois Press, 2007.

Toth, Anthony, "Qatar." In *Persian Gulf States: Country Studies*, edited by Helen Chapin Metz, 147–95. Washington, DC: GPO for the Library of Congress, 1993.

Trouillot, Michel-Rolph. "The Anthropology of the State in the Age of Globalization: Close Encounters of the Deceptive Kind." *Current Anthropology* 42, no. 1 (February 2001): 125–38.

Trouillot, Michel-Rolph. *Silencing the Past: Power and the Production of History*. Boston: Beacon, 1995.

Tsing, Anna. "What Is Emerging? Supply Chains and the Remaking of Asia." *Professional Geographer* 68, no. 2 (2016): 330–37.

van der Veer, Peter. *Religious Nationalism: Hindus and Muslims in India*. Berkeley: University of California Press, 1994.

Vejdani, Farzin. *Making History in Iran: Education, Nationalism, and Print Culture*. Stanford, CA: Stanford University Press, 2015.

Vitalis, Robert. *America's Kingdom: Mythmaking on the Saudi Oil Frontier*. London: Verso, 2009.

Vitalis, Robert. *Oilcraft: The Myths of Scarcity and Security that Haunt U.S. Energy Policy*. Stanford, CA: Stanford University Press, 2020.

von Bismarck, Helene. *British Policy in the Persian Gulf, 1961–1968: Conceptions of Informal Empire.* London: Palgrave Macmillan, 2013.

Vora, Neha, and Natalie Koch. "Everyday Inclusions: Rethinking Ethnocracy, Kafala, and Belonging in the Arabian Peninsula." *Studies in Ethnicity and Nationalism* 15, no. 3 (2015): 540–52.

Wang Hui. *The End of the Revolution: China and the Limits of Modernity.* London: Verso, 2009.

Watts, Michael. "Resource Curse? Governmentality, Oil and Power in the Niger Delta, Nigeria." *Geopolitics* 9, no. 1 (March 2004): 50–80.

Watts, Michael. "Righteous Oil? Human Rights, the Oil Complex, and Corporate Social Responsibility." *Annual Review of Environment and Resources* 30 (2005): 373–407.

Watts, Michael. "A Tale of Two Gulfs: Life, Death, and Dispossession along Two Oil Frontiers." *American Quarterly* 64, no. 3 (September 2012): 437–67.

Wezeman, Pieter D., Alexandra Kuimova, and Siemon T. Wezeman. "Trends in International Arms Transfers, 2021." *SIPRI Fact Sheet.* Stockholm: Stockholm International Peace Research Institute, March 2022.

Williams, Brandon Kirk. "Labor's Cold War Missionaries: The IFPCW's Transnational Mission for the Third World's Petroleum and Chemical Workers, 1954–1975." *Labor: Studies in Working-Class History of the Americas* 7, no. 4 (2010): 45–69.

Wohlmuth, Jerome S., and Rhoda P. Krupka. "The Taft-Hartley Act and Collective Bargaining." *Maryland Law Review* 9, no. 1 (Winter 1948): 1–27.

Woolbert, Robert Gale. "Pan-Arabism and the Palestine Problem." *Foreign Affairs* 16, no. 2 (January 1938): 309–22.

Wright, Andrea. *Between Dreams and Ghosts: Indian Migration and Middle Eastern Oil.* Stanford, CA: Stanford University Press, 2021.

Wright, Andrea. "'The Immoral Traffic in Women': Regulating Indian Emigration to the Persian Gulf." In *Borders and Mobility in South Asia and Beyond,* edited by Reece Jones and Md. Azmeary Ferdoush, 145–66. Amsterdam: Amsterdam University Press, 2018.

Wright, Steven. "Qatar." In *Power and Politics in the Persian Gulf Monarchies,* edited by Christopher Davidson, 113–34. New York: Columbia University Press, 2011.

Yang, Anand A. *The Limited Raj: Agrarian Roots in Colonial India, Saran District, 1793–1920.* Berkeley: University of California Press, 1989.

Yergin, Daniel. *The Prize: The Epic Quest for Oil, Money, and Power.* New York: Simon and Schuster, 1991.

Zahlan, Rosemarie Said. *The Creation of Qatar.* London: Croom Helm, 1979.

Zaman, Muhammad Qasim. *The Ulama in Contemporary Islam: Custodians of Change*. Princeton, NJ: Princeton University Press, 2010.

Zamindar, Vazira Fazila-Yacoobali. *The Long Partition and the Making of Modern South Asia: Refugees, Boundaries, Histories*. New York: Columbia University Press, 2013.

Zhou, Luyang. "Nationalism and Communism as Foes and Friends: Comparing the Bolshevik and Chinese Revolutionaries." *European Journal of Sociology* 60, no. 3 (2019): 313–50.

Index

Abadan refinery (AIOC): British support for, 20–21; British workers at, 27; communal violence at, 84–85; communism and, 39; expansion of, 26; former workers from, 55, 88, 108; Indian workers at, 18, 20–21, 22–23, 27, 38; job losses at, 88; living conditions at, 27, 38–39, 93; nationalization of, 16, 88; overview of, 18; production increase at, 26; statistics regarding, 26; strikes at, 17–18, 23, 37–38, 39–40; tensions at, 23; Tudeh Party (Iran) influence at, 18, 39; violence at, 84–85; wages at, 108; as wasteland, 21; working conditions at, 27

Abdullah I (King of Jordan), 123

Abrahamian, Ervand, 18

Abu Dhabi: contracting in, 170, 172–73, 190–92; foreign firms in, 252–53n82; International Labor Organization (ILO) and, 188; labor accommodations in, 171; labor department, 187–88; labor laws in, 171, 187–90; labor relations in, 170–74; migration regulations in, 187–90; oil industry in, 170–74, 190; oil nationalization, 190–92; in OPEC, 190, 196; police force of, 182–83; profit sharing agreement in, 179–80; reforms at oil companies in, 183–86; security measures in, 180–83; strike restrictions in, 186; strikes in, 169–70, 174–78, 181–82; tensions in, 177–80; unions in, 187–88; wages in, 171, 182, 185, 188–89; work permits in, 189–90; working conditions in, 171

Abu Dhabian workers, 169–74, 177–78, 186

Abu Dhabi Marine Areas (ADMA), 169–70, 175, 184–87, 191–92, 248–49n5, 251n60

Abu Dhabi Marine Operating Company (ADMA-OPCO), 248–49n5

Abu Dhabi National Oil Company (ADNOC), 249n5

Abu Dhabi Petroleum Company (ADPC), 169–70, 172–73, 174–77, 184–86, 187, 248n1
accommodations/living conditions: at Abadan refinery (AIOC), 27, 30–31, 38, 39; in Abu Dhabi, 170–71, 184; at Aden refinery (BP), 88–89, 92, 107, 110; at Aramco, 72, 73; in Bahrain, 70–71, 127; at Bapco, 72, 73, 81; of British Petroleum (BP), 106; complaints regarding, 16, 41–42; justifications of, 30, 31; at Kuwait Oil Company (KOC), 41–42, 55; nationality and, 9, 70, 72; in Qatar, 148; segregation and, 70–72; solidarity and, 3, 8, 38, 87, 91, 141, 171
Aden: British in, 44, 88; difference of, 90–91; government of, 91, 105; Indians in, 97, 102, 224n18; nationalism in, 113, 135, 152, 193
Adenese workers: in Abu Dhabi, 176; communism and, 36, 152; preferential hiring of, 90–91; in Qatar, 160; recruitment of, 111–12; at the refinery, 88, 111; strikes by, 112–13
Aden refinery (BP): camps at, 92; construction of, 88–89, 90–94; contracts at, 95; hunger strike at, 89–90, 94–95; Indian workers at, 89–90, 92–94, 106, 109–11; living and working conditions at, 88–89, 110; local workers at, 111–13; overview of, 88–90; racism at, 93; recreational facilities at, 93; recruitment practices of, 96–97; religious discrimination at, 99–101; spy system at, 109–10; strike at, 89–90, 112–13; wages at, 107–8; worker complaints in, 15–16, 88–89
agents. *See* recruiting agents
Ajman, 44
al Bakir, Abdur Rahman, 124, 131, 133
al Khalifa, Sheikh Salman bin Hamad, 118, 119, 126
al Nahyan, Sheikh Said bin Shakhbut, 176, 181, 186
al Nahyan, Sheikh Shakhbut ibn Sultan: criticism of, 177–82; efficacy of, 174, 176–77; ineffectiveness, alleged, of, 177–82; Labour and Worker's Law of, 171; local contracting and, 185; oil company tensions with, 178–80, 183, 253n88; removal of, 187; rumor tool of, 251n60; worker management and, 170, 186
al Nahyan, Sheikh Sultan bin Shakhbut, 176, 181, 186
al Nahyan, Sheikh Zayed bin Sultan, 179, 187, 244n31, 253n86
al-Nakib, Farah, 149, 242n178
al Sabah, Sheikh Abdullah al Mubarak, 142
al Sabah, Sheikh Abdullah al-Salem, 142, 143, 242n178
al Sabah, Sheikh Ahmed al Jaber, 141
al Sabah, Sheikh Jabir al Ahmed al Jaber, 142–43, 242n175
Alsayed, Wafa, 232n9
al Thani, Sheikh Ahmed bin Ali, 149, 244n31
al Thani, Sheikh Ali bin Abdullah, 147, 149, 244n31
al Thani, Sheikh Khalifa bin Hamad, 151, 154–55, 244n31
Ambedkar, Bhimrao Ramji, 86
American Oil Company (Amoco), 199n1

American workers, 49, 50, 68–71, 127, 169, 211n40, 216–17n15

Amin, Shahid, 5–6

Aminoil (American Independent Oil Company), 47, 51, 106, 211n49

Anglo-Iranian Oil Company (AIOC): British military and, 18; collective action against, 18, 37; colonial logics of, 29–31; communal violence at, 84; competition of, 26; contracting by, 39; deaths at, 17; former workers of, 42, 49, 69; Indian hiring ban at, 56–57; Indian workers at, 26, 49, 205n52; Iranian negotiations with, 129, 179, 250n37; Iranian viewpoint of, 30; Iranian workers at, 25–26; labor laws and, 39; management of, 27, 29, 31–33, 39; naming of, 24–25, 88; nationalization and, 16, 88, 129; overview of, 211n49; policies of, 19; recruiters for, 56–57; religious classification in, 83; social relations of, 30; Training Within Industry (TWI) and, 32; violence in, 84–85; wages at, 30; wildcat strikes at, 17. *See also* Abadan refinery (AIOC); Anglo-Persian Oil Company (APOC); British Petroleum (BP)

Anglo-Persian Oil Company (APOC): advantages of, 1; British support for, 1, 19–21; colonial infrastructure of, 22; concessions of, 46, 243n5; founding of, 19; Indian workers at, 21–24, 23; Iranian negotiations with, 24–25; Kuwait Oil Company (KOC) and, 211n46; labor relations at, 28; payment to Iran by, 24; Red Line Agreement and, 45, 46; renaming of, 24–25; World War I and, 1, 20–21, 22.

See also Anglo-Iranian Oil Company (AIOC); British Petroleum (BP)

anticolonial movements, 16, 36–37, 81, 17–18, 152, 198

anti-imperialism, 9, 36–39, 117, 127–28, 234–35n54, 236n74

Arab Federation of Petroleum Workers, 136, 160, 161, 165

Arab Federation of Trade Unions, 136

Arabian American Oil Company (Aramco): communism concerns at, 36, 251n47; concessions of, 46; fifty-fifty profit sharing by, 179, 251n47; Indian workers at, 74–76, 87; Italian workers at, 69, 72, 107–8, 217n17, 217–18n29, 219n48; labor force demographics at, 69, 216n12, 217n16; ownership of, 46, 68; Pakistani workers at, 80, 87, 221n69; Palestinian workers at, 140–41, 227n58; police in, 72; racism at, 68–70; recreational facilities at, 71; Red Line Agreement and, 209n24; religious classification in, 83, 227n58; Saudi Arabian agreement with, 179; Saudi Arabian workers at, 80, 123–24, 130; segregation at, 70–73; statistics regarding, 69, 217n16; strike response of, 74–76; strikes at, 75, 116; wages at, 130; worker demographics of, 68–69, 217n16; worker restrictions of, 140–41

Arabian Peninsula: boundary defining in, 47; British government role in, 47, 194; British market share in, 194; citizenship question in, 14, 16; colonial tropes in, 4–6; concessions in, 43–46; as indigenous, 44; oil production statistics of, 10; power

Arabian Peninsula (*continued*)
  influence in, 43; restrictions on worker actions in, 140–43; treaties in, 43–46; Trucial States in, 44. *See also specific locations*
Arab League, 153–54, 160, 165–66
Arab Oil Workers Union, 136
Arab workers, 69–70, 98, 124–28, 161, 245n56. *See also specific nationalities*
Awali, Bahrain, 1–2, 128, 199n2

Ba'ath Party, 152, 242n1
Bahrain: Bapco (Bahrain Petroleum Company) relations with, 128–29; British government in, 128–30, 132, 134; British treaties with, 44; citizenship in, 234n41; communal violence in, 84; Compensation Ordinance, 140; imperialism in, 128–30; Indian workers in, 77–78, 125; labor laws in, 118, 134–40, 187; Labor Ordinance, 139–40; Labour Federation, 124, 133, 137; legal cases in, 48, 134; oil discovery at, 1–2; oil industry in, 10, 120, 128–29; oil shipping from, 195; oil wealth of, 12; Palestine, support for, 84, 122; police force in, 2, 132; population growth of, 144; racism at US oil projects in, 68–70; refinery in, 128–30, 195; strike restrictions in, 135, 137–40; strikes in, 2, 7, 115–18, 131–34; union restrictions in, 135–37; unrest in, 118–21, 143–44; worker complaints in, 15–16
Bahraini workers: in Abu Dhabi, 182; at Bapco (Bahrain Petroleum Company), 68–69, 118–19, 127, 130; as citizens, 119; complaints of, 120–21, 131; as laborers, 118–19; migration of, 119; in Qatar, 161; as racialized, 69–70; solidarity of, 127–28; strikes of, 2–3, 115–18, 162, 195; tensions regarding, 144; training of, 119, 127; wages of, 120
Bahrain Petroleum Company (Bapco): Adenese workers at, 36; Americans at, 49, 68–69, 195; Bahraini workers at, 118–19, 127, 130; Bahrain relations with, 51, 128–29, 237n82; Caltex and, 200n4; chemist firing by, 66–67, 77–79, 82–83; communism concerns at, 36; compliance of, 51; concession by, 45–46, 119; concessions of, 45, 119; employment contracts of, 73, 81–82, 218n38; Foreign Service Agreement of, 73–74; hiring practices of, 127; Indian workers at, 2, 66, 81, 119, 126–27, 218n38; job hierarchies at, 68–70; labor force demographics at, 2, 68–69, 118–19, 120, 216n12; labor recruitment for, 73–74; labor relations at, 118–21; oil discovery by, 1–2; oil production interruption of, 195; ownership of, 1–2, 45–46, 68, 199–200n3, 200n4; Pakistani workers at, 126–27; protest response of, 122; racism at, 66–70; recreational facilities at, 71; redundancy at, 143–44; refinery of, 128, 129, 195, 255n5; religious classification in, 227n58; security at, 116, 122, 132; segregation in, 70–73; skilled worker complaints at, 81–82; strike role of, 12; strikes at, 115–18, 143–44; training by, 120; United States' dependence on, 195; workforce demographics of, 68–69; during World War II, 195
Balibar, Étienne, 9
Baluchi police officers, 132

Baluchi workers, 59, 148
Bechtel: in Abu Dhabi, 175; in Aden, 225n22; and Aramco, 72; experience of, 173; growth, 218n31; labor recruitment by, 91, 95, 96, 105, 110; religion of workers, 99–101; strikes at, 110, 112, 175; wages at, 107–8
Bechtel, Stephen, 72
Beinin, Joel, 137
Beling, Willard A., 143
Bhatia, Mr., case of, 150
Brass, Paul, 222n81
bribes, paid by Indian workers, 110–11
British/American Camp, at Aden refinery (BP), 92
British East India Company, 29–30
British Foreign Office, 20, 44
British government: Anglo-Persian Oil Company (APOC) and, 1, 19–20; in Bahrain, 128–30; communism concerns of, 33–36; concessions to, 43–44; defense forces of, 192–93; enemies of, 129–30; governance role of, 47; Indian workers abroad, after 1947 and, 76–77; Indian workers abroad, before 1947 and, 73–76; influence of, in Iran, 42–43; and jurisdiction of, 48, 52–55, 181, 183, 241n162, 249n7; and Kuwait Oil Company (KOC), 50–55; legal infrastructure of, 48; oil as security to, 194–95; oil importance to, 19–20; oil industry policies of, 1; Pakistani workers abroad, after 1947 and, 76–77; Palestine and, 121; pamphlets against, 131–32; political destabilization concerns of, 49; Qatar and, 47–48, 164–66; and representative governance, 195–96; role of, in Arabian Peninsula, 47, 194; security role of, 48; strike response of, 117–18, 133–34, 138–39, 177–80, 181, 193; tension viewpoint of, 232–33n20; Trade Disputes and Trade Unions Act of, 138; trade unions and, 32, 136; travel regulation by, 48; wage concerns of, 189; worker concerns of, 49; work permits and, 189–90
British Indians, 2. *See also* Indian workers
British Petroleum (BP): Abu Dhabi's concession with, 179; and ADMA, 184; and ADPC, 184; AIOC and, 88, 224n4; and Amoco, 199n1; Bechtel and, 91, 95; British government and, 129; contracting and, 91, 112–13, 192; contracts of, 196; defense of, 106; hiring process of, 91; Indian workers at, 97–98, 106; labor recruitment for, 91, 95, 98, 142, 225n22; local workers at, 90–91, 111–13; Mr. Diaz, case of, 104–5; naming of, 88; ownership of, 248–49n5; strike against, 112–13. *See also* Aden Refinery; Anglo-Iranian Oil Company (AIOC); Anglo-Persian Oil Company (APOC)
British workers: in Abu Dhabi, 169; in Aden, 92; in Iran, 27–29, 31, 38; in Kuwait, 53; as managers, 21, 56
Brown Drilling, 216–17n15
Burgan field (Kuwait), 51
Burja, Abdalla, 113, 231n113
Burmah Oil Company, 21, 204n25

California Arabian Standard Oil Company, 46
California Texas Oil Company (Caltex), 1, 45–46, 138–39, 190, 195, 196, 200n4, 240n155

capitalism, 15, 28
carbon, political action regarding, 12, 39
Central Council of Federated Trade Unions of Iranian Workers and Toilers (CCFTU), 17
Chakrabarty, Dipesh, 6
Chand, Jagdish, 125–26
chemists, Indian, 66–67, 68–70, 77–81, 82, 86–87
Chevron, 200n4. *See also* Standard Oil of California (SoCal)
Chittagonian language, 23
Christians, preferential hiring of, 83, 99–100, 101, 227n58
Churchill, Winston, 19, 20
CIA (Central Intelligence Agency), 136, 224n2, 242–43n1
Citino, Nathan, 190–91
citizenship: centrality of, 12–14, 127; codification of, 16, 40, 43; as duty to country, 31; human resources management and, 31–33; human rights and, 87; imperial, 14, 73, 77; in India, 8, 79, 81–84, 90, 94; in Iran, 18, 28; jurisdiction and, 64; in Kuwait, 59, 141, 214n90; laws and, 126, 128, 140; nationalism and, 39; nineteenth century conceptions of, 30; progress and, 19, 24, 33; in Qatar, 59, 146, 149–51; religion and, 83, 98–102; rights and, 14, 67–68, 81–82, 87, 94; secularism and, 102; strike effectiveness and, 8, 198; and worker organizing, 3, 14, 90, 140
Citizenship Law (Qatar), 149
class: in Abu Dhabi, 170; in Bahrain, 117; in Egypt, 122; Indians and, 36, 81–83, 86, 97–98; in Iran, 28, 37;

international solidarities and, 37, 39, 90; Poulantzas on, 201n32; in Qatar, 158
coal, 10, 12–13
Cold War, 19, 34, 198
colonial classifications, 14, 76, 82
colonial coup, 187
colonial governance, 6, 15, 29, 43, 79, 219–20n51
colonial infrastructure, 3–4, 16, 21–24, 49
colonialism, 15, 29, 230n99
colonial tropes, 4–6
communal violence, 76, 83–86, 101, 222n81
communism, 27–28, 31–37, 39, 54–55, 129, 136, 166
Communist Party of Great Britain, 37
Compagnie Française des Pétroles (CFP, later Total), 45, 248–49n5
Compensation Ordinance (Bahrain), 140
concessions, in the Arabian Peninsula, 43–46. *See also specific companies*
Conservative Party (British), 193
contracting, 11, 39, 91, 170, 172–73, 185–86, 190–93, 196
Contracting and Trading Company (CAT), 172
contract labor, 60, 61–62, 127, 160–61
contractors: in Abu Dhabi, 191–92; as exploitative, 61; local, 60, 185; worker issues with, 60–61, 151, 156, 170, 173. *See also specific companies*
corporate management, colonial logics of, 29–31
cost of living, 56, 107, 142, 156, 241n170
Crystal, Jill, 149
Curzon, Lord George Nathaniel, 45

INDEX 285

D'Arcy, William, 19
Darwish, Abdullah, 148
Darwish Brothers, 151
Das Island, Abu Dhabi, 169, 175, 176, 177–79, 181–83
democracy, oil connection with, 12–13
depoliticization, of labor, 194–98
development: economic, 27, 29, 31, 126, 151; national, 27–29, 31, 33, 123; of oil, 21, 45, 50, 58, 129, 253n88; pace of, 117; paternalism and, 116; of security, 154; social, 5, 29, 33, 130, 206n63, 206n69; state, 33, 43, 52; of unions, 152, 166; of workers, 31, 33, 59
Diaz, Mr., case of, 104–5
Dooley, C. R., 32
Dubai: British government and, 44; oil development and, 253n88; reform movements in, 3; restrictions on foreigners in, 150; support for Palestine in, 122; World War II and, 218n40

economic development, social development and, 30–31
economization of security, 194
economy, meanings regarding, 11
Eden, Anthony, 130, 137
effectual labor, 60
Egypt, 32, 117, 123, 129, 133, 136, 143, 160
Egyptian Trade Union Federation (ETUF), 137
Ehsani, Kaveh, 21
Eid al-Adha, 145, 152
Eisenhower, Dwight D., 254n101
emigration, 95–97, 103–6
Emigration Act (India), 22–23, 73, 103, 105–6

empire, in the early twentieth century, 19–21
energy consumption, growth of, 10

Farmanfarmaian, Manucher, 27, 206n54
Farouq (King of Egypt), 123
Fields, Barbara, 67
Fields, Karen, 67
fifty-fifty profit sharing, 11, 147, 179–80, 197, 251n47
flights, for emigration, 106
food provisions: in Aden, 89, 101, 108, 110, 113; by Aramco, 71, 74–75, 217–18n29; by CAT, 172; by KOC, 41–42
Foreign Service Agreement, 73–74
four freedoms, 79–80
France, 133, 142
Fromherz, Allen, 243n4
Fuccaro, Nelida, 124
Fujairah, 44

Gandhi, Mohandas Karamchand, 25, 67, 84, 94
Ghadar Movement, 36
global wealth inequalities, 15, 31, 106–9
Glover, William, 38
governance, human rights and, 79–81
Guha, Ranajit, 5
Gulf Oil, 46, 199–200n3, 209n21, 209n23, 211n46

Halul Island, Qatar, 155
High Executive Committee (National Union Committee), 117, 118, 124, 130, 131, 133
Hijazi, Sayyid A., 188
Hindu Indians, 82, 83–85, 90, 98–102
HMS *Striker*, 183

Hull, Matthew, 220n57
human resources management, 29, 31–33, 207n74
human rights, 66–67, 79–81, 82, 86–87, 134
hunger strike, 88–91, 94–95, 108–9, 113–14. *See also* strikes

illegal immigration, 189
imperial governance, 1, 5–6, 19, 42
imperialism, 128–30, 133
indentured labor, 4, 16, 22, 23, 49, 198
India/Indian government: citizenship question in, 14, 81; colonial, 29–30; communal violence in, 83–86; emigration and, 73, 95, 103–6; human rights role of, 80–82, 87; independence of, 8, 44, 78–79, 83–86, 97; Indian workers abroad, after 1947 and, 76–79; Indian workers appeal to, 95–96; job site inspections by, 104; jurisdiction of, 95, 106; migration policies of, 8; Ministry of External Affairs of, 98; nationalism, 25, 90; partition of, 76, 83–86; protection of Indian workers by, 111; reputation of, 96–98; secularism and, 102; strikes in, 2, 94; tensions in, 222n81; Trade Unions Act, 135
Indian Camp, at Aden refinery (BP), 92–93
Indian Employee Committee, 105, 108, 110
Indian nationalism, 5, 25, 90
Indian State Railway, 20
Indian workers: at Abadan refinery (AIOC), 18, 21, 22, 27, 38; abroad, after 1947, 76–79; abroad, before 1947, 73–76; in Abu Dhabi, 171, 175, 185, 192; at Aden refinery (BP), 88–90, 92–94, 106, 109–11; at Anglo-Iranian Oil Company (AIOC), 26, 34, 49, 205n52; at Anglo-Persian Oil Company (APOC), 21–22, 23; anticolonial movements of, 36–37; anti-imperialism of, 127–28; appeal to Indian government by, 95–96; at Aramco, 69, 72, 87, 217n16; in Bahrain, 78, 125; at Bapco (Bahrain Petroleum Company), 119, 127, 216–17n15; Bechtel and, 91; bribes to, 110–11; British government and, 73–77; as chemists, 66–67, 68, 77–81, 82–83, 86–87; as clerks, 97–98; coalitions of, 37–38; collective worker action of, 94; complaints of, 23, 103–4, 126–27, 141–42; contracts for, 73–74, 81, 95, 218n38, 226n44; as cooks, 96–97; current policies regarding, 198; descriptions of, 69; desire for, 21; emigration of, 94–96; food complaints of, 74–75, 101; Foreign Service Agreement regarding, 73–74; hiring increase of, 15; human rights demands of, 87; job security, lack of, 127; in Kuwait, 125; at Kuwait Oil Company (KOC), 53–54, 63; migration restrictions to, 119; pensions for, 245n56; at Petroleum Concessions, Ltd. (PCL), 49–50; police prejudice against, 72; policies regarding, 19; precarity of, 127, 197–98; preferential hiring of, 49; protesting by, 7; in Qatar, 147; at Ras Tanura refinery (Saudi Arabia), 74–76; recruiting of, 22, 49, 96, 110–11; as redundant, 168;

replacement of, 16, 192; restrictions on, 141; as skilled tradesmen, 26, 81–82, 126; solidarity of, 18, 127–28; statistics regarding, 22, 26, 49, 53, 205n52; strikes by, 23, 39–40, 74–76, 89–90, 94–95, 113–14, 141–42; tactics for control of, 109–11; tactics of, 16; wages of, 57–58, 78, 93; working conditions of, 15–16
infrastructure: British, 203n99; colonial, 3–4, 21–24, 49; legal, 48; military, 170; modernizing, 19; oil, 13, 19, 48, 99, 133, 190; recruiting, 14, 21–24, 49, 109; in the Trucial States, 5
International Confederation of Free Trade Unions, 136
internationalism, barriers to, 37
international labor movements, 161, 166
International Labor Organization (ILO), 32, 80, 138, 163, 164–66, 188, 247n90
international organizations, 163–67
International Petroleum Workers' Federation, 136
Iran: Anglo-Iranian Oil Company (AIOC) negotiations by, 250n37; British government influence in, 42–43; citizenship question in, 14; in the early twentieth century, 19; Great Depression and, 24; labor laws in, 39; oil discovery in, 19; oil industry influence by, 18–19; oil nationalization in, 88, 99, 129, 185; oil production in, 190; in OPEC, 196; Soviet Union (USSR) and, 33–34, 45; strikes in, 17, 18, 39–40; worker complaints in, 15–16
Iranian workers, 23, 25–26, 27, 35, 37, 41, 49, 57–59
Iranization, 24, 26, 27–28

Iraq, 45, 54, 142, 145, 192, 196, 202n35
Iraqi workers, 49, 54, 57–58, 242–43n1
Iraq Petroleum Company (IPC), 45, 46, 192, 209n24, 243n5, 248n1
Israel, 133, 153, 195
Italian Communist Party, 107
Italian workers: at KOC, 57; at Aramco, 69, 72, 107–8, 217n17, 217–18n29, 219n48

Japan, 26
Jassim, Abdul Karim, 242–43n1
Jebel Dhanna, Abu Dhabi, 169, 175, 176–77, 181
Jersey Standard (Standard Oil Company of New Jersey), 209n24
jet fuel, 1, 195
Jim Crow policies, 68, 93
Jinnah, Muhammad Ali, 25, 84
job hierarchies, 55, 68–71, 82–83, 87, 126–27, 198
job site inspections, 104
Jordan, 123, 135
Jordanian workers, 161, 247n90
Josephson, Leigh, 115–17
joyriding, 176, 250n28
Jumaa, Sayid Hassan, 188
jurisdiction, 53, 64, 210n31

kafala (sponsorship) system, 149, 197–98
khaliji workers, 16, 143, 156, 161–62, 167, 168, 169–70, 197. *See also specific nationalities*
Khilafat Movement, 23
Khreis, Director of Labor, 156, 158, 163, 164, 246n66
Kismet (film), 236n74

Kuwait: British treaties with, 44; citizenship in, 58–59; concessions in, 46, 47; fifty-fifty profit sharing and, 179; government of, 60–64; Indian workers in, 125; International Labor Organization (ILO) and, 165; Kuwaiti Nationality Law of, 59; nationality law in, 59, 141, 149, 214n91; oil companies in, 50–53; oil production of, 10, 190; in OPEC, 196; Palestinian workers in, 149–50; restrictions on worker actions in, 141–43; sovereignty in, 50–53; strike response of, 142; strikes in, 7, 35, 41, 55–56, 141–42; worker complaints in, 15–16

Kuwaiti workers, 52, 53, 58–64

Kuwaitization, 149–50

Kuwait Oil Company (KOC): British government conflict with, 50–55; communism concerns at, 35–36; complaints regarding, 41–42; contract labor and, 61–62; contracts at, 95; effectual labor at, 60; expelling of workers from, 35; hiring policies of, 57; Indian workers at, 53–54, 63; Italian workers at, 57; Kuwait agreement with, 179; Kuwaiti government and, 60–64; labor force reduction of, 60; living conditions at, 55; local workers and, 60–64; management responses of, 55–58; nationality concerns of, 58–60; non-effectual labor at, 60; overview of, 211n46; Palestinian workers at, 57; police in, 52; policies of, 53–54; salaries at, 26; security for, 47; strike at, 41, 55–56; strike response of, 142–43; supervisor guidelines at, 62–63; Tudeh Party influence at, 35–36; worker actions at, 55–58; worker demographics of, 53; worker restrictions of, 141; workforce management by, 58–60

labor laws, 12, 14, 118, 134–36, 143, 151–54, 193, 198. *See also specific laws; specific locations*

labor migration, 4, 21–24

Labor Ordinance (Bahrain), 134–35, 139–40, 241n162

labor relations, 118–21, 146–49, 163, 170–74

labor unions, 31–32, 134–40, 153, 163–67, 188

Labour Advisory Committee (Bahrain), 140, 153

Labour and Worker's Law (Abu Dhabi), 171

Labour Code (Qatar), 163–64

Labour Court Laws (Qatar), 152

Labour Department (UK), 32

Labour Federation (Bahrain), 124, 133, 137

Labour Law Advisory Committee (Bahrain), 130, 139, 140

Labour Laws (Qatar), 152

Labour Party (British), 134

League of Nations, 121

Lebanese Communist Party, 36

Limbert, Mandana, 235n61

Lloyd, Alexander, 193

local government, role of, 11, 87. *See also specific governments*

local workers, 2, 49, 87, 111, 125, 140–42, 174, 231n116. *See also specific nationalities; khaliji workers*

Lorimer, David, 4

Luce, William, 180–81, 183

Macaulay, Thomas Babington, 29–30
MacLean, Matthew, 176
MacNeill, Donald, 27–28, 29–33, 109
Mahdavy, Hossein, 12
Mamdani, Maulana Husain Ahmad, 25
Manama, Bahrain, 2, 84, 117, 122, 128, 131, 133, 234–35n54
Marx, Karl, 37
May Day parade (Iran), 17
migrant workers, current policies regarding, 198. *See also specific nationalities*
migration, 8, 187–90
militarization, to strikes, 193
Mina al-Ahmadi refinery (Kuwait), 51, 53, 55, 58
minimum wage law (Iran), 39
Ministry of External Affairs (India), 98–103, 105–6
Mir, Farina, 7
Mitchell, Timothy, 11, 12–13
mobile workers, governance and, 53–55
modernity, 201n28, 203n61
modernization, 18, 24, 141, 150, 206n63
Moharram, 117
Mohennedy tribe, 162
Mongia, Radhika, 15
Mosaddegh, Mohammed, 88, 195, 224n2
Muharraq, Bahrain, 133
Mukherjee, Janam, 218–19n40
Muscat, 45
Muscati police, 132
Muscati workers, 148
Muslim League, 85
Muslims, 25, 83–85, 99–101, 102, 221n69, 227n58

Nakba, 121–22, 124, 234n54
Naksa, 153

Nasser, Gamal Abdel, 123, 137, 178, 193, 243n1
nationalism: 1946 strikes and, 19, 27–29; communism and, 37; Indian, 5, 90; labor and, 6–7, 24–26; pan-Arab, 117–18, 121–29, 135–36, 148, 153, 160, 170; potential of, 36; racism and, 9; as strike response, 19; as threat, 65, 135, 144, 160; in worker solidarities, 9, 36–37, 82
nationality: categorization of, 69–70; as hiring consideration, 48, 64; job hierarchies from, 49–50, 55, 69–71; Kuwait Oil Company (KOC) and, 58–60; racialization of, 15–16, 67, 70, 72–73, 82, 86; religion and, 25, 83, 219–20n51; solidarity from, 9, 87, 90, 113; as territorialized, 14, 25, 65; wages and, 64, 93, 106–9; worker descriptions regarding, 69
nationality certificates, 59, 63, 64, 148, 149
Nationality Law (Kuwait), 59, 149
Nationality Regulations (Qatar), 149
nationalization, of oil: in Abu Dhabi, 170; Arab Federation of Petroleum Workers and, 160; concerns about, 129, 170, 190–92, 250n31; in Egypt, 250n31; in Iran, 16, 40, 88, 128–29, 185; in Kuwait, 196; protection against, 180, 190–92, 196; in Qatar, 196–97; in Saudi Arabia, 196; in United Arab Emirates, 196
National Oil Development Company (Qatar), 197
National Union Committee (High Executive Committee), 117, 118, 130, 131, 133
nation-state, 6–8, 11, 15, 36–39, 86, 198

Near East Development Corporation (NEDC), 45, 209n21
Nehru, Jawaharlal, 80, 228n72
networks: coal transport and, 13; exchange, 161; khaliji, 175; kinship, 123, 161; local, 39, 174–75; migration, 7–8, 110, 204n27; military, 193; political, 222n81; social, 6–8, 39, 123, 161; tribal, 167
No Objection Certificates, 125
Non-Aligned Movement Second Summit, 165
non-Arab workers, relations of Arab workers with, 124–28. *See also specific nationalities*
non-effectual labor, 60

oil: assumptions regarding, 10–11; coal as compared to, 13; as critical, 11; democracy and, 12–13; imperial governance importance of, 19; materiality of, 13; nationalization of, 190–92, 196–97; political action regarding, 12, 13; production scales of, 6–9; transportation process for, 13
oil industry: contracting in, 11; in the early twentieth century, 19–21; international and local politics regarding, 8; labor needs of, 21; segregation in, 3, 9; social lives in, 7; statistics regarding, 10; worker control in, 3. *See also specific companies; specific locations*
Oman, 10, 12, 210n29, 235n61
Omani workers, 59, 119, 148, 160, 214n91
Onley, James, 44
OPEC, 164, 190–91, 196, 254n101
Ottoman Empire, 23, 44, 45

Pahlavi, Reza Shah (Iran), 24–25, 26, 28
Pakistan, 8, 76, 83, 84
Pakistani workers: in Abu Dhabi, 171, 175, 185, 192, 254n111; at Aramco, 69, 72, 80, 87, 217n16; at Bapco (Bahrain Petroleum Company), 69, 119–20, 127, 216–17n15; British colonialism and, 200n10; British government and, 76–77; citizenship of, 76–77, 102; classification of, 102; communal violence and, 84–85; complaints of, 126–27; current policies regarding, 198; discrimination against, 83, 222n87; human rights demands of, 80, 87; at KOC, 36, 41–42, 53–54, 64; migration restrictions to, 119; pensions for, 245n56; precarity of, 127, 197–98; racism against, 221n69; as redundant, 168; replacement of, 16, 192; restrictions on, 141; strike by, 141–42
Palestine, 121–24, 128, 153, 159, 219–20n51, 235n54
Palestinian peasant movement, 2
Palestinian workers, 57, 140–41, 149–50, 161, 196, 227n58
Palmié, Stephan, 201n28
pan-Arab nationalism, 117–18, 121–28, 148, 160, 170. *See also* nationalism
Parsi Indian workers, 100
partition of India, 25, 26, 67, 76, 83–86, 101, 219n49, 219n51, 235n54
partition of Palestine, 65, 76, 121–22, 128, 219n51, 235n54
pensions, 156, 162, 245n56
Persia. *See* Iran
Persian Gulf Residency, 50, 128
petroleum, potential of, 13
Petroleum Concessions, Ltd. (PCL), 46, 49–50, 56, 210n26

Petroleum Concessions, Qatar, 85
Petroleum Development, Ltd. (PDL), 46
Petroleum Development, Qatar (PDQ), 56, 59, 146–47, 179, 212n70. *See also* Qatar Petroleum Company (QPC)
Petroleum Development, Trucial Coast, 179, 211n43
Philips radios, 150
policing: in Abu Dhabi, 182–83; in Bahrain, 130, 132, 144, 211n40; demonstrator killings by, 131; of Indian workers, 72, 126, 127; ineffectiveness of, 168; at Kuwait Oil Company (KOC), 52; of protesting, 122; in Qatar, 146; rationalization for, 118; of strikes, 2, 118, 170, 180, 186; in Trucial States, 193
Poulantzas, Nicos, 201n32
Pradeep, Kavi, 236n74
profit sharing, 11, 180. *See also* fifty-fifty profit sharing
Protector of Emigrants (India), 22, 23, 26, 57, 73–74, 76, 95–97, 99–101, 103–5, 126

Qatar: British concerns regarding, 49; British exports to, 194; British government control in, 47–48, 164–66; British treaties with, 44; citizenship in, 59, 149–51; concessions in, 197; demographics of, 161; elections in, 159; fifty-fifty profit sharing and, 179; government of, 196; Indian workers in, 147; International Labor Organization (ILO) and, 164–66; international organizations and, 163–67; Jordanian workers in, 161; labor laws in, 146, 148–49, 151–54, 163–64; labor relations in, 146–49, 163; Labour Code in, 163–64; Labour Court Laws of, 152–53; labor department of, 160–61, 163, 166–67; Labour Laws of, 152–53; leadership in, 244n31; nationalities in, 59; Nationality Regulations of, 149; oil discovery in, 146–47; oil importance to, 12, 153, 167; oil production statistics of, 10; oil profits of, 147, 153, 197; in OPEC, 196; Palestinian workers in, 161, 196; redundant workers in, 162; revenue of, 197; securitization in, 151–54; spending reductions in, 151; strikes in, 145–46, 148–49, 151–52, 154–57, 160, 242–43n1; taxation in, 197; in Trucial system, 44; unrest in, 148, 153–54; wealth inequalities in, 146; worker complaints in, 15–16; workers' committees in, 157–59
Qatari workers, 49–50, 145–46, 147–48, 151, 156, 167, 253n91, 245n56
Qatar National Petroleum Company, 197
Qatar Oil Company (Japan), 197
Qatar Petroleum Company (QPC), 145–46, 147–48, 157, 158, 159, 160–62, 245n56
Qishn, 44

racecraft, 67
racism: at Aden refinery (BP), 93; antagonism from, 72; at Aramco (Arabian American Oil Company), 68; at Bapco (Bahrain Petroleum Company), 66–67, 68; against Indian chemists, 66–67; job hierarchies

racism (*continued*)
and, 69; labor relations and, 14; as management technique, 14–15; nationalism and, 9; racecraft and, 67; territorialization and, 15; at US oil projects, 68–70

Ras al Khaimah, 44, 219n49

Ras Tanura refinery (Saudi Arabia), 72, 74–76

rations, demands for, 42

Reconstruction Finance Corporation (United States), 195, 255n8

recreational facilities, 16, 71, 92

recruiting agents, 7, 22, 49, 91, 95, 96, 110–11

Red Line Agreement, 45, 46, 199–200n3, 209n24

redundant workers: at ADMA, 192; in Abu Dhabi, 169–70; at Bapco, 143–44; consequences of firing, 161–62, 169–70, 254n109; contractors and, 60, 170, 173, 192; in government positions, 162; Indian and Pakistani, 168; issues over, 13; at KOC, 60; in Qatar, 156, 161; at QPC, 162

religion, 25, 81–83, 98–102, 123, 219–20n51

rentier states, 12

Rockefeller, John D., 203n11

Roosevelt, Eleanor, 80

Roosevelt, Franklin, 79–80

Roosevelt, Theodore, 203n11

Rose, Nikolas, 11

Roy, Manabendra Nath, 37

Royal Dutch Shell Company (Shell), 20, 45, 157, 204n15, 204n16, 245n56

rumor, 36, 106, 174, 176, 250n27, 251n60

Russia, 19, 21, 208n6. *See also* Soviet Union

Saudi Arabia: as British enemy, 129; British treaties with, 44; communism in, 36, 251n47; concessions in, 46; fifty-fifty profit sharing and, 179, 251n47; khaliji workers in, 143; labor laws of, 153; nationalism in, 69–70; nationalization of oil by, 196; oil production in, 10, 117, 128–29, 190, 195, 199n2; in OPEC, 196; Palestinian workers in, 140–41, 227n58; racism at US oil projects in, 68–70; as recipient of US arms exports, 254n2; restrictions on worker actions in, 140–41, 143; Standard Oil of California (SoCal) in, 46; strikes in, 7, 116, 251n47, 242n180; US involvement with oil production in, 14; wages in, 119, 130

Saudi Arabian workers, 59, 69–70, 71, 80, 123–24, 143

Sawt al-Arab (Voice of the Arabs) (radio broadcast), 174, 242–43n1

Sawt al-Bahrain (Voice of Bahrain) (magazine), 117

scale, as analytic, 6–9, 176

secularism, 102, 228n71, 228n72

securitization, labor laws and, 151–54

security, 48, 131–34, 144, 154, 182–83, 194–95

segregation, 3, 9, 70–73, 92–93, 109

Sharjah, 44, 84, 193

Sharwa Island, 197

sheikhs, authority boundaries for, 47. *See also specific persons*

Shell (Royal Dutch Shell Company), 20, 45, 204n16, 245n56

Shell Marketing Company, 155

Shell Oil Company, Qatar (SCQ), 145, 147, 154–62, 246n66

Sikh Indians, 84, 85–86, 100, 102, 223n104, 234–35n54
skilled workers, 26, 82, 120
Smith, Leslie (Caltex), 237n94
social development, economic development and, 30–31
Socotra, 44
solidarities, 7, 9, 14–16, 18, 113, 127
South Africa, Indian experiences in, 66–67
sovereignty: in Abu Dhabi, 176, 183; citizenship and, 64; imperial, 47–48, 55; in India, 67, 94–96, 106; in Kuwait, 50–55; state sovereignty, 87, 170
Soviet Union (USSR), 33–35, 45, 47, 129
Special Committee on Palestine (United Nations), 121
Spinneys, 42
spy system, of Aden refinery (BP), 109–10; 230n105
Sri Lanka (historically Ceylon), 190, 226n44
Standard Oil, 32, 203n11
Standard Oil of California (SoCal), 1–2, 45–46, 68, 199n3, 200n4, 209n23, 209n24
stateless workers, 55, 57
stereotypes, 4, 59, 70, 86–87, 167
strikes: of 1938, 2–3, 12; of 1946, 7, 17–19, 27–29, 30–39; of 1948, 41–42, 55–57; of 1953, 88–90, 116, 117, 141, 147; of 1954, 115–18, 139; of 1956, 112, 117, 131–34, 143–44, 148, 242n180; of 1963, 145–46, 149, 151–52, 169–71, 174–77, 242–43n1; of 1968, 154–60; in Abu Dhabi, 174–78, 181–82; at Abu Dhabi Marine Areas (ADMA), 169, 175; at Abu Dhabi Petroleum Company (ADPC), 169–70, 174–77; of Adenese workers, 112–13; at Aden refinery (BP), 89–90, 94–95; at Anglo-Iranian Oil Company (AIOC), 17, 29–31; Arab Federation of Petroleum Workers and, 160; at Arabian American Oil Company (Aramco), 116; attitudes regarding, 10 ; at Awali oil field, 2; in Bahrain, 2, 7, 115–18, 131–34; of Bahraini workers, 2–3, 115–18, 131–34; at Bahrain Petroleum Company (Bapco), 12, 115–16, 117, 143–44; British government response to, 117–18, 133–34, 138–39, 177–80, 181, 193; at British Petroleum (BP), 112–13; challenges of, 172; characterization of, 5; citizenship and, 198; coalitions of, 37–38, 41; commonality of, 2; conditions for, 6; as costly, 10; debates regarding, 134–40; demands in, 42; effectiveness of, 94, 113; failures of, 39–40; fragmentation of, 3; hunger, 90, 94, 113–14; against imperialism, 133; in India, 2; Indian nationalism and, 5; of Indian workers, 23, 39–40, 74–76, 89–90, 94–95, 113–14, 141–42; in Iran, 17, 18; of Iranian workers, 23, 27; of khaliji workers, 16, 169–70; in Kuwait, 7, 35, 141–42; of Kuwaiti workers, 64; at Kuwait Oil Company (KOC), 41, 55–56; labor laws regarding, 198; lawsuits over, 139; militarization against, 193; nationalism and, 27–29; nationalities in, 2–3; of Pakistani workers, 141–42; pan-Arab nationalism and, 170; political possibilities of, 134, 193; prevention of, 160–62, 192–93; in Qatar, 148, 151–52, 154–57,

strikes (*continued*)
160; of Qatari workers, 145–46; at Qatar Petroleum Company (QPC), 145–46, 157; restriction policies against, 186; rumors and, 36, 106, 174, 176, 235n54; in Saudi Arabia, 7; as security risks, 170; at Shell Company, Qatar (SCQ), 145–46, 157–58; solidarities in, 41; of students, 115–16; Taft-Hartley Act and, 139–40; in the United Kingdom, 2; in the United States, 2; violence in, 115–16; wildcat, 17; workers' committees and, 157–59
students, strikes by, 115–16
Suez Canal, 45, 88, 156
Suez Canal Company, 117, 133, 142
supervisors, guidance for, 32–33

Taft-Hartley Act (United States), 139–40
Takriti, Abdel Razzaq, 187
Tarif, Abu Dhabi, 169, 174, 176, 182
Tehran Agreement, 197
temporary labor, 61. *See also* contract labor
Texaco (Texas Company), 45–46, 200n4
Thadani, A. B., 96–97, 100, 105
Thomas, Lieutenant-Colonel, 34–35
Trade Disputes and Trade Unions Act (UK), 138
Trade Union Congress (UK), 157
trade unions, 31–32, 134–40, 153, 163–67, 188
Trade Unions Act (India), 135
Training Within Industry (TWI), 32–33, 207n74, 230n102
transportation, of oil, 13
treaties, in the Arabian Peninsula, 43–46

Trucial Coast, 44, 46, 48, 78, 150, 193, 209n20
Trucial Coast workers, 59, 211n43
Trucial Oman Scouts (TOS), 182–83, 187, 252n68
Trucial States, 5, 44, 176, 193
Trucial system, 44
Truman, Harry S., 80, 210n31
Tudeh Party (Iran), 17, 18, 27, 33, 34–36, 37, 39
Turkish Petroleum Company (TPC) (Iraq Petroleum Company, IPC), 45, 46, 192, 209n21, 209n22

Umm al Quwain, 44
unions, 31–32, 134–40, 153, 163–67, 188
United Arab Agencies (UAA), 150
United Arab Emirates, 10, 12, 196
United Kingdom, 2, 32, 62, 129. *See also* British government
United Nations, 79–80, 86, 121
United Nations Educational, Scientific and Cultural Organization (UNESCO), 164
United States: antiunion legislation of, 134–35; Bahrain Petroleum Company (Bapco) and, 49; contract labor in, 62; human resources management in, 31; involvement with oil production in Saudi Arabia by, 14; jurisdiction of, 210n31; Kuwait Oil Company (KOC) and, 49; oil as security to, 194–95; oil production statistics of, 10; OPEC and, 190–91; racism at oil projects of, 68–70; segregation at oil projects of, 70–73; strikes in, 2; USSR (Soviet Union) concerns of, 34
Universal Declaration of Human Rights, 80, 86

Vejdani, Farzin, 25
Venezuela, 196
Vietnam War, 195
violence, communal, 83–86
Vitalis, Robert, 11, 14, 68, 242n180, 251n47

wages: at Abadan refinery (AIOC), 108; in Abu Dhabi, 188–89; of Americans and Europeans, 93; of Bahraini workers, 120, 130; at Bahrain Petroleum Company (Bapco), 120, 130; calculation of, 107; in India, 78; of Indian workers, 57–58, 78, 93; of Iranian workers, 27; of Italian workers, 107–8; at Kuwait Oil Company (KOC), 54, 58, 142; labor laws and, 171, 182, 188–89; nationality and, 93, 106–9; of Qatari workers, 148; at Shell Company, Qatar, 156
Watts, Michael, 194
wealth inequalities, 15, 31, 106–9, 146
Wimpey, 99–101, 107–8, 110, 112–13
worker mobilizations, solidarities of, 6
workers, oil, overview of, 7–8, 9–10, 13, 15–16, 21. *See also specific nationalities*
workers' committees, 109, 146, 151, 154–56, 157–59, 160, 163, 246n63, 246n68, 247n87
work permits, 189–90
World Health Organization, 164
World War I, 1, 21
World War II, 1, 26, 31, 32, 51, 74, 80, 195

Yemeni workers, 92, 113, 160, 231n114

Stanford Studies in Middle Eastern and
Islamic Societies and Cultures

Laleh Khalili and Sherene Seikaly, editors
Joel Beinin, founding editor

The Incarcerated Modern: Prisons and Public Life in Iran   2024
GOLNAR NIKPOUR

Elastic Empire: Refashioning War Through Aid in Palestine   2023
LISA BHUNGALIA

Colonizing Palestine: The Zionist Left and the Making of the Palestinian Nakba   2023
AREEJ SABBAGH-KHOURY

On Salafism: Concepts and Contexts   2023
AZMI BISHARA

Revolutions Aesthetic: A Cultural History of Ba'thist Syria   2022
MAX WEISS

Street-Level Governing: Negotiating the State in Urban Turkey   2022
ELISE MASSICARD

Protesting Jordan: Geographies of Power and Dissent   2022
JILLIAN SCHWEDLER

Media of the Masses: Cassette Culture in Modern Egypt   2022
ANDREW SIMON

States of Subsistence: The Politics of Bread in Contemporary Jordan   2022
JOSÉ CIRO MARTÍNEZ

Between Dreams and Ghosts: Indian Migration and Middle Eastern Oil   2021
ANDREA WRIGHT

Bread and Freedom: Egypt's Revolutionary Situation   2021
MONA EL-GHOBASHY

Paradoxes of Care: Children and Global Medical Aid in Egypt 2021
  RANIA KASSAB SWEIS

The Politics of Art: Dissent and Cultural Diplomacy in Lebanon, Palestine, and Jordan 2021
  HANAN TOUKAN

The Paranoid Style in American Diplomacy: Oil and Arab Nationalism in Iraq 2021
  BRANDON WOLFE-HUNNICUTT

Screen Shots: State Violence on Camera in Israel and Palestine 2021
  REBECCA L. STEIN

Dear Palestine: A Social History of the 1948 War 2021
  SHAY HAZKANI

A Critical Political Economy of the Middle East and North Africa 2020
  JOEL BEININ, BASSAM HADDAD, AND SHERENE SEIKALY, EDITORS

Showpiece City: How Architecture Made Dubai 2020
  TODD REISZ

Archive Wars: The Politics of History in Saudi Arabia 2020
  ROSIE BSHEER

Between Muslims: Religious Difference in Iraqi Kurdistan 2020
  J. ANDREW BUSH

The Optimist: A Social Biography of Tawfiq Zayyad 2020
  TAMIR SOREK

Graveyard of Clerics: Everyday Activism in Saudi Arabia 2020
  PASCAL MENORET

Cleft Capitalism: The Social Origins of Failed Market Making in Egypt 2020
  AMR ADLY

The Universal Enemy: Jihad, Empire, and the Challenge of Solidarity 2019
  DARRYL LI

Waste Siege: The Life of Infrastructure in Palestine 2019
  SOPHIA STAMATOPOULOU-ROBBINS

For a complete listing of titles in this series, visit the Stanford University Press website, www.sup.org.

The authorized representative in the EU for product safety and compliance is:
Mare Nostrum Group
B.V Doelen 72
4831 GR Breda
The Netherlands

www.ingramcontent.com/pod-product-compliance
Lightning Source LLC
Chambersburg PA
CBHW032056230426
43662CB00035B/458

Since the dissolution of the Soviet empire in the early 1990s, churches in those lands have faced new opportunities and challenges, raising the need to examine afresh the nature and implications of Christian mission. Andrey Kravtsev provides readers with a timely and thorough examination of Russian Baptists' evolving understanding of mission and the various theological streams influencing that thinking. This case study offers insight and guidance for all who are seeking to biblically re-examine the mission of the church in a rapidly changing world.

Craig Ott, PhD
Professor of Mission and Intercultural Studies,
Director, PhD Program in Intercultural Studies,
Trinity Evangelical Divinity School, Deerfield, Illinois, USA

This is a much-needed study on the mission theology of Russian Baptists. Today the Russian Baptist Union is involved in local and global mission, in spite of continuous struggles within and without. Their models of mission are well presented in this study in comparison to a wider mission understanding. The perspective on the different phases of mission thinking and praxis in Russia shows that there is still much to learn and to do. With the current changes in Russia and worldwide, Dr Andrey Kravtsev's call through this book to a holistic mission is a call that needs to be heard even beyond Russia. Therefore, this thorough piece of research is a must-read for all who are interested in missions in Russia and in the region of Eastern Europe and Central Asia. It is an excellent book on mission with a helpful perspective and guidance on well-grounded mission theology and praxis.

Peter Penner, DHabil
Director of Advanced Studies,
Euro-Asian Accrediting Association
Professor for Mission and New Testament,
Campus Danubia, Vienna, Austria